KNOW THY ENEMY
Profiles of Adversary Leaders and Their Strategic Cultures

Edited by

Barry R. Schneider

and

Jerrold M. Post

USAF Counterproliferation Center

325 Chennault Circle

Maxwell Air Force Base, Alabama 36112-6427

July 2003

(Second Edition)

Disclaimer

The views expressed in this publication are those of the authors and do not necessarily reflect the official policy or position of the U.S. Government, Department of Defense, or the USAF Counterproliferation Center.

For sale by the Superintendent of Documents, U.S. Government Printing Office
Internet: bookstore.gpo.gov Phone: toll free (866) 512-1800; DC area (207) 512-1800
Fax: (202) 512-2250   Mail: Stop SSOP, Washington, DC 20401-0001

ISBN 0-9747403-0-6

Contents

Acknowledgments

We, the editors, wish to thank the authors of the various chapters in this volume for their expert contributions to our understanding of the personalities and strategic cultures of some of our most dangerous international rivals.

In addition, we are grateful for the support of the Advanced Systems and Concepts Office of the Defense Threat Reduction Agency (DTRA/ASCO) for their financial support of the USAF Counterproliferation Center's (CPC) "Adversary Project" that was essential to the production of this book and the conference that preceded it. Colonel Tim Lampe and Dr. Charles Galloway were instrumental in providing this support and we thank them.

Further credit should be given to Mrs. Jo Ann Eddy whose administrative and editorial work supported this project from cradle to grave, from the first grant proposal to the final printing and distribution of this extensive volume. Thanks also is due to the copy editing of Colonel Michael Ritz and the help of others on the CPC staff such as Mrs. Brenda Alexander and MSgt Patrick Ellis.

We also wish to thank Dr. Mitchell Reiss and the Wendy and Emery Reves Center for International Studies at the College of William and Mary for their support in hosting the International Rivals Conference where most of these papers were first presented in July 2002 in Williamsburg, Virginia. The editors also are indebted to CPC Associate Director, Richard Estes, who so capably organized that International Rivals Conference and provided such capable support to the CPC Adversary Project.

The authors also appreciate the partnership and help of Colonel Donald Karle, USAF (Retired), Executive Director of the Air University Foundation, for the financial support he and the Foundation gave in making the conference and book a success.

Our appreciation is also extended to Ms. Laurita Denny of Political-Psychological Associates, Bethesda, Maryland, for her assistance in preparing Dr. Post's chapters in this book and in coordinating extensively with the CPC in the editing and production process.

Finally, last but not at all least, the authors thank their spouses, Carolyn Post and Judith Keegan, for their continued love and support and many sacrifices that allowed us the time to do this important work.

Barry R. Schneider
Jerrold M. Post

CHAPTER 1

Deterring International Rivals From War and Escalation

Barry R. Schneider

Why do we seek to understand our enemies? If we are already at war with them the answer is we want to anticipate their actions so we are prepared to counter them effectively and minimize our losses. Forewarned is forearmed. The better we understand them, the more likely we are to win against them, the less likely we are to be surprised and defeated by them.

The ancient Chinese military strategist, Sun Tzu, put it this way:

> "One who knows the enemy and knows himself will not be endangered in a hundred engagements.
>
> One who does not know the enemy but knows himself, will sometimes be victorious.
>
> One who knows neither the enemy, nor himself, will invariably be defeated in every engagement."[1]

When engaging a modern day adversary armed with nuclear, biological, or chemical weapons capable of inflicting mass casualties, one should understand the enemy's red lines or likely trigger points when he would be most likely to escalate to the use of both conventional force and weapons of mass destruction (WMD).

To understand this, one ought to know things like the following:

- past cases when the adversary leader and his regime have used military force;

- past cases when the adversary has used weapons of mass destruction;

1

- propensity of the leaders(s) to escalate crises or conflicts when blocked or stressed;

- the likely doctrine of the regime in question;

- the reliability of the command and control of the rival's military forces;

- things the rival leadership values most and what kinds of retaliatory threats they most fear and believe likely;

- personal, bureaucratic, political or cultural factors that might influence a rival to escalate or de-escalate a crisis;

- information possessed by a rival and their perception of U.S. retaliatory capability, and willingness to escalate a conflict if provoked.

Classic Deterrence Theory

Classic "Cold War" theory states that for deterrence to be successful, four elements need to be present.

First, the United States must possess the capability to inflict a level of damage on the adversary that they consider to be unacceptable. In other words, the enemy would know the United States forces could mete out so extensive an amount of destructiveness that the adversary leadership would find the price too high to pay were they to attack.

Second, the rival leader(s) must believe that the U.S. president is willing to pull the trigger on that devastating response. The enemy must respect the U.S. Commander-in-Chief enough to be afraid of what he might order. In the year prior to the 1962 Cuban Missile Crisis, it appears that Soviet General Secretary Nikita Khrushchev had underestimated the fortitude of President John F. Kennedy, leading him to place Soviet missiles in Cuba as a means of closing the missile gap then facing the USSR. Once Kennedy showed his willingness to go to war and escalate to nuclear use, Khrushchev backed down.

The Soviet leader knew all along the U.S. had superior force at its command. What he did not know until October 1962 was that JFK also had the will to pull the trigger if necessary. This combination of capability and will is termed credibility and this is the coin of real deterrence.

2

Third, it helps deter the rival if you possess such overwhelming retaliatory capability even if he were to attack first. A robust deterrent cannot be disarmed by a surprise attack. Rather, in the parlance of Cold War nuclear strategy, the United States ensures crisis stability and escalation dominance by possessing a "second strike" force where the retaliation is both devastating and inevitable. Knowing this, an adversary should draw back from war and escalation of war.

Fourth, none of this works unless the adversary is both rational and well enough informed to understand the outcome of starting a war or escalating one to high levels with an aroused United States. It helps to spell out the threat precisely to dictators like Iraq's President Saddam Hussein who are both impetuous by nature and are surrounded by sycophants because of Saddam's propensity "to shoot the messenger" for delivering bad news or contrary advice. This is why, on January 12, 1991, four days before the coalition air attack began, President George Bush wrote the Iraqi dictator a warning letter spelling out the consequences of escalating the war. His letter emphasized this point:

> Let me state, too, that the United States will not tolerate the use of chemical or biological weapons . . . The American people would demand the strongest possible response. You and your country will pay a terrible price if you order unconscionable acts of this sort."[2]

In the 1990-91 Gulf War, President Bush attempted to deter Iraq from the use of chemical and biological weapons by threatening the use of nuclear weapons in response. This appears to have been persuasive.

Why did Saddam Hussein not use such chemical and biological weapons? It is likely he was persuaded that the U.S. leader was serious. Clearly, if he believed that Baghdad and his massed military forces were about to be annihilated by nuclear explosions, radioactive fallout, and the accompanying firestorms from a few well-placed atomic and hydrogen bombs delivered by U.S. forces with clear air superiority, it would be irrational to proceed.

Further, if Saddam Hussein were in President Bush's position, possessing such weapons, it would be difficult for him to imagine not using all the means at his disposal. After all, the Iraq dictator started his Ba'ath

Party career as a hit man. He rose to power as the bloody security chief, and once he had seized the Presidency he continued to ruthlessly kill his real and imagined opponents. He attacked Iran and then Kuwait. He has used chemical weapons on his own Kurds as well as on Iranian cities and armies. He has shown no regard for the lives of his countrymen since seizing power. It is easy to believe, when dealing with such a wielder of violence that he would find it all too easy to believe an enemy would use nuclear weapons if provoked by chemical or biological attacks.

Classical deterrence theory seems to have worked against Iraq in 1990-91. In this situation the United States had an overwhelming retaliatory force, postured in a secure second-state mode, led by a U.S. President who unmistakably meant business if pushed, and faced by a rational and informed enemy. In such conditions, peace not war should prevail and, if war were to begin, it should not escalate to strategic nuclear, chemical, or biological use. Given such conditions during the Cold War the peace was kept and some might argue that these conditions are all that are needed to work in the future.

In the years since Ronald Reagan's March 1983 speech calling for a strategic defense initiative, other U.S. defense analysts have also argued that classical retaliatory deterrence can also be improved by fielding effective air and missile defenses. The enemy, if knowledgeable about such defenses, could be deterred from attacks if he knew they would be ineffective. This kind of deterrence is called deterrence by denial.

Obstacles to Deterrence: Enemy WMD

However, there are numerous obstacles to successfully deterring an international rival from future war or escalation decisions.

First, many of our adversaries have or are close to acquiring a significant nuclear, radiological, chemical and/or biological weapons capability of their own. Once in place, their leaders like Kim Jong-il, Ayatollah Khamenei, Bashar al-Asad, and Muammar Qadhaffi might believe the United States to be deterred from attacking them if they were to invade or strike a U.S. ally, short of their launching a direct attack upon the United States. They might be willing to gamble that the United

States leaders would not be willing to put so many of its forces and citizens at risk in a WMD showdown in support of another country.

Indeed, one analyst of the 1991 Gulf War has argued that Saddam Hussein believed that his chemical arms and biological weapons gave him "top cover" against what he perceived as a casualty-adverse U.S. leadership at the time of his invasion of Kuwait.[3] If so, Saddam Hussein did not anticipate the American nuclear force trumping his chemical-biological cards.

Deterring Messianic Enemies

A second obstacle to a successful deterrence policy by the United States is that certain non-state terrorist groups such as al Qaeda, led by Osama bin Laden, appear to be willing to die in the process of striking murderous blows against U.S. citizens and facilities. U.S. retaliation may confer martyrdom, a price some are willing to pay.

Such messianic foes such as Mullah Omar of the former Taliban regime in Afghanistan may have been unwilling to compromise their militant policies despite the global reach of the United States or might simply be too ill informed or stubborn to believe the U.S. retaliation threat until it smashes their regime. Some may simply feel their Jihad is God's will and that they will go down in flames to implement it regardless of the disparities of military power arrayed against them.

Terrorist groups such as al Qaeda are particularly difficult to deter because in many cases their cells and other assets cannot be located for retaliation targeting.

Obstacle: Deterring the Deaf

Other adversaries might simply be too isolated or uninformed about U.S. capabilities and intentions to understand the likely outcomes of their actions. In each of the NASTI (NBC-Arming Sponsors of Terror and Intervention) regimes[4] like Iran, North Korea, Libya and Syria, the top leaders are caught up in a cult of personality where information flowing to them may well be biased, telling them what they want to hear rather than what they may need to understand. In some of these regimes, the top leaders have had limited foreign travel or exposure, and what they have experienced is highly selective and unlikely to fully inform them about the United States.

Obstacle: Weak U.S. Credibility

Another obstacle to successful U.S. deterrence of adversary warfare or escalatory moves, at least prior to the 1990-91 Gulf War, was a string of less-than-impressive U.S. actions against rivals.

The failures in Vietnam to win over an outgunned opponent, the 1983 withdrawal by Ronald Reagan of U.S. Marines from Beirut after losing 241 to lethal bomb attacks, and President Carter's failed rescue attempt to forcibly free U.S. hostages from Iran in 1980 all appeared to be weak responses to aggression. The U.S. withdrawal from Somalia after that peace operation began to cost U.S. lives also conveyed the idea that U.S. leaders were willing to withdraw U.S. forces rather than suffer many casualties.

Further, the ineffective U.S. retaliation against Iraq in response to an attempt to assassinate former President George Bush in Kuwait in 1993, and failure to force Iraq to fully comply with United Nations (U.N.) Resolutions after the Gulf War, all communicated a weak U.S. resolve during the Post-Gulf War decade.

Obstacle: No Equivalent Response

Other obstacles to successful U.S. deterrence of adversary aggressions and escalations are the lack of overwhelming and relatively simple responses available to the U.S. President if he does not want to employ nuclear weapons. The United States has signed and implemented the 1972, Biological Weapons Convention (BWC) and the 1993 Chemical Weapons Convention (CWC) and no longer has a tit-for-tat biological or chemical weapons response to the use of such weapons by an enemy.

Obstacle: Destruction of Nonproliferation Regimes

The use of nuclear arms could have many negative results even if their employment did destroy a rival regime and its military power. First, it would shatter the nuclear taboo that United States Presidents worked so many years to create. Second, U.S. nuclear first use would destroy any moral authority the United States might otherwise have in persuading non-nuclear states to remain so. Third, use of nuclear weapons, even in response to chemical and biological warfare (CBW) attacks, would violate a political pledge made by the United States at a Nuclear Non-Proliferation Treaty (NPT) review conference during the Carter administration. Countries would brand the U.S. a liar that backed out on its pledge not to attack non-nuclear foes who are members of the NPT and who refrain from acquiring nuclear arms.

Worse still, much of the world would regard the United States as a pariah for using such disproportionate weapons on the battlefield. This could trigger massive economic reprisals, particularly by those in the Muslim world if the weapon was used against a Muslim state like Iraq, Iran, Libya, or Syria. Another oil boycott along the lines of 1973 might be the reaction, causing serious economic repercussions in the United States and other industrialized states. Also, the use of nuclear weapons would likely galvanize a worldwide anti-nuclear movement that might do far more harm to U.S. global interests than any positive results that might flow from the use of such mega-weapons.

Obstacle: The "Use or Lose" Dilemma

Another obstacle to successful U.S. deterrence policies is the "use or lose" dilemma faced by enemy regimes whose WMD assets are being destroyed by U.S. allied conventional attacks in a conflict that has already begun. Will a dictator allow the U.S. to progressively destroy his end-game "ace-in-the-hole" without beginning to use this WMD capacity before it is extinguished? At what point does he launch his WMD salvos? When he has eighty percent of his WMD assets left? Fifty percent? Twenty-five percent? Is it reasonable to expect him to let the United States forces surgically remove them completely when the survival of his

7

regime in the war termination phase of combat might depend on that very capability to inflict fearsome damage on invasion forces or upon neighborhood allies of the United States?

Obstacle: Non-Rational Decisions

Finally, U.S. deterrence strategy success depends on the enemy leadership acting rationally and believing it has other successful options short of escalating to mega-weapons usage. No amount of profiling of potential enemy leaders can state with great assurance how they will act in a crisis situation, defined as an event characterized by surprise, a very short time for decisions to be made, involving life or death stakes. Crises produce maximum stress on leaders, and how individuals will perform under such burdens, even they might be unable to predict in advance of the event.

Decisions taken during periods of acute stress may be characterized by illogical or wishful thinking, simplification, extreme emotions, and over-reactions. Stress can also cloud analytic thinking, shrink creativity, increase stereotyping, lead to selective perception, and may lead to more we/they emphasis. Decision-makers under stress may exhibit less flexibility and more rigid thinking than normal, with greater emphasis on following habitual and past formulas for solving new problems. Stress can also bring out the dominant traits of those making decisions. Aggressive risk-prone policy-makers may become even more aggressive and adventuristic under stress. Passive decision-makers may become even more so when feeling acute stress.

Moreover, in a number of states, groups of decision-makers may collaborate on the policies chosen and the decisions may be a product of what psychiatrist Irving Janis labeled as "group think," not always the most rational of outcomes. In his classic study on the subject,[5] Irving Janis has examined how "group think" operated to produce U.S. fiascos in the 1961 Bay of Pigs crisis, in the 1950-53 Korean War, in the days before the Japanese attack on Pearl Harbor, and during the Vietnam War. Cohesive decision-making groups became dominated by "group think," according to Janis and, in each, crisis decisions were flawed in eight ways:

8

1. An illusion of invulnerability shared by most or all the members, which creates excessive optimism and encourages taking extreme risks;

2. Collective efforts were made to rationalize in order to discount warnings which might lead the members to reconsider their assumptions before they recommit themselves to their past policy decisions;

3. The group held an unquestioned belief in its inherent morality, inclining the members to ignore the ethical or moral consequences of their decisions;

4. Members held stereotyped views of enemy leaders as too evil to warrant genuine attempts to negotiate, or as too weak and stupid to counter whatever risky attempts are made to defeat their purposes;

5. There was direct pressure on any other member who expresses strong arguments against any of the group's stereotypes, illusions, or commitments, making clear that this type of dissent is contrary to what is expected of all loyal members;

6. Individuals engaged in self-censorship of deviations from the apparent group consensus, reflecting each member's inclination to minimize to himself the importance of his doubts and counterarguments;

7. They had a shared illusion of unanimity concerning judgments conforming to the majority view (partly resulting from self-censorship of deviations, augmented by the false assumption that silence means consent);

8. There emerged self-appointed mindguards, members who "protected" the group from adverse information that might shatter their shared complacency about the effectiveness and morality of their decisions.

Face-to-face groups also tend to make riskier decisions than the situation may warrant. Experimental psychologists have discovered that in small face-to-face decision-making groups a phenomenon called "shift-to-risk" tends to occur. They find that when making decisions the group as a whole tends to follow the most risk-prone members and will make a more escalatory or risky decision than would the individual members of that same group if polled privately.

Obstacle: Bureaucratic Politics and Procedures

Most regimes, even dictatorships, are power-sharing arrangements, and no one leader will make all the decisions alone. He will be influenced by the group he shares power with and group processes may influence outcomes.   States should not, as Dr. Alexander George writes in his chapter at the end of this volume, be regarded as unitary actors all acting with one mind. In some cases, like Saddam Hussein's Iraq, Stalin's Soviet Union, or Hitler's Germany, they may approach the totalitarian model, but most regimes are power-sharing networks where more than one decision-maker participates. This can yield uncertain and complex outcomes that may not square with the unitary state/rational decision-maker model implied by U.S. deterrence theory.

Within a government there are different sets of interests imbedded in different parts of the bureaucracy. Bureaucratic politics can influence government policies and this may or may not square with what is the most rational policy for that regime to follow.

Furthermore, when groups meet to make policy there may be considerable bargaining and outcomes may also be influenced by decision momentum where past policies are defended by groups previously mobilized to implement them.[6]

Beyond all this, there is declaratory policy and action policy, and the two do not always marry up. States are not unitary actors, rather, they are made up of various collections of individuals organized into several different departments, agencies, and services, each with its own domain for implementing decisions, each with its own interests and perspectives.

Decisions made may be the product of bureaucratic bargaining rather than the clear logical output of a single policy-maker. Also, different bureaucracies each have their own standard operating procedures (SOPs) for taking actions.

In his classic study of the October 1962 Cuban Missile Crisis,[7] Graham T. Allison described how Khrushchev and the Soviet Politburo made the decision clandestinely to place Soviet missiles into Cuba, hoping to present the United States with a fait accompli. The early part of the implementation of that decision went smoothly when the KGB secretly shipped the missiles to Havana in large cargo ships without detection because they were accustomed to operating using clandestine procedures. Deception and secrecy characterized all their operations.

However, once in Havana, the medium and intermediate range missile launchers, radars, and accompanying surface-to-air missiles, along with the offensive MRBMs and IRBMs were handed from the KGB to two different commands. First, the Soviet Air Defense Command was to install the SAMs, and then the engineers and technicians of the Strategic Rocket Forces were to install the offensive missiles. Their mode of operations did not include much secrecy, deception or camouflage. Rather, they operated in standard fashion, typical of how they did things within the borders of the Soviet Union. The SAM sites were erected in a trapezoidal pattern around the construction of the new MRBM and IRBM launchers just as they were normally constructed in the USSR, a sure tip-off to U.S. photo-reconnaissance experts that Soviet missiles were being installed. Carelessness gave away the operation. When unloading the missiles from the ships at Cuban docks, while Soviet technicians did not wear their uniforms, they nonetheless "formed in ranks of fours and moved out in truck convoys . . . These units (also) would display large insignia"[8] marked by "Red Army Stars" clearly visible to U.S. Intelligence.

Thus, the secret decision reached in Moscow, implemented capably in secret by the KGB, was revealed to U.S. intelligence by the SOPs of engineers and technicians in charge of erecting the missile launchers in Cuba.

This illustrates how verbal decisions made by central decision-makers can be skewed by how their subordinates carry out those orders, which rely on doctrine and standard procedures, which may or may not reflect the original intent of the orders.

Many Causes of a Failure to Deter

In summary, central decision-makers and those charged with implementation may make poorly informed decisions due to a lack of good information and biased perceptions. They may decide policy responses to U.S. warnings based on psycho-logic and "group think" rather than logic and clear thinking.

Thus, a rival's response may be distorted by the interplay of bureaucratic politics, decision momentum, stress on the decision-makers, standard operating procedures and doctrine. What central decision-makers thought they decided in a meeting at headquarters may be implemented quite differently by the organizations charged with carrying out the decisions reached.[9] This can happen even when everyone is trying to cooperate with their leadership.

Further, what also may occur may be that some members or groups, or those in a regime, will take unauthorized action and use regime assets in a way not wanted by the leadership.

Thus, international crises escalate and wars begin even when one would expect rational actors and unitary states to keep the peace, because governments are not always rational or unitary. Deterrence can fail even when the state attacked has superior military power.

Superior Strength is No Guarantee

Indeed, the history of warfare in the last two centuries shows many wars have been started by demonstrably weaker military powers initiating combat against clearly stronger enemies. This is counterintuitive and would not be predicted by deterrence theory.

One revealing study of the failures of deterrence in the 19th and 20th centuries showed that 22 percent of the wars from 1816 to 1924 (17 of 76 conflicts) were started by the much weaker party. Indeed, the record was higher in the 20th century when 33 percent or 14 of 43 wars were begun by significantly weaker states.[10]

There were many reasons why the weak would attack a much stronger adversary. In some cases the instigators of the conflict felt they had no choice, that it was a case of surrendering later or fighting now when the odds were better. In some cases, such as the Japanese attack on Pearl Harbor, those initiating the war gambled and lost, hoping that they could strike a compromise peace with the United States that would allow them to keep the Asian prizes that they had seized by force. The U.S. oil embargo imposed before the Japanese attack had placed the Tokyo leaders in a bind. They determined that without oil they either had to abandon their dreams of conquering an empire in SE Asia or had to smash the U.S. Pacific fleet and grab the territory and oil fields they coveted. These Japanese leaders in late 1941 were "beyond deterrence" and considered themselves in an "intolerable situation." In the words of one analyst, Japan "might lose, but defeat was better than humiliation and submission."[11]

In other cases, nationalistic fervor won out over good sense. In some wars, it was considered a matter of honor to oppose the stronger nation, regardless of the costs. As Patrick Henry said during the American Revolution, "give me liberty or give me death." Similar sentiments have propelled some weak states into ill-advised conflicts with stronger enemies. Some wars were accidental conflicts begun based on misperceptions. Some wars, such as the 1982 Argentine attack on the British in an attempt to seize control of the Falkland Islands, were started by the internal domestic pressures on the regime that started the bloodshed. A domestic crisis can precipitate an international conflict. In some cases there was an emotional rebellion against the policies of the stronger state. In a few cases, the causus belli was where smaller power terrorism was found out and retaliated against by the greater power. Such aggressive wars by weaker states have also begun out of hatred born of a clash of very different cultures.

In a few cases, wars were launched by leaders with severe psychological problems. One such case of a blindly irrational war was the War of the Triple Alliance (1864–1870) launched by Paraguay's crazy leader, Francisco Solano Lopez, who invaded Brazil, then declared war on Argentina, and finally also provoked Uruguay into joining the fray. Taking on three much larger and more powerful enemies at once almost annihilated the Paraguayan population, which was reduced from 1,400,000 persons in 1864 to only 221,000 by 1870. This Chaco War left Paraguay with only 29,000 living male adults by the war's end.

At the beginning of the 21st century, the United States and its allies are facing "holy war" declared by fanatical Islamists who follow Osama bin Laden and his Al Qaeda organization. To the independent observer, this appears to be a case of the flea attacking the flesh of the elephant, but perhaps the Al Qaeda attacks were meant to be provocations aimed at stimulating an overreaction by the United States that would, in turn, help mobilize the Muslim world in a we-they confrontation across the globe.

Whatever the reasons for such attacks, clearly weaker parties have not in the past always been deterred from war or escalation of war by the superior military strength of their opponents. Deterrence fails all too frequently.

13

Profiling Helps - Tailored Deterrence Needed

Clearly knowing one's enemy helps one to anticipate him, defeat him in battle, and can aid in efforts to deter him from war or escalation, but such understanding is no sure path to influence. Understanding the adversary is probably a necessary but not sufficient condition of successful deterrence. While such knowledge cannot by itself determine the outcome of events, it is a useful instrument in the tool kit.

When dealing with the Saddam Husseins, Kim Chong-ils, Bashar al-Hafezs, Muammar Qaddafis, and Mohammed Khameneis of this world there is probably no single deterrence policy that will work equally for all. Rather, actions and messages need to be tailored to each to maximize the effect on such different personalities, who are from very different strategic cultures, that the United States may be confronting in a number of very different scenarios.

Because there will likely be great disparities between adversaries, their perspectives, their relative military and political capability, their information about an unfolding situation, and a difference in the kind of crisis that could erupt, there likely should be a tailored U.S. deterrent policy for each. To put together a uniquely effective deterrence mix of actions and messages, it is first important to understand the adversary leaders and their strategic cultures. That is the purpose of the following chapters on Iraq, Iran, Libya, Syria, Pakistan, North Korea, al Qaeda, and the Muslim Brotherhood. Armed with such insights, U.S. and allied leaders will then be in a far better position to influence opponents and, hopefully, to deter conflicts or escalation of conflicts with such enemies.

Notes

1. Sun Tzu, *The Art of War,* translated, with introductions and commentary by Ralph D. Sawyer (Boulder, CO: Westview Press, 1994), 179.

2. "Statement by Press Secretary Fitzwater on President Bush's letter to President Saddam Hussein of Iraq," (Washington, D.C.: The White House, January 12, 1991).

3. Avigdor Haselkorn, *The Continuing Storm: Iraq, Poisonous Weapons and Deterrence* (New Haven, CT: Yale University Press, 1999).

4. See Barry R. Schneider, *Future War and Counterproliferation: U.S. Military Responses to NBC Threats* (Westport, CT: Praeger Publishers, 1999), 3-6.

5. Irving Janis, *Victims of Groupthink, A Psychological Study of Foreign Policy Decisions and Fiascoes* (Boston: Houghton Mifflin, 1972), 13.

6. See Barry R. Schneider, Chapter 3, "Decision Momentum," *Danger and Opportunity, Decision-making, Bargaining and Management in Three United States and Six Simulated Crises*, Ph.D. dissertation, Columbia University, 1974.

7. Graham T. Allison, *The Essence of Decision: Explaining the Cuban Missiles Crisis* (Boston: Little, Brown and Company, 1971), 102-113.

8. Ibid., 109.

9. The classic study of this is by Graham Allison, *The Essence of Decision: Explaining the Cuban Missile Crisis* (Boston: Beacon Press, 1996).

10. Barry Wolf, "When the Weak Attack the Strong: Failures of Deterrence," *A RAND Note*. N–3261-A (Santa Monica, CA: RAND Corporation, 1990).

11. See Keith B. Payne, *Deterrence in the Second Nuclear Age* (Lexington, KY: University of Kentucky Press, 1996), 10.

CHAPTER 2

Killing In The Name Of God:
Osama Bin Laden And Al Qaeda

Jerrold M. Post[1]

What manner of men are these, living in American society, for years in some cases, aiming to kill thousands while dying in the process? Surely, one would think, they must be crazed psychotics. No normal person could do such a thing. But, in fact, the al Qaeda terrorists were psychologically "normal." By no means were they psychologically disturbed. Indeed, terrorist groups expel emotionally disturbed individuals—they are a security risk.

In many ways, these new terrorists shatter the profile of suicidal terrorists developed in Israel. Seventeen to twenty-two in age, uneducated, unemployed, unmarried, the Palestinian suicide bombers were dispirited unformed youth, looking forward to a bleak future, when they were recruited, sometimes only hours before the bombing. The group members psychologically manipulated the new recruits, persuading them, psychologically manipulating them, "brainwashing" them to believe that by carrying out a suicide bombing, they would find an honored place in the corridor of martyrs, and their lives would be meaningful; moreover, their parents would win status and would be financially rewarded. From the time they were recruited, the group members never left their sides, leaving them no opportunity of backing down from their fatal choice.

The values communicated to the recruits by the commanders are revealed in their answers to questions posed in a series of interviews of 35 incarcerated Middle Eastern terrorists, who agreed to be interviewed in Israeli and Palestinian prisons. Twenty of the terrorists belonged to radical Islamic terrorist groups—Hamas, Hezbollah, and Islamic Jihad. The psychologically oriented interviews attempted to understand their life history socialization, and recruitment. They were asked to explain their attitudes towards suicide, which the Koran proscribes, and whether they had any moral red lines in terms of numbers of casualties and extent of destruction they were willing to inflict. Their answers are revealing.

One interviewed terrorist took umbrage at the term "suicide." "This is not suicide. Suicide is selfish, reflects mental weakness. This is "*istishad*" or martyrdom or self-sacrifice in the service of Allah."

One of the commanders interviewed was Hassan Salame, commander of the suicide bombers who carried out the wave of bombing in 1996 that precipitated the defeat of Prime Minister Shimon Peres and the election of Prime Minister Bibi Netanyahu. Forty-six Israelis died in the bombings. Salame is sentenced to 46 consecutive life sentences. Concerning suicidal terrorism, he said: "A suicide bombing is the highest level of jihad, and highlights the depth of our faith. The bombers are holy fighters who carry out one of the more important articles of faith." Another commander asserted: "It is suicide attacks which earn the most respect and elevate the bombers to the highest possible level of martyrdom."

Asked how they could justify murdering innocent victims, another interview subject bridled: "I am not a murderer. A murderer is someone with a psychological problem; armed actions have a goal. Even if civilians are killed, it is not because we like it or are bloodthirsty. It is a fact of life in a people's struggle. The group doesn't do it because it wants to kill civilians, but because the jihad must go on."

Asked whether there were any moral red lines, another leader responded: "The more an attack hurts the enemy, the more important it is. That is the measure. The mass killings, especially the suicide bombings, were the biggest threat to the Israeli public and so most effort was devoted to these. The extent of the damage and the number of casualties are of primary importance. In a jihad, there are no red lines."

The attitudes reflected in these statements characterize the ethos of radical Islamic terrorism. But there is a striking contrast between the Palestinian suicide bombers in Israel and the nineteen terrorists who carried out the attacks of September 11, an unprecedented act of mass casualty terrorism. They had lived in western society, in some cases for many years, exposed to its freedoms and opportunities. The leaders were older, in their mid-thirties and late twenties, and a number had received higher education. Mohammed Atta, the apparent ringleader, was thirty-three. Atta and two other hijackers had received graduate training at the technological university in Hamburg, Germany. Most came from financially comfortable middle class families in Saudi Arabia and Egypt. They blended in with society, eschewing the dress, customs and personal grooming of traditional Muslims. And yet, on the appointed day, like the Manchurian Candidate, they carried out their mission to hijack four airliners, and gave their lives while killing just over 3,000 people.

As I have come to understand them, the al Qaeda terrorists differ strikingly from the suicide bombers in Israel. Fully formed adults, they had internalized their values. They were "true believers" who subordinated their individuality to the group. They uncritically accepted the direction of the destructive charismatic leader of the organization, Osama bin Laden, and to them what he declares moral is moral, indeed it is a sacred obligation.

Osama bin Laden: A Political Personality Profile

What matter of man can inspire such acts? How could the son of a multi-billionaire construction magnate in Saudi Arabia become the leader of this powerful radical Islamic terrorist organization?

Osama bin Laden was born in Jeddah, Saudi Arabia in 1957, the 17th of 20-25 sons of Mohammed bin Laden, who had 52-54 children in total.[2] Originally an immigrant from Yemen, Mohammed bin Laden, by befriending the royal family, had established a major construction company and had amassed a fortune of some 2-3 billion dollars by the time of his death in a 1967 plane crash. Although estimates range from 18 million to as high as 200 million, it is most commonly agreed that Osama bin Laden inherited approximately 57 million dollars at age 16 from his father's estate.[3]

Osama was the only child of Mohammed and the least favorite of Mohammed's ten wives, Hamida, a Syrian woman of Palestinian descent.[4] Hamida was reportedly a beautiful woman with a free and independent spirit who, as a result, often found herself in conflict with her husband. Reportedly by the time Osama was born, Hamida had been ostracized by the family and had been nicknamed "Al Abeda" (the slave). As her only child, Osama was referred to as "Ibn Al Abeda" (son of the slave). Unlike the other bin Laden children who had natural allies in their immediate circle of siblings, Osama and his mother had no such natural allies in the family and, as a consequence, there may have been a defensive alliance between Osama and his mother against the larger family which treated "the slave and the son of the slave" with contempt. This familial exclusion was perhaps the basis of Osama bin Laden's later estrangement from his family. Reports are inconsistent as to how much of a presence Hamida was in her son's life during his early developmental years,[5] but it is clear that Mohammed bin Laden divorced Hamid prior to his death in 1967, when Osama bin Laden was ten years old.

Osama bin Laden attended King Abdul Aziz University in Jeddah. He is a certified civil engineer, and was working toward a degree in Business Management (although it is not clear that he completed his course work) preparing him to play a leadership role in the family's far flung business interests.[6] These two skill areas would serve him in good stead in Afghanistan.

An important influence on Osama bin Laden's political ideology was Abdullah Azzam, a radical Palestinian professor at the university who became an important intellectual mentor for bin Laden. It was Azzam, a noted Islamist, who provided the vision to bin Laden of what should be done in response to the invasion of the Muslim state of Afghanistan by the Soviet Union, and what role bin Laden could play. In particular, he conveyed to bin Laden the importance of bringing together Muslims from around the world to defend Afghanistan against the godless Soviet Union.

Demonstrating his already blossoming management skills, Osama bin Laden assisted Assam who founded the international recruitment network Maktab al-Khidamat (MAK - Services Office). The MAK advertised all over the Arab world for young Muslims to fight the Afghanistan jihad. In addition to the Arab and Muslim world, recruitment booths were set up in the United States and Europe. This massive international recruitment effort brought in Muslims from around the world – 5,000 were recruited from Saudi Arabia, 3,000 from Algeria, and 2,000 from Egypt. These were to become known as the Afghan Arabs, the nucleus of bin Laden's loyal followership.

A leader is not formed until he encounters his followers, and bin Laden's leadership experience during the struggle in Afghanistan against the Soviet invasion was crucial in the psychological development of bin Laden as a leader and was transformational for him. He came to Afghanistan unformed, and naïve. Using his own funds, he built clinics and hospitals, generously contributing to the *Mujahideen* movement. Eschewing an opulent life style, he lived an ascetic life in caves with his followers.

Regularly preaching about their holy mission, and inspirational in his rhetoric, bin Laden inspired his followers who came to adulate him. That they were able, with substantial American aid to be sure, to triumph over the Soviet Union, in what was to become the Soviet Vietnam, surely confirmed for Osama bin Laden and his followers the correctness of bin Laden's vision. In the Koran it is said that Allah favors the weak and the underdog. Surely they could not have triumphed over the godless Soviets unless God was on their side. This was the template of the destructive charismatic relationship between bin Laden and his religiously inspired Islamic warriors, the *Mujahideen.*

Bin Laden had not yet broken with the Saudi government, which after all was the main foundation of his family's wealth. But he had successfully vanquished one of the three major enemies identified by Muhammad Abdel Salam Farag, who wrote *The Neglected Duty: The Existing Arab State, the Western-Zionist Nexus, and the Communists.* Throughout the 1960s and 1970s, the critical enemy among this triad was the "enemy who was near," the Arab state, according to leading Islamic fundamentalists. In Farag's manifesto, he argued, "We must begin with our Islamic country by establishing the rule of God in our nation…the first battle for *jihad* is the uprooting of these infidel leaders and replacing them with an Islamic system from which we can build."[7]

Bin Laden came to see the Soviet superpower as a "paper tiger" that could be defeated, but also set his sights on the remaining super-power, the United States, as a next target. This represented a fundamental departure from the strategy of Farag, replacing "the enemy that is near" with "the enemy that is afar," the superpowers.

With the victory in Afghanistan, bin Laden the warrior king and his loyal Afghan Arab fighters were eager to continue to pursue the *jihad.* Bin Laden broadened his vision and determined to pursue the *jihad* on a worldwide basis, seeking to reconstruct the nation of Islam throughout the world, assisting Muslims who were in conflict: Algeria, Angola, Bosnia, Chechnya, Eritrea, Somalia, Sudan, and so forth.

While bin Laden was committed to the international struggle, Abdullah Azzam believed in focusing all efforts on building Afghanistan

21

into a model Islamic state, leading to increasing tension between Osama and his mentor. Following a split with Abdullah Azzam in 1988, bin Laden and Ayman al-Zawahiri, a founding father of the Islamic Jihad of Egypt, with the nucleus of their loyal followers established al Qaeda (The Base) as a direct outgrowth of MAK. The following year Abdullah Azzam died in a mysterious car bomb explosion. The most prominent theory has been that the Pakistani Intelligence Service (ISI) engineered the assassination.[8] Supporting this theory was that earlier that year Azzam had publicly and savagely attacked Pakistan, Saudi Arabia and the United States, accusing them of the "massacre" of thousands of *mujahideen* in Afghanistan.

Another key area of speculation has been the rivalry between the Egyptian and non-Egyptian members in the growing MAK/al Qaeda empire. There are reports that it was the Egyptians, directed by Zawahiri, who killed Azzam, with or without bin Laden's knowledge and acquiescence, thus removing a major obstacle to Zawahiri's growing influence over bin Laden. There has been widespread speculation that as a result of their diverging views of the future of MAK/al Qaeda it was Osama who engineered his mentor's death, but there has never been any proof linking him to the death of his one-time mentor. [9]

Regardless of who was responsible for the death of Azzam, bin Laden was left as the undisputed leader of the movement. Between the dismissal of U.S. help and the removal of Azzam from his leadership role, in the minds of both the leader and his followers, bin Laden became solely responsible for the victory over the Soviet superpower and the expansion of the jihadist movement.

With the defeat of the Soviet Union, the warrior king bin Laden and his loyal warriors had lost their enemy. As Eric Hoffer has observed, the power of a charismatic leader derives from his capacity to focus hatred against a single enemy, as Hitler did in the 1930s, unifying the German people in their hatred of the Jews. While in Sudan in 1993, bin Laden found his previous allies, the United States, with a military base on Saudi soil in the wake of the crisis in the Gulf. Decrying this "desecration" of holy Saudi soil by the infidel Americans, bin Laden had seamlessly transferred his enmity from the first defeated superpower, the Soviet Union, to the remaining superpower, the United States. As if to reinforce bin Laden's messianic vision to his followers, over the next decade al Qaeda had a series of triumphs against this new enemy.

Moreover, bin Laden actively criticized the Saudi royal family for their apostasy, decrying their stewardship of the land of the two cities, Mecca and Medina. The vigor of his criticism led Saudi Arabia to revoke his citizenship in 1994, and his family, which depended upon the Saudi leadership for their wealth, turned against him. Now bin Laden was righteously attacking the other two enemies in the triad of enemies, the Western-Israeli nexus, and one of the newly designated apostate Arab nations, Saudi Arabia. But he maintained the primary focus on the external enemy, the United States.

Yes, the leadership of the apostate nations had to be replaced, but now it was the United States that was the prime enemy, for America was responsible for propping up the corrupt leadership of these countries. Thus, he continued the strategy born in Afghanistan of focusing on the enemy who is afar, the Zionist-Crusaders, rather than the enemy who is near, the oppressive domestic rulers.

In the October 1996 Declaration of War, bin Laden justified his aggression as defensive aggression, asserting that the Islamic nation was under attack.

> *. . . The people of Islam had suffered from aggression, inequality and injustice imposed on them by the Zionist-Crusader alliance and their collaborators to the extent that Muslims' blood became the cheapest and their wealth looted in the hands of enemies. Their blood has spilled in Palestine and Iraq. The horrifying pictures of the massacre of Qana, in Lebanon are still fresh in our memory. Massacres in Tajikistan, Burma, Kashmir, Assam, Philippines, Somalia, Chechnya and in Bosnia-Herzegovina took place, massacres that send shivers in the body and shake the conscience.*[10]

With this, bin Laden and Zawahiri, who is widely believed to be bin Laden's pen, justified defensive jihad, while blaming the Zionist-Crusader alliance for every fight against Muslims. In 1996, the target was the American military in Saudi Arabia, with the stated goal of expelling the U.S. from Arabian soil, although the Declaration of War did expand the enemy to include not only military bearing arms but also non-combatants, justifying the attack in June 1996 on the American

23

military barracks in Dhahran, Saudi Arabia, Khobar Towers. Of course, to bin Laden's stated dismay, the enemy "that is afar," the United States, in fact, was near, indeed within the holy land of Arabia.

In 1998, a major expansion of the mission occurred, with the "Declaration of the World Islamic Front for Jihad Against the Jews and Crusaders" in which all Americans, civilian and military were declared to be the enemy, the civilians because they supported anti-Muslim U.S. policy.

From: Jihad Against Jews and Crusaders
World Islamic Front Statement (February 1998 Fatwa)

In compliance with God's order, we issue the following fatwa to all Muslims:

> *The ruling to kill the Americans and their allies -- civilians and military -- is an individual duty for every Muslim who can do it in any country in which it is possible to do it, in order to liberate the al-Aqsa Mosque and the holy mosque [Mecca] from their grip, and in order for their armies to move out of all the lands of Islam, defeated and unable to threaten any Muslim. This is in accordance with the words of Almighty God, "and fight the pagans all together as they fight you all together," and "fight them until there is no more tumult or oppression, and there prevail justice and faith in God."*

We -- with God's help -- call on every Muslim who believes in God and wishes to be rewarded to comply with God's order to kill the Americans and plunder their money wherever and whenever they find it.

According to bin Laden's fatwah, it is not bin Laden, but God, who has ordered religious Muslims to kill all the Americans. There is not an action that bin Laden orders that is not couched and justified in language from the Koran.

Al Qaeda: Ideology and Philosophy

The ideological and philosophical underpinnings of al Qaeda can be found in several important documents. During my service as expert witness in the spring 2001 trial of Osama bin Laden terrorists convicted for the bombings of the U.S. embassies in Kenya and Tanzania, I obtained a copy of the al-Qaeda operations manual. This document, introduced into evidence by the U.S. Department of Justice, was seized in Manchester, England in the home of Anas al-Liby, a fugitive charged in the al Qaeda terrorism conspiracy.

The provenance of the manual is somewhat obscure. Portions of it were circulating in radical Egyptian circles, suggesting that Ayman al-Zawahiri, Osama bin Laden's personal physician and designated successor, a founder of the Islamic Jihad of Egypt, probably played a central role developing the al Qaeda terrorism manual. Evidence in support of the conjecture that it is Zawahiri that is actually the author is the absence of references to Jews and Christians in the cited religious verses, for the main target of the radical Egyptians were Muslim leaders, referred to as apostates or murtid, those who renounce Islam.

This is an altogether remarkable document. On the one hand, it resembles nothing more than a basic tradecraft-training manual, concerned with how to operate in a hostile environment. There are detailed instructions on everything from ciphers to how to resist interrogation. But it is also a manual of terror, with no less than three of the eighteen lessons (chapters) devoted to techniques for assassination.

But it is not merely a list of instructions, for it is also written to inspire the undercover operator as he carries on his dangerous work. And the language at times is quite eloquent. The document reflects a sophisticated approach on the part of al Qaeda operational officials, for there is a continuing emphasis on lessons learned. Many of the chapters cite previous mistakes, which provide the basis for the points emphasized in the lesson. And they do not learn lessons only from their past mistakes, but from adversaries as well. In one section, they cite the astute observational skill of an Israeli Mossad counter-espionage agent who foiled a terrorist plot, and cite Soviet KGB sources in others. Thus, the manual reflects the adaptive learning of the organization, and the care with which al Qaeda prepares its operatives. No detail is too small, as exemplified by the instruction in lesson eight, which is concerned with Member Safety, "Do not park in no parking zones."

Many of the instructions are accompanied by elaborate justification, citing *suras* (verses) from the Koran, scholars who have provided commentary on the Koran, or *hadiths* (tradition). These elaborate justifications are offered especially when the instructions recommended seem to contradict Islamic teaching. In this text, the *suras* are not numbered, and while some are fairly well known, others are more obscure. Similarly, the sources of some of the *hadiths* are given, while the sources of others are not identified. The authenticity of many of the *suras* and *hadiths* is questionable, and several of the *suras* are taken out of context. For the Islamic youth taught to respect without questioning religious scholars, these can provide apparently persuasive religious authority justifying acts of violence. As Daniel Brumberg[11] sagely notes, in evaluating the authenticity of the sources, *sura* 3, 78, which speaks to Christians and Muslims, seems most aptly to apply to the writers of this manual.

> *There are among them (People of the Book)*
> *A section who distort*
> *The Book with their tongues*
> *(As they read the Book) you would think*
> *It is part of the Book*
> *But it is not part*
> *Of the Book: and they say*
> *"That is from Allah,"*
> *But it is not from Allah:*
> *It is they who tell*
> *A lie against Allah*
> *And (well) they know it.*

This document goes a long way towards explaining how the September 11 hijackers were able to maintain their cover, in the United States, "the land of the enemies." Lesson Eight, <u>Measures That Should Be Taken By The Undercover Member</u>, instructs the members to:

> *1. Have a general appearance that does not indicate Islamic orientation (beard, toothpick, book, (long) shirt, small Koran)*
> *2. Be careful not to mention the brother's common expressions or show their behaviors (special praying appearance, "may Allah reward you", "peace be on you", while arriving and departing, etc.)*

3. Avoid visiting famous Islamic places (mosques, libraries, Islamic fairs, etc.)

The explanation offered to "<u>An Important Question</u>: How can a Muslim spy live among enemies if he maintains his Islamic characteristics? How can he perform his duties to Allah and not want to appear Muslim?" in lesson eleven is compelling.

> "*Concerning the issue of clothing and appearance (of true religion), Ibn Taimia – may Allah have mercy on him – said, "If a Muslim is in a combat or godless area, he is not obligated to have a different appearance from (those around him). The (Muslim) man may prefer or even be obligated to look like them, provided his actions brings a religious benefit...Resembling the polytheist in religious appearance is a kind of "necessity permits the forbidden" even though they (forbidden acts) are basically prohibited.*"

Citing verses from the Koran, the instruction in effect says that Allah will forgive you for not living the life of a good Muslim, for it is in the service of Allah, in the service of jihad.

An interesting example of the manner in which episodes in the life of the prophet are employed to justify acts which Muslim tradition forbids is found in the section "Justification for Beating and Killing Hostages" in lesson eleven.

> "*Religious scholars have permitted beating. (The handbook provides an example from the life of the prophet.) The prophet – Allah bless and keep him – who was praying, started to depart saying, "Strike him if he tells you the truth and release him if he lies." Then he said, "That is the death of someone (the hostage)." In this tradition, we find permission to interrogate the hostage for the purpose of obtaining information. It is permitted to strike the non-believer who has no covenant until he reveals the news, information and secrets of his people. The religious scholars have also permitted the killing of a hostage if he insists on withholding information from Moslems. They permitted his killing so that he would not inform his people of*

27

what he learned about the Muslim condition, number and secrets. In the Honein attack, after one of the spies learned about the Muslims kindness and weakness then fled, the prophet – Allah bless and keep him – permitted (shedding) his blood and said, "Find and kill him."

The reference to religious scholars as the authoritative source is to be noted. These scholars "use a tradition" (i.e., a hadith) from Imam Mosallem, who in turn quotes Thabit Ibn Ans, probably a companion of the Prophet. The discussion is in the wake of the battle of Badr, in which a black slave was taken hostage, and apparently beaten on the orders of the Prophet himself. During the battle of Badr, there were two targets, one a line of traders with a wide variety of goods, led by Abu Sayfan coming from Syria, and the other a large army, which could not easily be vanquished. Mohammad had his men attack the latter, confirming the Muslims' virtue in their readiness to abandon worldly goods for their cause. And in the battle supreme enemies of the Muslims were killed.

There is, it should be emphasized, no reference in any of the relevant *suras* in the Koran (for example *sura* 8, 5-19, that Mohammad gave his permission to beat or to kill hostages. Rather, the key point is that the victory came only from Allah who (*sura* 9) provided "a thousand angels" and, as in *sura* 10, "there is no help except from Allah."

Thus, the battle is used as a parable to signify man's dependence on God, not to justify beating and killing hostages. Once again, by lifting the story of the battle out of context, the authors have misused religious stories and verses to provide justification for their goals. Furthermore, there is no reference in the Koran to the actions or statements attributed to Muhammad, although what the *hadith* claims may be accurate. But it is possible this story of the action and command of the Prophet was created to be persuasive. Indeed, the cold order attributed to the Prophet to "Find and kill him" is in jarring contrast to the image of the Prophet stressing mercy and compassion found throughout the Koran.

The assertion that the Prophet says, "Islam is supreme and there is nothing above it" can not be found in the Koran. The singular in the statement is discordant with many suras in the Koran, which while advancing the truth of Islam, do not imply that Islam is superior, nor are they meant to suggest that previous religions were intrinsically untrue.

In a more disturbing section of the training manual, the authors outline the "Characteristics of Members that Specialize in the Special Tactical Operations." Among the various characteristics listed are:

- Individual's physical and combat fitness (jumping, climbing, running, etc.)

- Good training on the weapon of assassination, assault, kidnapping, and bombing (special operations); Possessing cleverness, canniness and deception

- Possessing intelligence, precision and alertness

- Tranquility and calm personality (that allows coping with psychological trauma such as those of the operation of bloodshed, mass murder.) Likewise, (the ability to withstand) reverse psychological traumas, such as killing one or all members of his group. (He should be able) to proceed with the work with calmness and equanimity.

These characteristics resemble those of the stated requirements for members in general, but with some refinements. The member in general shall have a calm and unflappable personality that can tolerate murder. While the special operations member, according to the last point, shall not only be calm in the face of mass murder but must be able to kill "one or all members of his group," and to do this with calmness and equanimity – surely a description of a psychopathic personality.

The training manual's dedication provides perhaps one of the best insights into the al Qaeda leadership's view of their struggle:

In the name of Allah, the merciful and compassionate
To those champions who avowed the truth day and night ...
... And wrote with their blood and sufferings these phrases ...
The confrontation that we are calling for with the apostate
regimes does not know Socratic debates ..., Platonic ideals ...,
nor Aristotelian diplomacy. But it knows the dialogue of bullets,
the ideals of assassination, bombing, and destruction, and the
diplomacy of the cannon and machine-gun. . .

Islamic governments have never and will never be established through peaceful solutions and cooperative councils. They are established as they [always] have been
by pen and gun
> *by word and bullet*
>> *by tongue and teeth*

The literary quality and rhetorical force of this dedication is striking. Socratic debates, Platonic ideals, Aristotelian diplomacy—characteristics of a democracy—are dramatically contrasted with the absolutist, uncompromising nature of the confrontation with apostate regimes, referring to the moderate modernizing Islamic nations, who have strayed from the Islamist path, who will know only "the dialogue of the bullet, the ideals of assassination, bombing and destruction, and the diplomacy of the cannon and machine gun."

The three dangling last lines, in their pairing of qualities responsible for the establishment of Islamic governments pair words connoting violence (gun, bullet, teeth) with words reflecting persuasive rhetoric (pen, word, tongue.) Powerful rhetoric is highly valued in Arab leaders, and a notable aspect of Osama bin Laden's leadership is his capacity to use words to justify and to inspire.

Al Qaeda: Leadership, Structure and Organization

Al Qaeda is unique among terrorist organizations in its organization and structure. Perhaps reflecting his training in business management, bin Laden in effect serves as chairman of the board of a holding company ("Radical Islam, Inc."), a loose umbrella organization of semi-autonomous terrorist groups and organizations with bin Laden providing guidance, coordination, and financial and logistical facilitation.

Unlike other charismatically led organizations, such as Guzman's Sendero Luminosa (Shinning Path) of Peru, or Ocalan's terrorist PKK (Kurdistan's Workers Party) of Turkey, both of which were mortally wounded when their leader was captured, bin Laden has established a system by which designated successors are seamlessly promoted into open positions. Ayman al-Zawahiri has been designated as bin Laden's successor and number two. A leading Islamic militant, Zawahiri is a physician who founded the Egyptian Islamic Jihad and the new faction, Talaa'al al Fateh (Vanguard of Conquerors.) Zawahiri's group was responsible for the attempted assassination of President Hosni Mubarak of Egypt, and is considered responsible for the assassination of President Sadat. In fact, Zawahiri, who is responsible for more day to day decisions, can be seen as serving as CEO to bin Laden as Chairman of the Board. Chairman of the Islamic Committee and responsible for many of the Fatwas and other official writings of al Qaeda, Zawahiri indeed is reputed to be even more apocalyptic and extreme in his views than bin Laden. There has been speculation about the amount of influence Zawahiri has over bin Laden, with some believing that Zawahiri is the charismatic "behind the scenes" driving force of al Qaeda. The now deceased number three, Atef, also of the Islamic Jihad of Egypt, was chairman of the military committee and training before his death in Afghanistan in the fall of 2001 during U.S. raids following the September 11th attacks in the United States. In another example of the successor system, following Atef's death, Abu Zubaydah, formerly head of personnel and recruiting, became head of the Military Committee until his capture by U.S. and Pakistani forces in Pakistan in the spring of 2001. No doubt another successor has moved into the vacant position. Despite the fact that neither bin Laden nor Zawahiri has been seen in public since the fall 2001 U.S. attacks in Afghanistan, the fact that the al Qaeda's global network continues to operate is testimony to the effective leadership structure of the organization.

Conceptually, al Qaeda differs significantly from other terrorist groups and organizations in its structural composition. Unprecedented in its transnational nature, al Qaeda has proved a challenge to law enforcement officials. Its organizational structure, diffuse nature, broad based ethnic composition, emphasis on training, expansive financial network and its technological and military capabilities makes it not only a formidable force but difficult to detect.

Al Qaeda was reorganized in 1998 to enable the organization to more effectively manage its assets and pursue its goals. Gunaratna has characterized the revamped al Qaeda structure as having four distinct but interconnected elements: (1) a pyramidal structure to facilitate strategic and tactical direction, (2) a global terrorist network, (3) a base force capable of guerrilla warfare inside Afghanistan, and (4) a loose coalition of transnational terrorist and guerrilla groups. Strategic and tactical direction comes from al Qaeda's Consultation Council (Majlis al-Shura) consisting of five committees (Military, Business, Communications, Islamic Studies and Media), each headed by a senior leader in the organization, who oversees the operations of the organization.

It is believed that bin Laden himself oversees the Business Committee, which has developed and continues to oversee al Qaeda's extensive and sophisticated global financial resources. The committee, comprised of professional bankers, financiers and accountants coordinates the vast financial empire of al Qaeda, including legitimate institutions such as state and privately funded charities, banks and companies, as well as more clandestine entities. Although Gunaratna claims that many estimates of al Qaeda's funding for external operations have been exaggerated, he does place the annual budget of al Qaeda around $50 million.[12] Despite efforts by the international law enforcement community, al Qaeda's financial network appears to remain strong.

Ayman Al Zawahiri is believed to head the Islamic Studies Committee. Comprised of various Islamic scholars and religious clerics, this committee issues the organization's fatwas and other official writings. Although less has been written about this committee, it is clearly crucial to maintaining and generating the support of the masses of followers who subscribe to the organization's ideology.

The military committee, responsible for recruiting, training and operations is clearly one of the most powerful committees within the al Qaeda organization. Prior to his death in the fall of 2001 during the conflict in Afghanistan, Mohammed Atef headed this committee. Following his death, Abu Zubaydah seamlessly replaced Atef. In addition to maintaining and running the various training camps throughout the world, including those in Afghanistan, this committee reportedly planned and directed many of the organization's terrorist attacks. There has been a series of operational triumphs for al Qaeda over the past decade —Khobar Towers, the first World Trade Center bombing, the bombings of the U.S. embassies in Kenya and Tanzania, the attack on the U.S.S. Cole in Yemen and, of course, the most spectacular terrorist act in history, the events of September 11, the largest single act of mass casualty super-terrorism ever. Additionally, the military committee is responsible for developing the training methods and materials used in the various camps. As head of the committee, as in his previous position, Zubaydah screened applicants for al Qaeda training camps, and sent successful recruits to various places in the world to establish new al Qaeda cells. Following the capture of Abu Zubaydah by U.S. and Pakistani forces in March 2002, it is unclear who now heads this committee, although there is no doubt the position has been filled.

Al Qaeda also maintains its own guerrilla army, known as the 55th Brigade, an elite body trained in small unit tactics. This group, comprised of approximately 2,000 fighters, was reportedly the "shock troops" of the Taliban, having been integrated into their army from 1997-2001.[13] These elite fighters came from Arab states such as Egypt, Saudi Arabia, Yemen and others, Central Asian states such as Tajikistan, Uzbekistan, Kyrgyzstan and Kazakhstan, and Asian and Southeast Asian states, primarily Pakistan, Bangladesh, the Philippines, Indonesia and Malaysia. Most of the members had fought in either the Soviet/Afghan war or other regional conflicts, including conflicts in Kashmir, Nagorno-Karabakh and others.[14] Well-equipped with weaponry left by the Soviets after their retreat from Afghanistan as well as newer technology, this group remains a formidable presence despite having suffered serious losses during the fall 2001 U.S.-led attacks on Afghanistan.

Al Qaeda's global network consists of permanent or independently operating semi-permanent cells of al Qaeda trained militants established in over seventy-six countries worldwide as well as allied Islamist military and political groups globally.[15] The strict adherence to a cell structure has allowed al Qaeda to maintain an impressively high degree of secrecy and security. These cells are independent of other local groups al Qaeda may be aligned with, and range in size from two to fifteen members. Al Qaeda cells are often used as support for terrorist acts. Moreover, as was the case with the al Qaeda bombings in Kenya and Tanzania, locals who have been trained by, but are not official members of al Qaeda, may be activated to support an operation. Although the September 11 hijackers were members of sleeper cells in the United States, most cells are used to establish safe houses, procure local resources and support outside operatives as needed to carry out an attack.

Al Qaeda's approach of allying itself with various existing terrorist groups around the world enhances the organization's transnational reach. Al Qaeda has worked to establish relationships with diverse groups – not only geographically diverse, but they have also developed working relationships with organizations such as Hezballah and the Liberation Tigers of Tamil Eelam (LTTE) that do not necessarily follow the strict al Qaeda version of Salafi/Sunni Islam. According to Gunaratna, al Qaeda established relationships with at least thirty Islamist terrorist groups, including such well known groups as the Egyptian Islamic Jihad, Harakat ul-Ansar (Pakistan); Al-Ittihad (Somalia); Islamic Jihad and Hamas (Palestine); and Al Gama`a al-Islamiya (Egypt). In addition to its primary logistical base in Afghanistan, al Qaeda maintained a direct presence in Sudan, Yemen, Checnya, Tajikistan, Somalia, and the Philippines through relationships with Islamist organizations already existing in these countries.[16] In essence, bin Laden and his senior leaders have "grown" the al Qaeda "corporation" through mergers and acquisitions. Bin Laden has worked to minimize differences between the groups within the organization, emphasizing their similarities and uniting them with the vision of a common enemy – the West.

Having maintained bases in Pakistan, Sudan, Afghanistan and elsewhere as well as an ideological doctrine that rings true to much of the Islamic community, al Qaeda's membership base reaches every corner of the world, encompassing several dozen constituent nationalities and ethnic groups.[17] Its ideology has allowed al Qaeda to unite the previously unorganized global community of radical Islam, providing leadership and inspiration. Beyond the actual al Qaeda cells maintained in over 60 countries worldwide, al Qaeda sympathizers exist in virtually every country on earth. The sympathizers are not only the disenfranchised youth of impoverished communities, but include wealthy and successful businessmen in countries such as Saudi Arabia and Egypt.

Like many terrorist organizations, al Qaeda does not have a formal recruitment strategy; rather it relies on familial ties and relationships, spotters in mosques who identify potential recruits and the volunteering of many members. Al Qaeda members recruit from their own family and national/social groups, and once trained these members are often reintegrated into their own communities. Very similar to the Muslim Brotherhood, the concept of "brotherhood" draws on the concept that familial ties in the Islamic world are binding. Al Qaeda members refer to each other as "brother" and tend to view the organization as their extended family.

Al Qaeda training camps have trained both formal al Qaeda members as well as members of Islamist organizations allied with al Qaeda. According to reports, al Qaeda training is broken into essentially three separate courses: (1) Basic Training – training specific to guerrilla war and Islamic Law; (2) Advanced Training – training in the use of explosives, assassination and heavy weapons; and (3) Specialized Training – training in techniques of surveillance and counter-surveillance, forging and adapting identity documents and conducting maritime or vehicle-based suicide attacks.[18]

Al Qaeda has developed extensive training materials used in their camps and other training situations. In addition to paramilitary training, a great emphasis is placed on Islamic studies – Islamic law, history and current politics. The extensive training materials produced by al Qaeda, exemplified by the manual discussed at the beginning of this chapter, clearly demonstrate al Qaeda's twin training goals – the indoctrination of recruits in both military and religious studies.

Al Qaeda: What Next?

The unique and far reaching transnational nature of al Qaeda represents one of the greatest threats to international security. Following the attacks of September 11, 2001, on New York and Washington D.C., NATO, for the first time since its founding 52 years ago, invoked article V stating that an attack on one member state of NATO was considered an attack on all member states of NATO. A massive air and ground campaign was launched against al Qaeda, its operational bases and its Taliban supporters in Afghanistan. As a result of the campaign, al Qaeda has suffered severe losses, including the death and/or capture of several senior leaders. Despite these losses and the dispersal of members throughout the world, in testament to its organizational structure al Qaeda remains operationally intact – wounded for sure, but certainly not destroyed.

For many al Qaeda followers, the fall 2001 attacks in Afghanistan only served to reinforce their sense of righteous belief in their cause and their perception of the West as anti-Islamic aggressors. Although we have not seen a second large-scale al Qaeda attack, there is nothing to suggest that al Qaeda is no longer operational. Al Qaeda spends up to years planning a single operation, so it is quite conceivable they already have other terrorist events planned. Despite al Qaeda's Afghan base having been destroyed and its leadership dispersed, its cellular structure remains intact with active cells and sleeper cells throughout the world. Most likely though, due to the highly focused international attention, the next wave of al Qaeda attacks will be on a smaller scale and undertaken by cells operating independently.

There are several possible scenarios to consider for the future of al Qaeda following the September 11 terrorist attacks and subsequent U.S.-led war in Afghanistan:

1. In the event of Bin Laden's death or capture, al Qaeda's flat, dispersed organizational structure, the presence of a designated successor, the nature of bin Laden's and Zawahiri's leadership and charisma and their enshrined religious mission-all suggest that the terrorist network would survive. Bin Laden's loss would assuredly be a setback, but since Zawahiri is already running al Qaeda's daily operations, his transition to the top job would be virtually seamless. The organization's luster for alienated Muslims would dim, but within the organization, Zawahiri's considerable stature and charismatic attractiveness should permit him to carry on the network's mission. Bin Laden has not been seen in public since September 23, 2001. Bin Laden's death would surely lead to his designation as a martyr in the cause of Islam and might well precipitate terrorist actions. His capture could lead to retaliatory hostage-taking or other terrorist actions. In either event, al Qaeda would survive.

2. There have been various reports that Zawahiri had been killed or seriously injured in bombing raids in Afghanistan in the fall of 2001. A number of inner-circle members have also been said to have died. Should Zawahiri, in fact, be dead or incapacitated, and bin Laden survives, this would also be a major setback. But because it has systematically prepared individuals for and promoted them to leadership positions, al Qaeda, with bin Laden alive, would eventually recover and continue.

3. Should both bin Laden and Zawahiri, *as well as other key leaders*, be killed or captured, in effect eliminating the leadership echelon, this would be a major, possibly fatal, blow to the terrorist network, although the international jihadist movement inspired by al Qaeda and its senior leadership would no doubt continue. It is likely that in this scenario members of most al Qaeda cells would disperse and attach themselves to locally based groups, and reprisal attacks could be expected. Other groups inspired by al Qaeda's success and mission would continue to operate, most likely though limited to their regional area of operation. The transnational nature of the al Qaeda as an effective terrorist network in and of itself would most likely be destroyed.

4. Finally, should bin Laden disappear, the myth of the hidden imam would probably be infused with mythic power, and others might well speak in bin Laden's name in attempting to continue al Qaeda's terrorist mission.

President Bush and British Prime Minister Tony Blair have taken pains to clarify that the War on Terrorism is not a war against Muslims, but a war against terrorism. In contrast, seeking to frame this as a religious war, bin Laden has now laid claim to the title of commander-in-chief of the Islamic world, opposing the commander-in-chief of the Western world, President George W. Bush. Alienated Arab youth find resonance in his statements, and see him as a hero. For many al Qaeda followers the fall 2001 attacks in Afghanistan only served to reinforce their sense of righteousness in their cause and their perception of the west as anti-Islamic aggressors. Al Qaeda has become a catalyst for an international jihadist movement that will continue to grow independent of the original parent organization.

Notes

1. Jerrold Post is Professor of Psychiatry, Political Psychology and International Affairs at the George Washington University, Washington, D.C. He is the co-author of *Political Paranoia: The Psychopolitics of Hatred*, published in Germany.

2. There are varying reports about Osama bin Laden's exact location within the family, although 17th of 20/25 sons of 52 or 53 children is the most consistent figure available. Example sources include: Dickey, Christopher and Daniel McGinn. "Meet the bin Ladens," *Newsweek.* Found at: http://www.msnbc.com/news/639250.asp; Dorschner, John, "Osama bin Laden: The Mastermind of Terror." Knight Ridder Newspapers, September 24, 2001. Found at: http://www.freep.com/news/nw/terror2001/ osama24_20010924.html; Miller, John, ABC interview with Osama bin Laden, see, http://www.terrorism.com/documents/crs-report.shtml.

3. As noted, there is no single agreed upon figure as to the inheritance of Osama bin Laden and reports vary. Sources include: Beyer, Lisa. "The Most Wanted Man in the World," Time.com. Found at: http://www.time.com/time/covers/1101010924/ wosama.html; McFadden, Robert D. "Bin Laden's Journey From Rich, Pious Boy to the Mask of Evil," *The New York Times*, September 30, 2001.; Dorschner, John. "A Shadowy Empire of Hate was Born of a War in Afghanistan," Knight Ridder Newspapers, September 24, 2001.

4. Nearly all reports refer to Osama bin Laden as the only child (or the only son) of his mother with Muhammed bin Laden. Following her divorce, Osama bin Laden's mother remarried and subsequently started a second family.

5. While some reports claim that Muhammed had Hamida removed from the family before Osama turned one-year-old, other reports more consistently note that she was ostracized by the family but do not indicate that her departure from the family (following her divorce with Muhammed) was as early as that.

6. While most reports indicate that Osama did indeed obtain his civil engineering certificate and at least start his degree in Business Management, Rohan Gunaratna in his *Inside al Qaeda: Global Network of Terror* (New York: Columbia University Press, May 15, 2002) states that contrary to other reports, bin Laden did *not* study engineering.

7. Hashim, A. "Usama bin Laden's" Worldview and Grand Strategy," paper presented to conference at Navy War College, November 19,2001.

8. Adam Robinson, *Bin Laden: Behind the Mask of the Terrorist* (New York: Arcade Publishing, 2001).

9. See Gunaratna, op. cit.

10. *Declaration of War (1)* available on the World Wide Web at http://www.msanews.mynet.net/MSANEWS/199610/19961013.10.html.

11. The editor wishes to acknowledge his appreciation of the critical review of the text by Daniel Blumberg, an expert on radical Islam who is Professor of Government and

Middle Eastern Affairs at Georgetown University. Commentary on the *suras* draws on the analysis of Professor Blumberg.

12. Gunaratna, 60-63.

13. Gunaratna, 58.

14. Gunaratna, 59.

15. Countries believed to have active al Qaeda cells include: Britain, France, Germany, Bosnia, Croatia, Albania, Spain, Argentina, Brazil, Paraguay, Uruguay, Trinidad and Tobago, Australia, Papua New Guinea, Borneo, Brunei, Nauru, Fiji, Philippines, Indonesia, Malaysia, Singapore, Saudi Arabia, UAE, West Bank and Gaza, Egypt, Pakistan, Yemen, Somalia, Sudan, Comoros, Ethiopia, Kenya, Libya, South Africa, U.S., Canada, as well as a growing presence in South America. See Gunaratna, 79.

16. Gunaratna, Rohan. *Inside Al Qaeda: Global Network of Terror*, 5-6.

17. Gunaratna, 96.

18. Gunaratna, 72

CHAPTER 3

The Muslim Brotherhood and Islamic Radicalism

Gary M. Servold

Introduction

"God is our purpose, the Prophet our leader, the Qur'an our constitution, Jihad our way and dying for God's cause our supreme objective"[1] is the slogan of the Muslim Brotherhood, established in 1928 by Hassan Al-Banna. The Muslim Brotherhood or "Al-Ikhwan Al-Muslimum" (in Arabic) represents the "mother movement"[2] of the Islamic fundamentalist. With branches in "70 countries all over the world," [3] the Muslim Brotherhood is the most pervasive grass roots Islamic fundamentalist movement in the world. The Brotherhood was the first wide-ranging, well-organized, international Islamic movement of modern times.

The Muslim Brotherhood requires scrutiny because most of the leaders of the world's Islamic terrorist groups have their roots in this movement. Ramzi Yousef, the leader of the terrorist cell that attempted to blow up the World Trade Center in 1993, was recruited into the Brotherhood when he attended colleges in Wales. Osama bin Laden was similarly recruited while attending university classes in Saudi Arabia. They, and thousands of others now in terrorist organizations, have embraced the radical Islamist vision articulated by the Brotherhood.

If one is to understand the thinking of activists in al Qaeda, Hamas, the Islamic Jihad, and other extreme Islamic groups, the understanding of the Muslim Brotherhood is the place to begin.

Although recent statements by Brotherhood leaders articulate non-violent means for social change, Brotherhood members have resorted to violent measures. One of the most notable episodes of violence was the assassination of Egypt's President Anwar Sadat in October 1981 by Muslim Brothers. This organization serves as the breeding ground for both direct and indirect support to a wide variety of terrorist organizations, from Al-Takfir Wal Higra in Egypt to Hamas in Jordan and Lebanon. The Brotherhood is not a monolithic phenomenon. Internal factions and divergent approaches on a general theme characterize it.

The common theme within the Muslim Brotherhood is the rejection of the secularist approach that limits religion to a relationship between man and his creator. The Brotherhood views Islam not just as a religion but as a holistic system dealing with all aspects of life. Spreading the principle that Islam is " Creed and state, book and sword, and a way of life,"[4] it seeks to move Islam from the confines of the Mosque to the halls of government. Establishment of the Islamic sharia (law) as the controlling basis of the society and state is the first pillar of the Brotherhood. The Muslim Brotherhood seeks the creation of a Muslim state, the liberation of Muslim countries from imperialism, and the unification of Muslim nations as its second pillar. Through informal social programs focused on the disadvantaged low and middle class, the Brotherhood courts individuals, families, and communities in the creation of a state within a state of like-minded Islamists. The Brotherhood seeks to change the nature of the society and state in moderate pro-western governments of the Middle East through manipulation of the political process and infiltration of key institutions.

The group's international structure, history of violence, connections to terrorists, plan of action and beliefs, and its current political activism make the Muslim Brotherhood a major non-governmental strategic rival in the world. Within the Middle East, the secular pro-western moderate governments of Egypt, Israel, and Jordan face a substantial challenge from the Brotherhood. These governments are key to United States policy in the Middle East. This analysis will provide insights into the history, objectives, strategy, and organization of the Muslim Brotherhood. Also to be explored are the linkages between the Muslim Brotherhood and today's Islamic terrorist threats. Understanding the Muslim Brotherhood is important if U.S. policy-makers are to make informed Middle East engagement choices.

Evolution of the Middle East and Modern Fundamentalists

The history of the Muslim Brotherhood is rooted in events in the Islamic religion and during the formation of the nations of the Middle East. The legacy of reform in Islamic communities is considerable. In the 18th and 19th centuries Muslims saw a continual erosion of their traditional society by foreign colonial maritime powers and the influences of the Ottoman Empire's overlordship of the Arab world. The Ottoman Empire during the 18th century included Egypt and the area of the western Arabian Peninsula region of Hejaz, along the Red Sea. Through control of Hejaz, the Ottomans gained religious prestige and custodianship of the Holy Cities of Medina and Mecca. The Ottomans appointed local sharifs as the protectors and administrators of the holy cities.

It was in this setting in 1745 that one of the most pervasive radical reform movements was begun by Abd al-Wahhab, who began preaching a purification of Islam from the external influences of foreigners and their modern thinking. Abd al-Wahhab was heavily influenced by the thirteenth century teaching of Ibn Taymiya from the Hanbali school. Ibn Taymiya sought to eliminate any historic transformation of Islam and return to strict adherence to Sunna or traditions as practiced in the seventh century by Muhammad and the first four caliphs or successors.

Abd al-Wahhab was expelled from his home community for preaching the return to the strict Hanbali school of Islamic law and purification of polytheism from Islam. He resettled in Ad-Dir'iyah under the protection of its chief, Muhammad ibn Saud, and newest convert to Wahhabism.

Muhammad ibn Saud used the Wahhab's ideology to consolidate power and authority over the nomadic Bedouin tribes of central Arabia who had no nationalistic or unifying interests. Saud used warrior-preachers, Ikhwan, to spread the Wahhab fundamentalist revival throughout the center of the Arabian Peninsula.

The Ikhwan (Arabic for "brothers") established colonies of agricultural settlements and lived among and converted individuals, families, and tribes to an uncompromising Islam. The Ikhwan weaved the Wahhab ideology into the social fabric of the Bedouin tribes through teaching, fighting, and social integration.

43

The union of Wahhabism and Muhammad ibn Saud marked the beginning of a religious ideology used by three Saudi dynasties that vied for power and control of Arabia and the Holy Cities. Wahhabism and the Saud dynasty in the twentieth century created the Kingdom of Saudi Arabia and they drove the Hashemite family, the Sharifs of Mecca and Medina, from the Holy Cities.

Since the tenth century the descendents of the Hashemite family had served as Sharif of Mecca, Guardians of the Holy Places of Islam. The Hashemite families are direct descendents of the Prophet's daughter Fatima and son-in-law Ali, who was also the Prophet's cousin. They were entrusted with the guardianship of the Holy Cities. From 1916 to 1918, through the efforts of T. E. Lawrence ("Lawrence of Arabia"), the Hashemite Sharif of Mecca, Husayn ibn 'Ali aligned with the British to challenge and push the Ottomans from Transjordan and Syria in the Arab Revolt. By 1918, Husayn and his two sons, Faysal and Abdullah, had succeeded in dislodging the Ottomans. Faysal established a government in Damascus.

In 1920, the Conference of San Remo (Italy) created two mandates that separated the area covered by present day Israel and Jordan from Syria and Lebanon. The British mandate encompassed present-day Israel and Jordan. The French mandate encompassed Syria and Lebanon. The French with their mandate pushed Faysal from power in Damascus in 1920. In 1921, with British support, Faysal established himself as King of Iraq and Abdullah became the emir of Transjordan. The Hashemites, in disagreement with their benefactor, Britain, refused to agree to the terms of the Balfour Declaration approving a national homeland in Palestine for the Jews.

During the period from 1921 to 1924, the Saudi Wahhabis consolidated power on the Arabian Peninsula. Without the support of the British and allied Arabian factions, the Hashemites were not able to stem the expansion of the Saud dynasty into the Hejaz region. In 1924, the Saudi Wahhabis marched into Hejaz, ending the Hashemite rule over the Holy Cities. The British, in a protectorate role, acknowledged the sovereignty of The Hashemite Kingdom of Jordan in 1923 and the Kingdom of Saudi Arabia in 1927.

The Wahhabis wanted to continue their expansion in the Arab world by expelling the British and French. Ibn Saud broke with the Wahhabis in

1927 when the Wahhabis denounced him for selling out the cause. Ibn Saud seeing the reign of terror begun by the Wahhabi religious police, fearing loss of his country in a fight with the colonial powers, and desiring to pursue oil exploration concessions, began a brutal repression of the Wahhabis and many of the Ikhwan fled to Egypt and other Arab countries. Saudi Arabian Wahhabism played a critical role in the formation of the modern state of Jordan, Saudi Arabia, and in the spread Islamic fundamentalism across the Red Sea to Egypt.

With the completion of the Suez Canal in 1869 the British established de facto control of Egypt through military occupation and political maneuvering centered on the protection of the canal as a vital link to the British Empire. To prevent capture by Turkish or German forces, the United Kingdom formally expanded its role in 1914 by decreeing that Egypt was a British Protectorate.

Following World War I, an intense Egyptian resentment flowered against the British and the Suez Canal Company. The Wafd nationalist political party, the monarch proponents, and the British occupation forces struggled continuously to maintain control of Egypt from 1918 until 1956.

Egyptian society experienced a succession of different forms of government from constitutional monarchy to royal decree, characterized by intense rivalry among competing Egyptian political factions. Ever present was the British influence with the threat of military intervention to protect their Suez Canal holdings. In the backdrop of foreign influences, political instability, social upheaval, and Wahhabis influences the Muslim Brotherhood came to life.

The Muslim Brotherhood's Growth in Egypt

In 1928, armed with his devout Islamic family upbringing and formal education as a teacher at the Dar Al-Uloum School in Cairo, Hassan Al-Banna began preaching the principle that Islam was a comprehensive way of life to commoner patrons of cafes and coffee shops in towns along the Nile. Al-Banna's message struck a popular cord among all classes of Egyptian society. With a small group of six devout followers, Al-Banna formed the organization Al-Ikhawns Al-Muslimums, with the first goal of "fighting against the secular Egyptian constitution of 1923 to obtain the creation of an Islamic society on the pattern set up in the Arabian Peninsula by the Wahabites Ikhwans."[5]

The history of the Brotherhood unfolded in five phases. The first phase from 1928 to 1940 is the period of growth as a religious and social reform movement focused on gaining members through grassroots programs that established schools, youth clubs, centers, factories, and mosques. The organization's social welfare network distributed free meals to the needy. The path to change used by the Brotherhood was "mass Islamization through education, and information, acts of charity and welfare on behalf of the community."[6] This period marked the Brotherhood's establishment of a state within a state, filling a void in the government's social programs. Many influential future leaders of Egypt fell under the spell of Al-Banna, including a future Egyptian President, Anwar Sadat. Early in his career Sadat invited Al-Banna to teach his soldiers and he secretly participated in Al- Banna's seminars.

Key events in Phase I of the Muslim Brotherhood's growth were:

1928: Organization was founded by Hassan al-Banna as a youth club.

1936: The Muslim Brotherhood took a pro-Arab position following the Anglo-Egytian Treaty and the start of the Palestinian uprising against Zionist settlements in Palestine.

1939: The Muslim Brotherhood was defined as a political organization, that based itself on the Koran and the Hadith as a system that is applicable even for the modern society.

1940: The Brotherhood passed 500 branches, each with its own centre, mosque, school and club.[7]

In its second phase, from 1940 to 1948, the Brotherhood became politicized in the fight against the British occupation and the monarchy of King Farouk. When World War II started, El Banna sent two letters and emissaries to gain support from Adolph Hitler and Benito Mussolini for the "ejection of the British enemy and the downfall of the corrupt regime of King Farouk."[8] In 1942, Al-Banna convened the sixth Congress of the Muslim Brotherhood where he called for the establishment of an Islamic government through the political process in the future Parliamentary elections. During the Second World War, the Muslim Brotherhood formed an internal radical paramilitary wing "The Secret Apparatus"[9] that stole weapons, started clandestine military training, and collaborated against the British and the Egyptian monarchy. When the Parliamentary election was held in 1945, the Brotherhood candidates were defeated amidst vocal claims that King Farouk's men rigged the elections. This failure and the corruption of the election process spurred the Brotherhood's more militant apparatuses into action. They instigated riots, burned Jewish businesses, threatened journalists, bombed movie theaters, and murdered judges and ministers. After Egyptian Prime Minister Nokrashi outlawed the Brotherhood, they assassinated him.

Following the assassination, the Egyptian Government repressed and outlawed the organization, forcing many Brothers to move to Jordan, Syria, and Saudi Arabia. Thus began the globalization of their cause. Egyptian universities educating religious Arab men from all over the region also served as a means of exporting the Brotherhood ideology to other Arab countries. "Quickly there shot up branches of the Muslim Brotherhood in Syria, Sudan, Jordan, and in other countries."[10]

On the eve of the first Arab-Israeli War there were 38 branches in Palestine alone.[11] It is through the inspiration of the Muslim Brotherhood that the Palestinian Students Union was formed in Cairo. The Union membership included many of the future leaders of the PLO, including Yasser Arafat, Salim Zanum, and Abu Iyad. Sheikh Ahmad Yassin, father of today's Hamas terrorist organization, headed the growth of the Brotherhood in Gaza and Palestine under the name, Muslim Association. Following Al-Banna's guidance "... when words are banned, hands make their moves,"[12] thousands of Brothers joined Arab forces and fought in the First Arab-Israeli War in 1948.

Key events in the second phase of the Brotherhood's development included:

1940-45: During the World War II, the Brotherhood experienced a fast growth, and was joined by individuals from the lower and middle strata of the society.

1946: The Brotherhood claimed to have more than 5,000 branches, over 500,000 members and even more sympathizers, estimated at over three million. Over 50 branches were established in Sudan to begin the international expansion of the Brotherhood.[13]

1948: Brothers joined the Palestinian side in the war against the Zionists of Palestine. Many Egyptian officers were exposed to their ideology during this war.

> The Brothers blamed the Egyptian government for passivity in the war against the Zionists and launched terrorist attacks inside Egypt.
>
> *December:* The Muslim Brotherhood was banned by the authorities.
>
> *December 28:* Prime Minister Mahmud Fahmi Nokrashi was assassinated by a Brotherhood member. This leads to even more repression from the government.[14]

The third phase, 1948-1953 was marked by the Brotherhood's cooperation with revolutionary movements leading to the ousting of the monarchy by Colonel Gamal Abdel Nasser's Free Officers coup and its uprising against the British control of the Suez Canal. After this period of violence, Al-Banna realized he had lost control of the paramilitary wing. He stated that those who carried out the violence were "neither Brothers nor Muslim."[15] Despite his denunciation of violence, this episode was a harbinger of the future of the Brotherhood. The Brothers who had picked up arms in 1948 had the experience and the tools to pursue a more violent course. With Al-Banna's death the door was open for the development of a more violent ideology within the Brotherhood.

Key events in phase three of this movement were:

1949 *February:* Hassan al-Banna was killed in Cairo by Farouk's agents in retaliation for the assassination of Prime Minister Nokrashi.

1950: The Brotherhood was legalized as a religious body.

1951: Hassan Islam al-Hudaibi, a moderate, was elected leader of the Brotherhood.

1952 *January:* The Brotherhood actively supported the anti-British riots in Cairo.

> *July:* Free Officer's coup toppled King Farouk's monarchy. As a reward for their cooperation, the Brotherhood was not banned by the Free Officer's Revolutionary Command Council (RCC).[16]

The fourth phase, 1954 to 1981, was characterized by violent confrontation with Nasser's government, the second outlawing of the Brotherhood, and the rise of an extremist ideology within the Brotherhood that promoted violence to change the government from the top down. These Brotherhood members formed the violent offshoot terrorist organization that assassinated Anwar Sadat.

The Brothers blamed Nasser for failing to take a more aggressive posture against Israel, failing to institute Sharia (Islamic Law), and for the perceived unsatisfactory results of the Anglo-Egyptian Treaty of 1954 concerning control of the Suez Canal. A cycle of assassination attempts by the Brotherhood was followed by brutal repression, arrests, detentions, and executions by the Nasser government. During the crackdown, the third leader of the Brotherhood, Sayed Qutb (aka, Seid Kutub Ibrahim, Sayyid Qutb) was imprisoned.

Qutb was a virulent opponent of Nasser's socialist regime. While incarcerated, his writings were smuggled out of prison and attracted a following. Qutb's message in some twenty-four different books advocated the same program: destruction of the secular governments, revolution from the top down to establish an Islamic state, and the uncompromising pursuit of these goals by all means including violence. "With the infusion of Qutb's ideology, the Brotherhood became a powerful opponent of Nasser's regime."[17] Statements in his book "*Landmarks*" led to his arrest, conviction, and execution in August 1966 for plotting to overthrow the government. Following Qutb's death and the stinging Arab defeat in the 1967 Arab–Israeli War, opposition continued to grow.

After Nasser's death, Anwar as-Sadat appeased the Brotherhood with conciliatory gestures and the liberalization of Egypt's political system. Sadat's 1973 War with Israel to regain bargaining power and prestige brought significant domestic frustration. Although Sadat's efforts did facilitate the withdrawal of Israeli forces from the Sinai, the Brotherhood was strongly opposed to Sadat's 1977 address to the Israeli Knesset (Parliament) and the 1978 Camp David accords normalizing relations with Israel and establishing a framework for resolution of the Palestinian issues. Economic benefits from the United States aid that began in 1975 and reached one billion dollars by 1980 could not replace the loss of Arab funding that resulted from Sadat's peace overtures to Israel. Expulsion from the Arab League only heightened popular resentment. Sadat's democratization did not produce the level of economic revitalization needed. Economic hardships resulted in riots in Egypt's major cities in 1977. The government response left 79 people dead, 1,000 injured, and 1,250 in jail. In September 1981, Sadat, alerted by intelligence reports predicting another uprising, jailed another 1,300 members of the political elite who were made up mainly of Brothers.

In the shadows of this unrest and armed with Qutb's ideology, militant Brothers founded the Egyptian Jihad organization under the leadership of Mohammed Abed Alsalem Faraj. Participants in this group included Sheikh Omar Abed Elrahman, later convicted in connection with the 1993 bombing of the World Trade Center and Iman Zawahari, the reputed right hand operative of Osama bin Laden. On October 6, 1981, the Egyptian Jihad executed their plot to topple Sadat's government in a three-day campaign of terror that began with the assassination of Sadat. They then killed 120 soldiers at prayer in a mosque and another 90 police and security personnel at other locations. Vice President Hosni Mubarak with the help of loyal forces quelled the violence and began his twenty-year rule as the President of Egypt.

Key events in phase four of the Muslim Brotherhood included the following:

1954 *February:* Due to differences over by Egypt's system of government and law, Sharia or secular law, the Brotherhood was banned again.

> *October 23:* A Brotherhood activist, Abdul Munim Abdul Rauf, tried to assassinate President Nasser, but failed. Following this, he and 5 other Brothers were executed, 4,000 members were arrested. Thousands fled to Syria, Saudi Arabia, Jordan, and Lebanon.

1962-1967: Egypt engaged in armed conflict against Saudi Arabia in the Yemen civil war. Saudi Arabian supporters provided financial support to the Muslim Brotherhood in Egypt. Expatriated Brotherhood members in Saudi Arabia were influenced by Wahhabism and the Muslim Brotherhood eventually published and distributed the Wahhabist books "Minhaj al-Muslim" by Jabir al-Jaza'iri and "Fath al-Majid" (The "Gospel" of Wahhabism) by Ibn Abd al-Wahhad.[18]

1964: A general amnesty was granted to imprisoned Brothers. Nasser wanted them to join the newly formed government party, the Arab Socialist Union, to ward off the threat of communism. This conditional cooperation policy did not succeed, and Nasser was the target of 3 more assassination attempts by Brotherhood members.

1966: The top leaders of the Brotherhood were executed, and many other members were imprisoned.

1968 *April:* Around 1,000 Brothers were released from prison by President Nasser.

1970: With the death of Nasser, the new president, Anwar as-Sadat, promised the Brothers that Sharia shall be implemented as the law of Egypt. All Brotherhood prisoners were released.

1976: The Muslim Brotherhood was not allowed to participate in the general elections, so many Brothers ran as independent candidates or as members of the ruling Arab Socialist Party. Altogether they gained 15 seats.

1979: The Brotherhood strongly opposed the peace agreement between Egypt and Israel.

1981 *September:* About 2,000 dissidents were arrested, of which a majority are Brothers.

October 6: Four Brothers assassinated President Sadat.[19]

The fifth phase, from 1981 to the present, of the group's evolution has been characterized by the Muslim Brotherhood's shift from the violent active revolution ideology of Qutb back to Al-Banna's more moderate approach. The Muslim Brotherhood has tried to distance itself from the violent splinter groups spawned from the earlier Brotherhood ideology. The Brotherhood repudiated violent means as a method of creating their Islamic society. Now the focus of the Brotherhood is on changing the system through the existing political system. Although the Brotherhood remains outlawed as an official political party, they continue to create alliances with sanctioned opposition parties to gain seats in the Egyptian Parliament. They have successfully gained representation in the Egyptian Parliament and control the majority of Egypt's professional associations, despite counteractions by Mubarak's government to limit their influence.

51

Operating under twenty years of emergency law and Mubarak government domination, thousands of Brothers remain incarcerated in a swelling prison population numbering in the tens of thousands. As extremist groups executed a wave of violence designed to topple the Egyptian government through the destruction of the three billion dollar[20] tourist industry, the Muslim Brotherhood has been caught up in the extensive counter-insurgency efforts of the government.

Since rising to power President Mubarak has walked a hard-line on the liberalization of the political process and control of groups viewed as dangerous to the secular government. While allowing known Brotherhood members to participate in elections as individuals, the elections have always been marred by allegations of irregularities and impropriety by his ruling party. He has struggled with the question of how to channel violent opposition groups into a peaceful political process. On the other hand, the Muslim Brotherhood often cites the lack of access to the political process as the major cause of the violence.

The influence of the Muslim Brotherhood has been checked by the strong popular support given to Mubarak in the most recent elections. With 79 percent of the population voting, he received 94 percent approval in the referendum. Economic success, along with a growing disaffection for the radical Islamists, bolstered Mubarak's popularity. The economic boom in Egypt is one of the strongest in the world registering a 6 percent increase in Gross Domestic Product (GDP), 2 percent higher than the world average, and exceeding the population growth rate of 1.8 percent. The GNP per capita has increased every year since 1996 reaching 3.8 percent in 1999. Mubarak is continuing a privatization program that should continue to spur the economic improvement. He has also embarked on an infrastructure-rebuilding program that is gradually improving conditions in the country. With strong military and security forces support, business leader support, popular support, and international support, Mubarak has limited the Muslim Brotherhood's appeal.

Key events in the fifth period in the Muslim Brotherhood's evolution include:

1984: Brotherhood formed a coalition with the New Wafd party to gain eight seats in the 360 member People's Assembly.

1987: Brotherhood formed a tripartite alliance with the Liberal and Labor parties to gain 36 seats in the People's Assembly.

1990: Election law was changed that allowed individuals, as opposed to parties, to participate in elections. Previous law required parties to received eight percent of the votes to gain representation. Brotherhood boycotts the election at the national level but continues to field candidates at the local level.

1992: Brotherhood unveiled the "Islam is the solution" political campaign slogan signifying a major push in the political circles for the 1995 elections. The Brotherhood gained control of the prominent Lawyers' Association further solidifying their control of the major professional organization including the doctors', engineers', and pharmacists' professional associations. The Brotherhood controlled the majority of Egypt's 21 professional associations.

1993: Syndicate Law 100 was enacted that required 50 percent of the membership to vote for the election to be official.

1993: Brotherhood condemned the attempted assassination of the Minister of Information Safwat al-Sharif and the Minister of the Interior Hasan al-Alfi. They stated that, "the attack was a devaluation of the human soul…Religion cannot justify it."[21]

1995: Brotherhood fielded 150 candidates in a coalition of 120 Labour Party candidates to form the second largest force in the 1995 elections.

1995: Fifty-four Brotherhood members of professional organizations were arrested and sentenced to five years in jail for belonging to an illegal group and trying to control the professional organizations.

1995 *June 26*: Extremists were suspected of an attempted assassination of Mubarak while visiting Ethiopia.

1997 *November*: Gunmen attacked and killed 18 Greek tourists in Cairo. Mubarak security forces engaged in a counter-insurgency campaign that resulted in over 1,200 casualties between the militants and the police. Al-Gamaa al-Islamiya (the Islamic Group) and Islamic Jihad killed 58 foreign tourists at

Luxor. A government crackdown led to a swelling prison population estimated to be over 20,000.

1999: al-Gamaa al-Islamiya leadership renounced violence and declared it will cease all anti-government activities.

1999 *October*: Authorities arrested 16 Muslim Brotherhood members for plotting to infiltrate and subvert professional organizations.

2000: The Muslim Brotherhood won 17 seats in the People's Assembly, making it the largest opposition faction.

Brotherhood's Organization, Strategy, Objectives, and Regional Implications

The structure of the Muslim Brotherhood is not widely known outside the membership of the organization for reasons of security and self-preservation. While the exact number of members is not known, there are other indicators of the memberships' relative strength. In Egypt, Jordan, Algeria, Sudan, and Lebanon admitted Muslim Brotherhood members hold public office; this is an indicator of the organization's extensive strength and internationalism. A more sinister indicator of strength is the estimated number of Brotherhood members and sympathizers killed in Syria, 10,000 to 30,000, and the number of persons displaced, 800,000, in 1981. The bulging prison population of Muslim Brothers in Egypt is estimated to exceed 15,000. The rising number of Brotherhood non-governmental organizations (NGOs) like Islamic Relief, Mercy International, Muslim Association, Muslim Arab Youth Movement, and the Holy Land Foundation are just the identifiable tip of the iceberg of the Muslim Brotherhood's worldwide NGO support efforts. The Brotherhood's identifiable presence on college and university campuses spans much of the world, University of South Florida (US), Oxford College (UK), West Glamorgan Institute of Higher Education (UK), Cairo and Al Azhar University (Egypt), Khartoum University (Sudan), Amman University (Jordan), the University of Medina (started by the Brotherhood in Saudi Arabia), [22] University of Jeddah (Saudi Arabia), and Islamic University (Pakistan). While these examples and figures do not give an exact number of members, the sheer global nature of the organization suggests a membership in the many millions.

The Brotherhood uses an informal social network that is relatively impervious to authoritarian state control. The informal network is an indelible component of the Middle East social fabric. The basic building block is a five-man cell known as a "family"[23] in which the initial indoctrination to the Brotherhood occurs. Through everyday interaction the networks serve as the focal point for a mobilizing collective action. The Brotherhood uses weekly small group meetings (Halaqua), monthly multi group meetings (Katibah), trips, camps, course of instruction, workshops, and conferences to indoctrinate and educate members and coordinate action. The Brotherhood describe their organization as a spiritual worldwide organization that is:

(1) a "dawa" (call) from the Quran and the Sunna (tradition and example) of the Prophet Muhammed;
(2) a method that adheres to the Sunna;
(3) a reality whose core is the purity of the soul;
(4) a political association;
(5) an athletic association;
(6) an educational and cultural organization;
(7) an economic enterprise; and
(8) a social concept.[24]

The Brotherhood's worldwide branches work in accordance with the country's local circumstances to achieve their objectives. The leadership structure in each country is based on the guidance of the Supreme Guide or General Guide that is chosen by a shura council (advisory board). The Supreme Guide must be a member of the shura council. The shura council that chooses the Egyptian Supreme Guide has representation from branches outside of Egypt. This shura council has "120 members from the various governorates."[25] Because of the outlaw nature of the Brotherhood in Egypt, little information is available about the representation on the shura council. What is known is that the "shura council has not met in the past five years."[26] Current indications are that the shura membership is shifting to a younger generation called the doves that will push for a moderate Supreme Guide to replace the more hawkish Mustafa Mashhour. Essam El-Eryan, a senior Brotherhood figure stated, "Eighty percent of the Brothers elected to the People's Assembly (Egyptian Parliament) are under the age of 45." This is another indication that a younger, less violent group is taking over the leading roles in the Brotherhood. They are working within the confines of the political system to address their desires for change.

Deputy guides that work in functional areas or "secret bureau"[27] cells support the Supreme Guide. The actions, procedures, and policies of the organization are outlined in statutes outlined by Al-Banna in 1928 and amended in 1992. The Brotherhood uses a structure of charitable non-governmental organizations to formally pursue their youth, health, religious, education, and social welfare service programs. They establish small businesses and factories to generate income, employ members, and employ sympathizers. The Brotherhood uses membership in formal professional organization and syndicates as a vehicle to influence the national infrastructure.

The main objectives of the Brotherhood are:

1. Building the Muslim individual: brother or sister with a strong body, high manners, cultured thought, ability to earn, strong faith, correct worship, conscious of time, of benefit to others, organized, and self-struggling character [3].

2. Building the Muslim family: choosing a good wife (husband), educating children Islamicaly, and inviting other families.

3. Building the Muslim society (thru building individuals and families) and addressing the problems of the society realistically.

4. Building the Muslim state.

5. Building the Khilafa (basically a shape of unity between the Islamic states).

6. Mastering the world with Islam.[28]

The basic pillars or long-term plan of action of the Muslim Brotherhood includes, first, the establishment of Islamic Sharia law; second, establishment of Muslim states; and third, the unification of Muslim nations. These steps are directly tied to their Islamic doctrine. Likewise, the Brotherhood's objectives, goals, and funding are also directly related to Islamic doctrine. The first and foremost source of Islamic doctrine is the Quran or Koran. Muslims believe the Quran is the infallible word of God revealed through divine revelations to the Prophet

Muhammad in the seventh century A.D. The Quran identifies five pillars of faith: Profession of Faith to Allah and his apostle, Prayer, Almsgiving (*zakat* and *sadaquat*), Fasting, and Pilgrimage (hajj).[29] The Quran is organized in chapters or *suras* that are revered as the recited words of God. The suras constitute the basis for the ritual prayers performed by devout Muslims five times a day. This pillar of the Muslim faith serves as a unifying focal point for the Muslim Brotherhood. Prayer at mosques built by the Muslim Brotherhood provides a frequent forum for contact and promulgation of their fundamentalist ideology.

The Quran is a "doctrine of the absolute oneness of God"[30] that "refers to, and is concerned with, three religious groups: heathens, Jews, and Christians."[31] Since Islam's inception the "absolute oneness" and unyielding belief that the Quran expresses the literal words of God, served as a unifying point for the community of believers or the *umma*. Living among rival religions and hostile tribes necessitated a strong bond between like-minded believers. Physical struggles with non-believers forced Muslims to band together. While there are divergent sects and local variations in the practice of the Islamic faith, a clear distinction exists between believers and non-believers. The Muslim Brotherhood capitalizes on this unifying force as an ideology for the creation of a greater Muslim state and Islamic world. The Muslim Brotherhood exploits and promotes this communal religious unification as a protection measure, recruiting tool, and a call to arms for Muslims to defend their brethren throughout the world. It is this sense of religious ideological unity that mobilized the "Arab Afghans" to fight the Soviets in Afghanistan. From Bosnia to Sudan to Indonesia to the Philippines, protection of the umma is a familiar call to arms for militant Islamic fundamentalists and the Muslim Brotherhood. The protection of the umma is tied to the Islamic concept of *jihad*.

Jihad is word that is difficult to translate from Arabic to English. Its best translation is " a sincere and noticeable effort (for good); an all true and unselfish striving for spiritual good."[32] Jihad is a multi-dimensional concept with the primary focus on the individual.

At the individual level it is striving to live a good life in accordance with the Quran, being just, performing righteous deeds, protecting people's rights and freedoms, spreading the faith, and personally defending the faith. It is about the individual's spiritual struggle for "submission" (English for Islam) to God's will that is good and just, not evil.

At the collective level it is the development, expansion, and protection of a global Islamic community. Jihad at this level may involve addressing injustices through fighting to deter an attack, protecting the freedom to practice Islam, freeing the oppressed, and protecting oneself.

According to the Quranic verses, "God accepts only justice, fighting in the name of God is fighting in the name of justice."[33] The Quran does not consider war to be holy. In fact, the essence of the whole religion, submission to God's will, is predicated on peace not war. The Muslim Brotherhood's inclusion of "jihad our way" in their slogan has multiple meanings. It promotes a non-violent individual struggle for submission to God's will while allowing for the application of violent means, war in the name of God, when fighting a perceived injustice.

To fill the voids left by the Quran in the direction of everyday life, Islamic doctrine relies on two other documents, the *sunna* and *hadith*. The sunna is "the practice of the prophet or a tradition recording the same."[34] The hadith is "a technical term for a tradition of what the prophet said or did"[35] that is the underpinning of the sunna. The sunna-hadith are compilations of sayings, actions, and traditions attributed to the prophet that were formalized in the *Salih* compiled by al-Bukhari in the two hundred years following the prophet's death.[36] It combines ancient customs with past practices to outline the "ideal behavior of the prophet as enshrined tradition."[37]

The Muslim Brotherhood organization "adheres to sunna" as a main tenet of their operations. Within the Muslim scholarly world there is considerable debate about the importance and validity of specific meanings in the sunna-hadith. Because they were developed well after the prophet's death through reconstruction of hearsay evidence about Mohammed's actions, sayings, or practices, some scholarly Muslims express concern about the validity, interpretations, and the lack of appreciation for historical reasons, situations, or real intent. Questions arise about the application of the sunna-hadith in an evolving modern society. The Muslim Brotherhood's belief in strict adherence to sunna-hadith parallels the beliefs and demonstrates the influence of the Saudi Arabian Ikhwan Wahhabist.

Bard E. O'Neill, in his book *Insurgency & Terrorism: Inside Modern Revolutionary Warfare*, classified the Muslim Brotherhood as a "reactionary-traditionalist"[38] type of insurgency because of their insistence on the strict adherence to ancient religious customs, traditions, and practices. O'Neill states,

> "Traditionalist insurgences also seek to displace the political system, but the values they articulate are primordial and sacred ones, rooted in ancestral ties and religion…Within the category of traditionalist insurgents one also finds more zealous groups seeking to reestablish an ancient political system that they idealized as a golden age."[39]

This description applies to the Muslim Brotherhood considering its avowed desire to reestablish Sharia law and the Caliphate. Sharia law is a compilation of sacred laws resulting from *ijima* or consensus decisions by leading Islamic scholars, *qiyas* or analogy reasoning by judges, lawyers and scholars, the sunna-hadith, and the Quran. The Caliphate was the religious, military, and political structure that governed the Muslim people and lands after the death of the Prophet Muhammad in A.D. 632. The caliph, or successor to the prophet, served as the ruler of the Muslim community.

Through the first four caliphs the Muslim community rapidly spread through acts of conquest. Then an inter-tribal feud over the succession of the caliphate started a long period of conflict, hostilities, and division within Islamic community. One of the lasting results was a split in the Muslim community between the Sunni and Shi'a (or Shiite) Muslim sects over the rightful lineage of the Caliph. The caliphate for the next 600 years exercised varying degrees of control and influence over the Muslim community that stretched from India to North Africa to Spain and to Eastern Europe. Significant internal conflict existed during this period. The position of Caliph shifted between rival factions, resulting in the seat of power moving between a variety of locations, to include Medina, Damascus, Baghdad, and Egypt.

While the title Caliph extended to 1924, the actual influence and control of the entire Muslim world community was minimal after the thirteenth century. The Muslim Brotherhood's desire to see the return of the Caliphate raises substantial questions concerning their historical point of reference and definition of the Caliphate. The Muslim Brotherhood's desire to reestablish the Caliphate hinges more on pan-Arab revivalism than on acknowledgement of the turbulent nature of the Caliphate following the first four Caliphs.

In Islam, almsgiving or charity represents one of the five pillars of the faith. Charitable donations are as important as praying. Typically, Muslims give "2.5 % of their annual income"[40] to charitable causes. This is known in Arabic as "zakat." Much of this funding goes directly to grass root non-governmental organization (NGO) efforts. The Muslim Brotherhood's strategy relies heavily on this pillar of the Islamic faith to fund their social welfare programs that provide their base of popular support.

The Muslim Brotherhood draws heavily for financial support from diasporas from countries like Egypt, Algeria, and Syria where repression of the Islamic fundamentalists has resulted in massive relocations and emigration to Saudi Arabia, Jordan, Lebanon, Iraq, Europe, and America. A prime example of the magnitude of this phenomenon is Syria. In February 1981, the Syrian government, following a wave of Muslim Brotherhood inspired violence, brutally repressed the Syrian Muslim Brotherhood movement. The Syrian government's repression resulted in the complete destruction of the town of Hama and the estimated death of some 10,000 to 30,000 men, women, and children. Following this brutal suppression over 800,000[41] Syrian Muslim Brotherhood members and Islamic fundamentalist sympathizers fled the country to Jordan, Saudi Arabia, and Lebanon.

In Algeria, Tunisia, and Egypt the aggressive repression of the Muslim Brotherhood and like-minded Islamic fundamentalist organizations resulted in a massive emigration to Europe, the Middle East, and America. During recent decades, the Muslim population of France has grown to over five million.[42] Over one half of these emigrants hail from North Africa.

According to U.S. Immigration records, over 78,000 legal immigrants from Egypt and Syria entered the U.S. between 1989 and 1999. In both Europe and the United States these new immigrants, driven by a religious requirement, channel their charitable donations back to country organizations like the Muslim Brotherhood that have both a charitable and a political agenda.

When "zakat" is destined for charities outside the immediate local area or a person wants to transfer diaspora funds outside legal channels, the funds are transferred through an ancient Arab trader banking system known as "Hawala." Hawala is derived from the "Arabic word meaning change or transform."[43] "Hawala is a credit system for transferring funds over long distances, and it is centuries older than the Western banking."[44] This is how it works:

> "The hawala banker who takes a deposit writes down the phone number or address of the payer's representative in the receiving country. Then he instructs his partner—a money trader or group of traders in that country—to pay out the required sum. Generally the contact is made by telephone or email. A code word, or a recognized face or voice, is all that is required to complete the transaction. No cash is moved through the legal channels. The hawala money trader and his partner simply keep straight between themselves who owes what to whom and settle their own debts— in cash, gold or other commodities—when convenient."[45]

"The former Assistant Deputy Secretary of State Winer estimates that 25% to 50% of all transactions in the Middle East and South Asia are done outside formal banking channels."[46] Not only does this system allow money transfers to non-governmental organizations or NGOs, it has been linked to the money transfers of terrorist organizations. According to U.S. prosecutors, the hawala firm Dihab Shill[47] served as the al Qaeda funding conduit for the 1998 U.S. embassy bombings in Tanzania and Kenya. Hawala bankers have also moved funds to mujahedin guerillas fighting from Bosnia to Afghanistan. The hawala system provides a banking conduit, without legal oversight, that is equally adept at moving funds for NGOs and terrorists. Illegitimate NGOs can use the hawala banking system to move funds to terrorist organizations from virtually every corner of the world without the threat of government interference.

The Hamas (Islamic Resistance Movement) terrorist organization, which describes itself as the military arm of the Muslim Brotherhood in Palestine, is skilled in the use of charitable organizations in the U.S. to channel funds to Palestinian Muslim Brotherhood programs and to support the Hamas infrastructure in the Middle East. In the United States, Hamas operates a series of non-profit charitable organizations that serve as "a financial conduit for Hamas."[48] Steve Emerson, an investigative reporter and producer of the PBS documentary "Jihad in America," gave testimony before a U.S. Senate subcommittee that clearly shows the ideological, funding, and leadership ties between two supposed charitable organizations, the Holy Land Foundation for Relief and Development and the Islamic Association for Palestine (IAP) and the Muslim Brotherhood and its militant wing, Hamas.[49] Emerson's testimony lays out the linkage between Hamas and Musa Marzook, a principal founder and key leader-founder of the two organizations Holy Land Foundation and IAP. Marzook was arrested in the U.S., detained for twenty months pending deportation to Israel for terrorist crimes, and was then deported to Jordan as part of the political bargaining that led to the Oslo Peace Accords.

The organizations he founded were under FBI investigation but continued to operate until December 4, 2001, when their assets were frozen by President Bush's Executive Order 132224 that targeted terrorist financing. Years after Emerson's testimony, U.S. investigators discovered that in the year 2000, the Holy Land Foundation provided over 13 million dollars from U.S. sources to Hamas. Emerson reported that 23 of the 26 charities receiving Holy Land Foundation funding "are run by known Hamas activists."[50]

Emerson also points out that the Holy Land Foundation provides critical support to Hamas by giving financial support to the families of Hamas suicide bombers, deportees and detainees. The Holy Land Foundation actively pursued financial support for suicide bombers families from the Muslim Arab Youth Association that is "one of the largest constituent organizations of the Muslim Brotherhood"[51] in the U.S. The Muslim Arab Youth Association (MAYA) has chapters and has held conventions in Oklahoma, Arizona, California, Michigan, New Jersey, Illinois, Texas, and Missouri.[52]

Investigations revealed that Marzook was initially responsible for establishing the Muslim Brotherhood Organization in the U.S. that included the MAYA and the de facto Muslim Brotherhood lobby arm, the American Muslim Council, located in Washington, DC. He resigned from that position to take a more active role in Hamas activities. As part of his Hamas efforts, he sought to identify Muslim students within the MAYA that had the educational backgrounds, technical skills, and ideological mindset to support the production of conventional bomb, chemical, and biological weapons for Hamas's arsenal.

Marzook is now the second in command of Hamas operating out of Syria. In a recent interview with *60 Minutes* he confirmed that Hamas was developing a six-mile range missile to attack Israel from the occupied territories.[53] In a *Time Magazine* interview in August 2002, he espoused his unflinching support for his Hamas suicide bombers responsible for the rising death toll in Israel.[54]

The Muslim Brotherhood and the more violent organizations it has created, like Hamas, have found a very permissive, lucrative, and hospitable operational environment in the United States. They are following their organizational doctrine to build a coalition of likeminded fundamentalists whose non-violent, overt actions camouflage their acceptance and support of terrorist violence to accomplish their common objectives. The United States affords freedom of action, superb communication capabilities, a wealth of funding opportunities, and a recruitment base of educated talent.

Working through non-profit and tax exempt foundations, the Muslim Brotherhood has constructed a network of organizations. While there is no hierarchal command structure, they share a linkage through their core Muslim Brotherhood beliefs. These organizations provide the infrastructure that facilitates dissemination of propaganda, indoctrination of members, communication between organizations, appeals for financial support, access to a larger contact population, and the conscription of future terrorist recruits.

The structure of the Muslim Brotherhood provides a vehicle through which terrorist organizations can cooperate on a local level without the use of the traditional pyramid command structure. As was seen in the 1993 bombing of the World Trade Center, terrorists of five different nationalities, different organizational affiliations, and different agendas, were able to find a common ideological base in the doctrine espoused by the Muslim Brotherhood.

The Muslim Brotherhood's preferred course of action is to gain control of the governments through the ballot box. With control of the government secured, they then seek to institute their objective of "Islamizing" the nation. To accomplish this task the Muslim Brotherhood use a two-pronged approach. At the "intelligentsia" level, they seek to control social institutions by infiltrating and attaining prominent positions in professional organizations, government offices, institutions of higher learning, and labor unions. At the "proletariat" level, they seek to develop popular support through charitable and religious programs. The Brotherhood seeks to indoctrinate the population with their ideology in order to form a sympathetic voting block to push their objectives through the political system. Their slogan, "Islam is the solution," is a clever tool for drawing popular political support for their cause and is also a call to stem the modernization and globalization promoted by the Western world.

The Middle East, with over 260 million people, is increasingly urban, young, uneducated, and poverty stricken. Fifty-one percent live in cities,[55] 43 percent are under the age of 15,[56] 48.7 percent are illiterate,[57] and 33 percent earn less than a dollar a day.[58] These demographics describe a society with large segments of disaffected, disenchanted, disillusioned, disgruntled, and disappointed people. This embittered population sees the Western modernization and secular governments as unresponsive to their plight. The Muslim Brotherhood promotes a return to strict Islamic doctrine as the way to correct growing social inequities.

In countries like Jordan, where they have access to the political system, the Muslim Brotherhood has maintained a moderate and generally non-violent orientation. "To date the Brotherhood's most significant strategy in Jordan is its willingness to work within the system for the advancement of it goals."[59] The fear among secular or democratic governments is that if Islamic fundamentalists are elected and control the governments they will use their monopoly on power to set aside democratic institutions. These fears led the governments of Algeria, Tunisia, and Egypt to become undemocratic to prevent the Islamist from "revoking democracy itself."

In Algeria in 1992, the first round of the National Assembly elections was nullified by a Algerian military coup d'etat to prevent the Islamic fundamentalists, who won 188 of 231 seats, from taking power in the second round of elections. This put the Algerian military ostensibly in the position of "destroying democracy to save democracy."[60] The underlying reasons for the Islamic fundamentalists success had very little to do with religious fervor, but were instead a result of the dissatisfaction of the people with the incumbent political party and their failed socioeconomic programs.

The Algerian National Liberation Front or FLN was the political faction that fought the French for independence from 1954 to 1962. After independence, the FLN was the only political force and the only legal party in Algeria from 1962 to 1988. When the Algerian political process was opened to a multi-party participation in 1988, the Islamic fundamentalists were in the best organizational position to take advantage of the new system. The Islamic fundamentalists with their grassroots Muslim Brotherhood organizational structure were the only organization that could quickly and effectively present opposition political candidates. In Algeria's case, the circumstances have more to do with electioneering, dissatisfaction with incumbents, and anti-establishment attitudes than with theology.

In North Africa and Middle East, the transition from colonial or authoritarian governments has not left a wealth of strong democratic institutions or historical experience in self-governance. Consequently, the rigid structure espoused by the Islamic fundamentalist is an alluring alternative to potential chaos and lawlessness. The underlying problem is that threatened governments lack electoral accountability, an independent judiciary, a clear definition of individual rights, and strong parliamentary representation. Without these institutional tools, the existing governments are ill-equipped to mitigate the potential authoritarian goals of the Islamic fundamentalist.

Additionally, the governments cannot get Islamic fundamentalists to identify their definitive positions on key socio-economic issues and programs. Writer Asad AbuKhali illustrated this when he asked the Hizballah leader Sheikh Muhammad Husayn to define his programs for the impoverished Shi'ite of South Lebanon.[61] Husayn said, "We do not need programs. We have the Quran."[62] Muslim fundamentalists lack a comprehensive plan to deal with the pressing social and economic difficulties of their constituencies. As AbuKhali states, "While clerical leaders can afford to claim to rely solely on the Quran in their lives, poor peasants and workers can not use the Quran to pay their bills and feed their children."[63]

The lack of a coherent socio-economic strategy, and their uncompromising dogma, is creating challenges to the Islamists' legitimacy. The Jordanian Muslim Brotherhood, following initial electoral successes, saw the removal from office of three of their most influential activists after their first-term rhetoric was not translated into meaningful programs that benefited their constituents.

The rising number of elected moderates in Iran is another indicator that the fundamentalist agenda is failing to produce the results desired for their constituents. In Sudan, the Muslim Brotherhood-inspired military regime of General Umar al-Bashir has broken its ten-year ties to the Sudanese Muslim Brotherhood political party led by Hassan al Turabi.

Turabi's fundamentalist political party was responsible for the "Islamization" of Sudan that began in 1989. His agenda produced a rapid decay of Sudan's society and economy. Turabi was the power behind the Presidency until his Islamization programs lost the support of the population and the military. Turabi is now under house arrest. In July 2002, President Bashir met with rebel Christian leaders for the first time in an effort to end the nineteen-year civil war between Islamists and the southern Sudanese Christians who constitute one-third of the country's population. Bashir is aggressively attempting to improve relationships with the United States, his African neighbors, and is trying to distance himself from al Qaeda, the Islamic terrorist organization that once used his country as a sanctuary.

Syria, Egypt and Algeria with their weak democratic institutions lack the government controls, checks, and balances to allow a full accommodation with their Muslim fundamentalists in the political process. They rightfully fear the grass roots organizational capabilities of the Muslim Brotherhood. They know that through poor voter participation, the Muslin Brotherhood could gain political influence and control disproportionate to their actual political support from the population as a whole. The lack of details in the fundamentalists' governing agenda does little to assuage the apprehension of the governing leadership. These governments have also witnessed the violence used by Islamic fundamentalist splinter terrorist groups and fear that this violent behavior would increase if they were to gain more power.

These governments face many tough dilemmas. How does a secular government maintain a checks and balances system that nurtures political pluralism while preventing the radical overthrow of the governing system by participants bent on creating an authoritarian regime? How do they accommodate the fundamentalists' demand for the return to religious fundamentalism that links the mosque with the government through the legal system? How does a nation attract investment capital to address its social and economic problems if it transforms to an Islamic economic system that does not permit the charging of interest for investment loans? Capital investment is essential to create new jobs for the 300,000 Algerian and 500,000 Egyptian youth that enter the job market yearly. These core issues motivate secular governments to repress, ban electoral participation, and outlaw Islamic fundamentalist organizations. These coercive actions by governments are, in turn, met by radicalization and the creation of violent terrorist groups from the ranks of the Islamic fundamentalists.

Muslim Brotherhood's Terrorism Connections

The Muslim Brotherhood has ideological connections, leadership connections, and shared modus operandi with many terrorist organizations. The most common linkages between Islamic terrorist organizations and the Muslim Brotherhood are the shared goal of establishing an Islamic state or nation and the shared view of jihad as a means to this goal. Of the thirty-three organizations listed on the U.S. State Department's Designated Foreign Terrorist Organization List,[64] sixteen are engaged in terrorism to force the creation of an Islamic state.

The leadership and founders of many of the modern terrorist organizations had their early indoctrination in Islamic fundamentalist ideas through the Muslim Brotherhood. Ramzi Yousef, convicted in the bombing of the World Trade Center in 1993, "admitted he was a member of the Muslim Brotherhood, but left the group in the 1990s after deciding they were not adequately committed to the revolutionary Islamic cause."[65] He is believed to have received his indoctrination to the Muslim Brotherhood while attending college in the United Kingdom in 1986. Elements of the Muslim Brotherhood based in Britain were actively seeking mujaheddin for the war against the Soviets in Afghanistan. After spending the summer of 1989 in the victorious fight against the Soviets in Afghanistan, Yousef began a global terrorist career that would take him to America, Pakistan, Thailand and the Philippines. Osama bin Laden, founder of the al Qaeda terrorist network, recognized Yousef's terrorist talents. Bin Laden sent Yousef to the Philippines to teach bomb making to Islamic terrorists. Thus, a former Muslim Brotherhood member was instrumental in forming an alliance between two terrorist organizations seeking the creation of radical Islamic theocracies.

The influence of the Muslim Brotherhood is evident in the leadership, strategic objectives, and methods of the al Qaeda (The World Islamic Front for Jihad Against the Jews and Crusaders) terrorist network. This organization is a fusion of several groups, including the Egyptian Islamic Jihad, al-Gama'a al-Islamiyya, the Islamic Movement of Uzbekistan,

Harakat ul-Mujahidin, and Abu Sayyuf.[66] Some of the major militant influences on the organization, and its leader Osama bin Laden, were expatriate Muslim Brotherhood members in Saudi Arabia. Born in 1957, bin Laden was first exposed at an early age to a blend of Wahhabism and to the radical teaching of Muslim Brotherhood leader Sayyid Qutb, the "father of militant jihad."[67] In the 1970s, bin Laden was taught by Sayyid's brother, Dr. Mohammad Qutb, and a Jordanian Muslim Brotherhood member, Dr. Abdullah Azzam, the reported founder of Hamas. Azzam's ideas of non-compromise, violent means, and organizing and fighting on a global scale formed the basis for bin Laden's al Qaeda methodology.

During the Afghan war, bin Laden encountered many Muslim Brotherhood recruits who formed the nucleus of the "Afghan Arabs" numbering between 14,000 and 17,000.[68] One third, or about 1,000 Afghan Arabs under bin Laden's control, were from the Egyptian Islamic Jihad. [69] A prominent member of the Islamic Jihad was a former member of the Egyptian Muslim Brotherhood, Dr. Ayman Al-Zawahiri, who had a history of Brotherhood activism stretching back to 1966, when he was arrested at the age of fifteen.[70] He was also arrested in 1984 and jailed for three years for his involvement with the Islamic Jihad's assassination of Egyptian President, Anwar Sadat. Al-Zawahiri joined the "Arab Afghans" shortly after his release from prison and, in Afghanistan, he and bin Laden forged a lasting relationship. Al-Zawahiri traveled with bin Laden to Sudan at the invitation of Sudanese Muslim Brotherhood leader Hassan al Turabi who was the political leader behind Sudan's military regime. In Sudan, bin Laden observed the Turabi's Muslim Brotherhood organization and their Islamization of Sudan's society. Bin Laden was allowed to establish his terrorist network complete with business, banks, and training camps. Al-Zawahiri is considered to be bin Laden's intellectual and ideological mentor and second-in-command. Al-Zawahiri is considered the planner behind the 1993 bombing of the World Trade Center, the 1998 Luxor, Egypt attack by Islamic Jihad that killed 58 tourists, the 1998 U.S. embassy bombings in Kenya and Tanzania by al Qaeda, and the September 11, 2001 World Trade Center attack by al Qaeda operatives. These examples point to the significant roles that Muslim Brotherhood members have played as leaders of terrorist organizations, where they have adopted many of the Muslim Brotherhood's methods.

The use of charitable organizations and small businesses by the al Qaeda in the U.S., Africa, Afghanistan and Pakistan illustrates the Muslim Brotherhood's method of gaining financial resources and sustaining popular support. The Islamic American Relief Agency (IARA) in Columbia, Missouri is an example of their subversion of a charitable relief organization. This organization claims to provide aid to children and refugees in Africa, Asia, and the Middle East. It has even received funds from the U.S. Agency for International Development (USAID) and other U.S. government agencies totaling $5.8 million in 1998 and 1999. Their web site states: "Please help us to help victims."[71] A later U.S. Treasury Department investigation revealed the Islamic American Relief Agency funded foreign affiliated groups, such as Help African People and Mercy International Relief, employing people with ties to the al Qaeda terrorist network. It is now known that Ziyad Khalil, a U.S. fundraiser for the Islamic American Relief Agency, "supplied a satellite telephone that bin Laden used to plan the deadly bombings of the U.S. embassies in Tanzania and Kenya in 1998."[72] "Khalil also worked for the company that leased the charity's its web site domain name."[73] The activities of the IARA became known only after Khalil's arrest in Jordan and his subsequent cooperation with the FBI in the embassy bombing cases. The Islamic American Relief Agency still claims to have no ties to terrorists and boasts nearly $2.9[74] million in annual contributions despite the cancellation of U.S. government grants. Its web site emphasizing its accomplishments states it "steps in to provide the basic material necessities to the victims"[75] when tragedy happens.

Since the 1998 embassy bombing in Tanzania and Kenya and the 2001 World Trade Center attack, the linkage between Islamic NGO organizations and terrorist groups has attracted a great deal of attention. Because of this attention and the investigation these Islamic NGOs, the Al-Rashid Trust and Wafa Humanitarian Organization were placed on the U.S. Terror Exclusion List for their ties and support of al Qaeda. Both the Al-Rashid Trust and Wafa Humanitarian Organization are directly patterned on the Muslim Brotherhood's model and method. They use charitable donations and businesses to fund overt civic programs and covert violent terrorist groups. The Al-Rashid "charity" follows the Brotherhood's model by:

1. Providing financial and legal support to jailed militants around the world;

2. Pushing the World Food Program (WFP) out of Afghanistan so that they could take over "155 bakeries"[76] set up to feed over 300,000 needy people;

3. Sending 1,000 sewing machines to war widows;

4. Establishing a network of radical Islamist schools called madrassases in Afghanistan and "actually runs many of the madrassas and mosques in Pakistan;"[77]

5. Constructing 25 mosques along the Afghanistan highways leading out of Kandahar;

6. Setting up computer centers in Afghanistan catering to students;

7. Opening a medical clinic in Kandahar;

8. Sending 70 truckloads of relief supplies to the Taliban in Afghanistan;

9. Sacrificing $900,000[78] worth of livestock on the eve of Id-ul-Azha, a Muslim religious holiday involving the sacrifice of animals;

10. Establishing hundreds of offices in Pakistan to actively work with "vulnerable minorities,"[79] including opening a clinic in Pakistan, to provide medical care to minority orthodox Muslims in an area occupied by the Ahmedi who are considered a heretics by the orthodox Muslims;

11. Sharing offices and common fund raising cadres with the Jaishi-I-Mohammad, a militant Pakistani religious group that is on the U.S. Terrorist Exclusion List;

12. Producing the radical Islamist newspaper, Zarb-I-Momin, that praises the Taliban, al Qaeda, Jaishi-I-Mohammad, and Harakut-ul-Ansaar (listed on U.S. Terrorist Exclusion List) activities while spewing anti US, Western, Hindu, Christian, and Jewish "ultra – venemous propaganda;"[80]

13. Raising funds from the expatriated Pakistanis from around the world, the Middle East, Africa, and the United States to be used by al Qaeda,[81] advertising that shows that guns, jewelry, and money donated by the Pashtun tribes is "intended to be used for the Afghan holy war against the U.S.;"[82]

14. Aiding "widows and orphans of martyrs"[83] that experts believe provides direct financial support to families of suicide bombers and terrorists killed in pursuit of their cause;

15. Providing "jihad fighters with shelter and medicine inside Afghanistan."[84]

Although Al-Rashid does do charitable work, its efforts are specifically designed to promote a political agenda bent on violence, conflict, and support of terrorism. The pattern of mixing charitable NGO work with political and violent terrorist activities represents the most recent applications of the Muslim Brotherhood's model for "Islamizing" the world.

Responding to the Brotherhood's Challenge

The Brotherhood is a global organization with insurgency objectives and methods that threaten existing secular governments in North Africa, the Middle East, South Asia and South East Asia. The Muslim Brotherhood's strategic objective is the Islamization of society in strict adherence to selected Islamic doctrine and the establishment of Islamic theocracies.[85]

The Muslim Brotherhood's ideological ties to, and involvement in, the leadership of terrorist organizations threatens the security of U.S. citizens at home and abroad. The Muslim Brotherhood represents a challenge to U.S. goals of "enhancing security at home and abroad, promoting prosperity, and promoting democracy and human rights."[86] The Brotherhood represents a challenge to the U.S. values of freedom of religion, separation of church and state, equality of the individual, and human rights.

The Brotherhood's lack of definition as to how they would use power is a significant concern. Would they use power to reverse the democratic process to create theocratic authoritarian regimes? Their stated objectives leave little room for the democratic concepts of political compromise, majority rule, and minority rights. The Brotherhood everywhere advocates the integration of their interpretation of Islamic precepts into the existing secular government structure, the establishment of Islamic theocracies, the use of international terrorism to further their cause, the manipulation of NGOs to support their cause, and the use of Muslim Brotherhood mujahidin to serve as a Brotherhood foreign legion in the internal conflicts of other Islamic states.

Everywhere it exists, the Muslim Brotherhood's activities range from political party activism to promoting an insurgency that uses terrorism as a tool.[87] The Muslim Brotherhood's past strategies pointedly show how this supposedly non-violent organization aids and sustains radical Islamic groups who resort to violent means if their popular efforts are subverted. From the ranks of the Brotherhood, members have answered the call to "Jihad" in Palestine, Bosnia, Afghanistan, the Philippines, and Chechnya. In Algeria, Syria, and Egypt the Brotherhood serves as the umbrella organization promoting armed struggles.

The Brotherhood in different states moves between different phases of a classical insurgence. In some Islamic states they remain in the initial organizational phase where they initiate a pattern of organized activities and minor incidents. In other states, they operate at a second phase where the level of violence has grown to guerrilla warfare interspersed with terrorist acts to undermine the existing regime. Finally, in several states the Brotherhood has participated in a third phase, where there is open fighting between organized armed insurgent forces and the armed forces of the existing authority. The history of the Muslim Brotherhood in Syria, Egypt, and Israel provide examples of the Muslim Brotherhood's movement through successive insurgent phases. Syria and Egypt also demonstrate the Muslim Brotherhood's ability to revert to an earlier phase when government actions have defeated the insurgency and driven it underground.

With the population explosion, economic disenfranchisement, illiteracy, and under employment, the draw to religious fundamentalism will only increase in Muslim states. The United States and its allies must address the underlying issues that presently make the Brotherhood's slogan, "Islam is the solution," an alluring ideology. An alternative solution is needed to remedy the underlying socio-economic grievances that are not currently being addressed by the threatened governments. The seven characteristics of insurgency outlined in U.S. Army Field Manual, Foreign Internal Defense Tactics, Techniques, and Procedures for Special Forces, FM 31-20-3, relating to leadership, ideology, objectives, environment and geography, external support, phasing and timing, and organizational and operational patterns provide a useful construct for the development of an engagement and containment strategy.

Engaging the Brotherhood in dialogue is an important first step to reducing the potential for destabilization in many states. Jordan has long had an open dialogue with their Muslim Brotherhood organization that has prevented the escalation of violence and even served as a moderating influence on the more radical Islamists in their midst. Through very careful monitoring, regulation, and control the Jordanian monarchy has successfully prevented the radicalization of many attracted to the Brotherhood. Jordan has provided the Brotherhood with access to the political process as an opposition party loyal to the government. Meanwhile, Jordan also has strengthened its parliamentary institutions to limit the Brotherhood's potential impact through the democratic process. The Jordanian policy of accommodation with controls is a less volatile engagement strategy than found in Egypt, Syria, or Algeria. By gaining oversight of the funding and implementation of the Brotherhood's grass roots NGO social welfare programs, the Jordanian government minimized subversive influences. Additionally, the Jordanian government gained and maintained additional public support because of its involvement with the Brotherhood's programs.

Through engagement, work can begin on defining "Islam is the solution" in the context of a workable solution in the world today. The major challenge to Egypt and Jordan is working with the Brotherhood to define their objectives in specific terms. In the case of Egypt, they must first recognize the existence of the Brotherhood as a political party. Once the Brotherhood is openly recognized, work could begin on identifying areas of congruence and divergence leading to political strategies of compromise and cooperation. One major step would be codifying Islamic jurisprudence in terms of legal, economic, and governmental processes. This would bring to the forefront open discussion and

73

definition of the controversial issues of human rights, freedom of religion, economic structure, and governmental system.

Along with engagement, a deliberate program of containment to minimize the Brotherhood's influence is necessary. The United States should provide aid resources to threatened countries for the expressed purpose of filling the needs of the societal niche the Brotherhood targets for their popular support. Such aid must help replace the social services now monopolized by the Brotherhood. Education of children in the skills to succeed in the modern world and providing them follow-on opportunities is an essential component. Reversing economic decay through aid programs that establish sustainable economic growth and promote the redistribution of wealth is another essential element. These efforts require the deepest commitment, but will provide the greatest long-term benefits.

The containment program should also address the Brotherhood's support to "oppressed" Brothers in other countries. The containment program should seek to promote an information campaign supporting non-violent forms of "Jihad" in accordance with the Islamic values of peace, human life sanctity, and non-violence. The information campaign should support and promote the ideas of moderate scholars, leaders, and clerics with non-violent views. Aggressively countering the message of virulent clerics is an essential step in stemming the propaganda of violence.

Transforming Jihad into a war of words instead of terrorists and soldiers is an important step in undercutting and preventing militancy in the Muslim Brotherhood. The containment program should attempt to limit the international flow of mujahidin fighters from one country to another through the establishment of international immigration controls. While the United States supported mujahidin activity in the 1979–1989 Afghan-Soviet War, the longer term second and third order effects of this policy were not understood at the time. Facts show that many of these fighters too often became the core elements of future terrorist organizations.

The containment program also must find ways to limit and curb NGO external support to the Muslim Brotherhood. An alarming trend is the concealment of terrorist activities under the appealing banners of Islamic relief organizations. The misuse of so-called humanitarian organizations, aliases, information technology, and the Internet, have provided terrorist groups with support and worldwide access to potential contributors while concealing their more violent objectives.

Non-government organizations have in recent decades filled many of the voids in governmental social programs. As a result, the number of NGOs has skyrocketed, more than doubling since 1978. There are twenty times more NGOs than existed in 1951.[88] In 1999, the Union of International Associations reported that there were 16,586 such international NGOs in existence.[89] National NGOs have grown at an even faster rate and number in the hundreds of thousands. Bangladesh has 16,000 registered NGOs;[90] the Philippines, 21,000;[91] and Brazil, 100,000.[92] France has 54,000[93] NGOs. Britain's NGO community is growing at a rate of 4,000[94] per year. The bottom line is that the number of NGOs has overwhelmed the ability of governments, international government organizations, watchdog agencies, and the donator community to monitor NGO motives and operations.

The lack of NGO oversight, availability of new information technologies, and the use of aliases and misleading organization titles all-too-easily conceal the illegitimate organizations in this sea of NGOs. The NGO community, which is resistant to government oversight and involvement, is now at odds with governments over the issues of accountability, transparency, control, code of conduct, and ethics.

NGOs have access to billions of dollars from government, private, corporate, and religious donors that terrorists seek to divert to their activities. Terrorist organizations use the informal Hawala banking system of the Middle East and South Asia to move charitable donations from the "front" NGOs to more nefarious operators without any accountability trail or government interference. What is the answer to this challenge? Clearly the NGO community, United Nations, and national governments must work together to correct this situation and bring these nongovernmental organizations under greater control.

Several corrective steps need to be taken, namely:

1. Define what constitutes a legitimate NGO in both international and national laws.

2. Provide governmental oversight and access to NGO financial records, donor records, charters, objectives, and membership roles.

3.   Enforce a code of ethical performance.

4.   Outlaw NGOs that are unwilling to provide full disclosure of their activities and who they fund.

5.   Develop a policing program that prevents unlawful organizations from exploiting the Internet and using the Hawala banking system.

6.   Deny illegitimate NGOs access to public forums.

7.   Provide more aid through legitimate NGO programs to reduce the poverty, illiteracy, poor health, and sense of despair among the disaffected in society where illegitimate NGOs and terrorists best operate.

8.   Carefully evaluate the secondary effect of NGO programs to prevent inadvertent assistance or support to terrorists.

These actions will not be easy or inexpensive. They require unity of effort, money, a policing and oversight organization, and international cooperation. However, a new approach and operating environment is needed to prevent terrorist and political subversion of the NGO community. New programs of accommodation, engagement, oversight, and containment are essential to curb the influence of groups like the Muslim Brotherhood. The NGO community must work with governmental agencies to close the current paths by which terrorist are exploiting NGOs.

Summary

"I must tell you, this whole problem of terrorism throughout the Middle East is a by-product of our own, illegal Muslim Brotherhood—whether it's al-Jihad, Hizb'allah, in Lebanon, or Hamas. They all sprang from underneath the umbrella of the Muslim Brotherhood. They say they have renounced violence, but in reality, they are responsible for all this violence, and the time will come when they will be uncovered"[95]

President Mubarak, <u>The New Yorker</u>, 1994

The worldwide Muslim Brotherhood is the source of the core beliefs underlying most of the Islamic international terrorists. Its history demonstrates the influence of both internal and external factors that lead to violent militancy. It has also shown an ability in cases like Jordan to adapt and use peaceful means to address Muslim Brotherhood grievances. Although its objectives present many problems to secular governments, ignoring Brotherhood issues does not make those issues go away. Instead of waiting to become embroiled in Samuel Huntington's "The Clash of Civilizations," the United States needs to work with its Middle Eastern, African, and South Asian allies to engage and marginalize the Muslim Brotherhood with a mixed policy of controlled accommodation, engagement, and containment. To combat the Islamic terrorism of today, the United States and its friends must address the root of the problem, the Muslim Brotherhood.

Notes

1. "Politics in God's name," *Al-Ahram Weekly*, 16-22 November 1995, *Al-Ahram Weekly On-line*, on-line, Google, 12 Nov 2001.

2. Muslim Brotherhood Movement Homepage, 1-5, Google, 12 Nov 2001. Available from http://www.ummah.org.uk/ikhwan/.

3. Ibid.

4. Ibid.

5. "Muslim Brothers," *Middle East International*, February 1999, on-line, Google, 12 Nov 2001.

6. Ron Leshm and Amit Cohen, "*Islamic Terror: A History of the Muslim Brotherhood,*" October 29, 2001, on-line, Google, 14 Dec 2001.

7. Tore Kjeilen, "Muslim Brotherhood-Egypt," *Encyclopedia of the Orient*, on-line, Google, 12 Nov 2001.

8. Ibid.

9. Leshm and Cohen, 3.

10. Ibid.

11. Ibid.

12. Yasser Khalil, "Hassan al-Banna," *Huma's Homepage on Islam*, on-line, 10 Dec 2001.

13. Ibid.

14. Kjeilen, 2.

15. "Politics in God's name," 2.

16. Kjeilen, 2.

17. "Militant Islam: Roots, History, and Ideology," Hadassah Izaia Backgrounder, on-line, Google, 15 Dec 2001.

18. Shaykh Abdul Hadi, "Ask Ahlu-d-Dhikr if you don't know...,"on-line, Internet, 1 December 2001. Available from http://www.village.flashnet.it/users/fn034463/questions1.html.

19. Kjeilen, 3.

20. Grace Halsell, "Terrorism and Tourism in Egypt," Christian Science Monitor, 14 April 1995,Vol. 87 Issue 97, on-line, EBSCOhost, 28 Nov 2001.

21. Sana Abeb-Kotob, "The Accommodationists Speak: Goals and Strategies of the Muslim Brotherhood of Egypt", *International Journal of Middle East Studies*, Aug 95, Vol. 27 Issue 3, p. 321-339, on-line, EBSCOhost, 28 Nov 2001.

22. Jim Landers, "Islamic unity, by any means," *The Dallas Morning News,* 2 August 2002, p. 1-5, on-line, Internet, 2 August 2002. Available from http://www.projo.co/cgi-bin/include.pl/extra/binladen/20011021_dmn.htm.

23. Jim Landers, 5.

24. Sana Abeb-Kotob, 323.

25. Omayma Abdel-Latif, "Brotherhood signs," *Al-Ahram Weekly*, Issue No. 523 1-7 March 2001, *Al-Ahram Weekly On-line*, on-line, Google, 6 Dec 2001.

26. Ibid.

27. Ibid.

28. Muslim Brotherhood Movement Homepage, 2.

29. Alfred Guillaume, *Islam* (New York, N.Y.: Penguin Books, 1954), 55-77.

30. Guillaume, 63.

31. Guillaume, 5.

32. "Jihad in Islam (Submission)," *Welcome to Submission*, 1-5, on-line, Internet, 13 August 2002. Available from http://www.submission.org/muhammed/jihad.html.

33. Ibid.

34. Guillaume, 202.

35. Guillaume, 201.

36. Guillaume, 91.

37. Guillaume, 92.

38. Bard E. O'Neill, *Insurgency & Terrorism Inside Modern Revolutionary Warfare* (Dulles,VA: Brassey's,Inc., 1990), 18.

39. Ibid.

40. Laurie P.Cohen et al., "Bush's Financial War on Terrorism Includes Strikes at Islamic Charities," *Wall Street Journal Classroom Edition*, 25 September 2001, n.p., on-line, Internet, 20 December 2001. Available from http://wsjclassroomrdition.com/tj_092501_frz2.htm.

41. Guy Bechor, "It's Not So Easy To Murder Opponents Anymore" *Ha'aretz*, 3 September 1996, n.p., on-line, Internet, 2 August 2002. Available from http://www.mfa.gov.il/mfa/go.asp?MFAH08go0.

42. Milton Viorst, "The Coming Instability" *Washington Quarterly*, Fall 97, n.p., on-line, EBSCOhost, 4 December 2001.

43. Michelle Cottle, "Eastern Union," *New Republic*, Vol. 225 Issue 4526, 15 October 2001, n.p., on-line, EBSCOhost, 5 December 2001.

44. John Daniszewski and Paul Watson, "Age-Old Way of Moving Cash Leaves Little Trail," *Los Angeles Times*, 26 September 2001, *latimes .com*, n.p., on-line, 20 December 2001.

45. Ibid.

46. Borzou Daragahi, "Financing Terror," *Money*, Vol. 30 Issue 12, November 2001, n.p., on-line, EBSCOhost, 5 December 2001.

47. Cottle, 3.

48. Steve Emerson, "Prepared Statement of Steve Emerson before the Senate Judiciary Committee Subcommittee on Terrorism, Technology, and Government Information" Federal Information System Federal News Service, 24 February 1998, p. 1-31, on-line, Internet, 3 August 2002. Available from http://www.geocities.com/CollegePark/6453/emerson.html.

49. Emerson, 9-13.

50. Emerson, 15.

51. Emerson, 8.

52. Ibid.

53. Steve Kroft, "Official: Hamas Building Missiles, *CBSNEWS.com,* 24 January 2002, on-line, Internet, 8 August 2002. Available from http://www.cbsnews.com/stories/2002/01/24/60minutes/printable325480.shtml.

54. George Baghdadi, "Defining Terrorism", *Time Europe*, 8 August 2002, 1-6, on-line, Internet, 8 August 2002. Available from http://www.time.com/time/europe/me/daily/0,13716,227752,00.html.

55. Antoine B. Zahlan, "Labor Migration and Economic Integration in the Middle East," in *Middle East Dilemma*, ed. Michael C. Hudson, n.p., on-line, Internet, 6 August 2002. Available from http://www.ciaonet.org/book/hudson/hudso012.html.

56. Ibid.

57. Kowsar P. Chowdhury, "Literacy and Primary Education," *Human Capital Development and Operations Policy Working Papers, World Bank*, p. 2, on-line, Internet, 6 August 2002, available from http://www.worldbank.org/html/exdr/hnp/hddflash/workp/wp 00050.html.

58. Zahlan, 2.

59. Abeb-Kotob, 328.

60. Lt Col Randal K. James, "The Islamist Challenge in the Middle East and North Africa," Research Working Paper 118/96-04 (Maxwell AFB, AL: Air War College, 9

April 1996), 26.

61. Asad AbuKhalil, "A Viable Partnership Islam, Democracy, and the Arab World," *Harvard International Review*, Winter 93, Vol. 15 Issue 2, 22, 3-4, on-line, EBSCOhost, 5 December 2001.

62. AbuKhalil, 4.

63. Ibid.

64. U.S. Department of State, *Patterns of Global Terrorim 2001*, (Washington,DC.: Office of the Secretary of State, May 2002), 85.

65. Simon Reeve, *The New Jackals: Ramzi Yousef, Osama bin Laden and the Future of Terrorism* (Boston, MA: Northeastern University Press,1999), 118.

66. U.S. Department of State, *Patterns of Global Terrorim 2001,* 105.

67. John L. Esposito, *Unholy War Terror in the Name of Islam*, (New York NY: Oxford University Press, 2002), 8.

68. Reeve, 3.

69. Ed Blanche, "Ayman Al-Zawahiri: attention turns to other prime suspects," *Jane's Chem-Bio Web*, 3 October 2001, 1-5, on-line, Internet, 2 August 2002. Available from http://www.janes.com/security/international_security/news/jir/jir011003_1_n.shtml.

70. Blanche, 2.

71. Edward T. Pound and Lisa Griffin, "A Charity's Odd Ties," U.S. *News &World Report,* 12 November 2001, vol. 131 Issue 20, on-line, EBSCOhost, 5 December 2001.

72. Ibid.

73. Ibid.

74. Ibid.

75. Ibid.

76. Pepe Escobar, "The Roving Eye, Anatomy of a 'Terrorist' NGO," *Asian Times*, 26 October 2001, *Asia Times Online*, on-line, Internet, 20 December 2001. Available from http://www.atimes.com/c-asia/CJ26Ag01.html.

77. Escobar, 2.

78. Escobar, 2.

79. Escobar, 2.

80. Escobar, 2. "Publications it controls have also been promoting and directly praising the Arab suicide bombers who attacked the twin towers and the Pentagon."

81. Escobar, 2.

82. Smucker, 2.

83. Christopher H. Schmitt and Joshua Kurlantzick, "When Charity Goes Awry," *U.S. News & World Report*, 29 October 2001, Vol. 131 Issue 18, on-line, EBSCOhost, 5 December 2001.

84. Smucker, 2.

85. Nachman Tal, "A Decade of Fundamentalism: The Egytian and Jordanian Experience in Coping with Radical Islam," Jaffee Center for Strategic Studies Publication, 1-5, on-line, Internet, 6 December 2001. Available from http://www.tau. ac.il.jcss/tal.html.

86. The White House, *A National Security Strategy for a Global Age,* December 2000 (Washington D.C.: Government Printing Office), 1.

87. The Muslim Brother's strategic objectives and methods fit the definition of insurgency given in the U.S. Army Field Manual 31-20-3. FM 31-20-3 states, "An insurgency is an organized movement aimed at the overthrow of a constituted government through the use of subversion and armed conflict. In some cases, however, the goals of an insurgency may be more limited. For example, the insurgency may intend to break away a portion of the nation from the government control and establish an autonomous state within traditional or religious territorial bounds. The insurgency may also intend to extract limited political concessions unattainable through less violent means. Insurgencies generally follow a revolutionary doctrine and use forces as an instrument of policy."

88. Pamela Aall et al., *Guide to IGOs, NGOs and the Military in Peace and Relief Operations*, (Washington, D.C.: United States Institute of Peace Press, 2000), 89.

89. Aall et al., 89.

90. Thomas G. Weiss, International NGOs, Global Governance, and Social Policy in the UN System, March 1999, n.p., on-line, Internet, 17 December 2001, available from http://www.stakes.fi/gaspp.

91. Ibid.

92. Ibid.

93. Ibid.

94. Ibid.

95 Joel Campagna, "From Accommodation to Confrontation: The Muslim Brotherhood in the Mubarak Years," *Journal of International Affairs*, Summer 96, Vol. 50, Issue 1, on-line, EBSCOhost, 28 Nov 2001.

CHAPTER 4

Struggle for the Control of Pakistan:
Musharraf Takes On the Islamist Radicals

Stephen F. Burgess

Introduction

The attacks of September 11, 2001, underscored the fact that Pakistan has been a principal center for international rivals who have sought to attack the United States and its interests overseas. Al Qaeda and the Taliban, as well as Kashmiri and homegrown Pakistani Islamist militant groups, have maintained a presence and popularity in Pakistan, both among sections of the masses and elites. Post-September 11 attacks on the U.S. Consulate in Karachi, the journalist Daniel Pearl and French defense workers also in Karachi, and an Anglican Church congregation in Islamabad have demonstrated that Islamist terrorism is robust in Pakistan's cities. Al Qaeda and Taliban forces have moved from Afghanistan into western Pakistan, where the central government has little control, and some have moved into the disputed territory of Jammu and Kashmir on the Pakistan side of the Line of Control, where they hope to incite war between India and Pakistan. In response, the U.S. war on terrorism, Operation Enduring Freedom, is being fought inside Pakistan, as well as Afghanistan. Also, the Bush administration is working to stop Islamist militants in Kashmir from drawing Pakistani forces away from the Afghan border or starting a Pakistan-India war that could go nuclear.

Before September 11, 2001, it appeared that Pakistan was on the road to becoming an international rival of the United States. Relations between the military government of Pakistan, led by President/General Pervez Musharraf, and the United States were at a low point. U.S. sanctions against Pakistan for nuclear weapons development and testing and the 1999 military coup were hurting the economy and the military. The Clinton administration had begun tilting toward Pakistan's enemy, India, and the Bush administration signaled its intention to tilt even further. Pakistan's CIA, the Inter-Services Intelligence (ISI) Directorate, was backing the Taliban in Afghanistan, tolerating al Qaeda activities in Afghanistan and western Pakistan, and supporting Islamist militant organizations in Jammu and Kashmir. Islamist extremism within Pakistan was growing, thanks in part to Saudi-funded *madrassas* (Quranic schools) that were producing young militants who were joining or supporting Islamist extremist organizations, including al Qaeda. Islamist Pakistani scientists had established links with al Qaeda in Afghanistan and were assisting in efforts to develop weapons of mass destruction. If the terrorist attacks of September 11 had not occurred, Pakistan would have become increasingly Islamist, a U.S. rival, and perhaps even a candidate for the "axis of evil" list.

The September 11 attacks led the United States to seek from Pakistan basing and overflight rights in order to attack the Taliban and al Qaeda in Afghanistan. At first, it was uncertain if President Musharraf would assist the United States and, particularly, allow U.S. forces on Pakistani soil. However, President Musharraf apparently realized that Pakistan was at a crossroads and needed U.S. economic and political aid. He decided Pakistan should reject radical Islamism and move back toward secularism and closer relations with the United States in order to secure aid and prevent the United States from moving closer to India. Already, the United States was being offered bases by India to fight the war on terrorism, and Musharraf did not want to be out-maneuvered. He decided to allow the United States to enter Pakistani bases and use them to launch attacks on the Taliban and al Qaeda. Musharraf began to reorient Pakistan's security establishment by purging the armed forces and ISI of those who had managed the previous policy of consorting with Islamist radicals in Pakistan, Afghanistan, and Kashmir.

After an attack by Islamist terrorists on the Indian parliament on December 13, 2001, Indian and U.S. pressure led Musharraf to offer, in a speech delivered on January 12, 2002, support in combating cross-border terrorism from Pakistan into Indian-controlled Jammu and Kashmir. However, Musharraf has found it difficult to follow through on his commitments to India's satisfaction without risking his own position within Pakistan. Pressures on Musharraf by India and the United States have continued and saber rattling and the prospect of a nuclear exchange have mounted.

The focus of this chapter is on international rivals to the United States from within Pakistan. The approach is to provide background and understanding on the development of these rivals and the Pakistani government's ability to cope with them. The rivals are described, profiled, and analyzed and the degree of threat that these groups pose to the United States and its allies in Pakistan is assessed. At issue is whether or not Pakistan will collapse into anarchy, which would serve the interests of al Qaeda and other U.S. rivals. A related issue is whether or not al Qaeda and other radical Islamist groups will escalate war in Kashmir and attempt to cause a nuclear exchange between Pakistan and India, which would also hurt U.S. interests. Particular attention is paid to anti-U.S. factions within Pakistan and what the Musharraf government is doing to contain them. In assessing whether or not the Pakistani government can cope with rivals, the chapter provides a profile of President Musharraf.

The Rise of Rivals to the United States in Pakistan

Pakistan was established in 1947 as a state that promised Muslims a safe haven from the persecution that many had suffered at the hands of Hindus in British-ruled India. Pakistan was founded as a secular state that was predominantly Muslim, with largely secular political parties. Soon after independence, Pakistani forces invaded Jammu and Kashmir, attempting to annex the predominantly Muslim principality. However, the Indian army stopped Pakistani forces after they had seized half of the territory but not the main population center in the "Vale of Kashmir" and the capital, Srinagar.

Since the 1947 conflict over Kashmir, Pakistan and India have remained enemies and have fought four wars, most recently in Kargil along the "Line of Control" in Kashmir. In the 1950s, Pakistan established close relations with the United States as a partner in the Cold War. With the majority of the population from the Punjab Province and a fairly strong landed and political elite, Pakistan was a fairly stable state for the first 30 years. In the 1950s and 1960s, the military seized and held on to power but eventually handed authority back to civilians. The one great exception to the stability rule was the 1971 secession of East Pakistan and creation of Bangladesh with the help of an Indian invasion.[1]

In the first decade of independence, the largely secular Muslim League dominated Pakistan's politics. The first Islamist challenge came from the Jamaat-e-Islami (Islamist Party), which contested the 1951 general election and has competed in every subsequent general election, except the one in 1997, which it boycotted.[2] The Jamaat-e-Islami was founded in 1941 as one of the first Islamic revivalist movements in the world. The party led the campaign for the Islamization of politics and society and the grounding of the constitution and institutions in Islamic law. The Jamaat-e-Islami has had a large component of Mojahirs, who came from India especially to the Karachi region, Sind Province with the 1947 partition. They associated with the Islamist party and ideology as a way of competing for their rights with native Sindhis, who supported Zulifkar Bhutto's Pakistan People's Party (PPP). In 1950, the more puritanical and factional Jamiat-e-Ulema-i-Islami (Islamist Scholars and Priests Party) was founded.

From the 1950s onward, the Jamaat-e-Islami and Jamiat-e-Ulema-i-Islami opposed Pakistan's alliance with the United States. In the early 1990s, the Jamaat-e-Islami and Jamiat-e-Ulema-i-Islami supported Saddam Hussein and Iraq in the Gulf War and vigorously opposed Pakistan's support of the United States in the war. The Jamaat-e-Islami and Jamiat-e-Ulema-i-Islami remain rivals of the United States.

In 1977, the Pakistan National Alliance was formed to oppose the Pakistan People's Party (PPP) and the Prime Minister Zulifkar Bhutto in the March general elections. A faction of the Pakistan Muslim League joined with Islamist parties including the Jamaat-e-Islami and more puritanical parties, such as the Jamiat-e-Ulema-i-Islami (Islamist Scholars and Priests Party) and the Jamiat-e-Ulema-i-Pakistan (Pakistan Scholars and Priests Party). After the elections were rigged, the Islamist parties agitated against Bhutto and his regime to bring redress.

After a political crisis, General Zia ul-Haq led the military in overthrowing the Bhutto government and then saw to Bhutto's execution. Once in power, Zia became determined to remain there and, as a devout

Muslim, Islamize Pakistan. He adopted a number of initiatives to strengthen his position, Islamize government and politics, and weaken the established secular political order. Zia developed the ISI into a super intelligence agency with its own troops and the power to delve into domestic and international affairs. His Islamization package included the massive expansion of madrassas. By the 1990s, there were more than 40,000, with less than 5,000 registered.[3] They tended to define jihad in their instruction as Islamist guerrilla warfare and extremism, rather than the traditional definition of striving to become better Muslims. Subsequently, the Islamists became known as jihadis.[4]

Zia eased restrictions on Islamist movements and political parties and included Jamaat-e-Islami leaders in his cabinet.[5] He cultivated conservative, literal-minded Islamist elements that wanted to create a puritanical Islamist order. At the same time, Zia exercised control over Islamist parties and did not allow them to control policy matters outside of Islamic affairs.[6]

Zia opened the military and bureaucracy to Islamist activists. Ruling generals openly declared that they were Islamist in orientation and cultivated close ties with Islamist parties. Zia and his fellow generals represented a new wave of Pakistani officers who consciously moved away from western influences after the 1971 defeat in East Pakistan.[7] The 1979 Iranian revolution had a profound impact on military and civilian leaders alike and spurred on Islamization. Some even talked of an Islamic revolution in Pakistan.[8]

After the Soviet Union invaded Afghanistan in December 1979, the United States aided Zia's regime, as Pakistan became the principal ally in the war against Soviet occupation. The United States reversed its previous course toward Pakistan, dropped nonproliferation and human rights sanctions, and permitted Zia to develop a nuclear weapons program to counter India.

From 1979 onward, three million Afghans settled in Pakistani refugee camps and became the basis for the Mujahideen and, in the early 1990s, the Taliban. In the 1980s, the ISI and CIA worked together to aid the Islamist Mujahideen in Afghanistan in a jihad against the Soviet Union. In the 1980s, the CIA and ISI worked with the Jamaat-e-Islami in Pakistan and the Afghan Hezb-e-Islami, led by Gulbuddin Hekmatyar, as arms were shipped primarily to the Ghilzai Pushtun in central and northeast Pakistan.[9]

Zia supported not only the Mujahideen in Afghanistan, but also the ISI and the Jamaat-e-Islami backed Islamist militants in Pakistan and the Islamist fighters in Kashmir. The fighting in Afghanistan spilled over into Kashmir and touched off a wave of violence. The ISI's links to the religious-political organizations under Zia increased not only because he used religion to legitimize his rule, but also because the organizations were essential for recruiting to the ranks of the Mujahideen. The ISI built up links with fundamentalist parties such as the Jamaat-e-Islami and its offshoots, the Tableghi Jamaat (Evangelists Organization) and Markaz Dawa-al Irshad (Islamic Missionaries Organization - an Islamic fundamentalist grouping of Wahabi sects in Pakistan). This interaction allowed the Islamist parties in Pakistan to extend influence over armed forces personnel.[10]

During the 1980s, the United States and Saudi Arabia funneled more than $3.5 billion into Pakistan and Afghanistan. Pakistan cultivated close ties to Saudi Arabia and other Gulf Cooperation Council states. Wahabi groups from Saudi Arabia funded the Mujahideen, and Arab fighters, including Osama bin Laden, arrived in Pakistan and formed the basis for al Qaeda there. From 1987-88 alone, $25 million was contributed by private Saudi sources, including Osama bin Laden, to the Mujahideen. Private funding began to flow from Saudi Arabia, especially from Wahabi groups, to Pakistan and particularly to madrassas.[11]

In the 1980s, Zia encouraged the growth of militant Islamist groups that could rival the mass base of the PPP. These groups included Mohajirs, who challenged native Sindhis and the PPP in the Karachi region. Other groups were associated with Sunni Islam mainline sects, and others included the Wahabi/Deobandi sect and Shia sects. Contention between Shiite groups on the one hand and on the other Wahabi/Deobandi and mainline Sunni groups resulted in massive sectarian violence.

For example, the 1980 imposition of an Islamic Zakat tax led to sectarian violence between the Shia, who resisted the tax, and the Wahabi/Deobandi sect, which was violently anti-Shiite. Also, the Wahabi/Deobandi sect has been opposed to inequality and feudalism and has strong beliefs in egalitarianism for men and sequestering women. In 1985, the Anjuman Sipah-e-Sahaba was formed as a breakaway from the Jamiat-e-Ulema-i-Islami and resorted to violence in pursuance of its Islamist sectarian agenda, killing more than 3,600 Shiites over the next decade or more.[12]

1988-1999: The Rise of the Taliban, Al Qaeda, and U.S. Rivals

Zia ul-Haq died in a plane crash in 1988, but the damage had already been done by his rule to Pakistan's stability and secularism. He had strengthened the ISI and the military's dominance over politics and government. Zia had encouraged the growth of Islamist parties and groups in Pakistan, Afghanistan, and Kashmir. Subsequently, Pakistan's politics and society became more divided and unstable, as Islamist groups began to fight secularism and as Sunnis fought Shiites. In 1989, the United States turned away from Pakistan after the end of the Afghanistan war, and Pakistan pressed on to complete its nuclear weapons program.

In 1988, the secular Pakistan Muslim League and Pakistan People's Party (PPP) returned as the two dominant governing parties. The PPP returned to power and Benazir Bhutto became the Prime Minister. Soon afterward, the ISI worked to undermine the Bhutto government and unified the opposition to the PPP around the Muslim League in the Islami Jamhoori Ittehad, including Islamist parties such as the Jamaat-e-Islami and the Jamiat-e-Ulema-i-Islami.

Nawaz Sharif and the Islami Jamhoori Ittehad (IJI) came to power for the first time in 1990. During the same period, the Jamaat-e-Islami, Jamiat-e-Ulema-i-Islami, and other anti-U.S. forces in the government opposed U.S. intervention in the Gulf War and the Sharif government's support of the United States. The U.S. presence in Saudi Arabia from 1990 onward inspired the creation of al Qaeda, as well as anti-Americanism among Pakistani Islamist groups.

In the late 1980s and early 1990s, while the Mujahideen were fighting the Soviets and the Najibullah regime in Afghanistan, the Jamiat-e-Ulema-i-Islami was helping to create the Taliban in the region around Quetta, Baluchistan and in the NorthWest Frontier Province. The Jamiat-e-Ulema-i-Islami built a support base among Durrani Pushtun refugees who originated from the Kandahar region in southern Afghanistan. The establishment of madrassas was a key element, as militants in the Jamaat-e-Ulema-i-Islami, who were part of the Deobandi sect, passed their beliefs on to the Taliban students in the madrassas. The Taliban became even more extreme in their beliefs, especially in regard to women and Shiites. The future leaders of the Taliban, including

91

Mohamed Omar, fought against the Najibullah regime after the Soviets left in 1988. In 1992, the Mujahideen overthrew the Najibullah regime, and many future Taliban returned to Pakistan (especially around Quetta) to take advantage of the madrassas of the Jamiat-e-Ulema-i-Islami for themselves and their families.[13]

In the 1980s, President Zia supported Kashmiri militant groups who, after his death, launched a military and terrorist campaign and escalated the level of violence there. In 1989, the Kashmir conflict escalated, with the Jammu and Kashmir Liberation Front (JKLF) fighting for independence from India and Pakistan. In 1994, the Yasin Malik faction of the JKLF voluntarily ceased firing and disarmed.

By 1993, pro-Pakistani movements had replaced pro-independence movements and were sustaining the conflict. They were based in Pakistan, trained in Afghanistan, motivated by pan-Islamist fundamentalism, and filled with Pushtuns, Arabs, Punjabis, and Afghans (an estimated 40% of the fighters were not Kashmiris). Two of the most prominent of the Pakistani-based groups that became active in Kashmir were Harakat-ul-Ansar (Islamic Helpers Group) and Lashkar-e-Taiba (Army of the Pure). In 2000, the Jaish-e-Muhammad (Army of Muhammad) burst upon the scene as another major group.

Harakat-ul-Ansar was established as in the mid-1980s and changed its name to Harakat ul-Mujahedeen, Islamic Freedom Fighters Group, after 1995 when the State Department listed Harakat-ul-Ansar as a terrorist group. Associated with the Islamist Jamiat-e-Ulema-i-Islami and its leader, Maulana Fazlur Rahman, the Harakat was originally based in Pakistan, operated from Afghanistan, and had several thousand armed supporters in Pakistan and Kashmir, including Afghan and Arab veterans of the 1979-1988 Afghan war. Harakat members have also participated in insurgent and terrorist operations in Burma, Tajikistan, and Bosnia. In 2000, many Harakat members joined a new organization, Jaish-e-Muhammad.[14]

Lashkar-e-Taiba was founded in 1980 as the military wing of the well-funded Pakistani Islamist organization Markaz-ad-Dawa-wal-Irshad of Wahabi sects, which recruited volunteers to fight alongside the Taliban in Afghanistan. Almost all of Lashkar-e-Taiba's several hundred members have been non-Kashmiris and have been schooled in madrassas. Some have been Afghan war veterans. After launching operations in 1993, the

Lashkar-e-Taiba became the most brutal terrorist group in Jammu and Kashmir, killing large numbers of civilians. Headed by Mohammed Latif, the Lashkar-e-Taiba has operated in the Srinagar Valley and the districts of Poonch, Rajauri and Doda. Its training camps have been located at Kotli, Sialkot, and Samani in Pakistan-controlled Kashmir. Its professed ideology goes beyond merely challenging India's sovereignty over Jammu and Kashmir. The Lashkar's agenda has been outlined in a pamphlet titled, *Why Are We Waging Jihad?* It includes a call for the restoration of Islamic rule over all parts of India, as well as Israel, Ethiopia, Spain, Hungary, and Russia.[15]

In October 1993, the PPP and Benazir Bhutto returned to power. In striving to build a majority coalition, the secularist Bhutto turned to the Islamist Jamiat-e-Ulema-i-Islami and its leader, Maulana Fazlur Rahman. Upon joining the PPP coalition, Fazlur Rahman became Chairman of the National Assembly's Standing Committee on Foreign Affairs. He made numerous trips to Saudi Arabia and the Gulf States to seek financial and military help for the Taliban. He arranged hunting trips for Arab princes to Kandahar, where they made their first contacts with the Taliban.[16]

As the Taliban advanced in Afghanistan in 1994 and 1995, the Pakistan security establishment jumped on the bandwagon. Two Islamists, Interior Minister Naserullah Babar and ISI head Lieutenant General Javed Nasir, led the way in siding with the Taliban. In 1995, a coup attempt led by an Islamist general, Zaheer-ul-Islam Abbasi, enhanced fears of the penetration of religious extremists into the ISI and Pakistani military at the lower and middle levels.[17]

In 1996, the Taliban took control of Kabul and most of Afghanistan. Afterward, Osama bin Laden and al Qaeda decided to relocate their headquarters from Khartoum, Sudan to Afghanistan. The Taliban supported their former Islamist patrons in Pakistan and Kashmir. The Bhutto government's initial enthusiasm for the Taliban was tempered when, by 1997, only Pakistan, Saudi Arabia, and the United Arab Emirates had recognized the new regime. The extremism of the Taliban and its invitation to al Qaeda to base itself in Afghanistan were off-putting to many states.

As the Taliban advanced, the Jamiat-e-Ulema-i-Islami inherited camps used to train the Taliban, as well as al Qaeda fighters, for the jihad in Afghanistan. Pakistani Islamist militant groups used the camps to train a new generation of fighters. For example, the Harakat ul-Ansar trained recruits in Camp Badr near Khost on the Pakistan-Afghanistan border and sent the fighters to Kashmir, Chechnya, and Yugoslavia.[18] In 1995, the Harakat-ul-Ansar kidnapped four Western tourists, including one American, in Kashmir and killed them, which was a sign of rising Pakistani anti-Americanism. In response to the killings, the United States named the Harakat-ul-Ansar a terrorist organization, which subsequently changed its name to the Harakat ul-Mujahideen.

In February 1997, Prime Minister Bhutto, the PPP, and the Jamiat-e-Ulema-i-Islami lost power to Nawaz Sharif and the Pakistan Muslim League-led coalition. However, the Jamiat-e-Ulema-i-Islami had already helped launch the Taliban and helped put it in control of most of Afghanistan, and the Taliban and al Qaeda returned the favor by offering its support to the Jamiat-e-Ulema-i-Islami and related groups.

When Nawaz Sharif and the Pakistan Muslim League-led coalition returned to power, the Jamaat-e-Islami refused to return as part of the coalition, having become more radical and revivalist and rejecting the corruption of secular politics. The Jamaat-e-Islami created and was supporting the Kashmir-based Hizb-ul Mujahideen (Freedom Fighters Movement) to fight for Islamism. It was becoming one of the largest groups fighting in Jammu and Kashmir.

In May 1998, the Sharif government decided to conduct a nuclear weapons test in response to India's test earlier in the month. Subsequently, the fear of an "Islamic bomb" rose in some quarters in Israel and the West. Also, the fear of al Qaeda obtaining weapons of mass destruction grew. In August 1998, the United States launched cruise missiles attacks on al Qaeda bases on the Afghan-Pakistan border near Khost and in other locations in retaliation for the bombing of U.S. Embassies in Nairobi, Kenya and Dar es Salaam, Tanzania. The attacks killed Pakistani Islamist fighters, which led to an escalation of anti-Americanism inside Pakistan.

In early 1999, General Musharraf launched the Kargil operation to test India's resolve in Jammu and Kashmir, particularly with both countries in possession of nuclear weapons. Radical Islamist fighters from the Harakat-ul-Mujahideen and Lashkar-e-Taiba played in the Kargil operation, fighting alongside Pakistani troops. After weeks of fighting and the possibility of a nuclear exchange, India was able to repel the incursion by July 1999.

1999-2001: General Musharraf's Coup and the High Water Mark for U.S. Rivals

In October 1999, General Pervez Musharraf, Pakistani Army Chief of Staff, took power in a bloodless coup. He had taken hawkish positions in 1998, when Pakistan tested nuclear weapons for the first time and, in the first half of 1999, when he sent troops and insurgents into Indian-held territory in the Kargil war. General Musharraf led the coup against the elected government of Prime Minister Sharif, who was suspected of being too dovish in relations with India and who conspired to dispose of General Musharraf while the latter was flying back from a meeting in Colombo, Sri Lanka. Once in power, it was expected that General Musharraf would intensify the struggle against India over Kashmir by aiding Islamist militant groups and would move Pakistan toward the brink of confrontation with India, including the prospect of nuclear war. Until September 11, 2001, this scenario seemed to be unfolding.

The profile of Pervez Musharraf is one of a Western-influenced professional military officer, who also is a strong Pakistani nationalist but not an Islamist. Musharraf was born in Delhi, became a Mohajir, having immigrated with his parents to Pakistan after partition in 1947, and comes from a middle class Urdu-speaking family in Karachi. He spent his early childhood in Turkey (1949-1956) owing to his father's posting as a diplomat to Ankara, and he claims that Kemal Ataturk, that country's secular modernizer, is his hero. Returning to Pakistan, he attended Saint Patrick's High School and Forman Christian College. His mother worked for the International Labor Organization, and Musharraf has taken relatively progressive stands toward women.

His military education included Pakistan Military Academy, Command and Staff College, National Defence College, and the Royal College of Defence Studies in the United Kingdom. He fought in the Indo-Pakistan war of 1965 as a young officer and was awarded the Imtiazi Sanad for gallantry. He volunteered to be a commando and remained in the Special Services Group for seven years. He also participated in the Indo-Pakistan War of 1971 as a company commander in the Commando Battalion.[19]

From the 1960s to the 1990s, General Musharraf rose through the ranks, despite the fact that he did not belong to the predominantly Punjabi officer class of the Pakistani army. In fact, Prime Minister Sharif promoted Musharraf to the most powerful military position in 1998 because Sharif believed that Musharraf did not have a base of support among the Punjabi officer class.[20]

On December 25, 1999, four Pakistani Islamists hijacked an Indian Airlines flight from Katmandu, Nepal to Kandahar. They killed a passenger and demanded the release of 36 terrorists in Indian jails in exchange for the passengers. Indian authorities ultimately gave up three terrorists, Maulana Masood Azhar, Ahmed Omar Sayed Sheikh and Mustaq Ahmed Zargar. Masood Azhar reportedly had fought in Somalia against U.S. troops in 1993 and proceeded to found the Pakistani terrorist organization Jaish-e-Muhammad in February 2000 that would bomb the Jammu and Kashmir assembly on October 1, 2001, killing 36 persons. Omar Sayed Sheik had served five years in an Indian prison for kidnapping Westerners, became a prominent member of Jaish-i-Muhammad, and went on to kidnap Daniel Pearl in January 2002.

In July 2000, Abdui Majeed Dar, the leader of Hizb-ul-Mujahideen agreed to a cease-fire with the Indian army in Jammu and Kashmir coinciding with the visit of Jamaat-e-Islami leader, Ameer Qazi Hussain Ahmed, to the United States. However, the Muttahida Jihad Council of 14 jihadi groups refused to cease-fire. On August 1-2, 2000, the Lashkar-e-Taiba began a series of massacres, which spread over three districts of Jammu and Kashmir and led to the killing of more than 100 persons within a space of 24 hours.[21]

In October 2000, after the bombing of the USS Cole, the Clinton administration approached General Musharraf to assist in arresting and extraditing Osama bin Laden. However, Musharraf refused to serve as an intermediary for the extradition of bin Laden. The reluctance of Musharraf indicated that, before September 11, 2001, the position of al Qaeda and other U.S. rivals in Pakistan was fairly strong. The ISI continued to support several Islamist groups and al Qaeda enjoyed a degree of popular support in Pakistan.

In July 2001, General Musharraf named himself president in a bid to consolidate his grip on power. He went to India and held his first summit meeting with Indian Prime Minister Atal Behari Vajpayee at Agra. However, the two failed to make much headway in resolving the Kashmir dispute.

Post-September 11, 2001

After the terrorist attacks of September 11, 2001, the United States identified Taliban-ruled Afghanistan as the major target in the war on terrorism. The greatest challenge confronting the United States was how to gain access to land-locked Afghanistan, especially for U.S. air power. The only realistic avenue was through Pakistan. With some uncertainty, the Bush administration approached President Musharraf. The offer of economic aid and an end to some sanctions helped lead to his about face and the offer of overflight rights. However, before Musharraf could allow U.S. forces into Pakistani bases to attack al Qaeda and the Taliban, he first had to remove opposition within his own armed forces and especially the ISI.

Musharraf began a clampdown on Islamist generals and groups in Pakistan. With the start of U.S. military operations in Pakistan and Afghanistan on October 7, 2001, Musharraf carried out a shakeup of the military. He reshuffled the army, retiring the pro-Taliban ISI chief, Lieutenant General Mahmood Ahmed, and appointed the former Corps Commander in Peshawar, Lieutenant General Eshanul Haq, as Director General of the ISI. General Musharraf also retired Deputy Chief of Army Staff Lieutenant General M. H. Usmani, an Islamist tabligi (evangelist). Musharraf's differences with Lieutenant General Mohammed Aziz Khan, an Islamist and Taliban supporter, led the former to promote the latter from the powerful post of Commander IV Corps, Lahore, to the largely ceremonial post of the Chairman of the Joint Chiefs of Staff (CJCS) Committee. All three generals had been strong supporters of Musharraf in the 1999 coup against Prime Minister Sharif.[22]

A most significant change was the removal from the ISI of Lieutenant General Ahmed, who was supportive of and ethnically linked to the Taliban. He had provided covert support for jihadi activity from within the Pakistani military. During the September 11 attacks, Ahmed was in the United States. In October, President Musharraf sent Ahmed as the head of a delegation of Pakistani religious leaders to Afghanistan to negotiate the surrender of Osama bin Laden. Instead of asking for Bin Laden to be handed over unconditionally, Ahmed lauded the efforts of Taliban chief

Muhammad Omar in his fight against the United States and urged him to resist demands to hand over bin Laden.[23]

Another key move was the promotion of Lieutenant General Mohammed Aziz Khan to the largely ceremonial post of Chairman of the JCS. Aziz was a Punjabi-speaking Pathan (Pushtun) from Pakistan-administered Kashmir, who graduated from the British Royal Staff College. He shared the late President/General Zia ul-Haq's vision of a pan-Islamic state that would include Afghanistan and the Central Asian republics. As assistant director general of the ISI, Aziz was linked with the Taliban's push into Afghanistan in 1996 and had close dealings with its leadership and that of Islamist groups inside Pakistan.[24]

The Musharraf government moved to quash Islamist leaders who opposed his policy switch. On October 16, 2001, the Pakistan government charged Jamiat-Ulema-e-Islami leader Maulana Fazlur Rahman with sedition. He was accused of spurring violent protests against the U.S.-led attacks on Afghanistan and placed under house arrest. Sipah-i-Sahaba's chief, Maulana Azam Tariq, was also placed under house arrest. The Jamaat-e-Islami leader, Ameer Qazi Hussain Ahmed, was arrested and jailed. At the end of February 2002, he was released from prison and resumed his campaign of denunciation against President Musharraf. In May 2002, he publicly demanded Musharraf's resignation.

Also in October 2002, two Islamist nuclear scientists, Sultan Bashiruddin Mahmood and Abdul Majid, were arrested after they had visited al Qaeda and Osama bin Laden in August 2001 in Kabul, Afghanistan. They had conducted long discussions with bin Laden about nuclear, biological, and chemical weapons, according to Pakistani officials familiar with the interrogations of the men who were described as "very motivated" and "extremist in their ideas."[25]

Mahmood and Majid had used an Afghan relief organization, the Ummah Tameer-e-Nau, and a humanitarian mission as a cover to conduct secret talks with bin Laden. They reported that bin Laden indicated that he had radiological material acquired for him by the Islamic Movement of Uzbekistan. The scientists said they left the meetings believing that bin Laden had such material and that he had asked them how the material could be made into a weapon. They told him it would not be possible to manufacture a weapon with the material he had. The two scientists were eventually released in December 2001, but their case illustrated the dangers of Pakistani proliferation to U.S. rivals.[26]

The Islamists struck back at the emerging anti-terrorist coalition through Pakistani Islamists who operated in Jammu and Kashmir. On October 1, 2001, the Pakistani terrorist organization Jaish-e-Muhammad bombed the Jammu and Kashmir assembly, killing 36 persons. On December 13, 2001, Islamist militants attacked the Indian parliament. Indian authorities blamed the Jaish-e-Muhammad and the Lashkar-i-Jhangvi (Army of Mullah Jhangvi, headed by the Karachi financier Riaz Basra), backed by Pakistan and the ISI. In response, the Indian army mobilized and 700,000 troops moved toward the front line. President Musharraf countered by ordering 300,000 Pakistani troops to the front. On January 12, 2002, after considerable pressure from the United States and India, Musharraf gave a speech condemning cross-border terrorism and promised to stop it. Hundreds of suspected Islamist militants and fighters were arrested and detained. The U.S. government placed the Jaish-e-Muhammad and the Lashkar-i-Jhangvi on its list of international terrorists.

On January 23, 2002, Daniel Pearl was kidnapped by Ahmed Omar Sayed Sheikh and his Jaish-e-Muhammad associates in Karachi. The journalist was actually guarded and executed by Naeem Bukhari and his associates, who belonged to Lashkar-i-Jhangvi.[27] A Pakistani intelligence officer, Brigadier Abdullah, played a key role in nurturing the Jaish-e-Muhammad after its formation in 2000 and also helped facilitate Sheikh's frequent travels between Afghanistan and Pakistan. The intelligence officer was among those who were pushed aside as President Musharraf began his shake-up of ISI in October 2001.[28]

On March 17, 2002, the Lashkar-e-Omar (Army of Mohamed Omar) attacked an Anglican church in Islamabad, killing two Americans. In late March, a raid by Pakistani police and FBI agents in Faisalabad, Punjab Province, resulted in the capture of Abu Zubaida, the highest-ranking al Qaeda operative to be apprehended since the September 11 attacks in the United States. More than two dozen other al Qaeda members and a large number of computer disks were seized in the raid. The arrest was yet another sign that al Qaeda had infiltrated into Pakistani cities. Subsequently, Abu Zubaida has provided U.S. intelligence and law enforcement agencies with considerable information about al Qaeda.

By late March 2002, Musharraf had released many of the Islamist militants, who had been arrested in January. He was accused of using legal loopholes to release the militants. Previously, he had rounded them up under the Maintenance of Public Order Act, which had loopholes. Not one militant had been charged under the Anti-terrorism Act that had been amended with stronger penal provisions to curb religious extremists. A little over a month after the crackdown, the head of Pakistan's Interior Ministry's Crisis Management Cell, Brigadier Javed Iqbal Cheema said he was planning to release more than 2,000 suspected militants. They belonged to five banned groups, including Jaish-i-Muhammad and Lashkar-i-Jhangvi, who were believed to be responsible for the attack on the Indian Parliament on December 13, 2001.[29]

In Spring 2002, President Musharraf moved to further consolidate power. In March, he promoted 47 Brigadiers to Major General, which was a sign that civilians were being squeezed out of top positions and that military leaders who President Musharraf trusted were being put in their place. At the end of April, Musharraf staged a referendum on his presidency, which he won overwhelmingly, but which was not free and fair. Anticipating general elections in October 2002, Musharraf banned former prime ministers Bhutto and Sharif from contesting and has situated himself to remain in power.

An increasing number of retired and serving generals continue to espouse the cause of Islamism, support for jihadis, and oppose President Musharraf. These include General Aslam Beg (former Chief of Army Staff), Lieutenant-General Hamid Gul (former ISI chief), Lieutenant-General Javed Nasir (former ISI chief), Lieutenant-General Mohammed Ahmed (former ISI chief), and Lieutenant-General Mohammed Aziz, current Chairman of Joint Chiefs of Staff Committee (CJCS).[30]

In Spring 2000, the U.S. and coalition partners launched Operation Anaconda and other operations. U.S. personnel joined Pakistani troops in a hunt for al-Qaeda and Taliban fugitives in the North Waziristan semi-autonomous tribal area. It was the first time that foreign troops had landed in the area, where even the Pakistan Army had not been allowed to operate since independence in 1947. The hunt centered on Spin Wam, just 15 miles from the eastern Afghan province of Khost, which was the main center of operations of the U.S.-led coalition forces against the last vestiges of al Qaeda in Spring 2002. Pakistani and American officials suspected that Osama bin Laden and his men were hiding in the Waziristan tribal area, where the former Afghan Taliban regime had strong support.

Pakistani troops aided by U.S. personnel began combing the area, finding weapons but no terrorists. They angered tribesmen when they raided an Islamic seminary established by Jalaluddin Haqani, a former commander of Taliban forces. Pakistani tribesmen were being urged by their religious leaders to kill American soldiers.

About 200 Pakistani soldiers accompanied by a dozen American soldiers broke through the sprawling compound of the madrassa outside Miran Shah, headquarters of the North Waziristan tribal area, about 12 miles from the Afghan border, after reports that it was being used by al Qaeda as a hideout. Once a center for Islamic learning for the Afghan Taliban in the early 1990s, the madrassa was closed by the Pakistani authorities in December 2001 but later handed over to the local Islamic leaders. In a separate raid, a joint Pakistani and American team held the chief of another madrassa on suspicion of being an al Qaeda member. Pakistan, General Ehsan ul-Haq, and the ISI won praise from the United States for its support in the war on terrorism, particularly in rounding up more than 300 Qaeda members in Spring 2002.[31]

In recent months, Pakistani cities have filled with U.S. rivals, and terror attacks have pointed to worrisome links between local extremists and fugitive al Qaeda leaders who had filtered across the country into major cities. Hundreds of al Qaeda operatives who fled Afghanistan found refuge in Karachi, Lahore, Peshawar and Quetta. Their hosts have been Islamist militants who have joined forces with bin Laden's organization. Connections between Pakistani militants and al Qaeda foreigners increased al Qaeda's effectiveness. Bomb attacks in Karachi against the U.S. consulate and the French defense workers showed great planning and sophistication.

On June 14, 2002, a new Islamist group, al Qanoon (the Law), claimed responsibility for a suicide attack on the U.S. Consulate in Karachi. Most likely, al Qaeda plotted the attack. An ISI official said that signs pointed toward an al Qaeda link and an intensified collaboration between al Qaeda and indigenous terrorist groups, such as the Sunni Muslim extremist group Lashkar-e-Jhangvi. Pakistan's Interior Ministry estimated this year that the trained members of just five of the country's militant groups numbered 5,000. "Terror could hit the president, or anyone."[32]

In May 2002, reports emerged about Harka al-Jahad al-Islami, (Army of the Islamic Holy War) one of Pakistan's biggest jihadi militia, which had been headquartered in Kandahar. In Pakistan, very few had known the name of the outfit and its leader, Qari Saifullah Akhtar. A large number of its fighters made their way into Central Asia and Chechnya to escape capture at the hands of the Americans, while the rest stole back into Pakistan to establish themselves in Waziristan and Buner. Their military training camp (maskar) in Kotli in Azad Kashmir swelled with new fighters and the outfit has been scouting areas in the Northwest Frontier Province to create a supplementary maskar for jihad in Kashmir. It joined with Harkat-ul-Mujahideen to create Jamiat-ul-Mujahideen in order to cut the number of groups gathered together in Pakistan-held Azad Kashmir.[33]

In May 2002, three men were arrested for firing rockets toward the air base used by U.S. troops outside the southern Pakistan city of Jacobabad. They were identified as members of Sipah Sahaba Pakistan, a banned Sunni Muslim group. Implicated were both Sipah Sahaba Pakistan and Lashkar-e-Jhangvi, which had previously focused on attacking Pakistani Shiites, rather than Westerners.[34]

In May 2002, Islamist groups resumed their activities in Jammu and Kashmir after the snow on mountain passes had melted. Resulting tensions with India impaired Pakistan's ability to station troops and operate patrols along the border with Afghanistan, where American officials appear to have focused most of their concern.

On May 14, 2002, jihadi groups sent guerrillas from Pakistan's part of Kashmir into India's portion on a raid on an Indian army camp that led to the deaths of 34 people.[35] The incident brought the nuclear-armed neighbors to the brink of all-out war, which could have killed millions. The incident underscored the fact that field commanders rather than President Musharraf control Pakistan's nuclear forces.[36]

In the October 2002 elections, Islamist political parties made major gains in parliament. They also gained control of government structures in Boluchistan and North West frontier provinces. The Islamists are now a major political force in Pakistan.

Conclusions

This chapter has demonstrated that Pakistan is filled with some of the most dangerous international rivals that could harm U.S. interests in a number of ways. These rivals are Islamists, many of whom are prepared to die for their cause. Many have been schooled in Wahabi madrassas, to wage jihad against the United States, the West, India, and against secularism in Pakistan. They belong to a variety of groups and most are linked to al Qaeda and Osama bin Laden. The psychological profile of the leaders of these groups and their followers is similar to that of bin Laden and those who destroyed the World Trade Center and attacked the Pentagon on September 11, 2001. They have a burning resentment against all things Western and believe that dying for the cause is necessary and even desirable. They confirm that non-state actors, like Osama bin Laden, can be just as dangerous for the United States as Saddam Hussein or other heads of state.

Thus far, Islamist rivals to the United States in Pakistan have attacked soft targets with some sophistication. It is likely that these attacks will continue and will provide a disincentive for U.S. companies and non-governmental organizations that would like to operate in Pakistan. It is very difficult for the Pakistan government, backed by U.S. authorities, to root out Islamist groups that are filled with hundreds or thousands of fanatics and with more madrassa-trained volunteers waiting in the wings.

The greatest danger for the United States in Pakistan stems from efforts by Islamist groups to precipitate nuclear war between India and Pakistan over Jammu and Kashmir and to overthrow the governments of Pakistan and Afghanistan. The recent crisis between India and Pakistan demonstrates that additional Islamist attacks on Indian targets will bring Indian retaliation that could spiral into nuclear war, kill 12 to 15 million people, and devastate U.S. interests. A few thousand determined U.S. rivals could destroy the sub-continent and block international economic activity for decades to come.

Another danger is Pakistan-based Islamists helping to overthrow the U.S.-backed Afghan government of President Hamid Karzai. The present government is fragile and susceptible to attacks from various tribal warlords inside Afghanistan, who could be backed by Islamist allies in Pakistan. Thus far, U.S. and Pakistani forces have prevented Pakistani-based Islamists from linking up with their Afghan counterparts as they did during the anti-Soviet and Taliban wars. However, the border is so difficult to patrol that links will eventually be restored. If Karzai is overthrown, the door will be open for al Qaeda to return and to restore operations, including WMD development.

A third danger is for Islamists to join forces with sympathizers in the military in overthrowing the Musharraf government and moving Pakistan back in an anti-U.S. direction. If Islamists gained control of the government, they could shut down much of the U.S. war against terrorism, intensify operations in Kashmir that could lead to nuclear war, and help the Taliban to return to power in Afghanistan. An Islamist regime in Pakistan would most likely proliferate WMD and become part of the "axis of evil."

President Musharraf has done everything to prevent such a scenario, purging the military and ISI, clamping down on Islamist leaders and groups, and fortifying his own position as president and commander-in-chief of the armed forces. He has also moved carefully on the Kashmir issue, trying not to inflame public opinion against him. Musharraf will manage the October elections and the aftermath so that Pakistan does not return to the corrupt and divisive politics of the 1990s and Islamist groups are kept out of governing coalitions. Musharraf fits the profile of the "Ataturk of Pakistan."

In the long run, Musharraf faces a more daunting task in trying to secularize Pakistan than Ataturk had in transforming Turkey. Pakistan must provide a public education system and jobs as an alternative to the *madrassas* and the Islamist groups. However, heavy defense spending and the weak state of the Pakistani economy pose major obstacles to such a path. Fifty percent of the Pakistani budget is consumed by debt servicing and defense expenditure. The external debt is about $34 billion and internal debt is about 45% of GDP. In the 1990s the ratio of defense expenditure to health and education expenditure was 239:1. For Pakistan's democratic and economic restructuring to succeed these numbers have to change. Otherwise, Pakistan will continue to be a major source of rivals to the United States.

Notes

1. Shahid Javed Burki, *Pakistan: Fifty Years of Nationhood* (Boulder, Colo.: Westview, 1999).

2. S.V.R. Nasr, "Islam in Pakistan," in John L. Esposito, ed. *Political Islam: Revolution, Radicalism, or Reform?* (Boulder, Colo.: Lynne Rienner, 1997), 136-138.

3. Jessica Stern, "Pakistan's Jihad Culture," *Foreign Affairs,* 79, 6 (November/ December 2000), 117.

4. M. Ehsan Ahrari, *Jihadi Groups, Nuclear Pakistan, and the New Great Game* (Carlisle, Penna.: Strategic Studies Institute, U.S. Army War College, 2001).

5. Hasan-Askari Rizvi, *Military, State and Society in Pakistan,* (New York: St. Martin's, 2000), 170-76.

6. Nasr, "Islam in Pakistan," 136-138.

7. Stephen P. Cohen, *The Pakistan Army.* 2nd ed. (New York: Oxford University Press, 1999).

8. Rizvi, *Military, State and Society in Pakistan,* 245-48.

9. Ahmed Rashid, "Pakistan and the Taliban," in William Maley, ed. *Fundamentalism Reborn? Afghanistan and the Taliban* (New York: New York University Press, 1998), 74.

10. Ajay Behera, "Is Musharraf Spooked by His Spy Agency?" *Asia Times*, March 12, 2002.

11. "Saudi Arabia and Wahabism," *Issues in Foreign Affairs*, November 12, 2001, http://www.issuesinforeignaffairs.com/past/2001-11-12/issue5.html. Founded in the early 1700's by Mohamed Ibn Abd-al-Wahab, Wahabism preaches an uncompromising Islam. All other religions and sects of Islam are considered heretic. Foreign influences are considered to be prime evils. Wahabism is virulently anti-foreign and anti-West and forms the basis for the ideology of Osama bin Laden and al Qaeda.

12 Anatol Lieven, "The Pressures on Pakistan," *Foreign Affairs* 81: 1 (January/February 2002), 110.

13. Rashid, "Pakistan and the Taliban," 75.

14. Jonah Blank, "Kashmir: Fundamentalism Takes Root" *Foreign Affairs.* 78, 6 (November/ December 1999), 37.

15. "Jammu and Kashmir Rebels Advertise in Pakistan Papers," *The Asian Age*, February 8, 1999, 1.

16. Rashid, "Pakistan and the Taliban," 76.

17. Ajay Behera, "Is Musharraf Spooked?"

18. Rashid, "Pakistan and the Taliban," 108.

19. "Profile: General Pervez Musharraf," *BBC News,* September 24, 2001.

20. "Profile: General Pervez Musharraf."

21. See on Internet: http://www.expressindia.com/kashmir/kashmirlive/lashkar.html.

22. Ajay Behera, "Is Musharraf Spooked?"

23. Howard W. French, "Pakistani Intelligence Officials See Qaeda Peril In Their Cities," *New York Times*, May 29, 2002, 1.

24. Rahul Bedi, "Sidelining of Islamist generals puts Musharraf on safer ground," October 19, 2001. http://www.janes.com/security/international_security/news/misc/janes 011019_1_ n.shtml By *in New Delhi.*

25. Kamran Khan and Molly Moore, "2 Nuclear Experts Briefed Bin Laden, Pakistanis Say," *Washington Post*, December 12, 2001, 1.

26. Khan and Moore, "2 Nuclear Experts," 1.

27. A.B. Mahapatra, "Aziz Hand Seen in Kandahar Hijacking," *News Insight.net* November 8, 2001*:* According to this Indian news report, some diplomats and Indian officials believed (but could not prove) that the Pakistani military was behind the Christmas 1999 hijacking. They claimed that General Mohammed Aziz, Lahore corps commander, was coaching the hijackers in what demands to put and what to accept. They said that Aziz was heading what is known as the "Pakistani Army of Islam (PAI)." Supposedly, Colonel Pervez Musharraf of the Special Services Group and Colonel Mohammad Aziz raised the "Pakistani Army of Islam" from the students of 100 Deobandi madrassas in 1979-80. It was created on the orders of Pakistan's then martial-law administrator, General Mohammad Zia-ul-Haq. Zia ensured that, while Pakistan's military intelligence trained Arab and Afghan Mujahideen, with the assistance of American, British and French forces, the PAI was trained by Pakistani intelligence (the ISI) alone. Other Pakistani terrorist groups like the *Harakat-ul-Mujahideen* (banned by the United States), the *Lashkar-e-Taiba,* and the *Al-Badr* were supposedly constituents of the Pakistani Army of Islam. These claims cannot be substantiated, but they demonstrate that

many Indians believe that Islamist terrorism is orchestrated by the Pakistani government and army and, particularly, by the ISI.

28. Douglas Jehl, "Death Of Reporter Puts Focus On Pakistan's Intelligence Unit" *New York Times*, February 25, 2002, 1.

29. John Wilson, "The Bigger Coup in Pakistan," *The Pioneer*, March 6, 2002. Pakistani foot-dragging on arresting Islamist militants was evident in an inquiry conducted in Sindh Province on the directives of the Interior Ministry of Pakistan, which came out with a report that none of the *madrassas* and mosques in the province had anything to do with *jihadis*. This was in direct contradiction of the intelligence reports that spoke of 500-odd mosques and *madrassas* suspected to be breeding grounds for *jihadis*. The similar pattern applies in Punjab province where more than 2,715 *madrassas* and mosques have a total enrolment of 250,000 students.

30. Ajay Behera, "Is Musharraf Spooked?"

31. Zahid Hussain, "Tribesmen Urged To Kill American Soldiers," The Times, May 7, 2002.

32. Karl Vick and Kamran Khan, "Al Qaeda Tied To Attacks In Pakistan Cities: Militants Joining Forces Against Western Targets," *Washington Post*, May 30, 2002, 1.

33. Khaled Ahmad, "The Biggest Militia We Know Nothing About" *Friday Times* May 17 - 23, 2002 - Vol. XIV, No. 12 http://www.thefridaytimes.com/news10.htm.

34. Vick and Khan, "Al Qaeda Tied," 1.

35. French, "Pakistani Intelligence Officials," p. 1. The "new look ISI" now admits that their predecessors aided Islamist groups in their operations in Jammu and Kashmir.

36. David Blair, "Finger on the Nuclear Button is Not Musharraf's," *London Daily Telegraph*, June 7, 2002.

CHAPTER 5

Kim Chong-il's Erratic Decision-Making and North Korea's Strategic Culture

Merrily Baird

Introduction

In the more than 55 years since North Korea was created, the country has had but two leaders. The first, Kim Il-song, was born in a homeland occupied by Japan and spent his youth as a guerilla fighting to restore Korea's independence. Even after the Japanese withdrew in 1945, Kim looked backwards, building a nation which mirrored the preoccupations and operating culture of his guerilla days. This produced a leadership cadre that is still secretive, xenophobic, and convinced that only overwhelming military strength can guarantee the nation's survival.

Kim Chong-il, who succeeded his father and has ruled since 1994, is more intellectually agile and more intrigued by the notion of change. This has helped him to improve relations with China and Russia and to introduce some economic change. Moreover, because he better understands the problems North Korea faces and the strengths that South Korea enjoys, he seems less inclined to initiate a second peninsula war. Even so, North Korea remains a source of danger as the self-centered Kim is vulnerable to misinterpreting the intentions of foreign leaders and often relies on brinkmanship and threats as primary tools of diplomacy. Kim's ruthless personality, meanwhile, suggests that he would not hesitate to use weapons of mass destruction (WMD) if he believed foreign powers posed an imminent threat to either North Korea or him personally.

In late 2002, North Korean diplomats acknowledged that their country had violated a 1994 international agreement by resuming work on a clandestine nuclear weapons program. Clearly, this revelation and its consequences--a setback to rapprochement with Japan and a cutoff of Western assistance to the energy sector--are outcomes Kim Chong-il would have wished to avoid. Even so, Kim probably counts the secret nuclear program a worthwhile risk, and he may believe that acknowledging it now strengthens his country's deterrence posture. Kim's past behavior suggests that he may also believe that an opportunity exists to accept the imposition of new safeguards in exchange for progress on his own agenda, i.e., negotiating economic aid and realizing high-level talks with the United States.

The Supreme Leader: Kim Chong-il

Kim Chong-il was born in the early 1940s near Khabarovsk, where, under the protection of the Soviet military, Kim Il-song was at that time basing his guerilla operations. In August 1945, with Japan's defeat in World War II and the Soviets' assumption of control over the northern half of the Korean peninsula, Kim Il-song returned to P'yongyang. His wife and children followed a few months later, becoming North Korea's "first family" when the Soviets installed Kim in power in early 1946.

With the exception of two years spent in China at the start of the Korean War, Kim Chong-il grew up and was schooled in P'yongyang, and in 1964 he finished his education at Kim Il-song University, earning a bachelor's degree in political economy.[1] On leaving college, Kim went to work for the Korean Workers' Party (KWP), the main power base of his father. In quick succession he moved into managerial positions at three key departments.

The first and most significant of these appointments in the KWP was to the Organization and Guidance Department. This is not only the country's premier patronage-dispensing platform but also the coordinating body for managing the party's remaining departments and, through them, military, governmental, and economic activities. It was at and through the Organization and Guidance Department that Kim first had the opportunity to develop a comprehensive knowledge of political life in North Korea and the issues involved in running the country. Moreover, the assignment allowed him to begin building a personal power base, as is seen in the fact that many current second-tier leaders were his associates at the department in the 1960s and 1970s.[2]

Kim Chong-il used his next assignment, to the Propaganda and Agitation Department, to deepen ideological indoctrination. This helped enforce political conformity and justify rule by the Kim family, but it also strengthened a sense of national pride and uniqueness in an era when South Korea was beginning to flourish and North Koreans continued to suffer economic deprivation. Finally, Kim's assignment as head of the Culture and Arts Department of the KWP allowed him to focus on his personal passions--movies, opera, and theater--while making art more clearly serve political ends.

Leader-in-waiting. Changes in North Korean propaganda themes and other written materials indicate that Kim Il-song had decided on a family succession by the early 1970s. According to Han S. Park, the leading scholar of North Korean ideology, Kim Il-song sought to provide a basis not only for stability but also for a "perpetuation of the system characteristics that tend[ed] to be unique and peculiar."[3] Scholars agree that Kim Il-song was haunted by both the postmortem denunciations of Stalin and Mao's stumbling efforts to secure the Chinese succession. In these circumstances, the elder Kim turned to the only person he thought willing to preserve his legacy and able to lay claim—through blood ties—to his own legitimacy.

In connection with the succession plan, Kim Chong-il became a KWP secretary in September 1973 and a Politburo member in February 1974, and his authority grew rapidly thereafter. By the end of the decade he had assumed day-to-day control of government, party, and military affairs, even though Kim Il-song remained the final arbiter of policy. Precisely when Kim Chong-il obtained operational authority over the complex intelligence apparatus is not known. However, by 1978 he had at least partial control of covert operations and this allowed him to personally initiate an operation that, while relatively low risk, gained international attention. This was the pair of sequential kidnappings, from Hong Kong in 1978, of Kim's favorite South Korean actress and her movie-director husband.

In October 1980, at the Sixth Party Congress, Kim Chong-il was ranked second in the KWP. Although he was not formally designated his father's successor, in 1981 the media began referring to him by name and chronicling some of his activities.[4] Kim became first deputy chairman of the National Defense Commission in May 1990 and Supreme Commander of the Korean People's Army (KPA) in December 1991. He attained the military rank of marshal in April 1992 and became chairman of the National Defense Commission in April 1993. In July 1994, Kim Il-song—still the general secretary of the KWP and the head of state as President—died of a heart attack. Three years of national mourning followed, after which Kim Chong-il became KWP general secretary. However, instead of assuming the presidency, he rules as chair of the National Defense Commission.

Kim Chong-il's Managerial Style and Personality

Managerial style. Kim Chong-il is less public a figure than his father, as is evident from his behavior and pattern of activities. He does not view public appearances and public speeches as a critical element of his leadership style. North Korean television broadcasts of the 1980s show him to be patently bored at large, formal meetings and abrupt to the point of rudeness in greeting citizens on ceremonial occasions. In addition, Kim is a relatively solitary decision-maker, who, according to defector information, obtains information primarily by reading official reports, the foreign press, and the internet, and by watching foreign television.[5]

Micromanagement also characterizes Kim Chong-il's workstyle. No detail is too small to rivet his attention and no project escapes his decision-making reach. The media treats this managerial pattern as evidence of unparalleled talents and a deep care for the welfare of the people. However, Kim has a strong need for control. This first became clear in the mid-1970s, when he created the Three Revolutions Teams and sent college-age students to every production unit in North Korea. The students were charged with encouraging a greater use of modern technology, but the primary intent of the program was to give Kim Chong-il a means of control and a channel of information collection independent of those used by Kim Il-song.[6]

Personal characteristics. While capable of a studied charm, especially in the presence of foreign visitors, defectors indicate that Kim cares little whether he is liked. Indeed, he clearly prefers dominating by fear, especially when dealing with senior officials. Specific anecdotes related by defectors paint a portrait of a manipulative individual who controls people through a combination of bribery (i.e., the granting of special privileges), humiliation, and the threat of punishments. The most dire of these punishments is execution, and several defectors have named senior officials said to have been executed on Kim's orders. Even if some of these stories are more urban legend than fact, their widespread currency heightens Kim's ability to instill fear.[7]

Defectors also characterize Kim Chong-il as self-centered and lacking empathy, and they indicate that he tends to view nearly everything and everyone in a utilitarian manner. Kim believes that lesser beings exist to serve him. Kim also takes a utilitarian approach to ideas, according to examples given by defectors. On the negative side, this means that he has no enduring commitments to principles other than that of his own self-interest. On the more positive side, his non-sentimental approach makes him a more flexible thinker than his father. Kim thinks of himself as a highly creative and artistic individual, and he welcomes creative ideas offered by other people as long as they do not clash with his opinions or threaten his control. He especially appreciates novel ideas for earning greater foreign currency, manipulating the appearance of P'yongyang's architecture, and generally acquiring major benefits at minimal cost.

Both Kim's lack of empathy and sense of entitlement are revealed in his indulgent lifestyle, which contrasts with the struggle of most North Koreans to simply feed themselves. Defector reporting indicates that Kim maintains lavish villas in each of North Korea's provinces and has them furnished with imported luxury goods. He is the world's leading importer of high-end cognac, according to a report carried by the *Wall Street Journal* in the mid-1990s, and has squads of beautiful female entertainers maintained for his benefit.

A low regard for others is indicated by Kim's apparent involvement in overseeing two terrorist incidents (one in 1983 and another in 1987, as discussed later in this chapter) meant to take many lives. More recent events also testify to his comfort with tolerating high levels of deaths at home. In confronting North Korea's famine, saving lives has not been a top priority. Early in the famine cycle Kim cut off nearly all food supplies to the four eastern provinces and denied these provinces access to international aid.[8] Large numbers of deaths also occurred when, between

1997 and 1999 on Kim's orders, several hundred thousand people displaced by the famine were herded into camps where conditions allowed few to survive.[9] Moreover, according to the testimony of eyewitnesses, Kim has ordered the systematic killing of babies born in North Korea's camps for political prisoners.[10]

Decision-making Elites and Military Command and Control

Ruling elites. Kim Chong-il is the sole arbiter of who rises to senior levels of the party, government, and military and which individuals and institutions are allowed a voice on each decision-making occasion. The advisors closest to him form a hand-chosen kitchen cabinet of relatives and long-time allies. It is within this circle that Kim can let down his hair, so to speak, and obtain non-threatening policy advice and emotional support. The members of this group spend a good deal of leisure time with Kim, and they control mechanisms which earn substantial amounts of foreign currency, including that reserved for Kim's personal use. To the degree that North Korea is a kleptocracy, a political system managed to enrich a small number of leaders, the heart of that kleptocracy resides here.

This inner circle includes:

- Kim Kyong-hui, the younger sister of Kim Chong-il and his only full sibling. The South Korean press identifies her as deputy director of the KWP's Light Industry Department.

- Chang Song-taek, the husband of Kim Kyong-hui and the seniormost of the first vice directors of the KWP's Organization and Guidance Department. Through this department, Chang manages KWP headquarters operations, the procurement of goods and cash for Kim Chong-il, and smuggling by diplomats. Chang also reportedly heads the party-based Taesong Bank, and this may connect him to the flow of payments involved in North Korea's arms sales.[11]

- Vice Marshal Cho Myong-nok, the second ranking member of the National Defense Commission and political commissar of the KPA. In

October 2000, as a special envoy of Kim Chong-il, Cho visited Washington D.C. and met with President Clinton, Secretary of State Albright, and Secretary of Defense Cohen. Some years earlier he was commander of the Air Force and is reported to have negotiated the transfer of missiles and missile-related technology to Iran.[12]

- Kim Yong-sun, the KWP secretary in charge of rapprochement with Seoul, South Korean investment in the North, and covert action programs against South Korea.

- Kim Ki-nam and Kim Kuk-tae, longtime KWP secretaries and specialists in propaganda and personnel affairs, respectively.

A second, larger circle of officials shores up Kim Chong-il's power base and joins the inner circle in strategic decision-making. In recent years, representatives from the KPA have gained dramatically increased prominence within this echelon as have the KWP officials who oversee weapons production. Key members of this group are currently the Minister of the People's Armed Forces and the KPA Chief of the General Staff; the KWP secretaries and department chiefs for Chagang Province, weapons production, and general military affairs; the head of the General Staff's Operations Bureau; and the two deputy political commissars of the KPA.

Military command and control. On paper and in practice under current peacetime circumstances, control of North Korea's military policies and armed forces is vested in Kim Chong-il and flows down from him in two intersecting chains-of-command. One chain-of-command is based in the KWP, where the Central Military Committee works with the KPA's General Political Bureau to ensure party control of the military. The other administrative channel of control is the National Defense Commission in whose name Kim rules.

North Korean media reporting indicates that the National Defense Commission currently includes the head of the General Political Bureau, the Defense Minister, Chief of the General Staff, the three service commanders, the active-duty heads of major security organizations, and the two civilian KWP officials who manage the armaments industry. The Commission is North Korea's closest equivalent to the U.S. National Security Council but it lacks representatives from the foreign affairs establishment and the non-armaments economic sector.

It is not known how often the National Defense Commission meets, either as a full or partial group. Information on the dynamics of Commission discussions is also not available, but given Kim Chong-il's dislike of opinions that challenge his and his solo ability to dictate the Commission's membership, any question of his having to defer to Commission decisions may be moot. Consistent with this judgment is one journalist's report of Secretary of State Albright's discussion of missile-related issues with Kim in October 2000. After Albright had "commented that some of the questions were technical and might require study, Kim picked up the list and began immediately to provide answers one by one without advice or further study, in what Albright later called a 'quite stunning' feat, which could only be performed by a leader with absolute authority."[13]

Under Kim Il-song, the chain-of-command for implementing military orders originated with him and moved down through the Minister of Defense, to the director of the KPA's General Political Bureau, and finally to the Chief of the General Staff. According to the defector Hwang Chang-yop, Kim Chong-il has streamlined this process so that orders now flow directly from him to the Chief of the General Staff.[14] This reporting is consistent with a downgrading of the Defense Minister's portfolio under Kim Chong-il. For several years, Kim allowed the post to be encumbered by an official too frail to attend to his duties, and at several subsequent junctures he has allowed the position to remain unfilled for short periods of time.

North Korea's Political Culture

The underpinnings of ideology. In defining a policy path, Kim Il-song and his colleagues articulated an ideology of national self-reliance called *chuche* (pronounced 'jew-cheh'). Initially, Kim's preoccupation with independence grew out of past circumstances, for Korea is situated where the ambitions of three historically hegemonistic powers--China, Russia, and Japan—overlap. Of most immediate concern was Japan's colonial occupation which Kim Il-song and his fellow guerilla fighters had challenged.

Exaggerated in importance, Kim's days as a guerilla became the basis for his reinvention as the great liberator and for his political legitimacy.[15] The emphasis placed on Kim Il-song's guerilla days helped, in turn, underwrite a state ideology focused on defending the country's independence. For Kim Il-song, the major lesson learned from the Japanese occupation was that overwhelming military strength and a willingness to employ violent struggle were absolutely vital. North Korea's answer was to make massive investments in the military. Even today, under difficult economic conditions, Kim Chong-il and his ruling circle still calculate that military strength, rather than a vibrant economy, is the most critical need for the regime's and country's survival.[16]

At the same time that he addressed strategic issues, Kim Il-song molded *chuche* to serve two other ends. One was justifying his authoritarian rule, and the other was arguing that the socioeconomic system was superior to all others. In both instances, the leadership used utopian metaphors, describing North Korea as a paradise on earth whose citizens were uniquely blessed.

This utopian vision involved a social contract wherein the state would provide for all of the citizens' needs while the populace would cede to the government the right to make nearly all decisions, large and small, public and personal. The state's provision of housing, food, and daily necessities never produced anything approaching the lifestyles in the rest of Asia, but, through the 1970s and 1980s, most of the populace apparently believed that the leadership had fulfilled its obligations. The Kims, meanwhile, had gained what they sought, a culture of dependency in which the state was seen as the source of all beneficence while the populace was passive, disinclined to assume personal responsibility, and unaccustomed to think independently.[17]

The state of control. As a result of the Orwellian controls imposed by the Kims, North Korea lacks any voluntarily-organized associations, be it in the intellectual, scientific, artistic, recreational, religious, or economic domains. All activities and organizations are controlled by the state, as are all publications. One or two small political parties other than the KWP exist, but they—like several small churches—have been created to provide the illusion of democracy and religious freedom.

The minds and will of senior leaders other than Kim and of the general populace have also been affected by suffocating controls. In this vein, Hwang Chang-yop, the KWP secretary who defected in 1997, has reported that "some party members acknowledge that [North Korea is] in trouble...but they keep worrying without any plan to get out of it."[18] A larger sample of defectors interviewed by two U.S. scholars has indicated much the same. Although none of these defectors had anything positive to say about Kim Chong-il and expressed cynicism about his cult and propaganda, they reported having had "no energy to pursue their thoughts and certainly no opportunity to discuss them." Instead, like many other North Koreans, they had simply "become politically disengaged."[19]

While there remains no opportunity for opposition political activity, there are signs that Kim Chong-il and his ruling colleagues have lost some of the control they long enjoyed. This is most evident in how the population at large and even some officials have responded to the severe famine of the last decade. A sharp deterioration of controls can be seen in the regime's current inability to dictate the physical mobility of its citizens. In a country that had previously achieved a state of near total immobility by denying the population access even to bicycles, many people are now footloose gypsies who wander the countryside searching for food and who illegally crowd trains that will transport them towards the border with China.

At the same time, corruption has soared, especially in regions hardest hit by the famine. In the northeast, for example, officials have aided and abetted the illegal harvesting of trees and the cannibalizing of factories as they struggle to find goods that might be traded for Chinese food supplies. In Ch'ongjin City, this uncontrolled activity is said to have become so severe that in 1995 Kim reportedly removed both the civilian and military leadership, disbanding in the process the VI Corps headquartered in the city.[20]

Whether the senior leadership also lacks full control of its military operations is less easy to determine. Speculation to this effect surfaces periodically, as, for example, when a deadly naval skirmish occurred in June 2002 off the west coast. According to analysis carried in *The New York Times* after this incident, the North Korean provocation at sea may have reflected military dissatisfaction with conciliatory gestures towards both South Korea and the United States.[21]

The State of the Economy

The economic balance sheet. North Korean leaders have consistently given priority to developing military strength at the expense of building a consumer-oriented economy with global ties. For at least four decades, this strategy sufficed because P'yongyang's key supporters in the Communist world—the Soviet Union and China—were willing to prop up the North Korean economy with subsidized trade, concessionary prices on energy resources, and debt write-offs.

However, in the early 1990s, Moscow and Beijing turned their backs on these arrangements. Chronic shortages of petroleum, oil, and lubricants (POL) were one early consequence of this change, leading to serious power shortages. Combined with North Korea's long-term failure to maintain and upgrade its industrial infrastructure, these power problems resulted in a manufacturing sector operating at only a fraction of capacity.[22] In turn, widespread unemployment and underemployment resulted, and North Korea began to experience a run of negative growth statistics.

Reliable statistics are not published by P'yongyang, but the Central Intelligence Agency in 2001 reported an estimated growth rate of minus 3 percent in 2000 and a GDP of roughly $22 billion. Imports were pegged at $960 million and exports at $520 million. In contrast, CIA statistics for South Korea showed a positive growth rate of 9 percent, a GDP of $764.6 billion, imports of $160.5 billion and exports of $172.6 billion. These extraordinary differences in levels of economic activity are all the more striking because South Korea's population is little more than twice the size of the North's.[23]

In the agricultural sector, the situation is even more dire as North Korea has experienced nine consecutive years of crop failure. While the leadership blames these failures on weather disasters—several years of flooding followed by drought—outside experts attribute an overwhelming portion of the blame to the regime's dysfunctional policies.[24] Even the receipt of foreign food aid has failed to avert mass starvation, and studies by international experts set the number of deaths at roughly 2.5 million people, according to Andrew Natsios, currently serving as administrator of the U.S. Agency for International Development. If this estimated figure is correct, the loss equals more than ten percent of the population.[25] Surveys by the World Food Program and UNICEF further indicate that as many as 18 percent of children under the age of nine are suffering severe malnutrition, including body wasting, and that 62 percent are the victims of stunted growth.[26]

To deal with the food crisis, Kim Chong-il and his ruling colleagues have washed their hands of broad responsibility for feeding the nation and allowed most of the national food distribution system, which had been administered via the workplace, to collapse. Initially, local authorities were tasked with feeding their citizens, but in January 1998, Kim demanded that each family henceforth fend for itself. This has required people not previously engaged in agriculture to raise food directly or to barter their labor and non-food products for food supplies. Many citizens have relocated to the countryside to farm, while others have become foragers and several hundred thousand more have fled to China.

Prospects for reform. The senior leadership recognizes the severity of the economic crisis, and it has accepted the fact that changes in the food distribution system have led to a *de facto* privatization of many plots and farmers markets. Kim Chong-il made two recent visits to China (in 2000 and 2001), stopping to see special economic zones (SEZ) and such institutions as the Shanghai stock exchange, and while there—although not at home—praised China's economic achievements. Several sets of legal reforms have also paved the way for foreign investment, and a SEZ is already operating, albeit in the remote region of Najin-Songbong near the Tumen River.[27]

Despite these steps forward, the leadership has not signaled either a willingness to abandon a Stalinist model of development or a willingness to make strategic changes. According to the scholar Nicholas Eberstadt, getting North Korea back on a growth track would require an end to massive investment in the military sector, an end to spending on politically-oriented showpiece projects, the introduction of market-driven dynamics, and true integration into the world economy.[28] Such policy adjustments would involve a sea change in policy, and there are as yet few signs that Kim Chong-il is thinking in such ambitious terms. Instead it appears as if North Korea, for the time being, has opted to pursue one of its favorite types of balancing acts. This involves seeking the greatest payoff while incurring the lowest possible political risk and economic cost.

In the foreign investment domain, one such proposal fits this bill ideally: opening North Korean territory to rail transit rights that would give Russia a land connection to the markets of South Korea. This plan would maximize foreign currency earnings while minimizing the exposure of North Korean citizens to outside influences. In the domestic arena, meanwhile, experiments in localization are being pursued in Chagang Province in the mountainous north. Making a virtue out of necessity, this program calls for some relaxation of central planning in favor of making the province self-reliant in both food production and electricity generation.[29] It is telling that this experiment is being managed not by a local official but rather by a heavyweight dispatched from P'yongyang. This is Yon Hyong-muk, who is the former premier, the mastermind of North Korea's failed, centrally planned economy, and the KWP official also currently in charge of the weapons industry.

The Diplomatic Front

Because P'yongyang's approach to foreign affairs is driven above all by a sense of threat, it had traditionally been reactive and focused on preserving North Korean independence while denying South Korea legitimacy. For many years, this unimaginative strategy was played out in a world split and defined by ideology. The Socialist family of nations could be relied on to deny Seoul diplomatic recognition, to trade on a non-cash basis, and to offer significant aid without North Korea having to exert any great diplomatic skill to obtain it. In the 1980s and 1990s, however, these sureties were undermined by the irresistible draw of South Korea's robust economy, the disintegration of the Soviet bloc, and the unwillingness of Moscow and Beijing to continue subsidizing trade with P'yongyang.

As a result, Kim Chong-il has found it necessary to proactively rebuild ties of critical importance, and he has made Russia the front-burner issue. Russia too is seeking improved relations, for it wishes to avoid losing its voice in a potentially unstable region contiguous to its Far Eastern provinces. In February 2000, Moscow and P'yongyang initialed a revised friendship treaty, this time without security guarantees, and in July 2000, Vladimir Putin became the first Russian or Soviet head-of-state to visit North Korea. In April 2001, the two countries signed a Defense Industry Cooperation Agreement meant to benefit North Korea, and in the area of economic cooperation particular attention is focused on linking rail lines with a connection through to South Korea.[30]

P'yongyang's relations with Beijing, while benefiting from a greater sense of cultural affinity and the Korean War legacy, also took serious hits in the last years of Kim Il-song's rule. The establishment of U.S.-Chinese relations in 1979 brought rapprochement between North Korea's closest ally and worst enemy, and the following year China began trading with South Korea. In 1988, China, like the Soviet Union, participated in the Seoul Olympic games and four years later Beijing and Seoul established diplomatic relations. Still, China, like Russia, is unwilling to completely abandon North Korea. The Sino-Korean friendship treaty of 1961 remains in force, although some Chinese officials have suggested to Western interlocutors that Beijing no longer feels committed to dispatch troops to North Korea in time of war.[31]

The Armed Forces and Their Weapons Systems

Conventional military forces. The result of North Korea's massive investment in its armed forces is the world's most militarized country in terms of the standing army compared to the population size. Roughly 1.1 million personnel are on active duty status, while another several million citizens form a body of reservists operating under four umbrellas.[32]

The *ground forces* have slightly over one million personnel divided among 20 corps. Approximately 70 percent of these forces are in a forward deployment close to the Demilitarized Zone (DMZ), and this accounts for the U.S.-South Korea calculation that warning of war might, at best, come only 24 hours before hostilities begin. Approximately 90,000 of the army's troops are classified as special operations forces. These have been trained to undertake reconnaissance, penetrate South Korea to establish a second front, disrupt U.S. and South Korean facilities and command and control, and otherwise sow chaos and confusion.[33]

Major armaments in the inventory of the ground forces are an estimated 4,000 tanks and assault guns, 2,500 armored personnel carriers, 10,000 artillery pieces, 2,300 multiple rocket launchers, and five battalions of free rockets over ground (FROGs). Some analysts also assign to the ground forces operational control of North Korea's four ballistic missile systems (two deployed and two under development).[34]

Naval forces, believed to number between 46,000 and 60,000 personnel, are split among a command headquarters in P'yongyang, a East Sea Fleet, a West Sea Fleet, two sniper brigades, and two coastal defense missile regiments. Their mission is primarily defensive in nature. The navy has close to 1,000 surface vessels, some constructed indigenously and others acquired years ago from the Soviet Union and China. According to one estimate, 83 percent of the navy's vessels are smaller than 200 tonnes and none are of destroyer size or larger. Midget submarines and small semisubmersibles are used primarily as infiltration craft by the intelligence services.[35]

The *air force* has a personnel base estimated at 100,000 or less and approximately 1700 aircraft. Because the inventory of fighters is heavily skewed towards MiG-15s, 17s, 19s, and 21s, many planes are limited to daylight hour-use and good weather conditions. More advanced capabilities are available with the MiG-23 FLOGGERs, MiG-29 FULCRUMs, and Su-25 FROGFOOTs acquired from the Soviet Union in the 1980s, but these craft total just 98. The sole bomber in the inventory is the Il-28 (H-5), of which North Korea has about 80. Roughly 300 helicopters and 300 transport planes round out the inventory.[36]

Weapons of mass destruction and delivery systems. According to U.S. Government estimates, North Korea has a significant but uneven capability to produce and use WMD.

- In the nuclear area, P'yongyang is believed to have recovered enough plutonium from the spent fuel rods of the Yongbyon reactor to fabricate one or two weapons. As discussed at the conclusion of this chapter, a clandestine and unsafeguarded uranium enrichment program begun in the late 1990s may be providing another source of fissile material. Whether weaponization has occurred is not known.

- In the biological weapons area, P'yongyang has pursued a capability since the 1960s and appears to have the infrastructure needed to produce agents such as anthrax, cholera, and plague. Here too, it is not known whether weaponization has occurred.

- In the chemical weapons area, North Korea is believed to have large stockpiles of warfare agents (of the nerve, blister, choking, and blood types) and is known to have trained its own forces to survive in a chemical warfare environment.[37]

Delivery options available for WMD include ballistic missiles; anti-ship cruise missiles; fighters, bombers, and helicopters; artillery pieces;

rocket launchers and mortars; sprayers; and special operations personnel. The ballistic missile option is of greatest concern. North Korea, according to a recent U.S. Intelligence Community study, is nearly self-sufficient in developing and producing these missiles. In difficult economic times, it has financed this ambitious program via the export of weapons systems, components, and technology to countries in the Middle East and South Asia, and this has made P'yongyang the world's leading proliferator of ballistic missiles.[38]

Already deployed in large numbers in North Korea are three missile systems: the SCUD B and Scud C SRBMs and the Nodong MRBM. Another MRBM, the Taepo-dong 1, was successfully tested in August 1998, with a flight that moved eastward over the Japanese archipelago before plunging into the Pacific Ocean. Work also continues on the Taepo-dong 2, an ICBM.

- The SCUD B and SCUD C, with their ranges of several hundred kilometers each, provide coverage of South Korea and small portions of Northeast China and Siberia.

- The Nodong missile has a range of 1,300 kilometers and can reach all points in South Korea and Japan as well as parts of the Chinese and Russian maritime provinces.

- The Taepo-dong 1, with a range estimated by the Department of Defense at 2,000 kilometers, can reach all of South Korea, Japan, Taiwan, most of China's maritime provinces, and part of Siberia.

- The Taepo-dong 2, the ICBM, has not been flight tested under the terms of a moratorium that the United States negotiated with North Korea. The U.S. Intelligence Community estimates that in a two-stage configuration it could carry a payload of several hundred kilograms up to 10,000 kilometers. In a three-stage configuration, it is believed, it might attain a range of 15,000 kilometers, which would allow it to reach all of North America.[39]

Covert action assets. North Korea has a large cadre of officers trained to collect intelligence, build cells in South Korea, and undertake covert action. Under the control of the KWP are four organs, all supervised by Secretary Kim Yong-sun. These are the Social and Cultural Department, the Investigation Department, the Operations Department, and the Unification Front Department. Under the KPA is the Reconnaissance Bureau, which collects intelligence of relevance to the military and undertakes special operations. These organs have at their disposal a variety of military assets, most notably North Korea's minisubmarines and other craft suitable for seaborne infiltration of South Korea.[40]

The Strategic Paradigm

The post-Korean War paradigm. From the late 1960s until the late 1980s, senior leaders in P'yongyang assumed that they could unilaterally dictate the agenda for reunification, and, conditioned by their guerilla past, they expected to employ violence in doing so. They had factored in the possibility that China and Russia might not support another military adventure southward but still thought a second peninsula war a worthwhile gamble if:

- South Korea were attacked at a vulnerable time.

- Preconditions for unrest in South Korea had been fostered by North Korean covert action programs.

- U.S. military engagement on behalf of South Korea were limited.

- Massive, early damage were inflicted on Seoul.

Defector information, joined with a study of propaganda themes, North Korean behavior, and weapons deployment patterns, indicates that P'yongyang thought that an initial use of artillery followed by a push of armor would quickly level Seoul and force the South Koreans to sue for peace. To a generation of guerilla veterans accustomed to long-term struggles and inured to physical and economic hardships, the South Koreans were viewed as lacking a fighting spirit equal to that of their northern brethren and the Americans, especially after the war in Vietnam, were thought to lack the stomach for another Asian conflict.[41]

Covert action and terrorism. These assumptions regarding the ideal conditions for an attack shaped the blueprint for much of North Korea's behavior towards South Korea in this period. Of particular note was the two-pronged strategy that evolved to create an enabling environment for a quick collapse of the government in Seoul. On the one hand, the North Koreans sought to build cells and emplace sleeper agents in the South, so that chaos, confusion, and a collapse of U.S. and South Korean command and control could be orchestrated at the outset of hostilities. On the other hand, the North Korean leadership looked to the use of terrorist incidents to precipitate instability in the South.[42]

Activities involving covert action, intelligence collection, and penetrations of South Korea have been numerous and are presumed to be occurring regularly, even at the present time. Most involve small numbers of agents and go undetected, or, at a minimum, occur without fanfare. Some others however, have been ambitious and involved substantial bloodshed. The highest-profile operation of this type was an infiltration that, in late 1968, involved 120 commandos who penetrated the Ulchin-Samchok area seeking to initiate guerilla warfare. Twenty South Korean civilians and armed officers died before all the North Koreans were killed or captured. A more recent penetration that gained attention occurred in September 1996, when a small submarine ran aground in South Korea. All 26 crew members either committed suicide or were hunted down by South Korean authorities.[43]

Terrorist attacks against South Korea have numbered three.

- In January 1968, a 31-man commando team infiltrated Seoul in an unsuccessful attempt to kill President Pak Chong-hui at the Blue House.

- In October 1983, North Korean commandos set off a bomb in Rangoon, killing 17 visiting South Korean officials, including four cabinet ministers. Arriving late for the event, President Chun Doo-hwan escaped death.

- In November 1987, operatives planted a bomb on KAL Flight 858, which went down in the Andaman Sea and killed 115.

When the first of these three incidents occurred in 1968, Kim Chong-il was just four years out of college and beginning his work within the KWP. Although it is not known whether he participated in the decision-making and planning that preceded the Blue House raid, it seems safe to assume that he lacked at that juncture the authority to order such a high-risk operation. In fact, scholars such as Dae-Sook Suh identify the aggressiveness of hard-line guerilla veterans as being largely responsible for both the raid and the subsequent shooting down of a U.S. EC-121 reconnaissance plane in April 1969.[44]

By the time that the next two terrorist incidents occurred, Kim Chong-il's influence in policy matters and his day-to-day control of the military and the intelligence apparatus were substantial. At the same time, the guerilla veterans who had promoted the 1968 raid were long gone from the scene, having been purged by Kim Il-song after the EC-121 incident. In interviews, the agent who planted the bomb on the KAL aircraft is said to have identified Kim Chong-il as the initiator of the bombing.[45] It is not clear whether the agent would have had access to such sensitive information. However, what we know generally about the roles played by the two Kims in the 1980s suggests that neither the Rangoon bombing nor the KAL bombing could have occurred without Kim Chong-il's operational oversight and Kim Il-song's final approval.

Since 1987, North Korea has undertaken no terrorist incidents. The leadership has no religious or philosophical motive for creating chaos as an end in itself, and its inclusion on the Department of State's list of state sponsors of terrorism has precluded its accessing critically-needed sources of international financial aid. Most significantly, however, it is likely that, with the introduction of democratic reforms in South Korea, Kim Chong-il and his colleagues have been unable to identify any moment of vulnerability equal to that which they thought existed in 1983. The Rangoon bombing of October 1983 occurred just five months after large numbers of protestors in Kwangju—taking to the streets to protest the imposition of martial law—had been killed by President Chun Doo-hwan's dispatch of special forces troops to the city.

Dealings with the United States. Through the late 1980s, North Korean leaders had two major goals vis-à-vis the United States: weakening the alliance with Seoul and raising doubts in Washington about the desirability of U.S. military engagement on the peninsula. As a corollary to this second goal, North Korea also sought to compress the window of time that U.S. leaders would have in deciding how to respond to the start of hostilities. Here the forward-deployment of ground forces was critical, for it reduced the warning of war timeframe.

As a tactic for pursuing its goals vis-à-vis the United States, the senior leaders in P'yongyang decided that periodic reminders of how dangerous a place Korea is, produced a useful payoff. The most serious of these reminders were the seizure of the *Pueblo* in January 1968, the downing of the EC-121 in April 1969, and the axe murders of several U.S. servicemen at Panmunjom in August 1976. In handling these issues, as well as numerous lesser incidents, the United States dealt with North Korea through the U.N. armistice structure based at Panmunjom. Throughout this period and despite the seriousness of some of these incidents, North Korea failed to intimidate the United States into withdrawing its forces from South Korea and failed to engage Washington in senior-level, political talks outside the armistice venue.[46]

The more recent strategic paradigm. In the post-1987 period, information provided by the defector Hwang Chang-yop has indicated that North Korean leaders have continued to preach the same four articles of faith that informed strategic thinking through much of the 1980s.[47] However, they have added some new elements to the paradigm to reflect opportunities offered by their more threatening WMD capability and have sought accommodations with both the United States, Japan, and South Korea as a means of building a stronger economic base.

Objective conditions have changed dramatically over the past 15 years in North Korea, and Kim Chong-il has had to factor into his strategic planning severe economic problems, an end to the country's conventional military advantage, and an erosion of the military manpower base. In these circumstances, an interest in nuclear, chemical, and biological weapons undoubtedly reflects a judgment that WMD provides the best and only possible means for equalizing the broader balance-of-power when U.S. and South Korean military assets are aggregated. A WMD capability has also allowed North Korea's top leaders to place new emphasis on the concept of deterrence. According to Hwang Chang-yop, senior leaders view even the threat of using WMD against the United States and/or Japan as their ace card in convincing Washington to forgo involvement should another peninsula war begin.[48]

While leveraging threats regarding a WMD capability to his advantage, Kim has also tried to accommodate the United States. He views our country as uniquely well-positioned to help North Korea build a stronger economic base and, despite decades of railing against capitalism and singing the praises of *chuche*, he is not bothered by the ideological irony of this approach. At the same time, Kim appears motivated to lessen what he views as U.S. military pressure on North Korea. In this regard, three recent developments—President George W. Bush's inclusion of North Korea in the "axis of evil," the issuance of a Pentagon study discussing the potential use of nuclear weapons against nations such as North Korea, and the refusal of Washington to continue certifying compliance with negotiated nuclear agreements—may have motivated Kim in mid-2002 to seek a new round of bilateral talks.

Kim's interest in dealing with the United States on well more than the nuclear issue was signaled most clearly in October 2000, when he dispatched Marshal Cho Myong-nok, North Korea's second-ranked official, to Washington. Cho, who met with President Clinton, failed to get North Korea removed from the Department of State's list of state sponsors of terrorism, but U.S. officials were sufficiently encouraged by North Korea's interest in rapprochement that Secretary of State Albright quickly traveled to P'yongyang to talk directly with Kim Chong-il. At that time, Kim indicated North Korea's willingness to forgo further flight testing of the Taepo missiles under development.

Risk Taking and Escalation to Force

The early risk calculus. Scholars and other experts have characterized Kim Il-song's circle of guerillafighters as the most aggressive of North Korean leaders, but even they engaged in risk assessment.[49] The four-point paradigm outlined above reflected their view of what North Korea needed (South Korean instability, predisposing covert action, limited U.S. involvement, and massive, early damage) to tilt the balance in favor of success in another invasion. These assumptions can be tracked through the reporting of senior defectors and inferred from North Korean actions, propaganda, and force deployments.

Less easy to document are a few additional assumptions that likely informed the thinking of senior North Korean leaders. Identifying these working theses is necessary to appreciate how North Korea, confronted with devastation to its homeland in the 1950-1953 war and Washington's continued commitment to Seoul, could nonetheless contemplate initiating new hostilities.   One assumption appears to have been that, safely bunkered themselves, North Korea's senior leaders would not flinch from sacrificing soldiers and civilians in war. Another likely assumption was that, if hostilities could indeed be concluded very rapidly, what remained of South Korea's infrastructure would more than offset North Korea's material and human losses.

Through the mid-1980s, senior North Korean leaders were satisfied with the applicability of this body of assumptions for assessing risk. This was so because they believed their country to be operating from a position of strength.[50] The Socialist community of nations provided moral support, China and the Soviet Union had proven themselves ready to prop up the economy, the North still had a conventional weapons edge, and both South Korea and the United States had been willing to suffer acts of aggression and terrorism without retaliating militarily. At home, meanwhile, Kim Il-song was regarded as something akin to a deity and nothing seriously threatened his grip on power.

The new risk calculus. In the 1990s, the world as North Korea knew it changed dramatically, and this has likely changed how senior leaders now assess risk.   The North Korea that weighs its options today is diplomatically weak and has an economy in freefall, a shrinking population and military manpower base, and deteriorating control of its citizens.

Moreover, North Korea's inventory of conventional weapons systems has aged and what was once superiority in the weapons competition with South Korea has given way to inferiority. Budget figures reinforce the reality of this now irreversible trend. The CIA has estimated that for 1998 North Korea's military expenditures had an equivalent purchasing power of between $3.7 and 4.9 billion and that this consumed between 25 and 33 percent of GDP. South Korea, meanwhile, was able to allocate $12 billion to defense in 2000 by spending little more than 3 percent of GDP.[51]

It was in this broad context of strategic decline that North Korea's negotiations with the United States on both nuclear and missile-related issues unfolded in the 1990s. That segment of the negotiating process which culminated in the nuclear-related Agreed Framework of October 1994 began in April 1993. At that time, Kim Il-song's government precipitated a crisis by announcing its intent to withdraw from the Nuclear Nonproliferation Treaty and to spurn further inspections of safeguarded facilities. To defuse the crisis, Kim Chong-il (his father had died in July 1994) traded away North Korea's ability to unilaterally control and reprocess the spent fuel rods that would henceforth be removed from the Yongbyon reactor.

According to the defector Hwang Chang-yop, this decision displeased some military leaders.[52] However, this was far from the greatest risk that Kim faced, for U.S. officials had considered imposing economic sanctions against North Korea and some private voices in the United States had called for a preemptive strike against Yongbyon.[53]

Balanced against North Korea's concession, Washington promised to provide light water power reactors with a capacity of 2000 Mwe as well as oil until the reactors went on-line. Moreover, North Korea emerged from the negotiations still in control of whatever plutonium had already been reprocessed. The deterrence value of a nuclear capability, or an assumed nuclear capability, was thus preserved. The crisis, moreover, had motivated Washington to negotiate in political channels at a senior level, even absent diplomatic relations, and in the closing days of the Clinton Administration, there was even talk of a presidential visit to P'yongyang.

Further, the presumption that North Korea had a nuclear weapons capability had reminded Russia and China that they could not afford to walk away from a role in ensuring Northeast Asian peace, and it helped prompt international interest in maintaining a stable environment in North Korea via the provision of some limited economic aid.

Escalating to force. Whereas the strategic paradigm that informed North Korean thinking through most of the post-1953 period rested on an assumption that P'yongyang could deal from a position of strength, that type of planning is no longer possible. As a consequence, North Korean leaders today are devoting more energy to simply keeping the country afloat.

Deterring foreign interference and aggression remains the highest priority, and in this regard Kim Chong-il and his ruling circle still value a strategy of convincing other nations that North Korea is dangerous. However, they are now attempting to do this with implicit threats—such as the missile overflight of Japan in August 1998—without employing outright aggression. The result of these changes is a more nuanced method of manipulating risk and an abstention from acts of major aggression against South Korean or U.S. forces in Korea. In particular, while Kim and other senior leaders have worked to develop a deterrence based on fears of WMD programs, they have also sought to leverage these fears to wrest concessions of concrete benefit to North Korea.[54]

These changes notwithstanding, neither Kim Chong-il nor his country as a whole are about to renounce their commitment to one day reunifying the peninsula by force. Too much has been invested in the armed forces in terms of material wealth, ideological dogma, and the very legitimacy of the Kim family to jettison the priority in military investment and the threat of using military force. At the same time, Kim and other senior leaders seem less inclined than in the past to use their military card in launching unprovoked hostilities against the South.

Even if this perception of a less trigger-happy North Korea is correct, the country remains, just as Kim wishes it to be seen, a strategic pressure point of potential danger. Despite the leadership's greater exposure to the outside world and track record of having negotiated with the United States for the past several years, North Korean officials still find it difficult to read foreign intentions. Moreover, they remain hypersensitive about perceived foreign interference in their affairs, and they are still relatively inexperienced in knowing how to pursue national interests by leveraging other than explicit and implicit military threats. Outside North Korea, meanwhile, expanded engagement seems to have only deepened the confusion that foreign observers feel in assessing P'yongyang's intentions and actions.

These risks of miscalculation on both sides appear today to hold the greatest potential for a North Korean escalation to force. This danger was recognized in 1993 and 1994 when U.S. military and diplomatic officials feared that the imposition of economic sanctions against North Korea and a likely need to deploy more U.S. military assets to Korea risked provoking P'yongyang into going to war. Information on North Korea's thinking on possible military responses to real or imagined provocations is not available. However, the leadership appears ready to employ the full range of military assets available to it. Moral issues do not appear to factor into Kim Chong-il's thinking on any matter, and his decisions would undoubtedly reflect a determination to protect both his personal equities and those of his nation.

Risks linked to a succession fight. A nearly equal level of risk may be inherent in any internal power struggle to replace Kim Chong-il. It is tempting to believe that North Korea after Kim would suddenly produce a visionary and daring leader, clone Chinese-style economic reforms, and become a more constructive member of the international community. However, over decades the two Kims have taken pains to ensure that there is little breathing room for a Gorbachev or Deng-like figure to prosper, be it in the capital city or the provinces, the government and the party or the military.

It is also unlikely that, despite having an ideology which vests political authority in Kim Il-song and his blood descendants, that Kim Chong-il will be succeeded by his favorite son. Kim Chong-nam, 31 years of age, was raised and educated in Western Europe and Russia and, according to the South Korean press, currently heads the state Computer Committee. Both his upbringing and current responsibilities suggest that he has not had the opportunity to build a power base in North Korea.[55]

In a country that has neither a history of routinized leadership changes nor a long-established pattern of monarchial succession, it is difficult to predict whether North Korea will manage a stable transition. Kim Chong-il's leadership style has distorted normal institutional dynamics and made it seemingly inevitable that the military will step in and take an important role in the succession. Armed showdowns within the country could easily result and even carry the conflict beyond North Korea's borders.

The 2002 Nuclear Crisis

In October 2002, it was revealed that North Korea had for several years been operating a revamped nuclear weapons development program in violation of an international agreement, the so-called 1994 Agreed Framework, which bars such work. This revelation trained a klieg light on the opportunistic quality of Kim Chong-il's decision-making, the high priority that he assigns WMD, and the manner in which he often handles foreign crises.

According to information released by the White House, Foreign Ministry officials—while meeting with the visiting U.S. Assistant Secretary of State for East Asian Affairs in early October—were confronted with evidence of a clandestine nuclear weapons program and thereafter confirmed the program's existence. This program, according to unnamed U.S. officials cited in the *New York Times*, is designed to enrich natural uranium with gas centrifuges reportedly acquired from Pakistan. In the immediate aftermath of the revelations, North Korea did not claim to possess nuclear weapons, but it declared the right to do so in light of what it describes as the threatening posture of the United States.

As of late 2002, no foreign nation or group of nations was debating a military response to the breach of the 1994 Agreed Framework. Steps already taken in the economic domain, however, promise severe setbacks for North Korea's quality of life and the opportunity costs of other losses may eventually be even more dramatic.

- In mid-November, the U.S. Government announced that it would halt further financing of the monthly fuel shipments being sent to North Korea under the terms of the Agreed Framework. The agreement had called for the yearly delivery of 500,000 metric tons of fuel oil.

- Also in jeopardy is further progress on the supply of two light water reactors financed and constructed by a U.S., Japanese, South Korean, and European Union consortium per the terms of the 1994 Agreed Framework. Work on the reactor site in North Korea had begun in mid-2002.

- Food aid from other than U.N. agencies and non-governmental organizations is in jeopardy. The CIA recently estimated the value of food aid received from the same group of nations building the reactors at $300 million annually.[56]

- Further progress on diplomatic rapprochement with Japan is in question. In September 2002, Kim Chong-il and Japanese Prime Minister Junichiro Koizumi had signed an agreement to move toward the establishment of diplomatic relations. Had this process been concluded successfully, North Korea stood to receive aid from Japan totaling several billion dollars.

- Also at risk is a general warming of relations with Seoul that had gained significant momentum in the months prior to October 2002.

First-hand accounts of how Kim Chong-il decided to reinitiate a clandestine nuclear weapons program are not available, but it is clear that he is powerful enough to have given the program a green light even if individual or institutional objections had been raised. In fact, Kim would have been the sole arbiter of who was allowed a seat at relevant planning and decision-making discussions. In this regard, it is possible that foreign affairs and civilian trade officials were denied even knowledge of the program. On the other hand, key planning officials would have been those in Kim's inner circle who are most experienced in managing special channels for weapons sales and weapons technology procurements.

Whether Kim Chong-il sponsored a cost-benefit analysis of the decision to clandestinely produce weapons-grade uranium is also not known. What is apparent, however, is that his decision would have been strongly colored by abiding fears of the countries he considers enemies, particularly the United States, and by the stock he places in the deterrence value of WMD. In his arrogance, which has been reinforced by work in the fields of propaganda and theatrical illusion, Kim may also have calculated that he could once again, with time, manipulate much of his foreign audience into viewing him as a pragmatic reformer. The fact that he violated the 1994 Agreed Framework, meanwhile, is consistent with an unprincipled approach to nearly everything that crosses his radar screen: Kim's commitments last only as long as he perceives that programs, promises, and other people serve his utilitarian interests.

There seems little reason to doubt that Kim Chong-il would have preferred that the clandestine centrifuge program continue undetected and that progress achieved in dealings with Japan and South Korea remain on track. However, Kim's past behavior as well as recent North Korean statements suggest that Kim sees in the nuclear crisis some compensatory opportunities. The very fact that no nation wants to deal with North Korea on military terms is in itself a measure of P'yongyang's success in building a weapons inventory—both conventional and unconventional—that can deter aggression in other than extreme circumstances. Moreover, as occurred in the months leading up to the 1994 Agreed Framework, the world has been reminded that North Korea remains a dangerous nation, and this, Kim may believe, will serve him in his quest to continue negotiating economic aid and to realize high-level talks with the United States. Regarding Washington, Kim seeks above all a U.S. commitment to forswear aggression against North Korea.

Notes

1. Some scholars report that Kim Chong-il attended flight school in East Germany while in his late teens, but there is no corroborating evidence for this claim. Dae-Sook Suh, *Kim Il-sung: The North Korean Leader* (New York: Columbia University Press, 1988), 283-285.

2. Biographical information on Kim Chong-il and other leaders is available from the *Nkchosun.com*, an English-language internet site maintained by the *Chosun Ilbo* newspaper published in Seoul.

3. Han S. Park, *North Korea: The Politics of Unconventional Wisdom* (Boulder Colorado: Lynne Rienner Publisher, 2002), 149.

4. Adrian Buzo, *The Guerilla Dynasty: Politics and Leadership in North Korea* (Boulder, Colorado: Westview Press, 1999), 115-116.

5. A valuable body of defector reporting is available on the internet site of the National Intelligence Service, Seoul's counterpart to the U.S. CIA. See in particular the series titled *Testimonies of North Korean Defectors*.

6. Buzo, 88.

7. See Helen-Louise Hunter, *Kim Il-song's North Korea* (Westport, Connecticut: Praeger, 1999), for details on the privileged lives of the ruling elite.

8. Andrew S. Natsios, *The Great North Korean Famine: Famine, Politics, and Foreign Policy* (Washington D.C.: United States Institute of Peace Press, 2001), 106-107.

9. Ibid., 73-74.

10. "Defectors from North Korea Tell of Prison Baby Killings," *The New York Times*, 10 June 2002.

11. The Israeli newspaper *Ma'ariv* reported in April 1995 that Kim Il-song had earlier designated Kim Kyong-hui and Chang to negotiate with Tel Aviv on the subject of P'yongyang's missile exports.

12. "N. Korea's Air Force Chief Visits Iran for Closer Ties," *Washington Times*, 25 February 1994.

13. Don Oberdorfer, *The Two Koreas: A Contemporary History* (Basic Books, 2001), 438.

14. *Testimonies of North Korean Defectors: Hwang Chang-yop Speaks on Preparations for War in North Korea*, on the internet site of the National Intelligence Service.

15. See Park, for a historical examination of *chuche*.

16. Park, 24.

17. A culture of dependency is encountered frequently in political systems shaped by terrorists.   Robert S. Robins and Jerrold M. Post, *Political Paranoia: The Psychopolitics of Hatred* (New Haven: Yale University Press, 1997), 83-87.

18. *Testimonies of North Korean Defectors: Hwang Chang-yop Speaks on Politics in North Korea*, on the internet site of the National Intelligence Service.

19. Kongdan Oh and Ralph C. Hassig, *North Korea: Through the Looking Glass* (Washington D.C.: Brookings Institution Press, 2000), 35-37.

20. Joseph S. Bermudez Jr., *The Armed Forces of North Korea* (London and New York: I. B. Tauris Publishers, 2001), 59.

21. "North and South Korea Trade Charges Over Naval Clash," *The New York Times*, 30 June 2002.

22. *CIA Factbook*, Washington D.C.: Central Intelligence Agency, 2001.

23. Ibid.

24. Natsios, 109.

25. Natsios, 202-206.

26. Natsios, 105.

27. Marcus Noland, "North Korea's External Economic Relations," *Washington D.C.: Institute for International Economic Relations*, 2001, 6-7.

28. Nicholas Eberstadt, *The End of North Korea* (Washington D.C.: AEI Press, 1999), 120.

29. Park, 152.

30. Oh and Hassig, 154-155. Central Intelligence Agency, *Unclassified Report to Congress on the Acquisition of Technology Relating to Weapons of Mass Destruction and*

Advanced Conventional Munitions, 1 January Through 30 June 2001, Washington D.C.: January 2002.

31. Oh and Hassig, 156.

32. Bermudez, 1-8. The International Institute for Strategic Studies (IISS), *The Military Balance: 2001-2002*, London: Oxford University Press, 2001, 196-197.

33. Bermudez, 3-5.

34. Bermudez, 3-5. IISS, 196-197.

35. Bermudez, 5-6, 106-111. IISS, 196-197.

36. Bermudez, 147-149. IISS, 196-197.

37. CIA, *Unclassified Report to Congress on the Acquisition of Technology Relating to Weapons of Mass Destruction and Advanced Conventional Munitions: 1 January Through 30 June 2001*, January 2002, CIA/DCI;   Department of Defense, *Proliferation: Threat and Response*, January 2001, 9-13.

38. Department of Defense, *Proliferation: Threat and Response*, January 2001, 9-13; CIA, *Foreign Missile Developments and the Ballistic Missile Threat Through 2015* (unclassified summary of a National Intelligence Estimate), CIA/DCI.

39. CIA, *Unclassified Report to Congress on the Acquisition of Technology Relating to Weapons of Mass Destruction and Advanced Conventional Munitions: 1 January Through 30 June 2001*, January 2002, CIA/DCI;   Department of Defense, *Proliferation: Threat and Response*, January 2001, 9-13; CIA, *Foreign Missile Developments and the Ballistic Missile Threat Through 2015* (unclassified summary of a National Intelligence Estimate), CIA/DCI.

40. Bermudez, 177-195.

41. *Testimonies of North Korean Defectors: Hwang Chang-yop Speaks on Preparations for War in North Korea*, on the website of the National Intelligence Service. Buzo, 201-202

42. Apart from its desire to destabilize South Korea, North Korea has had other reasons to be associated with terrorism. In the past, training terrorists from other countries meshed with Kim Il-song's efforts to promote the stature of North Korea among Third World revolutionaries. Although North Korea continues to harbor the Japanese Red Army members who hijacked a plane in 1970, it has in recent years eschewed promoting terrorist capabilities overseas. Even so, its involvement with smuggling,

counterfeiting, and opium sales has resulted in contacts with terrorist groups. *Global Patterns of Terrorism*, 2001, Washington D.C.: Department of State, May 2002

43. Bermudez, 195.

44. Suh, 231-232, 238-239.

45. Kim Hyon-hui debarked from the KAL flight in Abu Dhabi after placing the bomb in an overhead luggage rack. Following the explosion, she was picked up elsewhere in the Middle East and transferred to Seoul, where she was interrogated and still lives. According to the journalist Don Oberdorfer, Kim Hyon-hui was told before departing P'yongyang that Kim Chong-il had ordered the KAL bombing to discourage participation in the 1988 Seoul Olympics. Oberdorfer, 183.

46. Oh and Hassig, 166.

47. *Testimonies of North Korean Defectors: Hwang Chang-yop Speaks on Preparations for War in North Korea*, on the website of the National Intelligence Service

48. *Testimonies of North Korean Defectors: Hwang Chang-yop Speaks on Preparations for War in North Korea*, on the internet site of the National Intelligence Service.

49. See, for example, Suh, 321-234.

50. Scott Snyder, *Negotiating on the Edge: North Korean Negotiating Behavior* (Washington D.C.: United States Institute of Peace Press, 1999), 13.

51. *CIA Factbook*, Washington D.C.: Central Intelligence Agency, 2001.

52. *Testimonies of North Korean Defectors: Hwang Chang-yop Speaks* on the internet site of the National Intelligence Service.

53. Leon V. Sigal, *Disarming Strangers: Nuclear Diplomacy with North Korea* (Princeton: Princeton University Press, 1998), 75-81

54. Snyder, 13-14

55. Kim Chong-nam gained international notoriety in 2001, when, accompanied by a toddler, he attempted to enter Japan on a falsified Dominican passport. Before being deported to China, he reportedly told the Japanese authorities that he had wished to visit Tokyo Disneyland and that he had illegally entered Japan on numerous occasions in the past.

56. *CIA Factbook*, Washington D.C.: Central Intelligence Agency, 2002.

CHAPTER 6

The Crucible of Radical Islam:
Iran's Leaders and Strategic Culture

Gregory F. Giles[1]

Introduction

U.S.-Iran relations have been strained ever since the Islamic Revolution. Those relations have witnessed open but limited conflict, as in the hostage crisis in 1979 and the naval clashes in the Persian Gulf in the late-1980s. The 1990s were largely characterized by Washington's efforts, through sanctions and other measures, to contain Iran (and neighboring Iraq). The election of reformist president Mohammad Khatami in 1997 raised hopes of a possible relaxation of U.S.-Iran tensions. Those hopes appear dashed for now with President Bush's recent declarations that Iran is part of an "axis of evil" and incapable of reform.

Against this backdrop of enduring and growing tensions, this analysis provides an assessment of Iran's current leadership. First, it is important to begin with a description of Iran's power structure and the underlying strategic culture. Second, this analysis profiles Iran's Supreme Leader, Ayatollah Khamene'i, and the national security policymaking structure over which he presides. Finally, we will look at Khamene'i's strongly held views on the United States and their impact on future U.S.-Iranian relations.

The Structure of Power in Contemporary Iran

Iran's system of governance is complex and does not readily lend itself to simple description. This complexity stems from multiple and competing centers of power located in both the formal and informal structure of governance. Shi'a doctrine infuses both of these power structures, further complicating understanding by non-Muslim observers.[2]

The central premise of Iran's post-revolutionary power structure lies in the concept of *velayat-e faqih*. This concept combines religious and state political authority in the person of the leading Shi'i jurisprudent, originally Grand Ayatollah Ruhollah Khomeini. The concept of *velayat-e faqih* was enshrined in Article 110 of the 1979 constitution and thus forms the legal basis of rule in contemporary Iran.

In essence, the *faqih* is the supreme leader of the nation, appointed for life. As originally conceived, the *faqih* is the absolute authority on all matters of religion and state. He has the power to mobilize the armed forces and declare war and peace. He also has the power over key appointments in the formal government structure, such as the head of the regular military (the *Artesh*), the Islamic Revolutionary Guard Corps (IRGC or *Pasdaran*), and the law enforcement forces. Upon his death in 1989, Khomeini was succeeded as *faqih* by Ayatollah al-Udhma Sayyid Khamene'i. While the transfer of power went relatively smoothly, it was not without controversy, which endures to this day.

Under the supreme leader, multiple and competing centers of power include the president, currently Mohammad Khatami; parliament (*Majlis*); and the judiciary. This separation of powers is in some cases analogous to western models. For example, the president and his ministers can be removed by a two-thirds majority vote of no-confidence by the Parliament. In other cases, the Iranian system breaks with that model. In particular, while the judiciary presides over civil, criminal, and clerical courts, it does not have constitutional review powers. Those powers are found elsewhere in the Iranian system, namely, the Council of Guardians.

The Council of Guardians reviews legislation passed by the parliament and rescinds those measures deemed "un-Islamic." The Council is comprised of 6 clerics appointed by the Supreme Leader and 6 lay jurists appointed by the Parliament on the advice of the head of the judiciary, who, it turns out, is appointed by the Supreme Leader. The Council of Guardians is empowered to interpret the constitution and a ruling by three-fourths of its members has the same weight as the constitution itself. Notably, the Council also decides if parliamentary and presidential aspirants are sufficiently Islamic and loyal to the regime to stand for election. This prerogative effectively limits the exercise of democracy in contemporary Iran.

Inherent in the relationship between the *Majlis* and the Council of Guardians is the potential for legislative gridlock. To counter this, yet another constitutional assembly was created as final arbiter, the Expediency Council. In addition to its power to resolve disputes between the Parliament and the Council of Guardians, the Expediency Council also has the authority to pass its own "emergency" laws. Such laws passed by the Expediency Council cannot be repealed by the *Majlis* or Council of Guardians.

The Expediency Council also provides something of a check on the Supreme Leader, forcing him to consult with the Council in the (rare) event that the Leader cannot resolve a state problem through normal means. Permanent members of the Expediency Council include the heads of the three branches of government and clerical members of the Council of Guardians. Other members are appointed to five-year terms by the Supreme Leader. The current Chairman of the Expediency Council is the former president and former speaker of the Parliament, Ali Akbar Hashemi-Rafsanjani. The secretary of the Expediency Council is former commander of the *Pasdaran*, Mohsen Reza'i.

The final constitutional body is the Assembly of Experts. The Assembly consists of 86 clerics who, after being vetted by the Council of Guardians, are popularly elected to 8-year terms. The purpose of the Assembly is to elect the Supreme Leader from within their own ranks. The Assembly can also remove the Leader if he his unable to carry out his duties or if he is determined to have lost one or more of the qualifications to hold the position. Most members of the Assembly also hold positions in other government or revolutionary institutions.

By design, Iran's formal government structure is decentralized and power is relatively dispersed. This stands in marked contrast to neighboring regimes. This multitude of government power centers, a number of them unique to Iran, has been created to keep political-ideological factions in a constant state of maneuver and negotiation and thus less likely to mount a coup threat.

Permeating this formal government structure is Iran's informal power structure, described as the "four rings of power."[3] In the center ring is the core group of politically powerful Shi'a clerics, referred to as the

143

"patriarchs." The patriarchs are led by Ayatollah Khamene'i. Religious hierarchy does not necessarily equate to level of influence among the patriarchs, however.

For example, a *hojjatoleslam* (proof of Islam) or mid-level cleric is subordinate to an *ayatollah* (sign of God). Yet, President Khatami, a *hojjatoleslam* is considered to have more influence in Iran than *Ayatollah* 'Ali Meshkini, the head of the Assembly of Experts. Similarly, *Hojjatoleslam* 'Ali Akbar Hashemi Rafsanjani, chairman of the Expediency Council, is considered more influential than President Khatami. Government office likewise is not a fully reliable measure of standing within the patriarchy, as *Hojjatoleslam* 'Abbas Va'ez-Tabasi, head of the Imam-Reza Foundation, is judged more influential than 'Ali Meshkini.

By all accounts, the patriarchs of all ranks represent a minority of Shi'a clerics both inside and outside of Iran. For example, there are approximately 28,000 *hojjatoleslam* in Iran, yet only about 2,000 are regime clerics. Similarly, while there are approximately 5,000 *ayatollahs*, only 80 are regime clerics. The rest are apolitical. At the more senior rank of grand ayatollah, which number about 20 worldwide, 14 reside in Iran. Of those, all but one, Hosein 'Ali Montazeri, are opponents of the *velayat-e-faqih* concept, the very foundation of the Islamic Republic.

The second ring of power is populated by the highest ranking governmental functionaries. These individuals are found in all branches of the government at the national and provincial level. The third ring comprises the regime's power base. It is made up of individuals who control revolutionary institutions, such as the para-statal foundations, the media, and security forces, like the IRGC. This ring is responsible for propagating the clerical regime's ideology and countering threats against it. The final ring is inhabited by formerly influential individuals and groups. These elements constitute a semi-opposition in that their goal is peaceful reform of the current regime from the inside.

The informal power structure in contemporary Iran is sustained by various shared experiences and family connections. The top leadership is bound not just by their status as Shi'a clergy, but also their direct personal connections with Ayatollah Khomeini and common struggle against the Shah. Educational experiences among the leadership provide additional linkages. For example, the current supreme leader also was a student of Ayatollah Khatami, the late father of the current president. Indeed, the

Khatami and Khamene'i families have been close friends over the years.[4] Inter-marriage further solidifies this elite. For example, President Khatami's sister-in-law, Zahra Eshrai, is the granddaughter of Ayatollah Khomeini.[5]

Such connections permeate Iran's national security structure, as well. For example, many of the top personnel in the Intelligence Ministry come from a leading theological school in Qom, the *Madrasse-ye Haqqani.*[6] Similarly, intermarriage among religious families is an important linkage among IRGC commanders. Thus, typical family functions become an informal opportunity for the IRGC leadership to share views with the religious/political elite.[7]

Commonalities among the top leadership cascade down through the power structure in the form of personal patronage networks. Individuals in power instinctively turn to immediate relatives to fill subordinate posts within an organization. In turn, these immediate relatives draw in relatives and friends of their own. While such patronage is by no means unique to Iran, it has been noted that its practice in the Islamic Republic undermines institutions and often puts the functioning of the government structure at its mercy.[8]

All of this is not to suggest the absence of disagreement within Iran's elite. Indeed, there are crucial differences over such issues as the economy, personal freedoms, and relations with the west. Nonetheless, the shared experiences and common background of the clerical leadership help set the boundaries for debate and compromise.

Iran's Strategic Culture

The Islamic Republic did not necessarily begin with a clean slate in 1979. Various historical and cultural influences continue to shape Iranian perceptions and actions, irrespective of the relative novelty of the current clerical regime. Indeed, the emergence of an Iranian theocracy has actually facilitated the inculcation of certain traditional Shi'a traits into the contemporary Iranian state. The culmination of these historical, cultural, religious, and geographic influences is considered to constitute Iran's "strategic personality" or "culture."[9] They provide yet another dimension to understanding Iranian behavior.

Modern day Iran sits atop a history of Persia that can be traced back nearly 3,000 years. An immense sense of identity and pride stems from this cultural continuity. A less flattering manifestation is Iran's sense of superiority over its neighbors. Against this backdrop, then-president Hashemi Rafsanjani revealed in 1995 a rather strident Iranian attitude toward its Gulf neighbors: "Half of the coast line belongs to Iran, so Iran alone has the same amount of rights and responsibility as all those [other littoral] countries put together . . ."[10] In more recent years, Iran has taken a more diplomatic tone towards its neighbors to the south, hoping to woo them out of defense relationships with the United States rather than intimidate them. Yet, few could doubt that Iran seeks to live up to its proud history by re-establishing its regional dominance.

Paradoxical to this sense of cultural superiority and manifest destiny is Iran's deep sense of insecurity. That insecurity stems from a series of conquests suffered by Persia over the centuries, which have left Iranians highly suspicious of foreigners. Indeed, these periods of foreign domination appear to have fundamentally shaped Iranian inter-personal and, by extrapolation, international behavior. Living under foreign rule imbued Persian life with a sense of uncertainty. Personal fortunes could rise or fall suddenly depending on how skillfully one anticipated the foreign master's whims. Tools such as artifice, flattery, dissembling, and treachery became standard for survival. Carried to the international arena, the need to outmaneuver greater powers induces Iranian diplomats to attempt to be more resourceful than their western counterparts.

Similarly, to cope with the uncertainty of life under foreign domination, belief in conspiracies was fostered as a way of explaining erstwhile random events. Indeed, the greater the power, the more clever it is assumed to be in secretly manipulating events. Iran's belief that the 1988 shoot-down of the Iranian Airbus by the *U.S.S. Vincennes* was not an accident but rather a deliberate act by Washington designed to coerce Tehran into accepting a ceasefire with Iraq is a modern manifestation of this proclivity for conspiracy theories. It is this mistaken belief in the omnipotence of the United States and its obsession with Iran that poses perhaps the greatest risk of inadvertent conflict between the two.

Specific attributes of Shi'ism, which was adopted by Persia in the sixteenth century, both reinforce and expand certain traits in Iranian strategic culture. For example, to protect the sect from mainstream Sunni

Islam and other early enemies, Shi'ism encouraged its practitioners to conceal their faith if their lives were at stake. This practice of *taqiyeh* adds a religious and moral justification for dissembling. That it can be practiced collectively by a group of clerics inevitably leads to doubts about the professed intentions of Iran's current leadership.[11]

Shi'ism also introduces concepts and drives Iranian behavior in ways that are not readily grasped by the west. In particular, the Shi'a attitudes toward war are less goal-oriented than western concepts. As evidenced by Khomeini's conduct of the 8-year war with Iraq, struggle and adversity are to be endured as a sign of commitment to the true faith.

Defeat is not necessarily equated with failure. This emphasis on continuing the struggle against oppression and injustice rather than on achieving "victory" is seen as producing a high tolerance of pain in Iran. The cult of martyrdom inherent in Shi'ism, specifically, the honor accorded those who give their life to defend the faith, may give Iran certain practical military advantages. How committed Iran remains to these concepts of warfare, now that the initial fervor of the revolution has long since passed and the Iranian economy has become more brittle, remains to be seen.

Profile of Ayatollah Khamene'i

At the apex of Iranian power stands Ayatollah al-Udhma Sayyid Khamene'i. He is very much a product of the Islamic Revolution, having held virtually every major government and revolutionary post. While a direct descendent of the Prophet Muhammad, his relatively limited religious credentials place tangible limits on his influence. Perhaps because of these limitations, his main motivation appears to be upholding the legacy of Ayatollah Khomeini rather than making his own mark on Iranian society.

Khamene'i was born on July 15, 1939 in the holy city of Mashhad in northeastern Iran. He was born into a religious family, his father being a *hojjatoleslam* and his grandfather, a prominent cleric who later migrated to the holy city of Najaf in Iraq. Biographies of Khamene'i typically stress that he grew up in poverty. His formal religious education began at age five, with classes on the Koran. In 1958, Khamene'i moved to Qom where

147

he studied under Ayatollahs Sheikh Hashim Qazwini, Ha'iri, al-Udhma Burujerdi, and Khomeini. In 1964, Khamene'i returned to Mashhad to care for his father.[12]

Khamene'i's political activism was first stirred by Nawwab Safawi in the early 1950s. Safawi advocated reviving Islam and establishing an Islamic government in Iran. Inspired by Safawi, who was later "martyred" by the Shah, Khamene'i participated in the Islamic movement of 1955-56, protesting, for example, against the mayor of Mashhad for failing to close the city's cinemas during the holy months of Muharram and Safar.

Khamene'i's activism in Mashhad caught the attention of Ayatollah Khomeini, who used him to organize the Islamic resistance in the Khurasan province. Between the early 1960s and the 1979 revolution, Khamene'i was arrested by SAVAK, the Shah's secret police, a half-dozen times. Khamene'i is credited with helping to found the *Ulama Mujahidin*, a precursor to Khomeini's Islamic Republican Party. Following Ayatollah Khomeini's exile to Iraq and then Europe, Khamene'i went underground in Iran, where he continued to agitate for an Islamic state. During this time, he spent nearly a year in a safe house with 'Ali Akbar Hashemi Rafsanjani, who also rose to prominence in the Islamic Republic.[13]

Khamene'i's key role in supporting the revolution from Mashhad was rewarded by his appointment to the Ayatollah's Revolution Command Council, which was charged with setting up Iran's forthcoming Islamic government. Khamene'i also helped set up the Ayatollah's reception committee to arrange his triumphant return to Iran, and was appointed head of the information bureau in Khomeini's Office of the Imam. Khamene'i held a quick succession of revolutionary, religious, and government posts, including the following:

- Commander of the IRGC

- Special Envoy to the Sistan and Baluchistan provinces

- Revolution Command Council representative to the National Defense Council

- Deputy Minister of Defense

- Imam's representative to the National Defense Council

- Friday Prayer Imam in Tehran

Khamene'i was also elected to the first Islamic *Majlis* in 1980, representing a Tehran constituency, and was a key figure in the Islamic Republican Party, serving as its Secretary General until it was disbanded.

Khamene'i fell victim to the violence that accompanied the revolution. On June 27, 1981, he was wounded in an assassination attempt. The next day, a bomb blast in Tehran killed the leading members of the Islamic Republican Party. Another bomb in August killed the newly elected President 'Ali Raja'i and Prime Minister Javad Bahonar. This prompted a new presidential election in October, which Khamene'i won.

Khamene'i was re-elected and served as president until Ayatollah Khomeini's death in June 1989. Under the 1979 Constitution, an extraordinary meeting of the Assembly of Experts was convened to select Khomeini's successor. Khamene'i was not generally considered to be in the running to succeed Khomeini.

The path for Khamene'i was cleared by two events, the first being the falling out between Khomeini and his officially chosen successor, Grand Ayatollah 'Ali Montazeri. The second was a decision by Khomeini and the clerical leadership to lower the religious requirements to hold the post of *faqih*.

In essence, an amendment to the Constitution in 1989 dropped the requirement for the *faqih* to be a grand ayatollah and *marja'-e taqlid,* or source of emulation for Shi'i. It was Khomeini's standing as a *marja* that gave authority to his religious pronouncements and edicts, or *fatwas.* Upon Khomeini's death, Khamene'i, then only a *hojjatoleslam*, was promoted to ayatollah, and after meeting for 20 hours, the Assembly of Experts elected Khamene'i *faqih*, reportedly by a vote of 60 out of the 74 members present.[14]

While lowering the qualifications to become *velayat-e faqih* helped ensure a smooth transition of power following Khomeini's death, it greatly compromised the legitimacy of his successor. It also offered no quick remedies. For Khamene'i to become a true *marja*, he would have to complete another three decades of religious study and write a major thesis that is recognized by other grand ayatollahs. An attempt by Khamene'i in 1994 to gain the title of grand ayatollah following the death of Grand Ayatollah Mohammad 'Ali Araki failed in the face of opposition from numerous leading Shi'i clerics from within and outside Iran.[15]

The limitations imposed on Khamene'i by his weak religious credentials are significant. While he cannot claim to be a source of emulation to Shi'as in Iran, he has staunchly claimed such a role for Shi'as outside of Iran.[16] Yet, in a key test of this claim, Hezballah's leaders have not adopted Khamene'i as their source of emulation.[17] This rejection of Khamene'i dilutes Iran's moral and religious influence over Hezballah, although other connections certainly exist. More importantly, Khamene'i is left open to attack by his religious and political foes within Iran.

A major challenge to Khamene'i's legitimacy was mounted in 1997 by Ayatollah Montazeri, Khomeini's would-be successor. In a sermon to his followers in Qom, Montazeri challenged the intervention of the *faqih* in all aspects of Iranian life, contending that the position was one of mere supervision to ensure conformity with Islamic rules and justice. Montazeri claimed that Khamene'i was unsuited to be *faqih* due to his insufficient religious credentials and therefore lacked the authority to issue a *fatwa.* Montazeri's challenge coincided with similar criticism from another prominent Ayatollah, Ahmad Azari-Qomi.

Conservative allies of Khamene'i rushed to his defense and Khamene'i himself censured Montazeri and Azari-Qomi indirectly, warning that foreign enemies were using "domestic agents" to target the leadership and should be tried for treason. Azari-Qomi was stripped of his membership in the Association of Seminary Theologians of Qom and reportedly put under house arrest until his death in 1999. Conservatives tried to embarrass Montazeri by publishing a 1989 letter from Ayatollah Khomeini to him, which laid out the reasons why Montazeri was not qualified to succeed him. He was also placed under house arrest.[18]

Opposition to the legitimacy of Khamene'i did not subside in 1997. Rather, the cause was joined by lay intellectuals and students and has become wrapped up in the broader political debate over individual freedom.[19] By March 2002, the issue was being debated in the Assembly of Experts itself. Thus, for the foreseeable future, Khamene'i will have to labor with this religious Achilles Heel.

Against this backdrop, the carefully managed image that the Office of the Imam portrays of Khamene'i is of a devoted Islamic scholar, constantly reading books on Islamic jurisprudence and meeting with prominent clergymen. He is also portrayed as a pious, frugal man. Interviews granted by those closest to him, including his wife, emphasize time and again the austere nature of his lifestyle.[20] These portrayals appear largely defensive. It has been suggested, for example, that by outdoing Khomeini's public austerity, Khamene'i is attempting to compensate for other inevitable shortcomings compared to his predecessor.[21] More practically, Khamene'i is also trying to guard against charges that he is raiding the public treasury to feather his nest, a ploy used against him in 1985 when he served as president.[22]

Khamene'i is depicted as being in excellent health despite his advancing age. In 1999, he was reported to go mountain climbing on a weekly basis. He is also described as a literary figure and poet. Although the specifics are lacking, Khamene'i apparently has good access to information. His office provides him with a press summary that he supplements with morning and afternoon newspapers. He also is reported to read weekly, monthly, and quarterly journals. He is particularly interested in reading editorials. In the evening, Khamene'i is said to watch television news.[23]

Khamene'i's typical work day begins at 8 a.m., following morning prayers. His morning revolves around official visits from civilian and military authorities. These meetings continue until the noon prayers, which he performs in the office. Lunch and rest follow, and he resumes his work at 4 p.m. Afternoon meetings last until maghreb prayers. In the evening, Khamene'i makes regular unannounced visits to the families of martyrs, those who gave their lives on behalf of the regime.[24]

In some sense, Khamene'i is an "accidental ayatollah." His background provides no indications that he aspired to become Supreme Leader. While he was active in the Khomeini movement, his appointments in various revolutionary bodies, such as the Revolutionary Command Council, appear to be of secondary importance. The assassination, death, or exile of more prominent religious and revolutionary figures appears to have cleared the way for Khamene'i's ascension into the highest levels of Iranian power, first as president and then as *faqih*.

Whatever his aspirations, Khamene'i appears to appreciate the immense burden placed on him as supreme leader. In essence, it is Khamene'i's duty for the remainder of his life to uphold the legacy of Ayatollah Khomeini and preserve the Islamic regime. This burden has forced a modification of Khamene'i's political orientation. Initially, Khamene'i was associated with the moderate wing of the revolutionary establishment.[25] Throughout the 1980s, his positions closely mirrored those of the pragmatic Hashemi Rafsanjani.[26] However, once elevated to the position of *faqih*, Khamene'i gravitated towards the conservative camp. This shift stems from the inherent weakness of Khamene'i's position. What Khamene'i lacks in religious qualifications to hold the position of supreme leader, he must make up for in hard-line positions that suit the most fervent supporters of the *veleyat-e faqih* concept, the conservatives.

Over time, Khamene'i has demonstrated more flexibility. In 1992, his public pronouncements facilitated the sacking of then-culture minister Mohammad Khatami for failing to be sufficiently vigilant against the western cultural onslaught. Yet, in response to the mounting crisis between conservatives and reformers in 1998 over the fate of the reformist mayor of Tehran, Gholam Hossein Karbaschi, Khamene'i sided with then-president Khatami. Khamene'i sided with Khatami again the following year, when mass demonstrations posed a serious threat to the regime. Specifically, Khamene'i compelled his own protégé and commander of the *Pasdaran*, General Yahya Safavi, to rescind IRGC threats of a coup d'état if Khatami did not abandon his reform program.[27]

What had changed in Khamene'i's attitude between 1992 and 1998-1999 was that Khatami had come to represent the vast majority of Iranians who were disenchanted with the failed policies of the conservatives and demanded real change. Khamene'i thus has demonstrated that he is willing to placate this increasingly powerful constituency at the expense of his conservative backers in order to hold the Islamic regime together. Some have speculated that the rise of Khatami's populist front as a major force in contemporary Iranian politics may actually enable Khamene'i to reduce his traditional reliance on the conservative camp.[28] Others have questioned whether conservative leaders such as Ayatollahs Ahmad Jannati and 'Ali Meshkini, chairmen of the Council of Guardians and Assembly of Experts, respectively, would allow Khamane'i to steer a more moderate course.[29]

National Security Decision-making

As with the division of powers at the national level, Ayatollah Khamene'i, as Commander-in-Chief, presides over a complex array of entities and agendas in the national security apparatus. This apparatus comprises the branches of the regular armed forces, or *Artesh*, a parallel force structure in the IRGC, and a large para-military force known as the

152

Basij. The motivation for these overlapping and competing organizations is to reduce the prospects for a military takeover of the government. Other key national security entities include the Ministry of Foreign Affairs and the Ministry of Intelligence and Security (MOIS).

Notably, the president is not part of the military command structure and has no authority over the intelligence services.[30] His influence is exercised mainly through the Foreign Ministry, although the Supreme Leader maintains his own emissaries abroad, thus making it difficult for Iran to act in a coordinated fashion or speak with a single voice. By virtue of his power of appointment and other special laws, Ayatollah Khamene'i has ensured that the coercive arms of the government are firmly in the hands of clerical and other loyalists.

The principal forum for national security decision-making is the Supreme Council for National Security (SCNS). Membership in the SCNS includes two representatives of the Supreme Leader, head of the Judiciary, Speaker of the *Majlis*, Chief of the General Staff, and head of the MOIS. The President acts as the SCNS chairman. Decisions of the Council only take effect with the approval of the Supreme Leader.

As with other dimensions of Iranian decision-making, the SCNS is the scene of vigorous debate between conservative and reformist elements. To achieve consensus, lowest common denominator positions tend to be adopted by the Council though they remain subject to constant renegotiation. Even then, there appears to be considerable latitude as to how the Council's decisions are implemented, resulting at times in inconsistent or conflicting Iranian behavior. Informal networks further complicate national security decision-making.[31]

Khamene'i has considerable experience in national security decision-making, dating back to his days as Ayatollah Khomeini's representative to the forerunner of the SCNS, the Supreme Defense Council. Later as President, Khamene'i acted as the day-to-day Commander-in-Chief on behalf of Khomenei throughout most of the war with Iraq. It appears that Khamene'i has upheld this pattern, leaving to the president and his top military commanders day-to-day decision-making on foreign and defense affairs.

Recent major decisions reached by the SCNS provide insights into the risk-taking propensity of Khamene'i. Iran had been wary of the Taliban's rise to power in Afghanistan in the mid-1990s. Basic friction between

Shi'a Iran and Taliban Sunni extremism escalated in 1998 after 11 Iranian diplomats and journalists in Afghanistan were killed by Taliban forces. As tensions mounted, the SCNS met in emergency session. Despite mounting support from conservative elements for a war with the Taliban, President Khatami and Expediency Council chair Rafsanjani, with the support of the *Artesh*, advised a diplomatic solution to the crisis. The Supreme Leader sided with Khatami and Rafsanjani.

Rather than risk a war which would jeopardize Iran's Islamic rehabilitation and invite meddling by the United States, Khamane'i opted for a considerable show of force along the border with Afghanistan and diplomatic negotiations brokered by the United Nations to reduce tensions. At the same time, Iran stepped up its support to anti-Taliban forces in northern Iraq.[32] Khamene'i adopted a similar course the following year, when Iranian and Turkish forces clashed along their common border. Rather than risk escalating to a potential war with a member of NATO and close ally of the United States, Khamane'i settled for a modest demonstration of force followed by diplomatic efforts to defuse the situation.[33]

In other areas, however, Khamene'i has been much more militant. Specifically, Khamene'i continues to publicly promote Palestinian groups that reject the peace process with Israel. He has openly called for Israel's annihilation and has praised Palestinian suicide bombers. He has also supported on oil embargo against Israel and its supporters. Behind the scenes, Khamene'i has sanctioned the training, funding and organization of such rejectionist groups as Hamas, Hezballah, and the Popular Front for the Liberation of Palestine – General Command. Such training is under the direction of the IRGC and is provided in Lebanon as well as Iran. Khamene'i's stance toward Israel and the Palestinians reflects both the desire to uphold Khomeini's legacy and extend Khamene'i's religious influence, such as it may be, beyond Iran's borders.

Khamene'i has similarly blessed the brutal repression of regime opponents. In 1997, a German court concluded that the assassination of four Iranian dissidents in Berlin in 1992 was authorized by Khamene'i, then-President Rafsanjani, and other senior government officials.[34]

Khamene'i and U.S. Relations

Another area where Khamene'i has been consistent rhetorically is his hostility toward the United States. Here, too, Khamene'i can be seen trying to preserve the legacy of Ayatollah Khomeini. Khamene'i has routinely denounced the United States for its arrogance, greed, and contempt for the Iranian nation.[35] As noted above, Khamene'i also sees the United States as leading a "cultural onslaught" designed to undermine the Islamic Republic. Thus, Khamene'i has echoed Khomeini's view that Iran has no need for the United States and should keep a safe distance from it. It has been suggested that Khamene'i intentionally uses this anti-Western ideology to keep reformist elements in check.[36]

President Khatami's desire to initiate a dialogue with the United States, expressed shortly after his inauguration in 1997, has opened an intriguing chapter in U.S.-Iran relations, one that features all the nuances of Iranian politics, as well as its ambiguities, particularly with regard to Khamene'i's intentions. No real progress was made in thawing U.S.-Iran relations by the end of the 1990s. Indeed, in June 2001, the United States publicly linked Iran to the 1996 bombing of the Khobar Towers in Saudi Arabia, which killed 19 American servicemen and injured 372 other Americans. However, the Al Qaeda terrorist attacks of September 11, 2001, provided a new stimulus for interacting with the United States. President Khatami quickly expressed Iran's sorrow for the attacks, which he condemned. In contrast, Ayatollah Khamene'i waited a week before publicly commenting, and only condemned the attacks generally, comparing them to other "acts of slaughter," such as Hiroshima, Nagasaki, Sabra and Shatilla, and Bosnia.

Wary that American retaliation for the terrorist attacks might somehow be directed against Iran, Khamene'i is reported to have turned to President Khatami and authorized him to take whatever actions were necessary to spare Iran any harm.[37] Evidently, Khatami used this opening to reduce Iran's own support for terrorism, at least temporarily, provide low-level cooperation to the U.S. war in Afghanistan, and resume efforts to put U.S.-Iran relations on a more normal footing.

Specifically, Tehran agreed to a U.S. proposal to rescue any American pilots that might be downed on Iranian territory and consented to allow food and humanitarian assistance to pass through Iran to northern Afghanistan.[38] Additionally, Iran lowered its profile abroad, withdrawing some 700 intelligence and military advisers, including IRGC advisers to Hizballah in Lebanon, a move reportedly sanctioned by the Supreme Leader in his capacity as Commander-in-Chief.[39] All the while, Khamene'i continued his verbal assault on the United States, rebuking President Bush by declaring that "we are not with you and we are not with the terrorists either."[40]

By early 2002, a series of events threatened to derail this potential opening in U.S.-Iran relations. Namely, the United States objected to apparent attempts by Iran to destabilize the interim government in post-Taliban Afghanistan. Washington was also concerned that Iran was harboring Al Qaeda operatives who had fled Afghanistan. Finally, the United States was dismayed by the discovery of a large shipment of arms sent from Iran to the Palestinian Authority aboard the freighter *Karine-A*.[41] It was against this backdrop that President George W. Bush labeled Iran part of an "axis of evil" in his January 29, 2002, State of the Union Address.

The impact of the Bush speech in Iran appears to have been two-fold. As to be expected, Iranians expressed unity and their readiness to defend the country against U.S. attack. Some of this rhetoric, particularly on the part of the IRGC, became quite inflammatory. Reportedly, at President Khatami's request, Ayatollah Khamene'i intervened and warned military commanders against interfering in foreign policy matters.[42] In turn, the potential for tensions to spin out of control led to a redoubling of efforts by Iranian officials to establish a dialogue with the United States.

Khamene'i's role in this matter has remained cloaked in ambiguity. In April 2002, it was reported that he had quietly authorized the SNSC to assess the merits of starting talks with the United States.[43] Other reports from Tehran stated that Khamene'i had given Hashemi Rafsanjani, who had previously advocated normalized relations with the United States, the go-ahead on secret contacts with Washington.[44] On May 21, for the first time in two decades, the *Majlis* debated in closed session the prospect of resuming relations with the United States. The following day, Khamene'i warned that establishing contact and holding talks with America ". . . is both treason and foolishness."[45] Shortly thereafter, the Judiciary banned Iranian media from reporting on the prospects of talks with the United States. By the end of May 2002, President Khatami, in a surprising move, urged his reformist allies in the *Majlis* to abandon their efforts to achieve better relations with Washington, citing growing U.S. belligerence toward Iran.[46]

Presumably, Khatami was referring to remarks by National Security Advisor Condoleezza Rice the month before that Iran's behavior with respect to terrorism and proliferation put it "squarely in the axis of evil," and that Iran's reformers were not yet capable of changing that behavior. Without naming Iran specifically, Rice added that, "We must recognize that truly evil regimes will never be reformed. And we must recognize that such regimes must be confronted not coddled."[47] On May 21, the U.S. State Department released its latest annual assessment of global terrorism and identified Iran as "the most active sponsor of terrorism in 2001."[48]

Given the complexity of Iranian politics, and the ambiguous relationship between Khamene'i and Khatami, this episode is open to multiple interpretations. One such explanation, consistent with this chapter's portrayal of Ayatollah Khamene'i and Iran's strategic culture is that Khamene'i and Khatami are in a tacit partnership to break the stalemate in U.S.-Iran relations. The motivations to do so are primarily economic and security in nature. Namely, Iran desperately needs to get more integrated into the global economy to shore up domestic support for Islamic rule.

Iran's fragile state makes it all the more important to avoid the wrath of the U.S. war on terrorism. Thus, according to this theory, Khamene'i is merely utilizing the Shi'a practice of *tarqiyah* to mask his true intentions by steadfastly denouncing the utility of normalized relations with America. The delicate balancing act comes from establishing the groundwork for improved ties without inadvertently stoking conservative and nationalist sentiments. Khamene'i's warning to the IRGC not to inflame U.S.-Iran tensions would be consistent with this theory. One can imagine that as Khatami made progress behind the scenes, i.e., winning some face-saving concessions from Washington, Khamene'i's rhetoric could soften to the point where dialogue with America could be tolerated. That Khatami appears to be the one to ostensibly pull the plug on the initiative suggests that he lost confidence in his ability to manage the normalization process carefully. What is of greater concern is the possibility that a crucial opportunity to avert conflict between Iran and the United States may have been missed.

Looking Ahead

Iran's support for terrorism and pursuit of nuclear, biological, and chemical weapons has put the country on a path of confrontation with the United States, now even more so in the wake of September 11th. Whether outright conflict can be avoided in the near-term hinges largely on who the real Ayatollah Khamene'i is. If he is genuinely and philosophically committed to the conservative camp, then little moderation of what U.S. leaders see as objectionable Iranian behavior can be expected. If, on the other hand, Khamene'i is a "closet pragmatist," only compelled to toe the conservative line because of his own insecurity, a tacit partnership with President Khatami to tone down provocative behavior, while maintaining the cleric moral high ground, may help Tehran stay out of harm's way. Information presented here supports both scenarios.

The United States will find Iran to be a formidable adversary should the march to confrontation go unabated. As noted above, competing and overlapping power centers, as well as informal mechanisms, bolster the Islamic Republic against political or military attempts at decapitation. Iran's religious leadership remains in tight control of the military and internal security apparatus. The military's possession of weapons of mass destruction, long-range missiles, and reliance on asymmetric strategies suggests that it can substantially raise the costs of military action against Iran. The Ayatollahs, as demonstrated time and again, can be ruthless in their suppression of meaningful dissent.

This is not to suggest that Iran is an impregnable juggernaut. The rifts in Iranian society are real and seemingly growing. The erstwhile center of gravity of the regime, the concept of *velayat-e faqih*, rests on a shaky foundation in light of Khamene'i's meager religious qualifications. The economy is in a shambles and Iran's unemployed youth, which number in the millions, are increasingly restive and dissatisfied with religious rule. Iran's leaders recognize these vulnerabilities if only for the potential opening they provide the United States to manipulate events in and ultimately undo the Islamic Republic. It is in their recognition of Iran's own vulnerabilities and the potential for enormous losses from a direct conflict with the United States that perhaps holds the greatest hope for encouraging prudent leadership in Tehran.

Notes

1. This chapter does not necessarily reflect the views of Science Applications International Corporation or any of its U.S. Government sponsors.

2. A notable exception in this regard is Wilfried Buchta's *Who Rules Iran?* (Washington Institute for Near East Policy and the Konrad Adenauer Stiftung, 2000), upon which this section draws heavily.

3. Buchta, 6-10.

4. Dariush Zahedi, *The Iranian Revolution Then and Now* (Boulder, CO: Westview Press, 2000), 176.

5. Daniel Brumberg, *Reinventing Khomeini* (Chicago: University of Chicago Press, 2001), 244.

6. Buchta, 166.

7. Daniel Byman, Shahram Chubin, Anoushiravan Ehteshami, and Jerrold Green, *Iran's Security Policy in the Post-Revolutionary Era* (Santa Monica, CA: RAND, 2001), 26.

8. Buchta, 6-7.

9. This section draws extensively upon Graham E. Fuller, *The "Center of the Universe,"* (Boulder, CO: Westview Press, 1991), 8-33.

10. Excerpts from Rafsanjani's interview with George A. Nader, editor of *Middle East Insight*, were reproduced in "From Tehran to Waco," *Washington Post*, July 9, 1995, C3.

11. Information in this paragraph was drawn from Nikola B. Schahgaldian, "Iran After Khomeini," *Current History*, February 1990, 62.

12. *A Brief Biography of Ayatollah al-Udhma Sayyid Ali Khamene'i,* Islamic Center, London, http://www.islam-pure.de/imam/biograph/biogricel.htm. This document contains autobiographical excerpts from Khamene'i.

13. Ibid. See also, "The Rahbar: 'Ali Khamene'i and the Iranian Culture Wars," *The Estimate,* vol. XII, no. 17, August 25, 2000, http://www.theestimate.com/public/082500.html.

14. "The Rahbar."

15. Buchta, 52-55.

16. Ibid., 55.

17. Byman, *et al*, 81-82.

18. David Menashri, *Post-Revolutionary Politics in Iran* (London: Frank Cass, 2001), 26-32.

19. Ibid., 32.

20. See, for example, "A Day in the Life of the Leader of the Islamic Revolution," *Ettela'at International*, January 6, 1999, 6.   Accessed through http://www.islam-pure.de/imam/others/others1999.htm#06.01.1999.   See also, "Interview with Mrs. Khamene'i, *Mahjubah, The Magazine for Mulsim Women*, Sept. & Oct. 1992, Accessed through http://www.islam-pure.de/imam/others/others1992.htm#September%201992 and "Mrs. Khamene'i Message on the Great Global Gathering of Women," *Mahjubah*, Sept. 1995. Accessed through http://www.islam-pure.de/imam/others/others1995.htm#01.09.1995.

21. Ali M. Ansari, *Iran, Islam and Democracy* (London: Royal Institute of International Affairs, 2000).

22. Bahman Baktiari, *Parliamentary Politics in Revolutionary Iran* (Gainesville, FL: University Press of Florida, 1996), 128.

23. "A Day in the Life."

24. Ibid.

25. Ansari.

26. Zahedi, 177.

27. Ibid., 186-192.

28. Ibid., 192.

29. Buchta, 55.

30. Ibid., 164. Anthony Cordesman, however, speculates that a subcommittee of the SCNS, comprising the President, Supreme Leader, and the head of MOIS likely oversee nearly all intelligence operations. See his book, *Iran's Military Forces in Transition*, 34.

31. Shahram Chubin, *Iran's National Security Policy* (Washington, D.C.:   Carnegie Endowment for International Peace, 1994), 69-70. See also, Daniel Byman, et al., 21-29.

32. Buchta, 146-148. See also, Daniel Byman, et al., 69-72.

160

33. Daniel Byman, et al., 65-69.

34. Ibid., 93-94.

35. See, for example, Menashri, 187-188.

36. Brumberg, 2.

37. Ali Nurizadeh, "Iran Makes Security and Military Preparations to Face a War on Its Eastern Border," *Al-Sharq al-Awsat*, September 18, 2001, 4, translated in Foreign Broadcast Information Service (FBIS), "Iran Reportedly Makes Military Preparations on Borders with Afghanistan, Iraq," GMP20010918000118.

38. Judith S. Yaphe, "U.S.-Iran Relations: Normalization in the Future?," *Strategic Forum*, No. 188, January 2002. Accessed through http://www.ndu.edu/inss/strforum/sf188.htm.

39. Parviz Mardani, "Iran to Recall Its Military and Intelligence Units From Abroad," *Iran Press Service*, November 8, 2001, http://www.iran-press-service.com/articles-_2001/nov_2001/iran_withdrawal_81101.htm.

40. "Statement by Supreme Leader of Islamic Revolution, Ayatollah Ali Khamenei," Islamic Republic News Agency, September 26, 2001. Accessed through http://www.mediareviewnet.com/irna.htm.

41. For an excellent account and assessment of this incident, see Robert Satloff, "The Peace Process at Sea: The Karine-A Affair and the War on Terrorism," *National Interest*, Spring 2002. Accessed through http://www.washingtoninstitute.org/media/satloff-peace.htm.

42. "Three Words That Shook Iran," *Iran Report*, March 11, 2002, vol. 5, no. 9. Accessed through http://www.rferl.org/iran-report/2002/03/9-110302.html.

43. Guy Dinmore, "Iran's Centrists Seek to Break Taboo of Talks With US," *Financial Times.com*, April 23, 2002, http://news.ft.com.

44. "…But the Possibility Brings Out Old Faces," *Iran Report*, May 6, 2002, Vol. 5, No. 16. Accessed through http://www.rferl.org/iran-report/2002/05/16-060502.html.

45. "Any Questions About U.S.-Iran Relations?," *Iran Report*, May 27, 2002, Vol. 5, No. 19. Accessed through http://www.rferl.org/iran-report/2002/05/19-270502.html.

46. "Iran Abandons Push To Improve U.S. Ties," *Washington Post*, May 30, 2002, A18. Accessed through http://www.washingtonpost.com.

47. Arshad Mohammed, "Bush Says Iran 'Squarely in the Axis of Evil,'" *Reuters,* April 30, 2002.   Accessed through http://asia.news.yahoo.com/020430/reuters/asia-102638.html.

48. U.S. Department of State, *Patterns of Global Terrorism 2001*, May 21, 2002. Accessed through http://www.state.gov/s/ct/rls/pgtrpt/2001/html/10249.htm.

CHAPTER 7

"Saddam is Iraq: Iraq is Saddam"[1]
(Until Operation Iraqi Freedom)

Jerrold M. Post[2] and Amatzia Baram[3]

Introduction

Operation Iraqi Freedom ended the Iraqi regime of Saddam Hussein in the Spring of 2003 even though the Iraqi leader may still be alive and in hiding. Identified as a member of the "axis of evil" by President George W. Bush, Saddam Hussein's Iraq posed a major threat to the region and to Western society. Saddam is believed to have doggedly pursued the development of weapons of mass destruction, despite U.N. sanctions imposed at the conclusion of the 1991 Gulf War. To deal effectively with Saddam Hussein required clear understanding of his motivations, perceptions, and decision-making as well as his Iraqi strategic culture.

Political Personality Profile

Saddam Hussein, the former president of Iraq, has been characterized as "the madman of the Middle East." This pejorative diagnosis was not only inaccurate but also dangerous. Consigning Saddam to the realm of madness could have misled decision-makers into believing he was unpredictable when in fact he was not. An examination of the record of Saddam Hussein's leadership of Iraq for the past 34 years reveals a judicious political calculator, who was by no means irrational, but was dangerous to the extreme.

Saddam Hussein, "the great struggler," has explained the extremity of his actions as president of Iraq as necessary to achieve "subjective immunity" against foreign plots and influences, all actions of the revolution are justified by the "exceptionalism of revolutionary needs." In fact, an examination of Saddam Hussein's life and career reveals this is but the ideological rationalization for a lifelong pattern: All actions were justified if they were in the service of furthering Saddam Hussein's needs and messianic ambitions.

Painful Beginnings—The "Wounded Self"

Saddam Hussein was born in 1937 to a poor peasant family near Tikrit, some 100 miles north of Baghdad, in central-north Iraq. But the central lines of the development of Saddam Hussein's political personality were etched before he was born, for his father died of an "internal disease" (probably cancer) during his mother's pregnancy with Saddam. His 12-year-old brother, too, died (of childhood cancer) a few months later, when Saddam's mother, Sabha, was in her eighth month of pregnancy. Destitute, Saddam's mother attempted suicide. A Jewish family saved her. Then she tried to abort herself of Saddam, but was again prevented from doing this by her Jewish benefactors. After Saddam was born, on April 28, 1937, his mother did not wish to see him, strongly suggesting that she was suffering from a severe depression. His care was relegated to Sabha's brother (his maternal uncle) Khayrallah Talfah Msallat in Tikrit, in whose home Saddam spent much of his early childhood. At age three Saddam was re-united with his mother. In the meantime, Sabha had married a distant relative, Hajj Ibrahim Hasan.[4] Hajj Ibrahim, his stepfather, reportedly was abusive both psychologically and physically to young Saddam.[5]

The first several years of life are crucial to the development of healthy self-esteem. The failure of the mother to nurture and bond with her infant son and the subsequent abuse at the hands of his step-father would have profoundly wounded Saddam's emerging self-esteem, impairing his capacity for empathy with others, producing what has been identified as "the wounded self." One course in the face of such traumatizing experiences is to sink into despair, passivity, and hopelessness. But another is to etch a psychological template of compensatory grandiosity, as if to vow, "Never again, never again shall I submit to superior force." This was the developmental psychological path Saddam followed.

164

From early years on, Saddam, whose name means "the One who Confronts," charted his own course and would not accept limits. According to his semi-official biography, when Saddam was only 10, he was impressed by a visit from his cousin who knew how to read and write. He confronted his family with his wish to become educated, and when they turned him down, since there was no school in his parents' village, he left his home in the middle of the night, making his way to the home of his maternal uncle, Khayrallah, in Tikrit in order to study there.[6] It is quite possible that Saddam somewhat embellished his story, but there is no mistaking his resentment against his mother and step-father that emerges from it.

Khayrallah Inspires Dreams of Glory

Khayrallah was to become not only Saddam's father figure, but also his political mentor. Khayrallah had fought against Great Britain in the Iraqi uprising of 1941 and had spent 5 years in prison for his nationalist agitation. He filled the impressionable young boy's head with tales of his heroic relatives, his great grandfather and two great uncles, who gave their lives for the cause of Iraqi and Arab nationalism, fighting foreign invaders. He conveyed to his young charge that he was destined for greatness, following the path of his heroic relatives and heroes of the medieval Arab-Islamic world. Khayrallah, who was later to become governor of Baghdad, shaped young Hussein's worldview, imbuing him with a hatred of foreigners. In 1981, Saddam republished a pamphlet written by his uncle, entitled: *Three Whom God Should Not Have Created: Persians, Jews, and Flies.*

Khayrallah tutored his young charge in his view of Arab history and the ideology of Arab nationalism. Khayrallah himself did not join the Ba'ath Party, but his worldview was close to its ideology. For Saddam, joining in 1957 was thus a natural choice. Founded in 1940, the Ba'ath Party envisaged the creation of a new Arab nation defeating the colonialist and imperialist powers, and achieving Arab independence, unity, and socialism. Ba'ath ideology, as conceptualized by its intellectual founding father, Michel Aflaq, focuses on the history of oppression and division of the Arab world, first at the hands of the Mongols, then the Ottoman Turks, then the Western mandates, then the

165

monarchies ruled by Western interests, and finally by the establishment of the "Zionist entity."

Thus inspired by his uncle's tales of heroism in the service of the Arab nation, Saddam has been consumed by dreams of glory since his earliest days, identifying himself with Nebuchadnezzar, the King of Babylonia (not an Arab, but seen by many in Iraq as such and certainly as a great Iraqi) who conquered Jerusalem and exiled the Jews in 586 B.C. Saddam was also fascinated by the exploits of Saladin (a Muslim Kurd regarded by many Arabs as an Arab) who regained Jerusalem in 1187 by defeating the Crusaders. But these dreams of glory, formed so young, were compensatory, for they sat astride a wounded self and profound self-doubt.

Saddam was steeped in Arab history and Ba'athist ideology by the time he traveled with his uncle to Baghdad to pursue his secondary education. The schools, a hotbed of a combination of Arab nationalism and Iraqi pride, confirmed his political leanings. In 1952, when Saddam was 15, Nasser led the Free Officer's revolution in Egypt and became a hero to young Saddam and his peers. As the activist leader of Pan Arabism, Nasser became an idealized model for Saddam, stating that only by courageously confronting imperialist powers could Arab nationalism be freed from Western shackles.[7]

At age 20, inspired by Nasser, Saddam joined the Arab Ba'ath Socialist Party in Iraq. In those days the party was still strongly pro-Nasser, seeing in him by far the most promising leader of the pan-Arab movement. Indeed, a few months after Saddam joined the party in Iraq, the Syrian branch turned to Nasser for a Syrian-Egyptian union and, upon his demand, even agreed to disband itself. In the 1960s, relations between the resuscitated Ba'ath Party and Nasser deteriorated and the United Arab Republic split up, even though both still claimed to believe in the unification of all the Arab states. But when Saddam joined the party all this was still unimaginable: Nasser was the hero.

Saddam quickly impressed party officials with his dedication. Known as a "street thug," he willingly used violence in the service of the party, and was rewarded with rapid promotion. In 1958, apparently emulating Nasser, Army General Abd al-Karim Qassem led a coup d'etat which ousted the monarchy. But unlike Nasser, Qassem did not pursue the path of pan-Arabism, and turned against the Ba'ath Party. The 22-

year-old Saddam was called to Ba'ath Party headquarters and given the mission to lead a small team assigned to assassinate Qassem. The mission failed, reportedly because of a crucial error in judgment by the inexperienced would-be assassins. But Saddam's escape to Syria, first by horseback and then by swimming across the Tigris, has achieved mythic status in Iraqi history.

During his exile, Saddam went to Egypt where he completed his high school education and started to study law, receiving a small allowance from Nasser. While in Cairo, he engaged in illegal Ba'ath Party activity there (the party had disbanded itself and was banned in the UAR). This won Saddam Nasser's wrath, but the Egyptian leader was keen to keep a radical anti-Qassem activist on his side, and refrained from any harsh measures.

Saddam returned to Iraq after the Ba'ath Party took over in Baghdad in February 1963. In March 1963, the party came to power also in Damascus. In Baghdad, Saddam then became a middle-level operative in the party's security apparatus. Aflaq, the ideological father of the Ba'ath Party, admired young Hussein, but Saddam still had a long way to go to get to the top. In November 1963, the party lost power in Baghdad, and Saddam and his comrades were arrested, then released, remaining under surveillance. In July 1968, they came to power again through a military coup d'etat.

Rivalry with Assad to be Supreme Arab National Leader

Rivalry over who is the true representative of the Ba'ath Party and the rightful leading elite of the Arab world, the Ba'ath regime in Damascus or the underground party in Baghdad, emerged in 1966, but it reached a political crescendo soon after the Iraqi Ba'ath Party came to power for the second time in 1968. At first this was a three-way struggle between Cairo, Damascus, and Baghdad, but Abd al-Nasser's death in September 1970 left only two contenders.

Until Saddam became president in 1979, this was a contest for legitimacy and Arab leadership essentially between an Iraqi duo, Vice President Saddam Hussein and his boss and distant relative, President Ahmad Hasan al-Bakr, on the one hand, and President Hafez al-Assad in Damascus on the other. This became increasingly bitter and led to acrimonious sparring between Saddam and Assad on the premise that there can be only one supreme Arab nationalist leader. In Saddam's mind, destiny had inscribed his name as Saddam Hussein. Some thawing in the late 1990s notwithstanding, the split and rivalry persisted until the death of the Syrian leader in 2000.

In July 1968, with the crucial secret assistance of military intelligence chief Abdul Razzaz al Naif, the Ba'athists, with Saddam playing a key role, mounted a successful coup. In gratitude for services rendered, two weeks after the coup, Saddam arranged for the capture and exile of Naif, and subsequently ordered his assassination. It is important to observe that Naif was ambitious, and that after he was ousted and exiled, he was engaged in anti-regime activity. Later, in 1970, Saddam ousted Minister of Defense Hardan Abd al-Ghafar al-Tikriti, another senior and ambitious associate, and a year later had him assassinated. In 1979, Saddam forced his senior partner, President Bakr, out of office and made himself president. Three years later the elderly ex-president died, widely believed to have been poisoned by his young successor.

The ousters and later assassinations represent a paradigm for the manner in which Saddam has rewarded incomplete loyalty or loyalty based on equality and the way in which he adhered to commitments throughout his career. He has a flexible conscience: commitments and loyalty are matters of circumstance, and circumstances change. If an individual, or a nation, is perceived as an impediment or a threat, no matter how loyal in the past, that individual or nation will be eliminated violently without a backward glance, and the action will be justified by "the exceptionalism of revolutionary needs." Nothing was permitted to stand in "the great struggler's" messianic path as he pursued his (and Iraq's) revolutionary destiny, as exemplified by this extract from Saddam Hussein's remarkable "Victory Day" message of 8 August 1990.[8]

> This is the only way to deal with these despicable Croesuses who relished possession to destroy devotion . . . who were guided by the foreigner instead of being guided by virtuous standards, principles of Pan-Arabism, and the creed of humanitarianism . . . The second of August . . . is the legitimate newborn child of the struggle, patience and perseverance of the Kuwaiti people, which was crowned by revolutionary action on that immortal day. The newborn child was born of a legitimate father and an immaculate mother. Greetings to the makers of the second of August, whose efforts God has blessed. They have achieved one of the brightest,

most promising and most principled national and Pan-Arab acts. Two August has come as a very violent response to the harm that the foreigner had wanted to perpetrate against Iraq and the nation. The Croesus of Kuwait and his aides become the obedient, humiliated and treacherous dependents of that foreigner . . . What took place on 2 August was inevitable so that death might not prevail over life, so that those who were capable of ascending to the peak would not be brought down to the abysmal precipice, so that corruption and remoteness from God would not spread to the majority . . . Honor will be kept in Mesopotamia so that Iraq will be the pride of the Arabs, their protector, and their model of noble values.

Capable of Reversing His Course

Saddam's practice of revolutionary opportunism has another important characteristic. Just as previous commitments were not permitted to stand in the way of Saddam's messianic path, neither would he persist in a particular course of action if it proved to be counterproductive for him and his nation. When he pursued a course of action, he pursued it fully. If he met initial resistance, he would struggle all the harder, convinced of the correctness of his judgments. Should circumstances demonstrate that he miscalculated, he was capable of reversing his course. Yet, he stuck to his guns on the strategic level: he never gave up on a dream. He would wait until circumstances changed, and then he would strike again. In these circumstances of a momentary reversal he did not acknowledge he had erred but, rather, that he was adapting to a dynamic situation. The three most dramatic examples of his revolutionary pragmatism and ideological flexibility concerned his ongoing struggle with his Persian enemies.

Yields on Shatt-al-Arab To Quell the Kurdish Rebellion

In March 1975, Saddam signed an agreement with the Shah of Iran, splitting the disputed Shatt-al-Arab waterway along the thalweg line, thus stipulating Iranian sovereignty over the Iranian (eastern) side. He did this in return for Iran's ceasing to supply the Kurdish rebellion. In 1970, Saddam signed an autonomy agreement with the Kurds, but in 1973, he declared that the Ba'ath Party represented all Iraqis, that the Kurds could not be neutral, and that the Kurds were either fully with the people or against them. In 1975, he destroyed the Kurdish autonomy and established a pseudo-autonomy, fully controlled from Baghdad. In 1979, he made the same point in regard to the Communist Party of Iraq, with whom he had a common "Patriotic Front": "Are you," he asked them, "with us in the same trench, or against us?" Then he cracked down on them with full force, imprisoning, torturing, and executing many. Indeed, this is another of Saddam's basic principles, "He who is not totally with me is my enemy." By 1975, the war against the Kurds had become extremely costly, having cost 60,000 lives in one year alone. Demonstrating his revolutionary pragmatism, despite his lifelong hatred of the Persians, Saddam's urgent need to put down the Kurdish rebellion took (temporary) precedence.

The loss of the Shatt-al-Arab waterway continued to rankle, and in September 1980, sensing Iran's military weakness as well as confusion in the Iranian political system, he declared the 1975 agreement with Iran null and void. Saddam then invaded the Khuzistan-Arabestan province. There were additional reasons for the invasion: fear of domestic Shi'ite unrest for one, but there may be little doubt that *revanche* was a major consideration. At first the Iraqi forces met with little resistance. However, following an initial success, Iran stiffened and began to inflict serious damage not only on Iraqi forces but also on Iraqi cities. It became clear to Saddam that the war was counterproductive.

Attempts to End the Iran-Iraq War

In May-June 1982, Saddam's forces were driven out of much of the areas they had occupied. He then reversed his earlier militant aggression and attempted to terminate hostilities, ordering a unilateral withdrawal from other areas and offering a ceasefire. Khomeini, who by now was obsessed with Saddam, would have none of it, indicating that there would be no peace with Iraq until Saddam no longer ruled Iraq. The Iran-Iraq War continued for another bloody 6 years, taking a dreadful toll, estimated at more than a million.

In 1988, an indecisive ceasefire was agreed to, with Iraq sustaining a military advantage. Saddam may have been able to reach a peace agreement, but this would have necessitated a return to the 1975

170

agreement, including renewed recognition of Iranian sovereignty over the eastern side of the Shatt. Saddam refused to make this humiliating concession, indicating that he would *never* yield, and that he would *never* withdraw from some Iranian territory he still held.

Reversed Policy on Disputed Waterway

But revolutionary pragmatism was to supersede this resolve, for Hussein was planning a new war, against a new enemy. He desperately needed the 500,000 troops tied up on the Iraqi-Iranian border, and he was in dire need of strategic depth. On August 15, 1990, thirteen days after he conquered Kuwait and found himself facing an ominous American troop buildup, Hussein agreed to meet Iranian conditions, promising to withdraw from Iranian territory and, most importantly, agreeing to share the disputed Shatt-al-Arab waterway. *Never* is a short time when revolutionary pragmatism dictates, which was important to remember in evaluating Saddam's vow of 1990 to *never* relinquish Kuwait, and his continued intransigence to Western demands.

Saddam's Psychological Characteristics: Malignant Narcissism

The labels "madman of the Middle East" and "megalomaniac" are often affixed to Saddam, but in fact there is no evidence that he was suffering from a psychotic disorder. He was not impulsive, only acted after judicious consideration, and could be extremely patient. Indeed, he has used time as a weapon.

While he was psychologically in touch with reality, he was often politically out of touch with reality. Saddam's worldview was narrow and distorted, and he had scant experience outside of the Arab world. His only sustained experience with non-Arabs was with his Soviet military advisors, and he reportedly only traveled outside of the Middle East on two occasions, a brief trip to Paris in 1976 and another trip to Moscow. Moreover, he was surrounded by sycophants, who were cowed by Saddam's well-founded reputation for brutality and who were afraid to contradict him. He ruthlessly eliminated perceived threats to his power and equated criticism with disloyalty.

In 1979, when he fully assumed the reins of Iraqi leadership, one of his first acts was to execute 21 senior officials whose loyalty he questioned. The dramatic meeting of his senior officials in which the 21 "traitors" were identified while Saddam watched, luxuriantly smoking a Cuban cigar, has been captured on film. After the "forced confessions" by a "plotter" whose family had been arrested, the remaining senior officials formed the execution squads.

In 1982, when the war with Iran was going very badly for Iraq and Saddam wished to terminate hostilities, Khomeini, who was personally fixated on Saddam, insisted there could be no peace until Saddam was removed from power. At a cabinet meeting, Saddam asked his ministers to candidly give their advice, and the Minister of Health suggested Saddam temporarily step down, to resume the presidency after peace had been established. Saddam reportedly thanked him for his candor and ordered his arrest. His wife pleaded for her husband's return, indicating that her husband had always been loyal to Saddam. Saddam promised her that her husband would be returned. The next day, Saddam returned her husband's body to her in a black canvas bag, chopped into pieces according to one story. This powerfully concentrated the attention of the other ministers who were unanimous in their insistence that Saddam remain in power.

Sometimes he seemed to want frank advice, but when those rare occasions arose it was difficult to determine if he really meant it or not, so the prudent inclination was to give him the advice one believes he really wanted to hear. When his mind was fully made up, he made it amply clear. On such occasions there is no room for the slightest dispute. Thus, he was deprived of the check of wise counsel from his leadership circle. This combination of limited international perspective and a sycophantic leadership circle sometimes led him to miscalculate.

Exalted Self Concept: Saddam is Iraq, Iraq is Saddam

Saddam's pursuit of power for himself and Iraq was boundless. In fact, in his mind, the destiny of Saddam and Iraq were one and indistinguishable. His exalted self-concept was fused with his Ba'athist political ideology. He believed Ba'athist dreams would be realized when the Arab nation was unified under one strong leader. In Saddam's mind, he was destined for that role.

172

Saddam's grandiose self-image and self-absorption was so extreme that he had little capacity to empathize with others. In many ways, he saw his advisers and inner circle as extensions of himself. This bears on the special meaning of loyalty to Saddam. For Saddam, loyalty was a one-way street. He could turn abruptly against individuals of whom he had become suspicious despite their demonstrated total loyalty throughout their careers. His fundamental distrust and wariness was so extreme that he was loath to trust anyone fully. He felt at ease only around people who either developed their career within his system and thus owed him great respect and loyalty, or people who belonged to a population group in Iraq that could not seriously aspire to power without his patronage. To the first category belong people like his own children, of course, but also the chiefs of his security system whom he molded for many years in his own image and, who totally owed their careers to him.

Saddam generally felt ill at ease around people with careers that were not developed under his patronage, and especially people with higher educational and professional credentials. Exceptions to this were Tariq Aziz, his foreign minister, who has a PhD from the University of Pennsylvania and Dr. Sa'dun Hammadi, Speaker of the Parliament, who has an MA from the University of Baghdad. Saddam was comfortable with these men because, in addition to being a Christian (Aziz) and Shi'ite (Hammadi), they totally owed their careers to him.

No Constraint of Conscience

In pursuit of his messianic dreams, there is no evidence Saddam was constrained by conscience; his only loyalty was to Saddam Hussein. When there was an obstacle in his revolutionary path, Saddam eliminated it, whether it was a previously loyal subordinate or a previously supportive country.

Unconstrained Aggression in Pursuit of His Goals

In pursuing his goals, Saddam used aggression instrumentally. He used whatever force was necessary, and would, if he deemed it expedient, go to extremes of violence, including the use of weapons of mass destruction. His unconstrained aggression was instrumental in pursuing his goals, but it was at the same time defensive aggression, for his grandiose facade masked underlying insecurity.

173

Paranoid Orientation

While Hussein was not psychotic, he had a strong paranoid orientation. He was ready for retaliation and, not without reason, saw himself as surrounded by enemies. But he ignored his role in creating those enemies, and righteously threatened his targets. The conspiracy theories he spun were not merely for popular consumption in the Arab world, but genuinely reflected his paranoid mindset. He was convinced that the United States, Israel, and Iran have been in league for the purpose of eliminating him, and found a persuasive chain of evidence for this conclusion. His minister of information, Latif Nusayyif Jassim, responsible for propaganda, his Vice President, Taha Yasin Ramadan, his Deputy Chairman of the Revolutionary Command Council, Izzat Ibrahim, and more generally speaking, his internal security apparatus probably helped reinforce Saddam's paranoid disposition and, in a sense, were the implementers of his paranoia.

It was this political personality constellation-messianic ambition for unlimited power, absence of conscience, unconstrained aggression, and a paranoid outlook, which made Saddam so dangerous. Conceptualized as malignant narcissism, this is the personality configuration of the destructive charismatic, who unifies and rallies his downtrodden supporters by blaming outside enemies. While Saddam was not charismatic, this psychological posture is the basis of Saddam's particular appeal to the Palestinians who saw him as a strongman who shared their intense anti-Zionism and would champion their cause.

Viewed Self as One of History's Great Leaders

Saddam Hussein genuinely saw himself as one of the great leaders of history, ranking himself with his heroes: Nasser, Castro, Tito, Ho Chi Minh, and Mao Zedong, each of whom he admired for adapting socialism to his environment, free of foreign domination. Saddam saw himself as transforming his society. He believed youth must be "fashioned" to "safeguard the future" and that Iraqi children must be transformed into a "radiating light that will expel" traditional family backwardness. Like Mao, Saddam encouraged youth to inform on their parents' anti-revolutionary activity. As God-like status was ascribed to Mao, and giant pictures and statues of him were placed throughout China, so too giant pictures and

174

statues of Saddam abounded in Iraq. Asked about this cult of personality, Saddam shruged and said he "cannot help it if that is what they want to do."

Probably Over-read Degree of Support in Arab World

Saddam Hussein was so consumed with his messianic mission that he probably over-read the degree of his support in the rest of the Arab world. He psychologically assumed that many in the Arab world, especially the downtrodden, shared his views and saw him as their hero. He was probably genuinely surprised at the fairly wide condemnation of his invasion of Kuwait. He was right, though, when it came to many Jordanians, Palestinian, and Syrians who did support him.

Political Personality Shaped Leadership Style

Saddam's leadership and operating style can be summarized in what Regis Matlak has dubbed "Saddam's Rules for Survival:"[9]

1. *Innocence is No Defense; Guilt is More Secure*: Although not necessarily the first recourse, Saddam has ordered execution of innocent officers to insure the removal of all coup plotters rather than be vulnerable to a residual threat. On the other hand, official complicity in crimes, that is to say "authorized" corruption, arbitrary arrest, and "official" torture and mutilation, are required to establish bona fides.

2. *Be Eternally Agnostic on Matters of Family and Loyalty*: For Saddam, it was an article of faith to be vigilant on appointments to coup-sensitive positions in his personal bodyguard and the broader palace-controlled personal, protective infrastructure.

3. *Never Trust a Fellow Conspirator.*

4. *Beware Dangerous Liaisons.* Saddam believed a coup plotter with luck and audacity is more likely to succeed than a conspirator with an extensive organization.

5. *Pre-empt the Building of Personal Power Bases or Political Factions, Particularly in Military and Security Organs*: Despite key assignments being restricted to family members and other members of the Tikrit power structure, Saddam did not permit a

175

long tenure in any one position ... Saddam viewed the establishment of a single independent power base as a de facto challenge to his leadership.

6. *Disregard "Intelligence" at Great Peril*: Saddam took seriously the human and technical information gathered from his pervasive intelligence and security networks ... Saddam also learned that acting on such intelligence with leniency has led the same conspirators to try again at a later time.

7. *Redundancy is "Security Effective," if not Resource Efficient*: There exist visible and shadowy organizational structures meant to pre-empt, control, or react to threats to regime stability ... This security apparatus is well practiced at penetrating military and intelligence centered cabals.

8. *Use Trojan Horses and Other Deceptions*: Saddam was not content to pursue only those who actively plan his removal. He also seeks out those who *might be tempted* to join a coup conspiracy if given the opportunity. This was done both through setting up "disloyal" senior offices to gather potential coup plotters, as well as the "perceived" Trojan Horse where a friend or family member heard unfavorable commentary about Saddam or the regime and was unclear whether this is a regime test knowing that if it is and they don't turn the person in they will pay the price.

9. *A Cult of Personality and a Perception of Invulnerability*: Saddam and the regime fostered a cult of personality. One of the primary objectives, at least for Saddam, was to create a perception that only Saddam can save Iraq from internal chaos, anarchy, and foreign encroachment; that Saddam and the regime were everywhere and all-powerful; and that it was futile to even think beyond Saddam. Saddam icons were located everywhere.

10. *Retribution is Good*: Individuals must know that there will be a high price to pay for taking action against Saddam. This characteristic was so strong in Saddam's operating style that it served to define Saddam's response to betrayal or attack.

Saddam at the Crossroads in the Gulf Crisis

It is not by accident that Saddam Hussein survived for more than three decades as his nation's preeminent leader in this tumultuous part of the world. While he was driven by dreams of glory, and his political perspective was narrow and distorted, he was a shrewd tactician who had a sense of patience. Able to justify extremes of aggression on the basis of revolutionary, pan-Arab and anti-imperialist needs, if the aggression was counterproductive, he showed a pattern of reversing his course when he miscalculated, waiting until a later day to achieve his destiny. His drive for power was not diminished by these reversals, but only deflected.

Saddam Hussein was a ruthless political calculator who would go to whatever lengths necessary to achieve his goals. His survival in power, with his dignity intact, was his highest priority. Soviet Foreign Minister Yevgeny Primakov, after meeting him in Baghdad during the Gulf War, suggested that Saddam was suffering from a "Masada Complex," which would cause him to jeopardize Iraq rather than compromise with other nations, preferring a martyr's death to yielding. This was assuredly not the case. Saddam had no wish to be a martyr, and survival was his number one priority. A self-proclaimed revolutionary pragmatist, he did not wish a conflict in which Iraq was grievously damaged and his stature as a leader destroyed.

While Saddam's advisors' reluctance to disagree with Saddam's policies contributes to the potential for miscalculation, nevertheless his advisors, by providing information and assessments, were able to make significant inputs to the accuracy of Saddam's evaluation of Iraq's political/military situation.

While Saddam appreciated the danger of the 1990-1991 Gulf crisis, it did provide the opportunity to defy the hated outsiders, a strong value in his Ba'ath ideology. He continued to cast the conflict as a struggle between, on the one hand, Iraq, leading the "Camp" of the decent and patriotic Arabs, the true Muslims, and honest people in the world at large, and on the other hand the United States, and even more personally as a struggle between the "Slave of God" Saddam Hussein versus the "Infidel" and "Imperialist" George Bush. When the struggle became thus personalized, it enhanced Saddam's reputation as a courageous strongman willing to defy the imperialist United States.

When President George H. W. Bush depicted the 1990-1991 conflict as the unified civilized world against Saddam Hussein, it hit a tender nerve for Saddam. Saddam had his eye on his role in history and placed great stock in world opinion. If he were to conclude that his status as a world leader was threatened, it would have had important constraining effects on him. Thus, the prospect of being expelled from the United Nations and of Iraq being castigated as a rogue nation outside the community of nations was likely very threatening to Saddam. The overwhelming majority supporting the Security Council resolution at the time of the conflict must have confronted Saddam with the damage he was inflicting on his stature as a leader, despite his defiant rhetoric dismissing the resolutions of the United Nations as reflecting the United States' control of the international organization.

Defiant rhetoric was a hallmark of the conflict and lent itself to misinterpretation across cultural boundaries. The Arab world places great stock on expressive language. The language of courage is a hallmark of leadership, and great value is attached to the very act of expressing brave resolve against the enemy in and of itself. Even though the statement is made in response to the United States, when Saddam spoke it was to multiple audiences. Much of his language was solipsistic and designed to demonstrate his courage and resolve to the Iraqi people and the Arab and Islamic worlds. There was no necessary connection between courageous verbal expression and the act threatened. Nasser gained great stature from his fiery rhetoric. Moreover, fiercely defiant rhetoric was another indicator of the stress on Saddam, for the more threatened Saddam felt, the more threatening he became.

By the same token, Saddam probably heard the Western words of President George H. W. Bush through a Middle Eastern filter. When a statement of resolve and intent was made by President Bush in a public statement, Saddam may well have discounted the expressed intent to act. This underlines the importance of a private channel to communicate clearly and unambiguously. The mission by Secretary of State Baker afforded the opportunity to resolve any misunderstandings on Saddam's part concerning the strength of resolve and intentions of the United States and the international coalition. There may be no doubt that, even though he refused to deliver President Bush's letter to Saddam, Tariq Aziz, who met with Baker in Geneva, delivered the message that the letter contained.

Still, Saddam remained inclined to believe that the U.S. would not attack.[10] This, like his more general assessment that invading Kuwait was a safe bet, demonstrated Saddam's predilection for wishful thinking.

The Iran-Iraq War and the Gulf Crisis Promote Saddam to World-Class Leader

Until he invaded Iran, Saddam Hussein had languished in obscurity, overshadowed by the heroic stature of other Middle Eastern leaders such as Nasser, Anwar Sadat, and Ayatollah Khomeini. With the invasion of Iran he assumed the role of the defender of the Arab world against the Persian threat, "the Guardian of the Eastern Gate" of the Arab homeland. But when the war was over, his economy was in shambles, his population was seething as a result of a crisis of socio-economic expectations, and his prestige in the Arab world was lower than it had been before he invaded Iran. In the 1990-1991 Gulf crisis, at long last, Saddam was exactly where he believed he was destined to be, a world-class political actor on center stage commanding world events, with the entire world's attention focused upon him. When his rhetoric was threatening, the price of oil rose precipitously and the Dow Jones average plummeted. He was demonstrating to the Arab masses that he was an Arab leader (qa'id) of historical proportions with the courage to defy the West and expel foreign influences.

Now that he was at the very center of international attention, his appetite for glory was stimulated all the more. The glory-seeking Saddam would not easily yield the spotlight of international attention. He wanted to remain on center stage, but not at the expense of his power and his prestige. Saddam would only withdraw if he calculated that he could do so with his power and his honor intact and that the drama in which he was starring would continue.

Honor and reputation must be interpreted in an Arab context. Saddam had already achieved considerable honor in the eyes of the Arab masses for having the courage to stand up to the West. It should be remembered that, even though Egypt militarily lost the 1973 war with Israel, Sadat became a hero to the Arab world for his willingness to attack, and initially force back, the previously invincible forces of Israel. Qadhafi mounted an air attack when the United States crossed the so-called "line of death." Even though his jets were destroyed in the ensuing conflict, Qadhafi's status was raised in the Arab world. Indeed, he thanked the

United States for making him a hero to the third world.[11] Thus, Saddam could find honor in the 1990-91 confrontation. He could even sustain very heavy casualties, provided that the battle would end with a draw, or with a defeat that could somehow be presented as a draw. And a draw with the United States, in itself, would be a kind of victory.

Saddam's past history reveals a remarkable capacity to find face saving justification when reversing his course in very difficult circumstances. Insisting on total capitulation and humiliation may have driven Saddam into a corner and made it impossible for him to reverse his course. He would only withdraw from Kuwait if he believed he could survive with his power and his honor intact.

By the same token, he would only reverse his course if his power and reputation were threatened. This would require a posture of strength, firmness and clarity of purpose by a unified civilized world, demonstrably willing to use overwhelming force if necessary. The only language Saddam Hussein understood was the language of power. Without this demonstrable willingness to use force, even if the sanctions were biting deeply, Saddam was quite capable of putting his population through a sustained period of hardship.

It was crucial to demonstrate unequivocally to Saddam Hussein that unless he withdrew from Kuwait, his career as a world-class political actor would be ended. The announcement of a major escalation of the force level was presumably designed to drive that message home. The U.N. resolution authorizing the use of force unless Iraq withdrew by January 15, 1991, was a particularly powerful message because of the large majority supporting the resolution.

The message almost certainly was received. In the wake of the announcement of the increase in force level in November 1990, Saddam intensified his request for "deep negotiations," seeking a way out in which he could preserve his power and his reputation. This, however, could only be achieved had he managed to pressure the United States to agree to leave a meaningful Iraqi presence in Kuwait, as well as to start pushing Israel out of the West Bank and Gaza. Alternatively, both he and his lieutenants had to be fully convinced that if Iraq did not withdraw they would lose power in Baghdad or, at least, be on the brink of losing power. That President Bush sent Secretary of State Baker to meet one-on-one with Saddam was an extremely important step. Yet, even the Geneva meeting failed to convince Saddam that the U.S. would go to an all-out war. In the interim leading up to the meeting, and following it, the shrewdly manipulative Saddam continued to attempt to divide the international coalition.

Considering himself a revolutionary pragmatist, Saddam was at heart a survivor. Even if in response to the unified demonstration of strength and resolve he did retreat and reverse his course, this would only be a temporary deflection of his unbounded drive for power. It was a certainty that he would return at a later date, stronger than ever, unless firm measures were taken to contain him. This underlined the importance of strategic planning beyond the immediate crisis, especially considering his progress toward acquiring a nuclear weapons capability. If blocked in his overt aggression, he could be expected to pursue his goals covertly through intensified support of terrorism.

Why Saddam Did Not Withdraw from Kuwait

In the political psychology profile prepared for the congressional hearings on the Gulf crisis in December 1990, it was observed that Saddam was by no means a martyr and was indeed the quintessential survivor. The key to his survival in power was his capacity to reverse his course when events demonstrated that he had miscalculated. It was believed he could again reverse himself if he concluded that unless he did so his power base and reputation would be destroyed, and if by so doing he could preserve his power base and reputation.

How can it be, then, that in 1990-1991 this self-described revolutionary pragmatist, faced by an overwhelming array of military power that would surely deal a mortal blow to his nation, entered into and persisted in a violent confrontational course? As pointed out above, Saddam may well have heard President Bush's Western words of intent through a Middle Eastern filter and calculated that he was bluffing. It is also possible he downgraded the magnitude of the threat, likening the threatened response to the characteristic Arab hyperbole. Even though he expected a massive air strike, he undoubtedly was surprised by the magnitude of the destruction wrought on his forces.

The Culminating Acts of Drama of His Life

But more importantly, the dynamic of the 1990-1991 crisis affected Saddam. What began as an act of naked aggression toward Kuwait was transformed into a dramatic moment in his life. Although he had previously shown little concern for the Palestinian people, the shrewdly manipulative Saddam had wrapped himself and his invasion of Kuwait in the Palestinian flag. The response of the Palestinians was overwhelming. They saw Saddam as their hope and their salvation, standing up defiantly and courageously to the United States to force a just settlement of their cause. This caught the imagination of the masses throughout the Arab world and their shouts of approval fed his already swollen ego as he went on a defiant roll.

Intoxicated by the elixir of power and the acclaim of the Palestinians and the radical Arab masses, Saddam may well have been on an euphoric high and optimistically overestimated his chances for success. For Saddam's heroic self-image was engaged as never before. He was fulfilling the messianic goal that had obsessed him—and eluded him—throughout his life. He was actualizing his self-concept as leader of all the Arab peoples, the legitimate heir of Nebuchadnezzar, Saladin, and especially Nasser.

His psychology and his policy options became captives of his rhetoric and self-image. He became so absolutist in his commitment to the Palestinian cause, to not yielding even partially over Kuwait until there was justice for the Palestinian people, and U.N. resolutions 242 and 338 had been complied with according to the Arab interpretation, that it would have been extremely difficult for him to reverse himself without being dishonored, and to lose face in the Arab world was to be without authority. Unlike past reversals, these absolutist pronouncements were in the full spotlight of international attention. Saddam had in effect painted himself into a corner.

The Bush administration's insistence on "no face-saving" only intensified this dilemma. Not only had Saddam concluded that to reverse himself would be to lose his honor, but he also probably doubted that his power base would be preserved if he dishonorably left Kuwait. For years he had been telling his people that a U.S.-Iran-Israeli conspiracy was in place to destroy Iraq and remove him and his regime from power, and doubted that the border of Iraq would limit the aggressive intention of the United States.

182

Earlier, Foreign Minister Aziz had indicated "everything was on the table," but by late December the semblance of diplomatic flexibility had disappeared, and Saddam seemed intent on challenging the coalition's ultimatum. Saddam, in our estimation, had concluded that he could not reverse himself and withdraw without being dishonored. He had concluded that he needed to risk entering into conflict to demonstrate his courage and to affirm his claim to pan-Arab and Islamic leadership as well as to traditional Arab values of manly valor (*al-futuwwa, al-muruwwa*) and honor (*al-sharaf*).[12]

Saddam expected a massive air campaign and planned to survive it. In the succeeding ground campaign, he hoped to engage the United States "Vietnam complex." As he had demonstrated in the Iran-Iraq War, his battle-hardened troops, he believed, could absorb massive casualties, whereas the weak-willed United States would not have the stomach for the heavy casualties it would certainly sustain. As protests mounted, the U.S. would stop its offensive and start negotiating, and a political-military stalemate would ensue, increasing his chances for a respectable draw.[13]

By demonstrating that he had the courage to stand up against the most powerful nation on earth, Saddam's credentials as pan-Arab leader and a manly hero alike would be consolidated and he would win great honor.

Saddam hoped to consolidate his place in history as Nasser's heir by bravely defying the U.S. and, if there was no other way, confronting the U.S.-led coalition. On the third day of the air campaign, his minister of information, Latif Nusayyif Jassim, declared victory. To the astounded press he explained that the coalition expected Iraq to crumble in 2 days. Having already survived the massive air strikes for 3 days, the Iraqis were accordingly victorious, and each further day would only magnify the scope of their victory.

It was revealed in January 1991, that under Saddam's opulent palace was a mammoth bunker, fortified with steel and pre-stressed concrete. The architecture of this complex was Saddam's psychological architecture: a defiant, grandiose facade resting on the well-fortified foundation of a siege mentality. Attacked on all sides, Saddam remained besieged and defiant, using whatever aggression is necessary to consolidate his control and ensure his survival.

Threats to Saddam's Survival After the Conflict

Iraqi domestic support for Saddam Hussein was drastically eroded after the Gulf War. By late 1996 a series of betrayals, failures, and disappointments had left him in a more precarious domestic position than at any previous time since March 1991. A principle of Saddam's leadership that had always been true was, if anything, intensified in the post-war period. Specifically, ensuring his domestic stability and eliminating internal threats to his regime was Saddam's central concern and, in a clash between his international position and internal security, internal security would win out.

Moreover, precipitating international crises could strengthen Saddam's internal position. The most damaging consequence of a setback internationally that proved him to be a failure as a leader would have been the consequent reduction in his internal prestige and threats to his regime's stability. Five events could have led his power base to seriously question Saddam's ability to lead Iraq:

- If Saddam's actions were to provoke the West to conduct a sustained powerful military campaign that destroyed important elements of his military power. (This, indeed, has happened.)

- If he could not have demonstrated to his power base that he would soon be able to bring to an end or, at least, continue to erode the U.N. inspections regime and with it the oil embargo;

- If he had been unable to guarantee the functioning of the national economy and to continue to support the relatively extravagant life style of his body guards and ruling elite

- If he had been unable to retain Iraq's WMD arsenal; or

- If he had lost the propaganda campaign he was waging within Iraq.

Accordingly, in addition to attempting to strengthen internal vulnerabilities, he also worked assiduously to strengthen his international position, both with his "far abroad,"—Russia, France, and China—as well as his "near abroad," Middle Eastern neighbor states.

Weakened Military

Immediately after the conflict terminated in March 1991, the military, Saddam's major source of support, was gravely weakened, its once proud reputation as the most powerful military in the Gulf shattered, its ranks and materiel depleted, its morale destroyed.

- Declarations of victory and medals distribution notwithstanding, the Iraqi armed forces, including the Republican Guard, became disillusioned with Saddam.

- The standard of living for soldiers had reached the lowest level ever. Logistical supplies were unavailable for the most part.

- They saw the no-fly zone over the north and south as humiliating. Moreover, Kurdish control over much of the north was a painful reminder that Iraq was powerless and at the mercy of the United States.

- The U.N. sponsored weapons inspections were a continuing humiliation and demonstration of Saddam's lack of control over Iraq's sovereignty. The sanctions were perceived as a serious detriment to the national economy and security.

- This, and the military defeat, led to a rising tide of desertions, which was one of the reasons for Baghdad's decision to demobilize units. The armed forces shrank from over one million to just over 400,000.

- The rising tide of disillusion and resentment led to repeated coup attempts.

- In March 1995, two regular army brigades suffered severe losses from clashes with Jalal Talabani's Kurds and The Iraqi National Congress (INC), further humiliating Saddam and the military.

Fractures in Tribal Loyalty

Within the larger Sunni tribal system there were signs of weakening solidarity. Of the five most important Sunni tribes that had once been the core of Saddam's support and were in leadership roles throughout the military, four fell under suspicion. A 1990 plot involved Jubbur members of the Republican Guards and regular army units. Jubburis live in Saddam's home-town, Tikrit, as well as south of Baghdad and south of Mosul. Officers of the 'Ubayd tribe, in and around Tikrit, were purged in 1993-1994, and very prominent members of another Tikriti tribe, the Jawa'inah, were purged in 1993 for an alleged plot. Al-Bu Nimr (of the Dulaym tribe) in and around Ramadi revolted against Saddam in 1995 and were crushed viciously by Udayy Saddam Hussein (Saddam's elder son) and his Saddam's Martyrs militia.

Frictions within Saddam's al-Bu Nasser tribe compounded problems, by late summer 1996 five "houses" within the tribe had grievances with Saddam or his family: parts of the Majid branch, to which belonged the Kamils (Saddam's paternal cousins and sons-in-law, whom his body guards gunned down soon after they returned from Amman, having defected there in August 1995); the Haza'; the Ibrahim Hasans (Saddam's half brothers), the Bakrs (the extended family of the late president), and the Msallat (the extended family of Saddam's maternal uncle). While Jubburis, Dulaymis, and 'Ubaydis, as well as members of the partly alienated "houses" in al-Bu Nasser continued to serve in Republican Guard and key security positions, they were removed from the most sensitive positions and were closely watched.

Overall, the threat of a large-scale tribal uprising remained remote, but when the regime was on the verge of collapse both in 1991 and 2003, many in these tribes and "houses" defected. When it comes to Shi'ite Tribes in the south, while many of them collaborated with the regime, only a few, if any, were fully committed. All were going through the motions of expressing unbound loyalty to the historical leader Saddam, but it was "loyalty at the barrel of a gun." At the first sign of disintegration many remained on the sideline to see where the wind was blowing and switched sides during Operation Iraqi Freedom once it was thought safe to do so. Many years of hardship in the volatile Iraqi countryside taught them harsh lessons and the need for caution.

Fault Lines in the Family

Udayy Saddam Hussein

The temperament and unconstrained behavior of Saddam's late elder son Udayy (born 1963), was a continuing issue. He had a reputation as the "bad boy" of Iraq, and was greatly feared among the population of Baghdad. He had been involved in several widely publicized incidents, but Saddam had regularly either overlooked Udayy's excesses or if the event was too public to ignore, dealt with it in the mildest of manner. In 1988, Udayy murdered Saddam's valet, Hanna Jojo, who had facilitated a love affair between Saddam and Samirah Shahbandar, the wife of Nur al-Din Safi, an official in Iraqi Airways. Eventually, Saddam had her divorce her husband and marry him; the ex-husband was promoted to chairman of the board and general manager as a consolation prize. He also received an apartment in the luxurious 28 April housing complex near al-Karkh Quarter in Baghdad.[14] In 1986, Samirah gave birth to Ali Saddam Hussein.

The affair angered Saddam's first wife (and maternal cousin) Sajidah to no end, and Udayy supported his mother in the dispute. Udayy beat the valet to death in full view of all the guests at a party in honor of Suzanne Mubarak, wife of Egyptian President Hosni Mubarak. As a result of this, Saddam jailed Udayy and put him on trial for murder, but family members of the victim "pleaded for leniency" saying that Udayy's deed was "the will of God," and thus he ought not be punished. Saddam released and exiled Udayy to Switzerland, where he lived with his uncle. A few months later Udayy was declared *persona non grata* by the Swiss authorities because he attacked a Swiss policeman. Udayy returned to Iraq and began reintegrating himself into the Iraqi power elite. He became the de-facto minister of youth; the czar of the Iraqi media and sports; and, in early 1995, his father allowed him to establish a militia force, Fida'iyyi Saddam (Saddam's Martyrs). This was a most unruly crowd, badly trained, poorly armed and remarkably dilapidated, but they were his to play with.

In 1995, Udayy shot his maternal uncle, Watban Ibrahim Hasan, in the leg. Watban was then the minister of the interior, in charge, among other responsibilities, of the police and General Security (*al-Amn al-'Amm*). The near-lethal confrontation was the culmination of at least two years of acrimonious political struggle, partly in the full glare of the Iraqi media, for prestige and power and, possibly, for wealth. This created a major crisis between Saddam and his half brothers, two of whom he had re-integrated into his security system only five-six years earlier (between 1983 and 1989 they were out of favor and out of jobs).

The night before the Udayy-Watban shooting incident, General Hussein Kamil defected with his brother, Saddam, their wives, who were Saddam Hussein's daughters, and a few cousins. Hussein Kamil was, at the time, in charge of the formidable Military Industrialization Organization (MIO) and one of the people responsible for the fearsome Special Security Organization (al-Amn al-Khass SSO) that was responsible for concealment of Iraq's weapons of mass destruction (WMD). Hussein Kamil's brother was a colonel in the Special Republican Guard. Once in Amman they started a series of revelations regarding Iraq's WMD that created a major crisis between the regime and the U.N. Their most important information related to Iraq's biological weapons.

Udayy was the main reason for this defection. Prior to the defection he threatened Kamil's life if the latter would not cease his attempts to re-take control over very lucrative assets Udayy had snatched from him while Kamil was recuperating from a brain surgery. According to some reports Udayy was also very involved—indeed central—in orchestrating the murder of Hussein Kamil and his brother after they returned to Iraq in February 1996. There is no doubt, however, that Saddam ordered the murder of Kamil and his brother ensuring in the process that those who did the killing took responsibility for it. The most remarkable fact about the assassination was that members of the hit team were carefully chosen to represent the five generations of Saddam's khams or lineage.[15] Saddam made sure that five generations of his family (Kamil was Saddam's cousin) would be involved in the murder, as this is the canonical structure of a tribal kham. In so doing, Saddam deflected guilt from himself and made it extremely difficult for an embittered extended family member to single him out as the target of a retributory blood feud.

Even before this, however, Saddam was outraged by the havoc his elder son was wreaking on his political-security system. He relieved Udayy of all his duties and even burned down a garage in the Presidential Palace compound housing a few of his son's most cherished (and expensive) vintage cars. This was the second time Udayy's recklessness placed his father at a disadvantage, but Saddam was unwilling to fully neutralize his elder son.

In December 1996 during an assassination attempt on Udayy, his car was raked with automatic gunfire, leaving him bedridden for at least six months with both his legs paralyzed.[16] By 2002, he seemed to have recovered from most of the adverse effects of his injury. No less importantly, his father re-instated him in all his previous duties, including control over the Fida'iyyun, now a 20-30,000 strong force, better equipped, and trained by the semi-professional General Muzahim Sa'b Hasan, a member of the clan.

From 1998 until his death in 2003, Udayy was free to sabotage his father's system for the third time. To limit his elder son's ability to do damage and to humiliate him, Saddam promoted Qusayy, Udayy's younger brother, above him and indicated that Qusayy was to be the heir apparent.

Qusayy

While Udayy was part of Saddam's problem, Qusayy was part of the solution. As reported to one of the authors (AB), even as teenagers the two brothers were very different from each other. Udayy was out of control, widely flaunting his privileges, while Qusayy was disciplined and hard working. Saddam could not help but notice it. Since 1989, Saddam had been preparing Qusayy for the duty of czar of internal security. Qusayy had worked closely with the former head of internal security General Abd Hamid Mahmud (or Ihmid Hmud). They were in charge of the SSO, the most formidable of all security bodies, and in charge of security inside all other security bodies, including the Himaya and the Special Republican Guard (SRG). The president's security rested mainly on them, but they were also in charge of the more lethal links of Iraq's non-conventional weapons in terms of concealment and deployment. Had Saddam given the order to launch non-conventional missiles they would have been the ones to do it, and there is a good chance they would have done so, since the SSO was considered to be the most disciplined organization in Iraq.

Qusayy was also the supreme authority for "prison cleansing," the execution of hundreds of political prisoners to make room for new ones in Iraq's crowded prisons. He also authorized executions of military and security officers suspected of disloyalty. Between 2001 and 2003, Qusayy was also a member of the Regional Leadership of the Ba'ath Party in Iraq, and Deputy Secretary of its important Military Bureau (*al-Maktab al-'Askari*).[17] According to the constitution, the chairman of the Revolutionary Command Council (RCC), who was also the president of the state, must come from among the RCC members, and RCC members must be from the wider body of the party's all-Iraqi Regional Leadership (RL). Thus, the promotion of Qusayy to the RL was probably the first step toward his planned inclusion in the RCC and, eventually, his promotion to the RCC Chairmanship and President, had the regime survived. According to unconfirmed reports Udayy, too, presented his candidacy to the RL, but failed. If true, then his anger and frustration were likely even greater. Ironically, the two brothers died together while on the run after the regime was toppled during OIF.

Strategic Shift

The family disarray culminating in Hussein Kamil's defection and assassination, together with the decline of Udayy and of Saddam's half brothers, signaled a certain change of strategy. No longer could the loyalty of the extended family be unquestioningly relied upon. Rather, it was necessary to strengthen the Ba'ath Party and rely more centrally on long standing party loyalists and on more distant members of the tribe, and the coalition of tribes. By 2002, the Ministers of Defense, Oil, Interior, the Director of Military Industrialization, and the Commander of the Republican Guards were no longer family members as in the past. At the end of the regime these sensitive positions were held by Ba'ath Party loyalists.

In a less formal fashion, Saddam also brought back into his political "kitchen" the most senior party member in Iraq, Dr. Sa'dun Hammadi, who, for many years, had been languishing in the political desert as member, then Speaker of the National Assembly. Udayy and Qusayy, too, were sometimes summoned to the "kitchen," and Cousin Ali Hasan al-Majid is almost always there, but it is more balanced than before. This is due to the fact that Ali Hasan was a party old timer, and other members were all old party hands. These included Tariq Aziz (whom Udayy had attacked viciously a few times before, demanding his ousting), Izzat Ibrahim, who since 1991 was Deputy Chairman of the RCC, and Vice President Ramadan.[18]

It should be emphasized that some distant cousins, and many tribe members and Tikritis were still placed in very important security positions, and they were indispensable as a security shield for the regime. However, save for Qusayy, the role of the extended family had clearly been reduced and the party old timers were becoming more prominent in the political arena and in the seam between the political and security realms, the ministries of defense and the interior. Accordingly, by mid-2002 Saddam relied on a more balanced party, Tikriti tribe and family power base.

Redemption and Restoration of Morale Courtesy of the Kurds

In late August 1996, Saddam Hussein authorized elements of the Republican Guard to attack the Kurdish city of Irbil following the Patriotic Union of Kurdistan (PUK)'s securing of limited military assistance from Iran. The Guard smashed the PUK and the U.S.-backed Iraqi National Congress (INC), as well as some CIA operations in Kurdistan. The seizure of Irbil was a major success for Saddam. This triumph, coming after a series of setbacks and reminders of their diminished status, restored the morale of the Republican Guard (and their faith in Saddam).

The success demonstrated the regime was still very much in control and was a major power throughout the country. It also showed the fractioned nature and impotence of the opposition movements in Iraq and was a powerful demonstration of the risk of rising against Saddam. This was a major turning point for the regime in terms of restoring its power position – had the Guard not taken Irbil it is likely that Saddam's support would be so undermined that his position would have been in grave jeopardy.

U.N. Resolution 986

Facing an imminent economic collapse in 1996, Saddam was forced to accept U.N. Resolution 986, the so-called oil-for-food deal. To Saddam, this represented a great humiliation because it glaringly infringed on the national sovereignty of Iraq, and indirectly on Saddam's personal honor. Saddam also feared it would undermine international pressure to lift the sanctions imposed on Iraq following the Gulf War.

Eventually Saddam had no choice but to accept the recommendations of his economic advisers. On November 25, 1996, Iraq announced its acceptance of the Resolution. Saddam's success in Irbil, combined with the

191

exposure of a military coup and the execution of the revolutionaries made the Resolution acceptable.

These events highlight Saddam's vulnerability in the summer of 1996. He needed a way to restore the Iraqi military morale and to demonstrate his own strength and power to his own people.

Advantages from accepting Resolution 986 were considerable. The sale of oil greatly improved Iraq's international and regional standing. That the food and medicines distributed to the population alleviated the people's suffering was less important to Saddam than the fact that, from now on, he could save the sums he previously had to spend on food for his impoverished people. The disadvantages were minor by comparison, as credit for the increase in supplies went mainly to the regime, not to the U.N. It did diminish the regime's ability to trumpet as loudly as before the suffering of the Iraqi people.

It may be that the crisis Saddam provoked with the U.N. in October-November 1997 over UNSCOM or UNMOVIC inspections could have been prompted by fear that the humanitarian issue would no longer be an issue, and that the embargo would remain. In reality, the Iraqi regime still trumpeted the suffering with considerable success, with the help of Western humanitarian groups.

Full cooperation with international inspections would be out of the question, for this would have meant disclosing voluntarily his remaining advanced weapons technological secrets. Retaining at least the perception of a WMD program was central to Saddam's leadership concept.

Strengthening International Support

In the events leading up to the 1991 Gulf War, Saddam had been extremely isolated, misjudging the impact of his actions not only upon his Arab neighbors, the so-called "near abroad," but also on major international actors on whose support he had previously been able to count, especially Russia and France. Grandiose and assumptive, ethnocentric, and surrounded by compliant sycophantic advisers, he had with regularity seriously miscalculated both the risks of his actions and the degree of his support. His foreign policy initiatives since have demonstrated a much surer and more sophisticated hand.

Petrodollars to Buy International Support

Since the end of the Gulf War and the establishment of the Northern and Southern no-fly zones, Saddam's political priorities were, not necessarily in the following order, to end the embargo and to end Western patrols over the zones. A lower priority was to reoccupy the autonomous Kurdish region. Since the George W. Bush administration came to office, Saddam's main priority shifted to the prevention of an American military offensive against him. A very important part of Saddam's campaign to achieve at least most of his priorities had been a diplomatic and economic "love offensive" directed mainly at his previous enemies. Faithful to his *modus operandi* inside Iraq, Saddam had been adding threats that an attack on Iraq will meet with a ferocious reaction against American interests.[19]

The main tool in Saddam's "love offensive" had been Iraq's growing buying power as a result of the accumulation of petrodollars in Saddam's personal coffers and in Iraq's New York Security Council escrow. Other tools, important as well, was an ostentatious "return" to Islam and high profile support for the Palestinian *intifadah* that erupted in September 2000.

The Near Abroad

Saddam was quite effective in his pre-2003 diplomatic efforts towards the "near abroad." He achieved a reduction of tensions with his lifelong enemy Iran, accomplished a significant rapprochement with both Saudi Arabia and Syria, the latter especially significant given Syria's September 2001 election as a non-permanent member of the U.N. Security Council. For economic and political reasons, even Jordan's distance from and tensions with Iraq were reduced. Saddam's strong embrace and support of the Palestinian cause was of great assistance in his courtship of these previously estranged Arab neighbors. Turkey's economic losses because of the sanctions against Iraq ($6-7 billion annually), coupled with their joint interests in countering their restive Kurdish population, regularly led Turkey to resist actions that would magnify Iraqi-Turkish tensions.

Recognizing these areas of joint interest, Iraq intensively pursued a diplomatic offensive to draw Turkey closer to it and away from the U.S. Significantly, Turkey refused the United States use of its territory, ports, or air space in Operation Iraq Freedom.

Syria

The most telling case in terms of Saddam's *modus operandi* when he feels weak and under great threat was provided by his tremendous resolve to mend his fence with his oldest Middle Eastern rival, President Hafiz al Asad and his son's successor regime. The years 1997-1998 saw the beginning of a new relationship between the two countries. Saddam extended an olive branch to Asad and the latter reciprocated in kind. Although ties were mainly limited to economic and diplomatic areas, this relationship was the beginning of Iraq's acceptance back into Middle Eastern politics.[20]

In November 2000, Syria announced the establishment of full diplomatic relations with Iraq. Less than three months later, in early January 2001, Syria announced "all Syrians can from now on travel to Iraq without any restrictions and all passports will not bear the 'excluding Iraq' sign."[21]

The two countries signed a free-trade agreement the result of which mutual trade volume was to grow from $500 million in 2000 to around $1 billion in 2001.[22] According to some reports, in 2001 mutual trade actually reached almost $2 billion.[23] These reports seem inflated, but even if the trade volume reached only $1-1.5 billion (most of it Syrian products sold to Iraq) this was of huge benefit to the Syrian economy. By the middle of 2002, it was estimated that the annual value of trade exchange between the two countries exceeded $3 billion.[24]

In November 2000, the old Kirkuk-Banyas oil pipeline, shut down by the Syrians in April 1982 in order to cripple the Iraqi war effort against Iran, was reopened. A few months earlier, in August 2000, a rail connection for smuggling Iraqi oil to Syria was opened. The old pipeline started delivering between 100-200,000 barrels a day.[25] To make detection difficult, Syria had been using the Iraqi oil for its own consumption, selling Syrian oil abroad instead.[26]

Iran

After taking power in 1997, Iranian president Khatami sought to improve relations with the U.S. and Saudi Arabia, something that worried Saddam a great deal. However, those relationships have not had the expected impact, which left more room for an improvement of Iraqi-Iranian relations.

Since the two countries signed only a ceasefire agreement in 1988, it is surprising that a slow rapprochement has taken place at all. From Saddam's viewpoint, burying the hatchet with the Iranians had been a very high priority. Confronting the Americans, British, and the Iranians was something that Iraq could simply not afford. Also, Iranian cooperation over oil smuggling was very useful to Iraq. Finally, as long as mutual relations do not reach rock bottom Saddam may reasonably expect that the Iranian support for the Shi'ite underground will be limited. The aggregate result is a very baffling cocktail of mutual acts of sabotage, mutual verbal attacks, mutual calls for improving relations, and occasional mutual visits of foreign ministers and other officials. There were a few fairly large-scale exchanges of prisoners of war, especially in 1998, and Iranian pilgrims were allowed to spend a week in Iraq, visiting the holy places of Najaf, Karbala, and Kazimayn (a Baghdad suburb where two Shi'ite imams are buried).

Turkey

Turkey supported the international coalition against Iraq in 1991. Yet, Saddam was happy to cooperate with it a short while after the war over the smuggling of oil through southern Turkey. Turkish-Iraqi economic ties saw a quantum leap since December 1996. This was when Kirkuk oil started to flow again through the old pipeline and Turkey started to reap legitimate oil transit revenues. Just before the invasion of Kuwait, Turkey's annual exports to Iraq amounted to around $400 million. In 2000, it reached almost the same annual rate as in 1990, $375 million, and in 2001, it almost doubled to $710 million.[27] By the end of 2001, it was estimated that in 2002 Turkey would be exporting to Iraq products to the tune of $2 billion.[28]

Turkey's strong ties to the United States and insistence on working with the U.S. on Iraqi matters were a great source of frustration for

Baghdad. Turkish military forays into autonomous Iraqi Kurdistan, too, elicited bitter condemnations from Baghdad. Even though Saddam was no longer in control of Kurdistan, such forays were seen in Baghdad as infringing on its sovereignty. Finally, the Iraqi regime was very critical of the strategic cooperation between Turkey and Israel. At the same time, though, Saddam was aware that Ankara would like to have sanctions lifted because it too suffered from the cut-off of trade and oil trans-shipment revenues from Iraq. He did everything in his power to whet the Turkish appetite, including open calls to breach the embargo. In 1997, the two countries signed an agreement to lay a 1,300 kilometer natural gas pipeline.

Additionally, the Turks were deeply wary of the possibility that if the Iraqi regime was toppled the Iraqi Kurds would declare independence. This might provide Turkish Kurds with a successful independence example and might result in a renewed Kurdish revolt in Turkey. The Turks were often unhappy with the indecisive way in which the Iraqi Kurds were handling the PKK.[29] Saddam used the lure of his business and the fear of Kurdish independence as his main charm points in Ankara, and he played them up continuously. This may have contributed to Turkey's decision not to cooperate with the United States in Operation Iraqi Freedom in 2003.

Jordan

While it did not participate in the international anti-Iraqi war coalition and was unwilling to confront Iraq politically either, Jordan has since the early 1990s, consistently distanced itself from Iraq. It did this in order to mend its fences with the U.S. and to make peace with Israel. The result was a major blow to Saddam's efforts to end his international isolation. When Hussein Kamil defected in 1995 he went to Jordan, where King Hussein publicly supported the notion of a regime change in Iraq. This support for the Iraqi opposition, however, appears to have diminished significantly as Jordan remains heavily dependent on Iraq for cheap oil and trade.[30]

It would seem, then, that much like Turkey, Jordan, too, was getting the best of both worlds: it kept on excellent relations both with the U.S. and Israel, including receiving U.S. economic aid; it thwarted, as best it could, Iraqi attempts to smuggle weapons through its territory to the Palestinians; and there is no evidence recently that they allowed illicit

196

goods into Iraq. Still, Jordan continued to receive cheap oil from Saddam and to trade with Iraq. Saddam was fully aware of the Jordanian practice, but he did not seem to care. For him, Jordan was an important avenue to the outside world.

Even more importantly, securing Jordan's objection to an American attack against him was then his top priority. He rightly feared Jordanian complicity with a U.S. offensive would mean his own immediate demise, as it will provide the U.S. with the most effective bridgehead from where to attack.

Saudi Arabia

Until March 2002, the Saudis remained opposed to the Iraqi regime and moved to improve relations with Iran as a counter to Iraq in the region should the United States not be able to live up to its commitments of security, or should the Saudi regime be compelled to ask the American forces to leave the country. The first deviation from this stance occurred in late 1997 and early 1998. Some Saudi newspapers started to call for leniency toward Iraq and against American attacks. In December 1997, Prince Abd Allah called upon the Gulf Cooperation Council (GCC) states to "overcome the past with its events and pains."[31] This was interpreted as a call for rapprochement with Saddam's Iraq.

In January 2001 the Saudis had already established a border crossing with Iraq and set up a trade office at Ar'ar in Northern Saudi Arabia. It expected to boost exports to Iraq to about $600 million in 2001 from about $200 million in 2000. The Saudis have been exporting mostly western goods to Iraq, which left Saudi Arabia with a sizeable profit.[32] Saudi Arabia did not go on record demanding an end to the embargo, and it continued to allow U.S. fighter planes to use its territory to patrol the Southern no-fly zone. The latter, rather than economic considerations, seems also to be the reason for the Saudi decision to deny the U.S. land forces any use of its territory when the United States decided to attack Iraq.

This again demonstrated Saddam's shrewd politics. He knew how to exploit his assets in the most effective fashion. He recognized the anti-American sentiment in Saudi Arabia. He also identified Prince Abd Allah's need to receive unanimous support in the Beirut Arab Summit and not to be embarrassed by any dissent. In March 2002, at the Beirut

Summit, Saudi Crown Prince Abd Allah hugged and kissed Izzat Ibrahim al-Duri, Saddam's Deputy Chairman of the RCC, in front of the world's TV cameras. This ended more than a decade of bitter hostility.

Other Gulf States

In Spring 2002, the UAE ratified a free trade agreement with Iraq that had been signed in November 2001. The most significant feature of this deal is that the six members of the GCC will merge their markets into a customs union in 2003. This will give Iraq open access to the entire GCC market. By mid-2002, the UAE was already one of Iraq's biggest economic partners in the region.

The only Gulf state that, by mid-2002, was still hostile to Saddam's regime was Kuwait. Despite Iraq's alternating offers of "friendship" and undisguised threats, Kuwait has steadfastly refused to improve bilateral relations. In January 2002, Saddam offered to allow Kuwaiti officials to visit Iraqi prisons to prove there were no Kuwaiti POWs being held. Kuwaiti officials refused and continued to be highly critical of the Iraqi regime. It seems that Kuwait was also sympathetic to the idea of an American-inspired violent regime change in Baghdad.

Egypt

Egypt was the main Arab participant in the anti-Iraqi coalition of 1990-91. Despite this, Iraqi-Egyptian relations started to pick up significantly the moment Iraq's buying power surged. Trade became meaningful and in January 2001 Iraq and Egypt signed a free trade zone agreement. According to Iraq's Trade Minister, Muhammad Mahdi Salih, upon his visit to Cairo, the mutual trade in 2000 reached $1.2 billion, triple the 1999 figure. The minister expressed hope that in 2001 the volume would go beyond $2 billion.[33]

The Iraqi Minister of Trade, Saddam's chief economic adviser, was not a shy man. He made it very clear to the Egyptian media that "lifting [the] international sanctions imposed on Iraq will provide Egypt an opportunity to export further goods and products to the Iraq market, a matter that would lead to increasing the volume of trade between the two countries. The Iraqi Minister explained that when the embargo was lifted, Iraq's oil revenues would reach $30 billion annually. This, he pointed out, was "a matter that would open the door for a real upsurge in trade between Egypt and Iraq." Egypt, he added, ranked first amongst Arab countries that have trade relations with Iraq. Egypt ranked fourth among Iraq's world trade partners [after France, Russia, and China, in this order].[34]

The Far Abroad

Ultimately, it was the "far abroad" that tried to come to Saddam's rescue. France, Russia, China (three of the permanent members of the U.N. Security Council which have the power of veto in addition to the United States and Great Britain) and more distant Arab countries, such as Egypt, were able to put pressure on the U.N., particularly the United States and Great Britain. Prior to Operation Iraqi Freedom in 2003, these countries took up the fight that sanctions were hurting the Iraqi people more than the regime and that lifting sanctions was the only way to alleviate the suffering of the Iraqi people – creating a sense that Washington, not Iraq, was increasingly isolated.

- Russia continued to speak out against using force to bring about resolution to the Iraq situation.

- France continued to actively speak out against sanctions, leading a bloc of European opposition to U.S. military operations by threatening to veto strong resolutions in the U.N. Security Council.

- China opposed the sanctions, but was more passive than Russia and France.

Saddam's patient diplomacy towards Russia and France, both of which have significant economic interests in an Iraq freed of economic shackles, permitted Saddam to challenge the UNSCOM inspections regime with relative impunity, knowing these Security Council powers could be counted upon to weaken reprisals against Iraq. China too supported his beleaguered regime in international forums.

Buying Off Superpowers: Russia as an Example

The oil pumps in Kirkuk had hardly started to send crude again through the Iraqi-Turkish pipeline to the Mediterranean port of Dortyol in December 1996 when Saddam Hussein realized the magnitude of his blunder in rejecting continuous U.N. offers to enter into oil-for-food arrangements. True, such arrangements were detrimental to Iraq's sovereignty, but there were other U.N. practices that followed the invasion of Kuwait that were far more damaging both to Saddam's pride and Iraq's sovereignty, a difference Saddam never fully grasped.

Saddam could not order everything he wanted. This was because all Iraqi contracts were monitored by U.N. Security Council 668 Committee, so when Iraq ordered dual-use items, they were usually rejected by the Committee or placed on hold. Still, Iraq was, at liberty to order humanitarian goods from whomever it wished. Very quickly this became Saddam's most important tool in his "love offensive" that was designed to buy off world superpowers as well as small and poor nations.

One demonstration of the newly acquired Iraqi popularity was the Iraqi annual trade fair in the fall of 2000. Some 1,450 firms from 30 countries, many of them in the West, laid out their wares there.[35] Even rich countries like France and superpowers like China and Russia could not ignore the lure of Iraqi buying power. It is important to note that Iraq owes Russia at least $7 billion, and France at least $4 billion. An end to the embargo may mean that Iraq could pay them back. Iraqi sources made no secret of the fact that they were using this power to bribe the superpowers and move them to support the Iraqi cause.

When one superpower would balk and refuse to obey Iraqi instructions (for example, Iraqi demands from Russia to start developing oil fields before this was approved by the Security Council), senior Iraqi officials would openly threaten that superpower with economic retaliation. When it came to clear cut violations of U.N. Security Council Resolutions, however, no country, including Russia and China, dared so far to confront the USA.

The Iraqi buying power and promises for lucrative oil field development contracts seemed to be at least one of the reasons that persuaded Russia, France, and China to show a more sympathetic position to Iraqi demands at the U.N.[36] Indeed, in an anti-embargo gathering in

200

Moscow, Yevgeny Primakov, a senior Russian Middle East expert, parliamentarian and ex-Prime Minister, made it very clear that "we would like Baghdad to create a regime of preferential treatment for Russian entrepreneurs." A Russian foreign ministry spokesman disclosed that Russia's overall losses as a result of the Gulf crisis and embargo against Iraq amounted in mid-2001 to $30 billion. Russia constantly has been pushing for, in the words of the foreign ministry, "new approaches to the problem of Iraq."[37]

Russia also objected strongly to the American patrolling of the no-fly zones in Iraq's north and south. For example, in January 2001, the Russian Foreign Ministry declared, "the establishment of the so-called no-fly zones over that country [Iraq] is absolutely illegitimate."[38] In exchange for these sympathetic Russian positions the Iraqis gave them some lucrative contracts, including the development of large oil fields.[39]

By 2001, not surprisingly, Iraq's leading trade partners were, in the following order: France, Russia, and China, followed by Egypt.[40] By mid-August 2002, the world media gave wide publicity to a new economic agreement in the making between Russia and Iraq. In itself it did not come as a surprise, but its order of magnitude was truly staggering at $40 billion. The information came from the Iraqi Ambassador to Moscow, Abbas Halaf. No doubt this was yet another Iraqi initiative designed to create tension between Russia and the U.S. and make it more difficult for the latter to attack Iraq, but the Russian government did not deny the information. The agreement was for five years and included new cooperation in oil, irrigation, agriculture, transportation, and electricity. According to American sources this deal represented a breach of the international sanctions on Iraq.[41]

Occasionally the Iraqi government also threatened other European countries with economic retaliation if their position in the U.N. were not sufficiently pro-Iraqi.[42] Poland, too, was forced to change its position and criticized the U.S. and Britain for their no-fly zone monitoring activities. The Iraqi threats were so effective that it took no more than eight days to change the Polish position, after they had implied support for an American-British attack on Iraqi ground-to-air battles.[43] There may be little doubt that the Iraqi tactic, combining punishment (that was not always needed) and temptation, was quite successful. Even countries whose trade relations with Iraq were rather limited, like Switzerland and

Norway, decided to open special offices in Baghdad, clearly an important diplomatic achievement for Saddam.[44]

Saddam's Propaganda Campaign in the USA

In the early 1990s, Saddam realized that he could not rely on greed when it comes to persuading the U.S. administration to lift the embargo. There is little doubt that many American oil companies and business men would have liked to do business with Iraq, but American political inhibitions in that respect were so powerful that the only deals were legitimate ones, within the framework of the oil-for-food program.

However, very early on, Saddam identified a promising avenue in the USA. Rather than greed, in the U.S. it was more promising to turn to idealism. His propaganda machine used the suffering of the Iraqi people as a political asset. A large number of well-wishing humanitarian organizations were caught in his net. Having allowed them to visit Iraq and often provide humanitarian aid, he took advantage of their fear that any criticism of his regime would result in denial of entrance visas.

Most humanitarian bodies also were ill prepared. They had very limited acquaintance with the Iraqi social, economic, and political system. Saddam thus managed to use them as his emissaries to the American public. These delegations did not realize, or were unwilling to realize, that most of the responsibility for the massive death and malnutrition of the children of Iraq was Saddam's. They reported the suffering, often greatly exaggerating it, taking the Iraqi propaganda machine data at face value, but they did not report the true reasons for it. Their conclusion was uniformly that the embargo should be immediately abolished.[45]

Busting the Embargo

After Saddam humiliated himself by reversing his initial decision to reject U.N. Security Council Resolution 986, once the Iraqi oil started to flow again to the world's markets the Iraqi president was under great pressure to demonstrate that the embargo, if not dismantled was, at least, dissipating. Doing this took time, but Saddam and his advisors eventually proved their competence. The embargo's main purpose—to prevent Saddam from being the sole arbiter where Iraq's oil revenues would go—succeeded, but he managed to erode many other aspects of the embargo.

Eroding the oil embargo essentially was accomplished on four different levels. By far the most important one was a substantial increase in the amount of oil smuggled out and sold illegally. The smuggling route through Turkey by tanker lorries had been functioning almost since the end of the Gulf War, but this was a limited avenue due to obvious logistical limitations. Oil sales to Jordan, too, to the tune of around 100,000 barrels per day, started a short while after the Gulf War, except these sales were approved by the United Nations. The official reason provided was that this was the only way Iraq could repay its national debt to Jordan of about $800 million. After a few years this debt was paid back in full. Still, the arrangement continued.

By the late 1990s, the Iraqi leadership felt the need to perform a quantum leap in its illicit oil sales. This happened through two new avenues. One was the Syrian pipeline, and the other was a maritime route from a specially constructed oil terminal south of Basra through the Shatt-al-Arab, hugging the Iranian coast within Iranian territorial water and then crossing the Gulf to the ports of the Arab Emirates.[46] By early 2001, the most reasonable assessment of how much the Iraqis were smuggling (excluding the U.N.-approved Jordanian part) came from Dubai and cited the quantity of 350,000 barrels a day. If this rate continued throughout the year, and the current prices for a smuggled oil barrel (around $12, roughly half the world market price) remained the same, then the annual revenue expected to go into Saddam's private pocket was to be around $1.5 billion.[47] This was, indeed, a quantum leap compared to the assessment of Iraq's illicit revenues of $600 million for the year 2000.[48]

Another avenue through which Iraq managed to earn illegal petrodollars was through a surcharge of between 15-30 cents per barrel, even though this was in contravention of Security Council resolutions. The U.S. and U.N. made efforts to stop it but only with partial success. Iraq had been circumventing the embargo also in the realm of imports, from new cars and luxury goods to spare parts for Iraq's military. Finally, there were numerous reports that Iraq bought legitimate goods but paid more than they were worth. The difference was handed back by the producers to Saddam's men and went into his private coffers.

It was just as important to the Iraqis to actually bust the embargo, as it was to boast about it. It was also to boost domestic morale and, at the same time, dishearten the U.N. and the U.S. Thus, for example, Under Secretary of the Foreign Ministry Nizar Hamdoon said to a Western reporter in Baghdad in early 2001: "Many people and businesses [in the world] are doing business with Iraq regardless of the sanctions regime . . . practically, the sanctions regime is crumbling."[49]

The Palestinians: Every Suicide Bomber Is Protecting Saddam

In Saddam's eyes, the Palestinian intifadah that started in September 2000 was the best guaranty against an American attack, because it kept the Arab world volatile, and threatened the moderate Arab regimes. He probably believed that the higher the flames, the more difficult it would be for the U.S. to attack him. As Saddam saw it, if, as a result of a large-scale Palestinian terrorist operation ("mega-terrorist operation," as it is called in Israel) the Israeli side may lose its inhibitions and perform a massacre, all the better, because such an atrocity might guarantee American paralysis over Iraq for a long time. Seen from Saddam's viewpoint, the intifadah should continue indefinitely. This demonstrated again what was one of Saddam's most salient characteristics, namely, his willingness to fight his battles at the expense of others, be it the Iraqi people or the Palestinians.

Unlike his military, that was in terrible shape, Saddam's coffers were full prior to his regime's demise in 2003. Accordingly, he had been giving financial support to families that lost their sons or daughters in the Palestinian intifadah. At first those were sums of $10,000 for each family that lost a son or daughter. Later, families whose sons or daughters became suicide bombers started to receive $25,000. The checks were handed over in small ceremonies by Saddam's representatives, members of the pro-Iraqi Ba'ath Party or of the pro-Iraqi Arab Liberation Front (ALF). On such occasions a poet would recite a panegyric praising Saddam, people would call for Saddam to bomb Israel, and certificates would be given to the families in addition to the check.[50]

In addition, Iraq informed the Palestinian authority and public that it had asked permission from the Security Council to dedicate one billion Euros (around $940 million) from its New York escrow to the intifadah.[51] There are other forms of support that, while not substantial, were still

204

serving Saddam's propaganda machine. For example, a few of the intifadah wounded were hospitalized in Baghdad.[52] Also, Iraq sent a number of lorries through Jordan and the Jordan River bridges to the West Bank full of humanitarian goods. Israel allowed these lorries to cross over. It is hardly surprising, therefore, that Saddam was highly popular with the Palestinians.

As reported by a foreign correspondent, in one case he witnessed a mother of a young man who died in a confrontation with the Israeli troops who shouted, "Saddam is the father of all the Arabs! He is the bravest example of how an Arab leader should be." Palestinian babies were named after Saddam and people called upon him to strike at Tel-Aviv again as he had done in 1991: "Dear Saddam, Hit, Hit Tel-Aviv!" (<u>Saddam ya habib, udrub udrub Tal-Abib.</u>)[53]

A "Return" to Islam As A Survival Technique

Since 1989-1990, Saddam Hussein's image in Iraq, and in large parts of the Arab world, was no longer that of a secular leader. Sometime towards the latter stages of the Iran-Iraq War (1980-1988) he realized that there was a shift in the Iraqi public toward more religiosity. He also had to defend himself against Khomeini's public accusations that he was an atheist (mulhid) and an enemy of Islam. His religious rhetoric escalated immediately following the invasion of Kuwait and the beginning of the American troop buildup in Saudi Arabia. He realized that his only help could come from the Arab and Islamic world and correctly believed that this world was far more religious and fundamentalist than he and his regime.

Since August-September 1990, Saddam had been presenting himself as the Slave of God (Abd Allah) who knows what God wants of him, of the Iraqis, of the Arabs and Muslims. As early as 1990-91, this new rhetoric won him tremendous admiration among Muslim fundamentalists in the Middle East. Probably the most interesting admirer he had was Shaykh Buyud Tamimi, leader of the Islamic Jihad Bayt al-Maqdas in Amman. This was, and still is, the most radical Islamist movement in Jordan. Shaykh Tamimi had attacked him during the Iraq-Iran War, but in 1990 he called Saddam "the New Muslim Caliph Marching From the East."

There is no doubt that the shaykh was well aware that in his life style Saddam was not a religious man, but he believed that Saddam's

205

rhetoric was a good beginning and that eventually he would become a good Muslim. Furthermore, Saddam represented to him, and to many others like him, the military might of resurgent Arab Islam, whatever his personal conduct. Indeed, Saddam became an Islamist (at least rhetorically speaking) two or three years before Osama bin Laden did, and their styles are very similar.

But this is not all. In 1994, Saddam introduced into Iraq the Qur'anic punishment of severing the right hand for the crime of theft. He then added the amputation of the left leg in the case of recidivists. He forbade the public consumption of alcohol in Iraq. In the late 1990s, he introduced the death sentence, in most cases by decapitation with a sword, for the "crimes" of prostitution, homosexuality, and providing a shelter for prostitutes where they can pursue their occupation. This was implemented in most part without proper trial and scores of young women were beheaded in front of their homes.

Since 1989, Saddam demonstrated to one and all that he prayed five times every day like a devout Muslim. Frequently, he stopped government meetings and meetings with foreign diplomats, retired to another room, either pretending to pray or actually praying, and then he returned to the meeting.

According to an extensive report by the prestigious *al-Sharq al-Awsat* that came out in five parts between January 6–10, 2001, the new emphasis on religious studies at all levels of education, including universities, was enhanced by the end of the 1990s to the extent that it reportedly "disrupted the education program." That the regime used mosque preachers for anti-American propaganda was not new, or the fact that all public ceremonies opened with a prayer. But that more and more female party members donned the veil was indeed new. An Iraqi weekly magazine, al-Zaman, asked Iraqi actresses, "Why don't you don the veil and pray?" The magazine lamented that these actresses had been following "the suggestions of Satan," with their "nakedness and hot kisses." One can see more and more portraits of the president kneeling in prayer. The President of Saddam University for Islamic Studies, Muhammad al-Sa'id, praised the regime for "communicat[ing] the Islamic thought to people through television, radio, newspapers and seminars."[54]

Another component of the Islamization campaign was the construction of extravagant mosques. For example, the Grand Saddam Mosque, under construction since 1999 and located on the way to the International Airport, was huge, second only to the one at Mecca in size. Saddam built the Mother of All Battles Mosque in central Baghdad, a very unusual architectural creation. Surrounding the dome are eight minarets. Four of them are shaped like Scud Missiles sitting on a launching pad, the other four like anti-aircraft guns. Inside the mosque lies a Qur'an inscribed, as reported, in the blood of the Iraqi leader. The visitors were told that Saddam donated no less than 50 pints of blood to write the holy book.

Shaykh Qaysi, the mosque's preacher, explained: "Our leader, the great believer, Saddam Hussein, always called on people to go back to religion and real values . . . He is our example, our school in religion and faith. Our great project now is to start teaching the sayings of the Iraqi president in universities." Western journalists report, however, privately many Iraqis complain about the exorbitant amount of money invested in building these mosques.[55] The mosque's preacher must have been fully aware of the implication of what he said, namely, that Saddam was encouraging his people to see him as anything between a Mahdi and a prophet.

Last but not least, the regime was worried about Shi'ite loyalty in the case of a military confrontation with the United States. General religiosity that applies to both the Sunni and Shi'ite creeds was believed to be of help, but Saddam felt the need also for some special gestures towards the Shi'a in particular. Most notably since the rise of Ayatollah Khomeini to power in Iran, Saddam "nationalized" the main Shi'ite occasions and presented himself as the genetic offspring of the first and third Shi'ite Imams, Ali and Al-Hussein, and of the Prophet.[56] In January 2001, Udayy Saddam Hussein declared that he is studying "Shi'ite rite in depth" and Shi'ite thinking in general and he criticized his own ministry of religious endowments for not building enough mosques in the Shi'ite areas.[57] It is not clear how helpful all these religious practices were to Saddam, but they do show how flexible he was in his approach to his own ideology, tossing it overboard whenever expediency dictates.

At the same time, however, Saddam did not toss overboard his old time supporter, the Christian Deputy P.M. Tariq Aziz. Apparently, this would have looked like total capitulation to the fundamentalists, and this is where concessions stop. Also, there are Christians among his bodyguards and it would be a mistake to arouse their wrath. It is clear that loyalty was a one-way street and only those who were seen to be serving Saddam with total loyalty would survive.

Why Weapons of Mass Destruction?

Beginning in 2001, apparently in response to the Bush administration's declaration of resolve to change the regime in Baghdad, Saddam started meeting regularly and publicly with his nuclear scientists. In these meetings he and his scientists were dropping hints that can only be interpreted as intended to tell the U.S. that, in case of an attack on Iraq, the latter may have some nuclear surprises up its sleeve. For example, when Saddam met with his head of the atomic energy organization, Dr. Fadil Muslim al-Janabi and his men in February 2001, he told them: "the bottom line is to defend Iraq. In so doing we defend the Arab nation . . . We will never hesitate to possess the weapons to defend Iraq and the Arab nation."[58] In a similar meeting a few months later Dr. Janabi made a pledge in the name of his organization: "We swear to be a formidable force . . . in the service of Iraq and its proud people, and when the confrontation and noble battle against the Zionists and the Americans would start."[59]

It is very clear that to Saddam, the first reason for developing non-conventional weapons was to deter external enemies. The USA is not the only enemy. On Iraq's Eastern front there is Iran, with a long history of confrontations and with three times Iraq's population and territory. To the North there is Turkey, again much larger and with a much larger and better equipped armed forces. Iraq is locked in an unresolved dispute with Turkey over the water of the Euphrates. In May 1990, Saddam threatened Turkey's Prime Minister, Yilderim Akbulut, upon the latter's visit to Baghdad, Turkey was exposed, with NATO having fallen apart.

But Saddam's *modus operandi* implied that such weapons were necessary also for domestic purposes, and for regional offensive ones. In the first place, the use of chemical weapons against the Kurds, especially in March 1988, which caused widespread panic in Iraqi Kurdistan, proved to be an extremely effective weapon against unprotected populations. It is not far-fetched to suggest that, in the case of another wide-scale Shi'ite revolt in the south, a few chemical bombs or artillery shells on a densely populated area would nip in the bud any popular revolt.

Biological and nuclear weapons are useless in a domestic context because they contaminate the area for a long time. Such weapons, however, are very useful for anyone aspiring to regional hegemony and international recognition as a superpower. Indeed, in April 1990, Saddam threatened Israel with annihilation ("I shall burn half of Israel"), unthinkable without weapons of mass destruction. There is every reason to believe that, if Saddam ever had nuclear weapons to match those of Israel, he would have been rattling them and offering every Arab and Islamic State that would request his protection the Iraqi nuclear umbrella. In fact, even before he became a nuclear power, Saddam promised the Arabs such an umbrella against Israel and even promised Arafat to use the Iraqi missiles in order to push Israel out of Jerusalem and the Palestinian territories.

In a meeting between Saddam's younger half brother, Watban Ibrahim Hasan, and Iraqi nuclear physicist Ali al-Shaharastani in 1979, the former told the latter that Iraq needed nuclear arms "to change the map of the Middle East." It is not clear what exactly this meant, but it could conceivably mean an Iraqi takeover of the Arab side of the Persian Gulf, and Iraqi leadership of the Arab world.[60] Finally, in his ongoing contest for prestige and authority with his army officers, Saddam needed WMD to demonstrate to them how he can win wars literally single-handedly. True, one cannot win wars without an army, but the relative weight of the WMD component within the armed forces, especially if Iraq had become a nuclear power, was of the essence, and Saddam could have been trusted to rub it into his officers' heads.

To Saddam, to be understood to have nuclear weapons, and WMD in general, was considered important. Major leaders have major league weapons. Moreover, for a person with tremendous insecurities as Saddam, these weapons can offer security that cannot be matched by any other, a necessary deterrent, especially since the Iraqi military was grievously wounded by the 1991 conflict. Moreover, defying the international community on this matter was a regular reminder to the military that Saddam would not capitulate.

To make sure that these weapons were always at his disposal and could be used ruthlessly and indiscriminately without any qualms and

209

inhibitions exactly when and where he wanted, Saddam is believed to have placed them in the hands of the SSO. These were the people who are closest to him by blood (most of them hail from his own tribe) and who were regarded, together with the Himaya, as the most disciplined and obedient to him. In other words, these people, who would push the buttons, were the closest to what one would see as an extension of Saddam's self. After all, Saddam molded these people in his own image.

Weapons of mass destruction also could have provided Saddam with an extremely potent tool with which he believed he could fulfill his manifest destiny, i.e., to unify all the Arab lands under his leadership, to put Israel in its right place, and to become a world leader no less important than any leader of the superpowers. Since 1990, he had also been aspiring to be recognized as the single most important Islamic leader. No wonder, then, that Saddam had been so reluctant to part with his WMD program, even though this obstinacy cost him, between 1990 and 1997, at least $100 billion, and thereafter still cost him in terms of his inability to fully control most of his petrodollars.

A nuclear-armed Saddam would have taken a quantum leap in power, and his already swollen ego would be further enlarged. One could well anticipate a game of nuclear threats and counter threats within the region, especially towards Israel, as he did in 1990 when Saddam threatened "to burn half of Israel." It is likely that Saddam would have attempted to dictate oil prices internationally and would likely have entered a state of permanent nuclear brinkmanship.

Weapons Inspections

Despite tactical retreats in Oct-Nov 1997, and Jan-Feb 1998, Iraq succeeded in winning important concessions on the sanctions front relating to weapons inspections. This was crucial in continuing to build Saddam's support among the Iraqi people – it was seen as a victory. The embargo was dissipating slowly, and yet Saddam did not have to be seen giving up his WMD. Before the regime's demise in 2003, the Iraqi people had achieved in Saddam's last year a better standard of living, many aspects of the embargo being gone.

Saddam's message on sanctions changed over the years. While still defiant in the face of the West, in his last years in power he claimed that sanctions were a disaster, so full of holes there is no point in continuing with them. Sanctions fatigue was an argument commonly used by outside observers in support of lifting sanctions. Increasing international dissent on sanctions highlighted by efforts of France, Russia, and China as well as some Arab states to lift sanctions continued to strengthen Saddam's argument that there is no real point to sanctions by the late 1990s. For example, Russian, French, and Arab pressures prevented the U.S. from adopting military measures to force Saddam to accept weapons inspectors after they left in December 1998.

- Following intense pressure from France, Russia, and China a compromise was reached ultimately allowing Iraq to export as much oil as they wanted while the international community continued to limit imports (ineffectively). This compromise dramatically weakened the impact of international sanctions.

- Saddam continued his propaganda by claiming that sanctions seriously limited medical supplies to the Iraqi people, resulting in untold deaths. All the while, he continued to rebuild his military machine.

- In the fall of 1997, U.N. weapons inspectors were refused entry to "presidential sites" on the basis that it would "impugn national dignity and sovereignty." Although weapons inspectors claimed that Saddam used these presidential sites as storage facilities for his WMD arsenal, there were no inspections. This defiance of the international inspection regime bolstered Saddam's image internally.

Indeed, when UNSCOM left Iraq in December 1998 and inspectors were not allowed back, this was a major victory for Saddam in the eyes of many Iraqi people. The United Nations had been forced out of Iraq, and Saddam was unscathed. Until forced to reverse policy in late 2002, the challenge to the U.N. inspections regime in particular had strengthened his internal support, diminishing the internal threat, as he demonstrated his ability to weaken and challenge the international coalition and still retain the coveted WMD program. The divisions within the U.N. that Saddam helped promote were so deep that Saddam concluded he was essentially immune to U.N. reprisals for pursuing unconventional weapons programs, which became all the more important to him given the weakening of his military in terms of personnel, conventional weaponry, and materiel. Since 1999, there were no meaningful coup attempts. Those officers who might have challenged a leader perceived to be a loser did not dare challenge a leader who challenged President Clinton for eight years and emerged victorious. The re-imposition of inspections in 2002, under threat of war by the U.S. and the U.K., may have caused some Iraqis once again to reevaluate their support.

Return to International Community / Change of Image

After the 1991 Gulf War, Saddam continued to work to increase his standing in the international community, seizing on opportunities to bolster his image within the Arab community.

- In October 2000, a hijacked Saudi airliner landed in Baghdad. All passengers were released unharmed and returned to their home countries resulting in a great deal of international praise for Saddam Hussein.

- The offer in January of 2002 to allow Kuwaiti officials to inspect Iraqi prisons, which was turned down, was a calculated step to garner international favor.

- The unrest of the Palestinian people following Sharon's visit to the Temple Mount was another opportunity Saddam capitalized on. Saddam spoke out against the visit, unlike many of his Arab counterparts who were hindered in doing so because of their relationships with Israel and the United States, earning him a great deal of admiration in the Arab world. Saddam pledged $881 million (USD) from oil revenues for the Palestinian people.

- In October 2000, signaling the change in Iraq's position in the Arab community, Iraq was invited by the Arab League to participate in their annual meeting for the first time since the invasion of Kuwait.

- In August 2000, Venezuelan President Hugo Chavez bucked international convention and traveled to Iraq to meet with Saddam Hussein. He was the first head of state to visit Iraq since the Gulf War, again signaling Iraq's growing acceptance in the international community.

• In January 2001, humanitarian flights began arriving daily from abroad. Iraqi airlines began operating (even in the no-fly zones), and oil-production recovered to pre-war levels. Food rations increased, power cuts were less severe, drinking water and sewer services dramatically improved.

• Baghdad International Airport re-opened in the fall of 2000, another sign of normalcy returning.

The Use of International Crises: Sustaining Power and Weakening Internal Threats

Saddam found that, in times of domestic unrest, international crises are helpful in his retaining power in his country, and allowed him to stunt the growth of the internal opposition. Naturally, whenever he triggered an international crisis, Saddam also believed he would emerge from it not only intact but also victorious, with tremendous prestige and authority, at least in the Arab world. But even when this latter hope was dashed, he managed to pull through by switching his *modus operandi* from trouble-making to trouble-shooting.

This was the case in 1980, when he tried to solve the Shi'ite problem by attacking Shi'ite Iran. Even before that, in 1977, he tried to deflect Shi'ite anger by accusing Syria of plotting to mass murder Shi'ite pilgrims in Karbala. This brought relations with Syria to a new low.

In 1990, he invaded Kuwait in order to "escape forward" from a desperate economic crisis that resulted from a very dangerous crisis of expectations inside Iraq. The paradox during the last few years was that over this time the foreign arena saved him from very serious domestic problems by eroding the embargo and giving him much diplomatic support. France, Russia, China, and some Arab states have demonstrated to one and all inside Iraq that, to them, Saddam was the legitimate leader and that he was gradually winning the diplomatic battle against the U.S. This strengthened his position domestically.

In short, emergencies Saddam fabricated helped him a great deal in his efforts to terrorize his own population. It is not clear whether, had he known that the international crisis he was going to initiate would cost him years of hardship, he still would have initiated it. After all, years of hardship produce their own domestic dangers. Still, so far, whenever he grossly miscalculated the risk, he also managed to wriggle out of the danger zone he created for himself. He did this mainly through patient, pragmatic foreign policies that looked like the complete or partial reversal of his previous behavior of high stakes gambling. He relied on foreign countries, mostly Russia and France, but even the U.S. once, to save him, and he was never wrong. His string of foreign policy successes, while gradual and earned through patience and long-term planning, strengthened him domestically.

Even when he challenged a world power, he always managed to manipulate other major powers and some Arab states, getting them to support him and prevent his downfall. For Saddam, success was not limited to the elimination of domestic opposition. Such elimination was only a pre-condition to achieve his great ambitions in the Middle East and world arenas. However, in order to be able to become a world-class leader he needed, in the first place, to control the domestic scene, and in his mind control meant absolute control, namely, the complete elimination of any opposition. In order to achieve this, Saddam was always ready to confront anybody, including world powers.

Saddam found that international crises were helpful in retaining power in his country, and his string of foreign policy successes allowed him to stunt the growth of internal opposition. For Saddam, success primarily meant strengthening his domestic position even at the expense of his international posture. The most damaging outcome of any crisis was one that showed him a failure as a leader. Thus, Saddam regularly promoted international crises to shore up his internal position.

While assuredly Saddam's position prior to Operation Iraqi Freedom was much weaker than it was on the eve of the invasion of Kuwait in 1990, he demonstrated a more sophisticated leadership both in terms of internal security vulnerabilities, and also diplomacy both with his Arab neighbors, the "near abroad" as well as with the "far abroad," and accomplished a great deal to reduce his vulnerabilities and to strengthen his position, both internally and internationally.

Conclusion

Saddam's survival in power was always his continuing goal. A life out of power was seen as akin to death for Saddam. A rational calculator who could bob and weave and was astutely Machiavellian, Saddam shrewdly managed to sustain the loyalty of his military and to weaken the international opposition for 24 years until Operation Iraqi Freedom ended his regime.

That he has been sophisticated and better attuned to the context of his leadership both internally and internationally does not lessen a still persistent danger, that when Saddam is backed into a corner, his customary prudence and judgment might have been apt to falter. On these occasions he could have been dangerous to the extreme, violently lashing out with all resources at his disposal. The persistent calls for regime change may have moved him into that dangerous "back against the wall" posture had not U.S. military strikes removed him from power.

The setting afire of the Kuwaiti oil fields as he retreated in 1991 is an example that might well have been repeated with his own Iraqi oil fields, as if to say, "If I can't have them, no one will."

The question then is the degree to which he continued to sustain the loyalty of his senior military commanders until Baghdad fell or whether they were induced to disobey Saddam when placed in extremis in order to safeguard their own futures. The melting away of this force in Iraq after several divisions of the Iraqi Revolutionary Guard were destroyed by allied bombing answers the question of regime loyalty. Once bloodied south of Baghdad, the rest of the force in Baghdad dispersed.

The explicit statement of Secretary of Defense Rumsfeld suggested Iraqi military officers could play a role in the reconstruction of a post-war Iraq, but if they become involved in WMD, all such bets are off. Similarly, President Bush's recommendation that senior military commanders disobey Saddam's orders were aimed at splitting Saddam from his senior leadership. The leafleting of the battlefield indicating that any commander who ordered the use of weapons of mass destruction would be held guilty under the war crimes act further consolidate the information operation.

At this writing, it is uncertain whether Saddam is dead or alive. It was thought that Saddam would not go down to the last flaming bunker if he had a way out, but that he could have been extremely dangerous and might have stopped at nothing if he was backed into a corner, if he believed his very survival as a world-class political actor was threatened. It was believed that Saddam could have responded with unrestrained aggression, ordering the use of whatever weapons and resources were at his disposal, in what would surely be a tragic and bloody final act.

But note the word "ordering." As noted above, the information campaign which attempted to split Saddam from his senior military leadership may well have led them to disobey his orders. Moreover, Saddam could not have used these weapons too early, for the disarray in the international community that he had fostered would surely dissolve, were he to reveal that he possessed these weapons. The success of the information operations campaign in concert with the rapid effectiveness of the U.S. air strikes in Operation Iraqi Freedom may well have blocked Saddam's capacity to escalate the war and employ possibly hidden weapons of mass destruction.

Notes

1. This assessment draws extensively on "Saddam Hussein of Iraq: A Political Psychology Profile" by Jerrold M. Post, M.D. presented in testimony to hearings on the Gulf crisis by the House Armed Services Committee, December 5, 1990 and the Foreign Affairs Committee, December 12, 1990, and *Building Toward Crisis: Saddam Hussein's Strategy for Survival*, Amatzia Baram, 1998, The Washington Institute for Near East Policy.

2. Professor of Psychiatry, Political Psychology and International Affairs, The George Washington University, Washington, D.C.

3. Professor of Middle Eastern History, University of Haifa, Israel.

4. The details of Saddam's pre-natal and early childhood history are based on an extensive interview with Nasimah, an elderly member of the Jewish family that saved Sabha's life and looked after her just before and after she gave birth to Saddam, conducted by one of the authors (AB) in Tel Aviv, February 2, 1991. These details were confirmed again by Nasimah's son, Yigal, in a telephone conversation on July 1, 2002. For more details, see a report by Peter Waldman of A.B's 1991 interview with Nasimah

in *The Wall Street Journal*, February 7, 1991. Also: Amir Iskandar, *Saddam Hussein, Munadilan wa Mufakkiran wa Insanan* (Paris, Hachette, 1980), 15-19.

5. See, for example, Judith Miller and Laurie Mylroie, *Saddam Hussein and the Crisis in the Gulf* (New York: Times Books, 1990). Also: personal interviews. In an interview with his biographer Saddam exposed his hate for his step-father that seems to corroborate these interviews. See Iskandar, Ibid., 353.

6. See Iskandar, 22-25.

7. For Saddam's admiring, yet ambivalent approach to Nasser see Amatzia Baram, "Saddam Hussein and Nasirism," in *Orient* (Hamburg), 3/2000, 461-472.

8. *FBIS*, Near East Report, 8 August 1990.

9. Matlak, Regis, *Inside Saddam's Grip*, NSSQ. Spring 1999.

10. Based on an interview in 1999 in Washington, D.C. with a senior ex-UNSCOM official who, in his own turn, interviewed General Hussein Kamil in Amman. Kamil was with Saddam when the first bombs fell on Baghdad.

11. DeHart, James and Jerrold Post, "Responding to Qaddafi," *The Christian Science Monitor*, January 7, 1992.

12. See Amatzia Baram, "Neo-Tribalism in Iraq: Saddam Hussein's Tribal Policies 1991-96," in *International Journal of Middle East Studies*, Vol 29 (1997), 13-14.

13. See Amatzia Baram, "Calculation and Miscalculation in Baghdad," in Alex Danchev and Dan Keohane, *International Perspectives on the Gulf Conflict 1990-91* (NY-Oxford: St. Martin's Press and St. Antony's College, 1994), 44-46.

14. Al-Majalla (London), Sept 5-11, 1999, 31-41.

15. See Baram, op. cit., 15 for a detailed breakdown of the assassins and their family lineage.

16. For details see Amatzia Baram, *Building Toward Crisis: Saddam Hussein's Strategy for Survival* (Washington, D.C., The Washington Institute for Near East Policy, 1998), 8-20.

17. Al-Hayat (London), June 18, 2001, 2, in *FBIS-NES GMP20010618000048*, June 18, 2001.

18. For example, *Baghdad Republic of Iraq Radio Main Service* in Arabic, March 12, 2001, in *FBIS-NES GMP20010312000090*, March 12, 2001. And for more, see Baram, "Building Toward Crisis," 37-44.

19. For example: Saddam on Victory Day, Baghdad Radio, August 8, 2002; Taha Yasin Ramadan, Radio Baghdad, August 17, 2002.

20. For details of the period 1991-1998 see Baram, *Building Toward Crisis*, 87-96.

21. *Reuters* from Damascus, January 4, 2001.

22. *HaAretz*, Feb. 1, 2001.

23. *MENA Report.com*, May 27, 2002.

24. *Iraq Press*, June 25, 2002.

25. *Iraq Press*, June 10, 2002, as reproduced by Washington Kurdish Institute, June 11, 2002. *Reuters*, March 7, 2001, Evelyn Leopold reporting from the UN. And see report by Peg Mackey from Dubai, *Reuters*, Feb. 14, 2001, according to which the oil flow to Syria was then 170,000 barrels per day. Also *AP* from Baghdad, January 23, 2001, in *WKI*, January 23, 2001.

26. Barbara Crossette, *The New York Times*, March 7, 2001. *AFP*, Brussels, Feb. 27, 2001.

27. *Turkish Daily News*, June 26, 2002.

28. *Anatolia*, Nov. 2, 2001.

29. For details, see Baram, "Building Toward Crisis," 109-122.

30. Ibid., 123-136.

31. *Jordan Times*, Dec. 24, 1997.

32. *Reuters*, Jan 24, 2001, in Washington Kurdish Institute, Jan. 24, 2001.

33. *Xinhua* (the official Chinese News Agency), Feb. 14, 2001, in Washington Kurdish Institute, Feb. 14, 2001. *MENA*, in English, Jan. 18, 2001, in *FBIS-NES- Serial GMP 2001 0118000178*, Jan. 18, 2001.

34. An interview by Salih to *MENA*, in English, Cairo, Jan. 18, 2001, in *FBIS-NES Serial GMP 2001 011 8000028*, Jan. 18, 2001.

35. Jason Burke, *The Observer*, Jan. 21, 2001.

36. See for example Iraq's Trade Minister, Muhammad Mahdi Salih threatening France that "it will not be given preference in trade transactions...because of its support

of the stupid anti-Iraq draft resolution on sanctions." On the other hand the minister promised that "Syria, Jordan, Turkey and Russia will be given priority...in the upcoming stage in appreciation of their stands rejecting the wicked U.S.-British draft resolution". *Baghdad Republic of Iraq Radio Main Service in Arabic*, July 9, 2001, in *FBIS-NES Serial GMP2001 0709000143*, July 9, 2001. See also *Babil*, Internet version in Arabic, July 9, 2001, implied threat, urging China and France to reconsider their "opportunistic" position regarding the new sanction proposal in the Security Council.

37. *Associated Press*, from Moscow, April 9, 2001.

38. See Moscow's "extremely negative reaction" to these patrols, *Moscow Interfax in English*, reporting a foreign office communiqué, Jan. 30, 2001, in *FBIS-NES Serial CEP2001 013000 0151*, Jan. 30, 2001.

39. See for example, Russian "penetration" into the West Qurna field, to the chagrin of the European powers, Andrew Boroweic, *The Washington Times*, Jan. 18, 2001.

40. *Xinhua*, April 2, 2001.

41. *HaAretz*, Aug. 18, 2002, 1, 3.

42. See for example, threats by Baghdad's *al-Thawra*, March 1, 2001: "The Italian Government must rectify its position of which we have taken note." Denouncing the Italian Foreign Minister Lamberto Dini, the party daily added, "the stupid statement [by Dini] will affect relations between the two countries."

43. See Trade Minister Muhammad Mahdi Salih announcing that Iraq is lifting the restrictions on imports from Poland after the Polish government modified its position on the US-British "aggression" against Iraq. Iraq had decided to stop its commercial dealings with Poland and Canada on Feb. 20, 2001. The Polish government "officially clarified...it does not support or back" the air patrols. *Baghdad Republic of Iraq Radio Main Service in Arabic*, Feb. 29, 2001, in *FBIS-NES Serial GMP 2001 0228 000129*, Feb. 28, 2001.

44. For Switzerland, *Reuters*, from Baghdad, Feb. 1, 2001; Norway opening an embassy, an announcement by Foreign Minister Thorbjoen Jagland, quoted by Simeon Kerr, *Countries*, Jan. 26, 2001, in *Washington Kurdish Institute*, (WKI @ Kurd.org), Jan. 26, 2001.

45. For an example of such a delegation, see details of a US Muslim delegation calling for the end of sanctions, *Dawn*, April 8, 2001. Other such groups are for example, Voices in the Wilderness, and even some UN agencies. For an analysis of the causes of the suffering and its results see Amatzia Baram, "The Effect of Iraqi Sanctions: Statistical Pitfalls and Responsibility," in *Middle East Journal*, Vol. 54, No. 2 (Spring, 2000), 195-223.

46. See for example, *AFP*, from Dubai, Feb. 5, 2001, quoting British officials in the Gulf.

47. Peg Mackey, *Reuters*, from Dubai, Feb. 14, 2001. The assessment was that close to 150,000 barrels a day went through Turkey, 170,000 barrels a day went through Syria and the rest through Iranian territorial waters and some illicit exports to Jordan. A somewhat more liberal assessment puts the Iraqi earnings from illicit oil sales at around $2 billion. See *Financial Times*, Feb. 6, 2001.

48. *Reuters*, Feb. 6, 2001.

49. *Toronto Star*, Feb. 3, 2001.

50. See for example, *Baghdad Republic of Iraq TV*, in Arabic, Feb. 9, 2001, in *FBIS-NES Serial GMP 2001 10209000194*, Feb. 9, 2001.

51. *AFP*, Jan. 24, 2001.

52. *The Christian Science Monitor*, Feb. 2, 2001.

53. See, for example, Nidal al-Mughrabi, reporting from Gaza, *Reuters*, Jan. 17, 2001.

54. Mariam Fam, *AP* from Baghdad, Feb. 2, 2002. See also similar observations about more people frequenting mosques and more veils seen in the streets of Baghdad. Kim Ghattas, *BBC*, April 25, 2002.

55. Kim Ghattas, *BBC*, April 25, 2002. See also, Hala Jaber, *Sidney Morning Herald*, Nov. 11, 2001.

56. See Baram, "Re-inventing Nationalism," *The Princeton Papers*, Ibid.

57. *Al-Quds al-Arabi* (London), Jan. 10, 2001, p. 3, in *FBIS-NES-Serial GMP 2001 0110000146*, Jan. 10, 2001.

58. *Baghdad Republic of Iraq TV*, in Arabic, Feb. 1, 2001, in *FBIS-NES Serial GMP 2001 0227000217*, Feb. 27, 2001.

59. *Babil*, (internet version in Arabic), July 8, 2001.

60. For details about Saddam's non-conventional strategy see, Amatzia Baram, "An Analysis of Iraqi WMD Strategy," *The Non-Proliferation Review* (Summer 2001), Vol. 8, No. 2. 25-39.

CHAPTER 8

Syria Under Bashar al-Asad: Clinging To His Roots?

Christopher Hemmer

Introduction

"When there is a storm the need is greater to cling to the roots, to principles and to the constants which are our roots. No matter how long the storm might last it is going to stop and when you try to stand up after the storm you will not be able to unless you have roots."

-Bashar al-Asad[1]

Upon the death of Hafiz al-Asad in June 2000, *The Economist* quipped that Syria had seemingly "lost a dictator and gained an ophthalmologist."[2] The transfer of power from a long-time military strongman to his medically trained and politically inexperienced son was bound to raise expectations of change in a society whose stability under 30 years of Hafiz al-Asad's rule bordered on paralysis. The challenges Bashar and Syria face are formidable. As Glenn Robinson notes, Syria is in many ways an anachronism, it is a minority dominated authoritarian state in the age of democracy and a statist economy in the age of the market.[3] Internationally the challenges are just as stiff. The ongoing conflict with Israel over the Golan Heights, continuing regional challenges from Iraq and Turkey, a Lebanon increasingly restive under Syrian rule, and a United States paying more attention to Syria's support for international terrorism, all pose challenges that Bashar will have to grapple with.

The initial transfer of power from father to son went far smoother than many had expected, a significant accomplishment in a country where as David Sorenson notes, coups are the traditional means for succession.[4]

Within days of his father's death, Bashar quickly assumed leadership positions in the three most important formal governing institutions in Syria; the armed forces, the Ba'th Party and the central government. Colonel Bashar quickly became Lt. General Bashar, the head of the Syrian armed forces, and he was also selected to replace his father as Secretary General of the Ba'th Party. At the same time the Syrian Parliament amended the constitution to lower the minimum age for the presidency from 40 to 34, which in a stunning stroke of good fortune for Bashar just happened to be his age at the time.[5] The Regional Command of the Ba'th Party then nominated Bashar for the presidency, a nomination that was quickly seconded by the Syrian Parliament. One month after the death of Hafiz, the Syrian people played its role in a presidential referendum in which Bashar's elevation was approved by a vote of 8.6 million ayes to 22,000 nays. While some may see 97.29 percent of the vote as a landslide, it represents a precipitous fall from Hafiz's 99.98 percent in his previous anointing as president.

What previously had been seen as a rather unlikely succession scenario had come to pass.[6] Beyond some quickly silenced grumbling from Hafiz's brother Rif'at from exile in Europe, Syria's transformation into a hereditary republic went virtually unchallenged. With these initial leadership hurdles cleared, Bashar now has to face Syria's problems. The purpose of this chapter is to offer an early assessment of Syria's direction under Bashar, focusing especially on Syria's foreign policy dilemmas and its relationship to the United States. The following section explores Bashar's personal history and worldview. Since many of Bashar's most important initial actions focused on economic and political reforms at home, the third section explores the status of the reform process and how the political power structure within Syria affects Bashar's decisions. The implications of this analysis for Syrian-U.S. relations under Bashar is the subject of the fourth section, with Syria's position in the current war on terrorism discussed in the fifth section. The chapter ends with a brief discussion of U.S. policy options regarding its relations with Syria.

In trying to forecast the future course of Syrian foreign policy, an understanding of Syria's international position and Bashar's domestic position will be just as, if not more, critical than understanding the personality and worldview of the Syrian President himself. Since internationally and domestically Bashar finds himself in much the same position his father did, the United States and the world can expect more continuity than change from Syria as the challenges Bashar faces will lead him to cling to the legacy and policies of his father. When Patrick Seale ended his monumental biography of Hafiz al-Asad, he asked his subject how he would like the biography to end. Hafiz's response was "Say simply that the struggle continues."[7] Bashar has now inherited that struggle.

Four Faces of Bashar al-Asad

In trying to sort out what Bashar al-Asad is like as a leader, four competing images are prevalent. Some see Bashar as a westernizing reformer, others as a virtual clone of his father, others as a political novice ill-prepared for the task of holding power in Syria, and still others see him as youthful statesman whose inexperience could lead to crises and a worsening of regional tensions. Since each of these views offers some insight into Bashar al-Asad, the purpose of this section is to explore each of the four.

Bashar was never supposed to become president; his older brother Basil was the one everyone expected to step into his father's shoes. It was Basil that was given the grooming, positions, and exposure thought necessary to prepare for an important role in Syrian politics. Basil's unexpected death in a car accident in January 1994 changed Hafiz's plans and Bashar's life, as the young ophthalmologist was called home just months short of the end of his residency at a hospital in England. At this point Bashar's medical training ended and his apprenticeship in Syrian politics began. Upon returning to Syria, Bashar was a captain, within a year he was promoted to major, the next year to Lt. Colonel, in 2000 to Colonel, and after the death of his father, to three-star general and commander in chief of the armed forces.[8] The new heir apparent was also placed in charge of Syrian relations with Lebanon and headed a high profile anti-corruption campaign.

Those who see Bashar as a nascent reformer stress his experiences prior to assuming his brother's mantle. Looking at his medical training, his years spent living in England, his enthusiasm for the internet and other forms of modern technology, highlighted by his leadership of the Syrian

Computers Users Association, some see Bashar as a westernized modernizer. This impression is particularly prevalent in western media accounts of the new Syrian leader. Capturing this image well is a *Salon* article that asks whether Syria's president is a "geek," noting his image as a "gentle, Westernized man with an interest in computers."[9] Hafiz's quasi-official biographer Patrick Seale sees the new president as "a computer nerd,"[10] arguing that it is "abundantly clear" that Bashar is looking to lead a "profound transformation" as the "protector—even the patron—of the new liberal movement."[11] After meeting Bashar at Hafiz's funeral, U.S. Secretary of State Madeline Albright praised him, hoping he would fulfill his potential to be a "modernizing reformer."[12]

A competing view of Bashar portrays him as his father's son, rather than as a son of modern technology and the West. His brief two-year stint in England, in this view, should not overshadow the fact that, as Bashar himself put it, he was brought up "in the home of Hafez Al-Assad."[13] It is debatable, however, how much interaction he had with his father while growing up and how much he can be considered, as one Syrian writer put it, "a branch of that blessed tree."[14] Upon assuming positions of high responsibility, Hafiz saw little of his family and spent most of his time working.[15] Bashar was not born until September 1965, well into his father's ascent to the upper realms of the Syrian power structure. An indication of Bashar's somewhat distant relationship with his father may be seen in his curious habit of regularly referring to Hafiz not as his father, but as "President Hafiz al-Asad."[16] Indeed, Hafiz's legacy as President will probably weigh far heavier on Bashar than Hafiz's legacy as a father.

A third view, similar to the reformist view discussed above, also sees Bashar as quite different than his father. The emphasis here, however, is on his political inexperience, rather than any alleged reformist tendencies. Referred to, at times clearly dismissively, as "Dr. Bashar" the stress here is on how Bashar's medical training has ill-prepared him for the competitive and often bloody world of Syrian politics. "The Doctor Will Lead You Now" is how one magazine chose to encapsulate this disjuncture between Bashar's professional training and his current responsibilities.[17] Bashar "has not taken to the rough and tumble of Syrian politics" is how Glen Robinson sees it.[18]

A final view, which also stresses Bashar's inexperience, focuses on the dangers this holds for Syria's foreign relations, rather than on Bashar's hold on power domestically. Here Bashar is seen as novice statesman prone to ill-considered rhetoric, hasty moves, and risky behavior that the cautious Hafiz would have abjured. In this vein, some have pointed to a number of inflammatory statements offered by Bashar in the early days of his presidency. At the November 2000 meeting of the Organization of the Islamic Conference, Bashar accused Israel of practicing a "new Nazism" and in falsifying history in its claims on Jerusalem.[19] In January 2001, Bashar painted Israel as "a state based on loathsome racist values and hatred toward Arabs and Islam."[20] In a speech to the 2002 Arab Summit in Amman, Bashar was seen as condoning attacks on Israeli civilians with his argument that the problem was not any particular leader in Israel, the armed forces, or the government, but inhered in Israel's racist society.[21] Upon welcoming the Pope to Syria, Bashar made international headlines by accusing the Israelis of trying "to kill all the principles of divine faiths with the same mentality of betraying Jesus Christ and torturing him."[22] Unlike Hafiz, who came to power considerably chastened by defeat in the 1967 war,[23] Bashar has no direct experience with war, which some worry could lead him to accept risks his father avoided. The major international event that coincided with Bashar's rise to power was not defeat in war, but the Israeli pullout from Lebanon. Possibly learning from this event that Israel can be defeated, Bashar, some fear, may be willing to rush in where his father feared to tread.[24]

Each of these perspectives on Bashar captures some portion of the truth. Bashar has had exposure to the West and to modern technology, he did serve his political apprenticeship under his father, and notwithstanding that, he is relatively inexperienced both internationally and domestically. Which side of Bashar emerges in any particular instance will depend greatly upon the specific situation he is in. Understanding Syria under Bashar will require grappling with the interaction of his temperament with his and Syria's situation.[25] The following section demonstrates how this interaction of personality and situation can help explicate the ups and downs of domestic reforms in Syria under Bashar.

Bashar at Home: The Structural Limits of Reform

Bashar's inauguration speech, which stressed the need for new ideas and active political participation by all segments of Syrian society, gave some measure of hope to reformers within Syria that significant economic and political changes were in the offing.[26] The main impetus for these reforms was the troubled state of the Syrian economy. The debate regarding Syria's economy is not whether it is in need of reforms or not, but is instead a debate over how serious the current problems are.[27] In the early 1990's, with the influx of aid money from the Gulf States following Syria's stand in the Gulf War, an increase in remittances from Syrian workers in the Gulf States, and the discovery of significant pockets of oil within Syria, the Syrian economy experienced a modest boom. Today, these sources of revenue are decreasing rapidly. Syria's oil fields are drying up, as is the aid money and remittances from the Gulf States.[28]

This economic downturn is coming at an especially difficult time given the youth of Syria's population. Close to 45% of Syria is under age 15, which means that large numbers of young adults will be continuing to enter the job market for years to come.[29] By one estimate, the labor force is currently growing well over twice as fast as job opportunities, this in a country with an already high unemployment rate.[30] Moreover, a significant portion of Syrian jobs remains in the inefficient public sector, which is currently losing the equivalent of 10% of Syria's GDP every year.[31] Given this large demand for jobs, it is not surprising that Bashar has prioritized job creation over privatization.[32]

Slow economic reforms had begun under Hafiz, such as the creation of new laws to encourage foreign investment and the Bashar-led charge to bring the internet and cell phones to Syria. Economic reforms have continued under Bashar with the creation of a unified exchange rate and new laws to allow private banks, even some with partial foreign ownership, the right to operate in Syria.[33] While there have been no significant reversals in the economic reform process, the slow pace of change has disappointed many Syrians.

Syria's model in the reform process seems to be China. Wanting to avoid the political collapse that hit the Soviet Union and its East European allies following attempts to reform, Syria prefers a slower paced set of reforms that operate within the existing political system. Another potential model closer to home is Egypt, where economic reforms, some political debate, and elections all take place within the framework of what remains an authoritarian system.[34] This has meant, however, that the political reform process has gone even slower than the already sluggish economic reforms, and that this process has suffered some significant reverses in recent months. The half-hearted nature of the reform process can be found in its most visible slogan, which offers the clunky and far from stirring call for "change within stability and continuity."[35]

Early in Bashar's reign there were some signs that significant political reforms were at hand. For example, Bashar ended the monopoly the Ba'th Party had on Syrian newspapers and has allowed political parties affiliated with the Ba'th in the National Progressive Front to begin publishing their own newspapers and Bashar has also approved the publication of a satirical newsmagazine.[36] Bashar has also discouraged the public display of pictures of himself and his father that are virtually omnipresent in Syria,[37] he has announced that when his seven year term is up he would like to hold a presidential election rather than a simple referendum,[38] and he has released large numbers of political prisoners.[39] When in September 2000 and January 2001 groups of Syrian citizens promulgated calls for increasing political reforms (the Manifesto of the 99 and the Manifesto of the 1,000 respectively), the regime initially did nothing to target the authors or halt the circulation of the petitions.[40] Some of the figures behind these two manifestos were also active in organizing and taking part in private gatherings of political discussion groups throughout Syria. Again, initially, the government tolerated these civil society forums.

The signs of this "Damascus Spring" soon came to an end, however. In February of 2001, the government banned the independent civic forums, requiring all such meetings to receive governmental permission. In September, Bashar issued a decree expanding the number of constraints and regulations on the press, and in August and September some of the leaders of the emerging civil society groups were arrested, including two independent members of Parliament. These two parliamentarians have since been found guilty of "aiming to change the Constitution by illegal means" and sentenced to 5 years in prison.[41]

Much of the explanation for the limits of these reforms, both economically and politically, can be found in the structure of the Asad

227

regime that Bashar inherited. The starting point for most analyses of the Asad regime is its minority nature.[42] Although Alawis, like Hafiz and Bashar al-Asad represent only about 12 percent of the Syrian population, the upper levels of government have been heavily Alawi since even before Hafiz came to power at the head of his "corrective movement" in 1970. While Alawis claim to be and are recognized by many as a legitimate sect of Shi'i Islam, the persistent doubts some hold about this conclusion is perhaps best seen in the continuing ardent efforts of Alawis to have their Shi'i identity recognized by others. For example, in the later years of his rule, Hafiz al-Asad departed from the strictly secular nature of his Ba'thist ideology and began to emphasize his own and his regime's Islamic nature.[43] In some ways, the minority Asad regime is not as surprising as it might seem at first. As Nikolaos van Dam notes, Sunni Muslims represent only 57.4 percent of the population, with the rest being composed of religious or linguistic minorities.[44] The Ba'th revolution that helped pave Hafiz's road to power was built on overturning the dominance of the traditional Sunni/Arab elite, and the minority nature of Bashar's regime could somewhat paradoxically be a source of strength as many Syrians continue to view an Alawi regime as less of a threat than a potential return of Sunni/Arab dominance.

The political coalition that Hafiz passed to Bashar is in actuality much broader than simply an Alawi-dominated military regime, or even a regime dominated by different minority groups. For example, although the revolution that brought the Ba'th Party to power was hostile to the traditional Sunni elite of Syria's major cities, Sunni leadership from rural areas played a key role in stabilizing the Asad regime. This portion of the Asad coalition is still represented by such powerful figures as long-time Defense Minister Mustafa Talas, long serving Foreign Minister Farouk al-Shar' and current Prime Minister Mustafa Miru.[45] Moreover, Hafiz al-Asad, from the very start of his reign, attempted to woo the traditionally dominant urban Sunni business class into his coalition, successfully creating what some have called a "military-merchant complex," combining an Alawi-dominated military establishment with the Sunni urban business elite.[46] The continuing expansion of the state structure under Hafiz also created a significant base of support for the regime in the civil service.[47]

Another pillar of the Asad regime is the network of formal institutions that Hafiz encouraged. As Hafiz himself put it, "I have always been a man of institutions."[48] In addition to the military and the intelligence services, there are also the formal governing structures of a Parliament, a Prime Minister, his cabinet, and a series of executive agencies. On top of the government structure is the apparatus of the Ba'th Party, which has been transformed from its early days as an ideological party to a mechanism for the distribution of patronage.[49] In order to prevent any single institution or its leadership from becoming too powerful and threatening the control of Hafiz and now Bashar, these institutions, especially the military and intelligence services, are often divided, given vague and overlapping mandates, and are put in competition with one another.[50]

Although the Asad regime is broader than an Alawi dictatorship, there is no doubt that as one moves through these organizations, from the formal government, to the party, and to the military and intelligence agencies, and as one moves up each organization, the Alawi presence becomes more and more predominant.[51] As Eyal Zisser notes, while Alawis are only 12 percent of the population, close to 90 percent of the heads of the military and security services are Alawis. This Alawi dominance is especially pronounced in the so-called Praetorian Guards, the military units stationed in and around Damascus.[52] Moreover, Sunni military commanders are usually paired with Alawi deputies and vice versa.[53] These institutions help explain, in part, the ease of the transition to Bashar because institutions are far easier to bequeath to a successor than are personal allegiances.[54]

Since Bashar has assumed power, three broad trends are evident in his dealings with the circle of leadership that surrounds the presidency. First, in a continuation of the last few years of Hafiz's rule, there has been a steady purging of those suspected of opposing Bashar's elevation.[55] Recently, the continued consolidation of Bashar's position has focused on purges from the armed forces especially in the military intelligence branches.[56] The second trend has been moves toward bringing new faces to head the cabinet departments responsible for economic policy, with the Ministry of Finance and the Ministry of Economy and Foreign Trade going to men believed to be in support of reform.[57] The third trend has been continuity in the top jobs under the President, including the Prime Minister, and the Ministers of Defense and Foreign Affairs. For example, Mustafa Talas, long time political ally to Hafiz al-Asad, who had been rumored to be on his way out, has been asked to stay on for at least two more years, even though he is past the legal age for retirement.[58]

Potentially, one of Bashar's most far-reaching personnel moves may have been his choice for First Lady, Asma al-Akhras, a member of a prominent Sunni family from Homs who was born and raised in England. The new First Lady, who holds a degree from King's College in computer science and has worked as an economist for Deutsche Bank and JP Morgan, symbolizes in a very concrete way Bashar's openness to working with the traditional Sunni business elite in pursuing the economic reform process.[59]

Playing down any potential tensions between reformers and traditionalists in Bashar's cabinet, Defense Minister Talas argued that "Syria does not have an old guard and a new guard, but one guard."[60] Despite such assurances, it is clear that any potential economic and political reforms will face an uphill battle given the nature of the Syrian political system. Bashar faces the eternal dilemma that confronts any reformer in office, which is that substantial reforms are likely to jeopardize the political base that put him into power in the first place.[61] Bashar faces the same equation his father did, namely that "key constituencies are likely to be threatened by liberalization, while liberalization's agents and beneficiaries are historic regime rivals."[62] Paring down the bloated and inefficient government sector may make economic sense, but public employees are a key pillar of the current regime's support base. Deregulation of certain industries may make economic sense, but it will also hurt regime supporters whose profits depend on government protection. Decreasing corruption may make economic sense, but access to corrupt profits is one of the most important rewards the regime bestows on its loyal supporters in addition to providing a useful tool that Bashar can and has used to get rid of potential rivals by selectively prosecuting them for corruption.[63] Even though Bashar has continued his father's efforts to bring the Sunni business elite into his coalition, the interests of this group is likely to increasingly diverge from the regime with regard to the pace and direction of reform.[64]

The slow pace of domestic reforms so far under Bashar is indicative of the political constraints he is operating under, regardless of what his personal preferences may be. These and similar constraints must also be kept in mind when thinking about the future course of Syria's foreign policy under Bashar, including the relationship between Damascus and Washington.

U.S.-Syrian Relations: A Persistent, but Moderate Rivalry

Although Syria was not included in George W. Bush's axis of evil, it does possess axis of evil credentials, especially with regard to its support of international terrorism and its Weapons of Mass Destruction (WMD) programs. Washington is also critical of Syrian polices toward the Middle East Peace Process and somewhat more quietly, of the continued Syrian military presence in Lebanon.[65] The purpose of this section is to explore the possibilities for a change in U.S.-Syrian relations with the accession of Bashar. Looking specifically at the Syrian position on relations with Israel, WMD development, its domination of Lebanon, and its policies toward with Iraq, the overall argument of this section is that given Syria's interests and the interests of the Bashar regime in staying in power, the U.S.-Syrian relationship is likely to remain one of low-key rivalry.

Starting with the Syrian relationship with Israel, there seems to be little prospect of Bashar adopting a policy any different than the one pursued by his father. As Bashar has stressed in his public utterances since his earliest days in office, the return of the entire Golan Heights, defined as an Israeli withdrawal to the lines prior to the outbreak of the 1967 war, is a matter of honor and national dignity, not a matter for negotiation.[66] Given that not bowing to the wishes of Israel is seen as one of the greatest accomplishments of Hafiz's reign, it is unlikely that the newly installed Bashar could reverse over thirty years of Syrian policy on such a central issue.[67] In addition to making Bashar look like he can not measure up to his father, any compromise settlement with Israel would reduce Syrian claims on aid from the Gulf States based on Syria's position as a frontline state against Israel.[68] In addition, peace with Israel would also take away a large part of the justification for the retention of authoritarianism at home.[69] Given the collapse of the peace process, which has reinforced Syria's long contention that the Oslo process was flawed from the start,[70] and given recent criticisms within Israel that Ehud Barak's pull-out from Lebanon helped lead to the intifada by making Israel look defeated, both Israel and Syria seem unlikely to make the concessions necessary to meet the demands of the other.

This does not mean that conflict between Israel and Syria over the Golan Heights is likely. Indeed, since 1967, this border has probably

231

been Israel's quietest. While Syria demands the eventual return of the entire Golan, it is also prepared to wait for it, as it has for over 35 years now. The most dangerous aspect of the Israeli-Syrian relationship centers on Syrian support for Lebanon's Hizballah, which will be discussed below in the section on Syrian support for terrorism.

Syria also possesses an extensive chemical weapons arsenal, a biological weapons program, and missile and aircraft programs designed to allow for the delivery of weapons of mass destruction.[71] When asked about this arsenal, Syrian officials sometimes deny they possess such weapons, sometimes maintain they need these weapons to provide a deterrent to Israel, or for those untroubled by logical inconsistencies, sometimes offer both answers simultaneously. Given Israel's possession of nuclear weapons, the continuing hostile relations between the two, and Syria's conventional inferiority in that relationship, Syria's desire to possess a WMD capability is understandable from a national interest standpoint. Even leaving Israel out of the equation, Syria would also have an interest in keeping these weapons as a deterrent against Iraq and Turkey.

While Syria's possession of WMD is likely to remain a source of tension between the United States and Syria, there is little reason to expect this tension to be particularly acute. Syria has viewed these weapons purely as deterrents and as weapons of last resort and Damascus has shown little interest in exporting these weapons to other states or terrorist organizations. Thus, while the Syrian WMD program is unlikely to go away any time soon, it is also unlikely to pose a serious threat to the United States.

The same can basically be said for Syria's domination of Lebanon, where since 1976, Damascus has retained somewhere in the neighborhood of 25,000 troops. In the interest of stability and in the interest of keeping Syria a part of the Gulf War coalition, the U.S. has tended to tacitly accept Syria's military presence in Lebanon.[72] Israel's exit from Lebanon in May 2000 did little to change Syria's calculations.[73] Lebanon remains economically vital to the Asad regime. Its relatively freer economic climate offers an outlet for the Syrian business class, it provides an important source of income for the military commanders stationed in Lebanon, and thousands of Syrians travel to Lebanon to find work.[74] While the death of Hafiz al-Asad may have encouraged certain groups within Lebanon to escalate their calls for a Syrian exit,[75] and despite some recent troop redeployments within Lebanon, Syria is in no hurry to leave.

The situation with regard to Syria's eastern neighbor, Iraq, is more fluid. Although the Ba'thist regimes in Damascus and Baghdad have historically had an uneasy relationship, upon coming to power, Bashar initiated a brief rapprochement with Hussein's Iraq. The Syrian-Iraqi border became increasingly open to trade, official visits between the two capitals became more common, and the pipeline connecting the Kirkuk oil fields in Iraq to the Syrian Mediterranean port of Banyas was the largest single hole in U.N. sanctions against Iraq.[76] The primary driver behind this improved relationship was Syria's economic interests. Damascus was moving to position itself to take advantage of the eventual lifting of U.N. sanctions and while those sanctions were still in effect, cheap oil from Iraq offered an economic windfall during a time when Syrian supplies were dwindling. Further, Damascus' opening toward Baghdad gave concrete form to common complaints heard in the region regarding U.N. and U.S. double standards. As Bashar expressed it, "Iraq is destroyed for the sake of U.N. resolutions and U.N. resolutions are destroyed for the sake of Israel."[77]

At first, the United States took a low-key approach regarding Syria's improving relations with Iraq, choosing even to ignore Bahsar's reneging on a pledge made to Secretary of State Colin Powell to shut down the Iraqi oil pipeline. The U.S. invasion of Iraq, however, put a spotlight on the ties between Damascus and Baghdad and further strained U.S.-Syrian relations. Syria was outspoken in its criticism of the U.S.-led invasion and it was accused of providing direct support for Hussein by shipping arms and by allowing irregular forces to cross into Iraq from Syria. Worries in Washington that Damascus intended to play a disruptive role in post-war Iraq increased following reports that high-level members of the deposed Hussein regime had taken sanctuary in Syria. The result was a brief war of words between Washington and Damascus that subsided almost as quickly as it arose. A brief visit by Secretary Powell as well as Syria's decision to evict a small number of Iraqis and better seal the border, quickly returned U.S.-Syrian relations to their steady, albeit uneasy state.[78]

Syria's Support for International Terror

Given the current war on terrorism, Syria's support for international terrorist groups stands out as the most important item on the agenda of U.S.-Syrian relations. Syria has been on the American list of state sponsors of terrorism since that list was initiated in 1979 and the most recent version of the list, although acknowledging that Syria has not been directly implicated in an act of terrorism since 1986, maintains that Syria continues "to provide safe haven and logistical support to a number of terrorist groups."[79] These groups include the Lebanese group Hizballah as well as the Palestinian Hamas, The Popular Front for the Liberation of Palestine, The Popular Front for the Liberation of Palestine—General Command, and the Palestine Islamic Jihad. Syria allows these groups to retain offices in Damascus, enjoy refuge and basing privileges in Syrian-controlled Lebanon, and allows for the transit of weapons through Syrian territory. Syria's position on this list prevents it from receiving U.S. aid, requires the U.S. to oppose loans to Damascus from international financial institutions, imposes a ban on all U.S. arms sales, and restricts trade in certain dual-use items. Otherwise, U.S. trade with Syria is allowed.[80]

Bashar and the Syrian government were quick to condemn the terrorist attacks of September 11 and to call for worldwide cooperation against terror.[81] At the same time, Syria has resisted cleanly fitting into President Bush's Manichean declaration that in the war on terrorism, "you are with us, or you are with the terrorists." Having fought a long and costly domestic campaign against an Islamic-based opposition that employed terrorism, culminating in the government's bloody destruction of the city of Hama in 1982, the Asad regime shed no tears for al-Qaeda and the Taliban. Bashar even suggested to a visiting U.S. congressional delegation that America could learn a lesson or two from the Syrians about how to quash terrorist threats.[82] This does not mean, however, that Syria is ready to cut its ties with all the groups designated by the U.S. as terrorist. As the State Department notes, Syria is trying "to have it both ways" in cooperating in the crackdown against al-Qaeda, but continuing to support groups like Hizballah and Hamas.[83]

To explain this distinction, Bashar argues that "there is a difference between terrorism and resistance . . . . the difference between one who has a right and the other who usurps this right."[84]   Seeing the Lebanese and Palestinian attacks on Israel as legitimate resistance to occupation, groups like Hizballah and Hamas do not qualify as terrorist groups in Syrian eyes. Beyond this, Bashar's government also insists that the U.N. and not the U.S. should head any war on terror and that instead of just condemning terror, the international community should solve the underlying grievances that spur terrorism.[85]

While Syria's definition of terrorism is certainly subject to debate, what is less debatable are the clear and concrete advantages Syria accrues by adopting this definition and continuing to support certain terrorists groups.   From a strategic standpoint, Syria's central international dilemma is that it is a state with broad regional ambitions, but a lack of resources with which to pursue those objectives. Syria aspires to play an influential regional role, but is decisively outclassed in terms of power resources by three of its immediate neighbors, Iraq, Israel, and Turkey. Support for terrorist groups is a relatively cheap and low-risk way to increase its influence in regional discussions.   Syria wants to regain the Golan but does not have the military or economic capability to make Israel's holding of the territory particularly costly to Jerusalem.   The best weapon the Syrians have in making Israel uncomfortable and giving it an incentive to negotiate is the support Syria offers to groups like Hizballah and various Palestinian groups. Similarly, what means of influence does Syria possess to persuade Turkey to come to a mutually acceptable water sharing agreement? For years, Syria's strongest card was the support it provided to the Kurdistan Workers Party (PKK). Even in Lebanon where Syria has military superiority, support for terrorist groups has also proven an effective way of solidifying Syria's dominance.

Beyond these benefits, Syrian support for terrorist groups has helped it improve its relations with Iran, justify Syria's claim to be the leading Arab state in the struggle against Israel, and serve as a source of revenue for the regime and its supporters. Moreover, support for these groups is also domestically popular, an especially important consideration for a politically inexperienced eye-doctor trying to prove that he is indeed tough enough to lead Syria.[86]

So far, the White House has been reluctant to seriously pressure Syria to cease its support for these groups. While President Bush has stated that it is time for "Syria to decide which side of the war against terror it is on," National Security Adviser Condoleezza Rice, although rejecting any distinction between good and bad terrorism, noted that "the means we use with different countries to get them to stop harboring terrorists may be very broad."[87] The administration's methods with Syria at this point seem to be limited to verbal encouragement. Reasons for this include the value the U.S. puts on Syrian intelligence cooperation against al-Qaeda, a desire not to close off a potential Syrian role in the peace process, and the hope that Syria can be persuaded not to attempt to undermine U.S. efforts to build a new regime in Iraq.

Another important factor limiting the extent of pressure the U.S. is willing to exert on Syria over its support for terrorist organizations is that Syrian support for terrorism has been deliberately crafted to limit the direct threat it poses to U.S. interests. In addition to the use of proxy terrorist groups that distances Syria itself from these actions and restrictions on launching attacks directly from Syrian soil, Damascus has also made a clear choice to discourage attacks on American or Western targets more generally. Even with regard to attacks on Israeli targets, where Syria has shown far less restraint, these attacks are also designed to minimize the dangers of escalation. Syria puts great stress on the implicit "rules of the game" regarding Hizballah attacks and has at times put definite restraints upon Hizballah. Evidence of Syria's desire to continue the terror attacks as a way to pressure Israel while minimizing the chances for escalation can by seen in Syria's lack of response to two Israeli attacks on Syrian positions in Lebanon, which killed Syrian soldiers, in April and June 2001. Rather than respond militarily to these strikes, which had been precipitated by Hizballah attacks on Israeli targets, Syria opted instead simply to continue its support for Hizballah—neither escalating nor lowering the conflict. While the possibility of miscalculation and unintended escalation remains a danger, Syria realizes that a major conflict with Israel or the United States is not in its interests.[88] Although Senator Bob Graham has argued that the threat stemming from terrorist training camps in Syria and Lebanon are "more urgent" than any threats emanating from Iraq, this remains a distinctly minority position in Washington.[89]

Conclusion: Dealing With Syria Under Bashar

Given this analysis, what should U.S. policy be toward Syria under Bashar al-Asad? Here the news includes the good, the bad, and the ugly. The bad news is that there is little the United States can do to stop Bashar from pursuing what the U.S. sees as hostile policies on the most important items on the American-Syrian agenda, like terrorism, WMD, and the peace process. The good news is that this hostility and the extent of rivalry between the United States and Syria is likely to remain limited as neither side has any desire to challenge the core national interests of the other.   The ugly news is that this uncomfortable situation of moderate rivalry is likely to last a long time.

Starting with bad news, when you consider the domestic, international and economic benefits Bashar and Syria accrue from their policies toward Israel, WMD development, and support for terrorism, U.S. resources to encourage a change in these policies come up short.[90] What could the United States offer to Syria to sign a peace agreement with Israel or cut its ties to terrorist organizations that would compensate for the domestic popularity, regional influence, aid from the Gulf States, and the sense of pride Syria feels in its long term refusal to knuckle-under to the pressure of the Israelis and the Americans?   Similarly, what could the U.S. offer Syria to make Damascus willing to expose itself to potential nuclear blackmail from Israel and give up its most credible deterrent to a broad conventional attack from Israel, Iraq or Turkey?

Theoretically, the United States may possess the carrots and sticks to change Syria's calculations, but in reality it is difficult to envision a situation where the United States would see it as in its interests to expend the resources that would be needed. U.S. trade with Syria is fairly minimal, aid is non-existent, and there seems little reason to suspect that there would be political support in Washington for massive aid for Syria. On the stick side, the costs of any military intervention would greatly outweigh the gain, and measures short of that, such as further unilateral sanctions, are likely to be ineffective. The last 35 years of Syrian policy has demonstrated the accuracy of Bashar's contention that Syria is "poor and can tolerate more than expected."[91]

One state that has succeeded in getting Syria to drop its support for international terrorist groups is Turkey. In 1998, Ankara did extract from Damascus a promise to withdraw its support from the PKK, an agreement that Syria has largely abided by. Is the "Turkish model" a potential roadmap that the U.S. could follow?[92] Probably not. In order to get that agreement, Turkey had to risk, threaten, and mobilize for a large-scale conventional war. Turkey was also willing to pair that threat with concessions on a water sharing agreement. While this certainly shows that Damascus is susceptible to military pressure, the United States may be hard pressed to make a similarly credible military threat. Although the toppling of Hussein in Iraq, as well as the Taliban in Afghanistan, certainly demonstrated the capability of the United States to unseat hostile regimes if sufficiently provoked, Damascus has been and will likely continue to keep its provocations well below any threshold that could spark a similar U.S. move into Syria. In addition, the costs and difficulties of reconstruction and state-building efforts in Afghanistan and Iraq, combined with the possibility of increased instability in Iran, also increase the incentive on the American side to keep any confrontation with Syria limited.

Moreover, Syria's benefits from support of groups like Hizballah and Hamas are far greater than anything Damascus gained from its support of the PKK. While Israel certainly presents a credible military threat to Syria, it has not been able to induce Syria to sign a peace agreement or cut its ties to these terrorist groups, and any increased Israeli military pressure on Syria will likely do more to complicate than ease America's policy problems in the Middle East. Any hope of using the Turkish model to get Syria to cut its ties to Lebanese and Palestinian terrorism is likely to be as misguided as any hopes that Hizballah's success in chasing the Israelis out of southern Lebanon can serve as an effective guide for driving the Israelis from the Golan Heights or the West Bank. Just as the Golan and the West Bank mean far more to Israel than southern Lebanon, Syria gains far more from Hizballah and Hamas than they did from the PKK.

The good news with regard to U.S.-Syrian relations is that to a large extent American deterrence has worked and Syria, although a rival, is a moderate one. Syria has been deterred from directing the terrorist groups it supports against U.S. targets, it has treated its weapons of mass destruction as weapons of last resort, and Syria has shown no interest in precipitating a war with Israel over the Golan Heights, a war it would almost certainly lose.

While Syrian policies on the peace process, weapons of mass destruction, terrorism, Lebanon, Iran, and Iraq are far from desirable from the U.S. standpoint, they are also far from a dire threat to important U.S. interests.

The ugly conclusion of this analysis is that the United States and Syria are likely to remain in a state of limited rivalry for the foreseeable future. There is no black and white answer for what U.S. policy should be toward Syria. Limited sanctions are an appropriate response to the limited threat Syria poses and limited incentives are an appropriate response for the limited cooperation Syria is willing to engage in. The precise mix of carrots and sticks is going to vary over time and issue area.

An adviser to Bashar argued that "he does not derive his legitimacy from the fact that he is the son of the late president, but from his adherence to his father's political legacy."[93] As long as that legacy is one of authoritarian induced domestic stability, a lumbering state-centric economy, distant relations with the West, and lack of compromise with Israel, Syria is going to remain a rival to the United States in the Middle East. A more promising legacy upon which to base solid U.S.-Syrian relations could be found in the development of democratic legitimacy in Syria along with economic growth based on integration in the world market. While U.S. investment and encouragement can play a role in pointing Syria in that direction,[94] that role is likely to be marginal and the results not visible for some time. In some ways, the less the United States government does to openly encourage reforms in Syrian domestic and foreign policy the better. Nothing is as likely to doom the reform process than for it to be viewed as an American imposition. The greater the storm, the more Bashar will cling to his roots. Such an outcome would be harmful to both the United States and Syria, for like his father, Bashar may find that the only way to hold Syria together is to hold it in place.

Notes

1. Speech to the Arab Summit Conference in Beirut, *Syria Times*, April 28, 2002.

2. 355, 8175 (June 17, 2000), 24.

3. "Elite Cohesion, Regime Succession and Political Instability in Syria," *Middle East Policy* 5, 4 (January 1998), 159.

4. "National Security and Political Succession in Syria," *Mediterranean Quarterly* 9,1 (Winter 1998), 74. For an overall account of the turbulent post-independence years of Syrian politics see Patrick Seale, *The Struggle for Syria: A Study of Post War Arab Politics, 1945-1958* (London: Oxford University Press, 1965).

5. Article 83 of the Syrian Constitution contains the age requirement.

6. Robinson, "Elite Cohesion, Regime Succession and Political Instability in Syria," 176-177.

7. *Asad of Syria: The Struggle For The Middle East* (Berkeley: University of California Press, 1988), 495.

8. Rachel Bronson, "Syria: Hanging Together or Hanging Separately," *The Washington Quarterly* 23, 4 (Autumn 2000), 96.

9. Flore de Préneuf, "Is Syria's next president a geek?" *Salon.com*, June 13, 2000.

10. Matt Rees, "Does Bashar Have What It Takes to Rule: Assad's son and the real succession question," *Newsweek* 135, 25 (19 June 2000), 22.

11. Patrick Seale, "Dramatic Initiatives," *The World Today* 57, 3 (March 2001), 7 and 9.

12. Fouad Ajami, "A Master of the Realm: Hafez Assad bequeaths that most elusive prize, power, to his son," *U.S. News and World Report* 128, 25 (26 June 2000), 32.

13. "An Interview with Bashar Al-Assad" *Middle East Media Research Institute (MEMRI)*, Special Dispatch Series #244 (July 20,2001). This and all subsequent *MEMRI* documents were acquired from http://www.memri.org.

14. Cited in Eyal Zisser, *Asad's Legacy: Syria in Transition* (London: Hurst & Company, 2001), 161.

15. Seale, *Asad of Syria*, 179 and 344.

16. For examples see, "Syrian President Bashar al-Asad's Interview with *Le Figaro*" *Foreign Broadcast Information Service (FBIS)*, (24 June 2001).

17. Christine Gorman, "The Doctor Will Lead You Now," *Time* 155,25 (June 19, 2000), 44.

18. "Elite Cohesion, Regime Succession and Political Instability in Syria," 176.

19. Bashar al-Asad "Speech to the 9th Summit of the Organization of the Islamic

Conference," (November 12, 2000) *Syrian Arab News Agency (SANA)*. This and all subsequent *SANA* documents were acquired from http://www.sana.org.

20. "Anti-Israeli Statements by the President of Syria," *MEMRI*, Special Dispatch Series, #177 (January 12, 2001).

21. "Syria's Bashar Assad's Speech at the Arab Summit," *MEMRI*, Special Dispatch Series, #202 (April 4, 2001).

22. "Speech Welcoming Pope John Paul II to Damascus," (May 5, 2001), *SANA*.

23. Seale, *Asad of Syria*, 143-144.

24. Eyal Zisser, "The Lebanon-Syria-Israel Triangle: One Year After Israeli Withdrawal," *PeaceWatch*, #326, (May 22, 2001), The Washington Institute For Near East Policy. This and all subsequent cites to the Institute's *PeaceWatch* and *PolicyWatch* series were acquired at http://www.washingtoninstitute.org/watch.

25. For an argument that the imperatives of his situation will overwhelm any temperamental factors, see Charles Foster, "Assad is Dead: Will Assad Live Long," *Contemporary Review* 277, 1617 (October 2000), 221-224.

26. Bashar al-Asad Inauguration Speech, (July 17, 2000), *SANA*.

27. For a pessimistic view of the Syrian economy see Steven Plaut, "The Collapsing Syrian Economy," *Middle East Quarterly* 6,3 (September 1999), 3-14. For a slightly more optimistic account, although one that also stresses the need for reforms, see Volker Perthes, "The Political Economy of Syrian Succession," *Survival* 43, 1 (Spring 2001), 143-154.

28. See Ali A. Bolbol, "Syrian Economic Development," *Middle East Insight* 17, 1 (January-February 2002), 53-58 and Peter Kiernan, "Syria's Economic Dilemma," *The Middle East*, #288 (March 1999), 35-37.

29. Perthes, "The Political Economy of Syrian Succession," 144.

30. Nimrod Raphaeli, "Special Focus: Syrian Economy," *MEMRI*, Middle East Economic News Report #17 (December 31, 2001).

31. Josh Martin, "Syria: Let The Reforms Begin," *Middle East* #310 (March 2001), 29-30.

32. "An Interview with Bashar Al-Assad," *MEMRI*, Special Dispatch Series, #103 (June 19, 2000).

33. See Martin, "Syria: Let the Reforms Begin," and Sami Moubayed, "Syria's New President Bashar al-Assad: A Modern Day Attaturk," *Washington Report on Middle East Affairs* 19, 9 (December 2000), 31-32.

34. See Perthes, "The Political Economy of Syrian Succession," 150-151; Robinson, "Elite Cohesion, Regime Succession and Political Instability in Syria," 162; and Alan Makovsky, "Syria Under Bashar Al-Asad: The Domestic Scene and the 'Chinese Model' of Reform," *PolicyWatch* #512 (January 17, 2001).

35. Zisser, *Asad's Legacy*, 213 and Najib Ghadbian "The New Asad: Dynamics of Continuity and Change in Syria," *Middle East Journal* 55, 4 (Autumn 2001), 641.

36. See Eli Carmelli and Yotam Feldner, "The Battle for Reforms and Civil Society in Syria-Part I," *MEMRI*, Inquiry and Analysis Series #47 (February 9, 2001); and Sami Moubayed "Tug Of War In Syria," *Washington Report of Middle East Affairs* 20, 3 (April 2001), 31.

37. Moubayed, "Syria's New President," 31.

38. Carmelli and Feldner, "The Battle for Reforms and Civil Society in Syria-Part I."

39. Ghadbian, "The New Asad," 637.

40. For the text of the Manifesto of the 99, see "Statement By 99 Syrian Intellectuals" *Middle East Intelligence Bulletin* 2,9 (October 5, 2000). This and all subsequent documents from the *Middle East Intelligence Bulletin* were acquired at http://www.meib.org. For the initial reaction of the government to both manifestos see Sami Moubayed, "Voices From Damascus," *Washington Report on Middle East Affairs* 20,2 (March 2001), 26-27; Carmelli and Feldner, "The Battle for Reforms and Civil Society in Syria-Part I," and Eli Carmelli and Yotam Feldner, "The Battle for Reforms and Civil Society in Syria-Part II" *MEMRI*, Inquiry and Analysis Series #48 (February 12, 2001).

41. For the trial and sentencing of the two Parliamentarians, see "Syria: Dissident Trials," *Middle East International* 674 (May 3, 2002), 22-23. For the overall crackdown on the Damascus Spring, see Human Rights Watch, *Human Rights Watch World Report, 2002* (New York: Human Rights Watch, 2002), 466-469. See also Yotam Feldner, "The Syrian Regime vs. the reformers; Part I: Backlash, The Regime Fights Back," and "The Syrian regime vs. the Reformers; Part II: The Battle of Ideas," *MEMRI*, Inquiry and Analysis Series #50, 51 (February 27-28, 2001).

42. For an excellent study of Syrian politics that stresses sectarian and ethnic divisions see Nikolaos van Dam, *The Struggle For Power In Syria: Politics and Society Under Asad and the Ba'th Party* (London: I.B. Tauris Publishers, 1996). For an examination of Syrian Politics that takes an explicitly class centered focus, see David Waldner, *State Building and Late Development* (Ithaca: Cornell University Press, 1999), 74-94.

43. Raymond Hinnebusch, "Syria: The Politics of Peace and Regime Survival," *Middle East Policy* 3, 4 (April 1995), 82-83.

44. *The Struggle For Power in Syria*, 1.

45. Zisser, *Asad's Legacy*, 7, 20.

46. The coiner of this term is Syrian analyst Sadiq al-'Azm, see Robinson, "Elite Cohesion, Regime Succession and Political Instability in Syria," 161 and Seale, *Asad of Syria*, 318-319 and 456. See also, Hanna Batutu, *Syria's Peasantry, the Descendants of Its Lesser Rural Notables, and Their Politics* (Princeton, Princeton University Press, 1999), 208-216; Waldner, *State Building and Late Development*, 88-89 and Raymond A. Hinnebusch, "The Political Economy of Economic Liberalization in Syria," *International Journal of Middle East Studies* 27, 3 (August 1995), 306.

47. Waldner, *State Building and Late Development*, 91.

48. Seale, *Asad of Syria*, 174.

49. Sorenson, "National Security and Political Succession in Syria," 73-74.

50. On the divisions within the military and intelligence services, see *Middle East Intelligence Bulletin* "Syria's Intelligence Services: A Primer" 2,6 (July 1, 2000); "Syria's Praetorian Guards: A Primer" 2,7 (August 5, 2000); and Richard M. Bennet, "The Syrian Military: A Primer" *Middle East Intelligence Bulletin*, 3, 8 (August/September 2001).

51. van Dam, *The Struggle For Power in Syria*, 75-88 and Batutu, *Syria's Peasantry*, 217-225.

52. *Middle East Intelligence Bulletin*, "Syria's Praetorian Guards."

53. Hinnebusch, "Syria: The Politics of Peace and Regime Survival," 79.

54. Ariel A. Ahram, "Iraq and Syria: The Dilemma of Dynasty," *Middle East Quarterly* 9, 2 (Spring 2002), 40.

55. For the steady elimination of possible rivals to Bashar, see Zisser, *Asad's Legacy*, 166-167 and Gary C. Gambill, "Syria's Night of Long Knives," *Middle East Intelligence Bulletin* 2, 5 (June 1, 2000).

56. See, "Military shake-up" *Middle East International* 668 (February 8, 2002) and Gary C. Gambill, "The Military-Intelligence Shakeup in Syria," *Middle East Intelligence Bulletin* 4, 2 (February 2002).

57. "Syrian President Issues Decree Forming New Council of Ministers," *FBIS*, 12/13/01 and Sami Moubayed, "Ushering in the New," *Al-Ahram Weekly Online* 565 (December 20-26, 2001) found at http://www.ahram.org.

58. "Report Views Motives for Extending Term of Syrian Defense Minister, Domestic Reforms," *FBIS*, (24 May 2002).

59. Gary C. Gambill, "Dossier: Asma Assad, First Lady of Syria," *Middle East Intelligence Bulletin* 3,6 (June 2001).

60. "Syria: Talas Discusses Al-Asad, Peace, Bashar, Arab Ties," *FBIS*, (15 July 2000).

61. Ghadbian, "The New Asad," 625.

62. Hinnebusch, "The Political Economy of Economic Liberalization in Syria," 307.

63. Ghadbian, "The New Asad," 635.

64. Robinson, "Elite Cohesion, Regime Succession and Political Instability in Syria," 160 and 177.

65. For overall accounts of U.S. Syrian Relations, see, Alfred B. Prados, "Syria: U.S. Relations and Bilateral Issues," *Congressional Research Service Issue Brief For Congress* (April 4, 2002); Erik L. Knudsen, "United States-Syrian Diplomatic Relations: The Downward Spiral of Mutual Political Hostility (1970-1994)," *Journal of South Asian and Middle Eastern Studies* 19, 4 (Summer 1996); and C. Ernest Dawn, "The Foreign Policy of Syria" in L. Carl Brown, ed., *Diplomacy In The Middle East: The International Relations of Regional and Outside Powers* (London: I.B. Tauris Publishers, 2001), 159-178.

66. See Bashar's Inauguration Speech, July 17, 2000; and Yotam Feldner, "All Quiet on the Eastern Front, Almost . . . Bashar Assad's First Interview" *MEMRI*, Inquiry and Analysis Series, #49 (February 16, 2001).

67. Henry Siegman, "Being Hafiz al-Assad: Syria's Chilly but Consistent Peace Strategy," *Foreign Affairs* 79, 3 (May/June 2000), 2-7.

68. Hinnebusch, "Syria: The Politics of Peace and Regime Survival," 74.

69. Sorenson, "National Security and Political Succession in Syria," 81 and David Wurmser, "Does Syria Want Peace?" *American Enterprise Institute* (February 2000).

70. See Bashar's interview with *Corriere Della Serra*, (February 14, 2002), *SANA*.

71. On Syria's WMD program see, Lawrence Scheinman, "NBC and Missile

Proliferation Issues in the Middle East," in Barry R. Schneider, ed., *Middle East Security Issues: In the Shadow of Weapons of Mass Destruction Proliferation* (Maxwell: Air University Press, 1999), 1-27; M. Zuhair Diab, "Syria's Chemical and Biological Weapons: Assessing Capabilities and Motivations," *The Nonproliferation Review* 5, 1 (Fall 1997), 104-111; *Middle East Intelligence Bulletin*, "Syria Continues to Bolster Chemical Weapons Arsenal," 2, 1 (January 2000); and Yedidya Atlas, "Syria's Stealth Strategy" *Insight on the News* 15, 23 (June 21, 1999), 38.

72. Eric V. Thompson, "Will Syria Have To Withdraw from Lebanon?" *Middle East Journal* 56, 1 (Winter 2002), 88-92.

73. See "Bashar al-Assad and Lebanese PM, Emile Lahoud on an Israeli withdrawal from South Lebanon," *MEMRI*, Special Dispatch Series, #75, (March 13, 2000); and *MEMRI*, "An Interview with Bashar Al-Assad," (June 19, 2000).

74. Thompson, "Will Syria Have To Withdraw from Lebanon," 93; Ghadbian, "The New Asad," 629; and Robinson, "Elite Cohesion, Regime Succession and Political Instability in Syria," 172.

75. Eyal Zisser, "Leaving Lebanon?" *Tel Aviv Notes*, #20, found at http://www.tau.ac.il/jcss. See also Robert J. Rabil, "The Maronites and Syrian Withdrawal: From 'Isolationists' to 'Traitors'?" *Middle East Policy* 8,3 (March 2001), 11-25.

76. Gary C. Gambill, "Syria's Foreign Relations: Iraq," *Middle East Intelligence Bulletin*, 3,3 (March 2001). See also "Syrian President Al Asad on Palestinian Intifadah, Arab Ties," *FBIS*, (5/13/02).

77. Bashar al-Asad "Speech to the 9th Summit of the Organization of the Islamic Conference."

78. Alan Sipress and Colum Lynch, "U.S. Avoids Confronting Syrians on Iraqi Oil," *Washington Post*, February 14, 2002, 1. Neil MacFarquhar, "Syria Is Forced To Adapt To A New Power Next Door" *New York Times*, April 22, 2003, and Alan Sipress, "Syrian Reforms Gain Momentum In Wake of War: U.S. Pressure Forces Changes in Foreign, Domestic Policy" *Washington Post*, May 12, 2003.

79. United States Department of State, *Patterns of Global Terrorism 2001* (May 2002), 68.

80. Ibid, 64. See also David Schenker, "Removing Syria from the List of State Sponsors of Terrorism," *PeaceWatch*, #239, (January 5, 2000).

81. See Bashar al-Asad's letter to George W. Bush, (September 12, 2001).

82. "Bashar Assad Teaches Visiting Members of U.S. Congress How to Fight Terrorism," *MEMRI*, Special Dispatch Series, #332, (January 16, 2002).

83. *Patterns of Global Terrorism*, 63.

84. "Speech to the Arab Summit Conference," March 28, 2002.

85. See "Syria's position: Define Terrorism Not Fight It," *MEMRI*, Special Dispatch Series #283 (October 7, 2001); Bashar's interview with *Corriere Della Serra*, and *FBIS*, "Syrian President Al-Asad on Palestinian Intifadah, Arab Ties."

86. Reuven Erlich, "Terrorism as a Preferred Instrument of Syrian Policy," International Policy Institute For Counter-Terrorism, (December 10, 1998), see also his October 10, 2001 update. Both found at http://www.ict.org.il.

87. Bush statement of April 4, 2002; and Rice interview with al-Jezeera, October 16, 2001. Both found at http://www.whitehouse.gov.

88. See Department of State, *Patterns of Global Terrorism 2001*, 68; Erlich, Terrorism as a Preferred Instrument of Syrian Strategy," and Yotam Feldner, "Escalation Games: Syria's Deterrence Policy, Part I: Brinksmanship" and "Escalation Games: Part II: Regional and International Factors," *MEMRI*, Inquiry and Analysis Series, #56 and 57 (May 24, 25, 2001).

89. See his comments on *Meet The Press*, July 7, 2002.

90. For an array of policy options available to potentially counter state-sponsored terrorism see, Boaz Ganor, "Countering State-Sponsored Terrorism," International Policy Institute For Counter-Terrorism (April 25, 1998), found at http://www.ict.org.il.

91. *MEMRI*, "An Interview with Bashar Al-Assad," July 20, 2001.

92. On the Syrian-Turkish agreement see, Ely Karmon, "A Solution To Syrian Terrorism," *Middle East Quarterly* 6,2 (June 1999), 23-32.

93. Patrick Seale, "Patrick Seale on Bashar's Handling of Crisis in Region, Ties with Neighbors," *FBIS*, (12/7/00).

94. For recommendations in that direction see Ghadbian "The New Asad," 641 and Yossi Baidatz, "Hizballah's Kidnapping: An Opportunity to Test Bashar Al-Asad," *Peacewatch*, #285 (October 13, 2000).

CHAPTER 9

Muammar Qaddafi and Libya's Strategic Culture

Craig R. Black

Introduction

In September of 1969, Muammar al-Qaddafi—then a virtually unknown army officer in his late twenties—rose to the leadership of Libya. Armed with a vision of Arab unity and anti-colonialism, he led a small group of his fellow officers who called themselves the Free Officers' Movement. In a virtually bloodless coup, they ousted the aging (and absent) King Idris Al-Sanusi and established Libya as a republic. During the 30 years since, Qaddafi has emerged as a charismatic and complicated leader. Considered by Westerners to be bizarre and irrational, he has been branded a terrorist and a rogue. Among some of his fellow Arabs, he is praised as a virulent anti-Zionist and anti-imperialist, while others condemn him as a plotter and an adventurer whose zealous pursuit of Arab, African, and Islamic unity has only resulted in destabilization.

Qaddafi remarked in 1976 that "atomic weapons will be like traditional ones, possessed by every state according to its potential. We will have our share of this new weapon." In 1987 Reuters quoted him as saying: "The Arabs must possess the atom bomb to defend themselves, until their numbers reach one thousand million and they learn to desalinate water and until they liberate Palestine."[1] Qaddafi places little faith in his armed forces and dreads a repeat of the 1986 U.S. air strikes against Tripoli and Benghazi. Reflecting on the air strikes, Qaddafi has wistfully spoken of possessing a ballistic missile capability that could threaten New York.[2] Few state leaders have expressed such single-minded determination to obtain chemical, biological, and nuclear weapons. This

247

determination, coupled with Qaddafi's long-term association with terrorism, has caused grave concern among other nations—especially the United States and Israel.

In this chapter, I will analyze Qaddafi's personal history, his leadership style, and the support structure of his regime. From this analysis, I will attempt to identify methods to deter him from employing weapons of mass destruction.

Libya Today

Libya has been described as an accidental and reluctant state. It was created in the aftermath of World War II at the behest of the Great Powers, its three culturally diverse provinces—Tripolitania, Cyrenaica, and Fazzan—loosely joined under the monarchy of King Idris. Independence occurred in 1951. Oil was discovered in 1959, soon to be followed by extensive investment by western oil companies.[3] After the 1969 revolution, a 12-member Revolutionary Command Council (RCC) was established, and one of its first actions was to demand the withdrawal of U.S. forces from Wheelus Air Force Base near Tripoli. Washington acquiesced.[4] During the 30 years since then, relations between the U.S. and Libya have been marked by one crisis after another: Qaddafi's efforts to overthrow moderate Arab regimes; Libya's apparent collusion with the Soviet Union during the Cold War; attempts to restrict freedom of navigation within the Gulf of Sirte; sponsorship of international terrorism; and pursuit of weapons of mass destruction.

Libya exists today as an isolated and distrusted nation. The cumulative effects of a depressed oil market and the U.N. sanctions imposed for Libya's alleged complicity in the Pam Am 747 bombing over Scotland strain its economy. On its western border is Tunisia—capitalistic and pro-Western. To the east is Egypt, a friend of the U.S. and the first Arab state to recognize Israel. Algeria, Libya's other neighbor on the Mediterranean, is the source of much of the Islamic extremism that threatens the Qaddafi regime.

Personal History

Qaddafi was born during World War II in a Bedouin tent in the desert, about 20 miles south of the seaside town of Sirte. His parents, descendants of the Qathathfa tribe, were herders of camels and goats, eking out an existence in one of the poorest countries in the world. Qaddafi attended a Koranic elementary school followed by high school at Sebha in the Fezzan, Libya's southernmost province. There, at the age of 15, he began to listen to Egyptian president Gamal Abdel Nasser on the radio, memorizing the speeches and reciting them, word for word, to his classmates whom he had organized into a revolutionary cell. Among his classmates were Abdel Salen Jalloud, who would become Qaddafi's most trusted deputy; Mustafa al-Kharoubi, who would be his intelligence chief; and Abu Bakr Yunis Jabir, the future commander-in-chief of the armed forces.[5]

Qaddafi insisted that that his fellow cell members observe what he called "revolutionary disciplines," avoiding alcohol and dissolute ways. Qaddafi's puritanism has been attributed to his Bedouin origins as well as to a reaction against the creeping corruption spread by the foreign oil companies and contractors, maneuvering for positions and favors under the monarchy. Qaddafi would be expelled from Sebha for political trouble making, in particular for leading demonstrations against King Idris for his lack of support for Nasser and the Palestinian cause against Israel.[6]

A summary of his early ideology:

> *He had soaked up the Arab revolutionary ideas which poured out of Egypt under Nasser and, although he seemed to have no clear ideology of his own, he had produced a potent cocktail of revolution and Islamic extremism. He was disciplined and immensely hard-working, and he had tapped into the reservoirs of underground discontent that existed in Libya under King Idris. He was poised to plan the revolution and, taking the advice of his mentor, President Nasser, and his Egyptian schoolmaster in Sebha, he decided that the most fertile ground lay in the Libyan armed forces.[7]*

Qaddafi attended military college in Benghazi where he continued his dissident activity, establishing the beginnings of the Free Officers'

Movement. After graduation in 1966, he traveled to England for several months of training with the British signal corps. He was a poor soldier, frequently being put on report for rudeness and insubordination, and even for suspicion of complicity in the summary execution of a fellow soldier. It is clear that Qaddafi's intention was not to serve a distinguished career in the service of the monarchy, but to overthrow it.[8]

During the next three years, Qaddafi molded his group of fellow officers into a full-fledged underground movement, ultimately overthrowing the monarchy. He would turn this coup into a revolution, attempting to change Libya from a conservative, colonial state into a modern, progressive one. This involved a major transformation of society—changes in roles, attitudes, and behavior—all codified in *The Green Book*, Qaddafi's philosophy of the Revolution. Qaddafi initially put the RCC in charge of the government and ruled by decree, campaigning to rid the country of corruption and the symbols of Western imperialism. The Americans and British left, the Italians were expelled, and Arabic was restored as the official language. Corrupt politicians and military officers were purged. Oil leases were renegotiated and many of the companies nationalized. With the suspension of the constitution and the outlawing of political parties, Qaddafi made himself the undisputed leader and architect of his country's future.[9]

Ideology and Style of Government

Since 1969, Qaddafi has dominated Libya's policies by the sheer force of his personality and leadership, seizing every opportunity to implement his revolutionary ideology. He has devoted Libya's considerable oil wealth to building roads, schools, and hospitals. Villages have been electrified and the desert irrigated. He has done as much as any other Arab leader for women's liberation and providing for popular decision-making in government.[10]

Initially, as chairman of the RCC, Qaddafi controlled both the legislative and executive functions of the government, experimenting with the socialist policies employed in Nasser's Egypt. Beginning in 1973, dissatisfied with the level of revolutionary zeal displayed by the Libyan people, Qaddafi launched his "Cultural Revolution." He dismantled the traditional apparatus of government and reorganized the country's political structure to follow his Third Universal Theory—a disavowal of capitalism and communism in favor of socialism, popular democracy, Arab unity, and progressive Islam. He set up what he envisioned as a direct democracy, in which the instruments of government were placed in the hands of the people. People's Committees and popular congresses were formed at the local, regional, and national levels to promote mass participation in the nation's decision-making process.[11] What resulted though was a stifling, overly rigid system that proved to be better at promulgating top-level policy than it was at cultivating popular participation.[12]

Although Qaddafi renounced all official posts and titles in 1979, he has continued to dominate the political scene in his capacity as the "The Leader of the Revolution." A journalist with unprecedented access reports:

> *Called simply "the Leader," he (Qaddafi) is not, technically the head of state. The ministers report to the people's congresses, not to him, and diplomats do not present him their credentials. Western diplomats say he probably has a veto power over official acts and that certain security agencies still report to him. Yet few Libya-watchers pretend to understand his precise role.*[13]

Qaddafi is supported by an extensive security network consisting of his personal bodyguards, several elite military units, and the various local People's Committees. The result is multiple and overlapping layers of surveillance that monitor and control the activities of anyone deemed a threat to the regime. The regime's security forces are regularly accused by international human rights organizations of murder, torture, and intimidation.[14]

Qaddafi's inner circle is made up of long-time revolutionary colleagues who have survived his frequent purges. A clear chain of command is difficult to draw since the members of his inner circle and security apparatus go by a misleading system of ranks and titles. A lieutenant colonel might report to a captain who works for another official with no rank at all. No one outside Libya—and perhaps even inside— knows for sure who controls exactly what. The vagueness and obscurity of this system is said to be of Qaddafi's own design, intended to confuse potential competitors within the regime.[15]

A generation of younger, more hard-line regime members is reported to be moving up. Qaddafi keeps these ambitious underlings in check by playing them off one another. No political heir has been designated and there does not appear to be any blood relatives capable of taking the reins. A report from a U.S. news magazine emphasizes this point:

> *For sheer intrigue, none of the succession struggles in the Mideast can top Libya's. The erratic but cunning Col. Muammar Qaddafi, 56, has survived several assassination attempts. If one finally succeeds, it is unlikely that any of his five sons will be able to hold power. The oldest, Saif al-Islam, has inherited his father's quirkiness: He bought two rare Bengali tigers, named Fred and Barney, for $15,000 from a Milan zoo and brought them along when he studied in Austria. U.S. officials point to one incident when asked what to expect if Qaddafi disappears from the scene: In July 1996, two of his sons, backing opposing soccer teams, got into a dispute over a referee's call. The match ended in a shootout between each son's retinue of bodyguards.*[16]

Qaddafi has managed the personnel assignments within his regime by paying close attention to tribal membership, thereby consolidating alliances and, by ensuring that no single tribe holds a monopoly on key positions, guaranteeing his security.[17] The predominate tribe within the regime and the one critical to Qaddafi's survival is his own, the Qathathfa. From the Qathathfa, Qaddafi has promoted junior officers in the armed forces and entrusted them with sensitive military posts.

Making up a core of colonels responsible to the preservation of the regime are, among others, Ahmad Qathf al-Damm, responsible for the Cyrenaica region; Masoud Abdul-Hafith, commander of military security; Misbah Abdul-Hafith, responsible for the Benghazi sector; Khalifa Ihneish, commander of armaments and munitions; Omar Ishkal, Al-Barani Ishkal, commander of domestic security; Mohamad al-Majthoub al-Qaddafi, leader of the revolutionary committees; Sayed Qathaf al-Damm, director of information and propaganda; and Ali al-Kilbo, commander of the Azazia barracks and in charge of protecting Qaddafi's residence.

These assignments feature a great deal of overlap and are subject to frequent revision making it difficult for even members of Qaddafi's own tribe to gain leverage over him. Qaddafi has had to eliminate at least one member of his extended family when his primacy was threatened. His cousin Hassan Ishkal, in charge of domestic security and Libyan troops in Chad, was gunned down by regime supporters after it became clear that he was no longer willing to adhere to Qaddafi's orders.[18]

Other important but less strategic positions within the regime have been filled by the Warfala tribe which enjoys blood ties to the Qathathfa. A third tribe from which regime members have been recruited is the Magharha.[19]

Qaddafi has had a falling out with Abdel Salen Jalloud, his number two man since the revolution. Jalloud, a member of the Magharha tribe, was often cited as a possible successor to Qaddafi and as such, was perhaps perceived by Qaddafi as a competitor. He has been stripped of his power and replaced by Abdallah al-Sanussi, another member of the Magharha tribe and Qaddafi's wife's brother-in-law.[20] Sanussi is said to lead a "dirty tricks department" that acts on Qaddafi's authority. Sanussi, along with five other Libyans, was recently convicted in absentia by a French court for the 1989 bombing of a UTA DC-10 over Niger. He has kept a low profile in recent months, perhaps to distance Qaddafi from the bombing or even because he has been banished from the inner circle.[21]

Abu Bakr Yunis Jabir, another revolutionary comrade of Qaddafi's, continues as the commander-in-chief of the armed forces but is said to possess little real power. Mustafa al-Kharoubi has retained his position as head of military intelligence but, like other members of the original RCC, is struggling for his political survival.[22] Two members of the original RCC, Omar al-Maheshi and Bashir Hawadi, have led coup attempts, earning themselves life prison terms and execution for their followers.[23] It would appear that Qaddafi distrusts long-serving regime members, especially those from tribes other than his own. Influence and political standing are no doubt what attracts a regime member to the inner circle but, once attained, guarantee his decline.

Libya-watchers describe Qaddafi's decision-making process as being haphazard and rarely following any given theory or ideology. His quirkiness and idiosyncrasies make great news copy. He receives Western journalists and African dignitaries in a camel-skin tent, attired in a Bedouin robe over western-style casual wear. His admirers claim that, by living an austere life, Qaddafi is being true to his Bedouin nature. His critics dismiss the tent, the rugs, and Bedouin garb as conceit.[24]

Insight into his personality can be gained by examining the policies of this regime. Two examples of Qaddafi's idiosyncratic leadership:

(In Qaddafi's Libya) the Gregorian calendar has been replaced with a new solar calendar that begins with the migration of the Prophet Mohammed in 622. The names of the Gregorian months have been replaced with names invented by General Qaddafi. The traditional Lunar Islamic calendar used by all Muslim countries has also been changed to begin with the death of the Prophet rather than his migration. Hence, the simple task of determining the day and date has become confusing because Libya neither follows the standard lunar Islamic calendar nor the global solar calendar. Every year a new set of rules and regulations telling Libyans what to wear, eat, say, and read is enacted by the regime.[25]

The domestic policies of the Libyan regime have often bordered on fiction. A case in point is a 1977 edict whereby the Libyan leader suggested that in order to achieve self-sufficiency every Libyan family had to raise chickens in the home. The cages and birds were imported and, for an obligatory fee of fifty-seven dinars ($150 at the 1977 exchange rate), were distributed by the government to Libyans. To many city dwellers in small apartments, raising chickens in their kitchens was a difficult if not impossible affair. The result was that many ate the birds and found other uses for the cages.[26]

Qaddafi's ideology and rule are constantly changing, sometimes in different directions. Always experimenting, he tinkers with the Revolution and its ideological mix, employing Islam, socialism, and populism in varying degrees to suit the situation at hand. The Revolution of today is unlike the Revolution of ten years ago, and almost certainly unlike what it will be ten years from now.

Foreign Relations

Not since Nasser has an Arab leader attempted such an ambitious foreign policy as has Qaddafi. Driven by his opposition to colonialism and

Zionism, as well as his vision of Arab unity, Qaddafi has pursued a world order in which Libya and other Arab nations would take top billing. But his revolutionary zeal and temperamental personality have progressively isolated his regime.

Libya's relations with its North African neighbors have been volatile. He has plunged into armed conflict with five of his six neighbors. Niger, the only neighbor he has not clashed with, is too weak to stand up to Libya and has adopted a policy of accommodation towards the Qaddafi regime.[27] Qaddafi has threatened to support opposition groups in Algeria and Tunisia as penalty for not supporting Libya against the U.N. sanctions.[28] Egypt, Libya's closest friend during the early years of the Revolution, attacked Libya in 1977 in a brief, punitive war after Israeli intelligence informed President Sadat that a Libyan assassination attempt was brewing.[29] Libya has staked claim to the Auzo strip of Chad since 1974 for ideological reasons and economic gain from Chad's rich uranium deposits. A protracted conflict ensued, ending in a devastating and embarrassing defeat for Qaddafi's forces.[30]

Qaddafi has meddled in the internal politics of virtually all of sub-Saharan Africa. In an effort to undermine Western and Israeli influence on the continent, he has provided aid, both military and economic, to a veritable *Who's Who* of African bad guys—Amin in Uganda; Bokassa in the Central African Republic; and Mobuto in Zaire.[31] These efforts earned him the dubious distinction of being the first political leader to be denied the chairmanship of the Organization of African Unity (OAU). [32]

In the greater Arab world, Qaddafi's insistence on a violent solution to the Palestinian problem has alienated Libya from the governments of Saudi Arabia, Jordan, and the Gulf States; while Libya's support for Iran during the Iran-Iraq war turned even Saddam Hussein against Qaddafi.[33]

Cut off from the world by U.N. sanctions and resentful at the Arab world for turning its back on him, Qaddafi has attempted to redefine his foreign policy efforts in Africa. Evidently abandoning pan-Arabism for the time being and embracing "pan-Africanism," he has reached out to South African President Nelson Mandela and attempted to mediate conflicts in Congo, Sierra Leone, Eritrea, Liberia, and Sudan. At the June 1998 OAU summit, African leaders declared that they would ignore the U.N. airline embargo against Libya. In gratitude, Libya rewarded African heads of state with large cash gifts for each visit that violated the embargo.[34]

Qaddafi's association with state-sponsored terrorism has earned him the enmity of both the Arab world and Western democracies. He is reported to have supported some 50 terror organizations and subversion groups, in addition to more than 40 radical governments in Africa, Asia, Europe, and America.[35] Among the terrorist groups that continue to receive direct support from his regime are Abu Nidal and Hamas.[36] An analysis of the terrorist groups and causes Qaddafi has supported does not reveal a clear ideological pattern. His indiscriminate sponsorship of groups as diverse as Hamas (the liberation of Palestine), the Irish Republican Army (Irish independence), and the Red Brigades (Marxist upheaval) suggests that he considers terrorism not so much as a tool to advance the Revolution but as a weapon to be used against his perceived foes—Israel and the Western democracies.

Libya's alleged involvement in the 1986 bombing of a Berlin nightclub that killed two U.S. servicemen resulted in U.S. air strikes against Tripoli and Benghazi, killing 36 Libyans, including Qaddafi's 16-month-old daughter.[37] Less violent but even more damaging to Libya were the U.N. sanctions prompted by the 1989 Pan Am bombing. U.N. sanctions, in effect from 1992 to 1999, crippled the Libyan economy and isolated the country from the world community. [38]

But the incidence of Libyan-sponsored terrorism during the 1990's appears to have declined, if not ceased. This could be a result of U.N. sanctions and/or the U.S. air strikes. An Australian study of worldwide terrorism, conducted in 1996, shows that Libyan-associated terrorist groups were substantially less active during the 20 months after the air strikes than before. The terrorist activity that persisted shifted away from acts of high and medium severity toward acts of low severity—evidence that military force might have some value in deterring terrorism, at least for the short term.[39] In interviews with western journalists, Qaddafi and his ministers insist that if Libyans have been involved in terrorist acts, they were not implementing Libyan policy.[40] This contrasts sharply with Qaddafi's public rhetoric of the 1970s and 1980s when terrorists were exalted as heroes and martyrs.

Qaddafi has paid a high price for his revolutionary zeal. He has virtually no friends or allies outside of Libya's borders. His support for terrorism, rather than advancing the Revolution and enhancing his political clout, has increased Libya's isolation, leading to a crippled economy and emboldened internal opposition groups. Although Qaddafi has displayed relatively good behavior for the past 10 years, his hatred of imperialism and Zionism likely remains the root of his ideology and the driving force of his foreign policy.

Threats to the Regime

Qaddafi, though possessing a monopoly on wealth and power, faces opposition from multiple segments of Libyan society. The regime's redistribution of property and the nationalization of virtually all industry and commerce have alienated Libya's middle class. Intellectuals and students have been scarred by a series of barbaric hangings carried out at the country's universities. The Muslim clergy view Qaddafi as a heretic for his reinterpretation of the Koran. Military officers are infuriated by Qaddafi's plans to raise a people's militia to replace the regular army.[41]

As Qaddafi has become more isolated, he has become less tolerant of criticism, repressing Islamic extremist groups and imposing brutal control over ethnic and tribal minorities. Tribes such as the Berbers, Tuaregs, and Warfalla are the bedrock of Libyan social structure and their growing disenchantment with the regime does not bode well for Qaddafi.[42] The tribal tension has even extended to his own Qathathfa tribe whose members have been accused of plotting to assassinate him.[43]

One of the many inconsistencies in the Qaddafi regime's policies has been its long-standing support of international Islamic opposition groups. Within Libya, though, the same groups have been the objects of brutal repression. Although by all accounts a devout Muslim, Qaddafi has long been distrustful of religious organizations since they often become involved in politics, breeding factionalism, and undermining his revolutionary objectives.   As part of his campaign to eliminate independent sources of power that could challenge his ideology and leadership, Qaddafi has attacked the Islamists as agents of reaction and obstacles to the progress of the Revolution.[44]

Religious groups, especially the Muslim Brotherhood, have objected to Qaddafi's efforts to concentrate religious power in his own hands and to make himself the sole interpreter of the Koran. They are resentful of the socialist changes that have taken place and critical of Qaddafi's promotion of his doctrine over that of traditional Islamic teachings. The Brotherhood's appeal is growing among city dwellers and the poor who respond to its vision of reformulating Arab institutions along Islamic ideals.[45]

The National Salvation Front is the other group that poses a threat to Qaddafi. Established in 1981, this party has attempted to craft a platform that accommodates both secular and Islamic opponents of Qaddafi. Of special significance has been this group's effort to establish connections with members of the Libyan armed forces. Two recent arrivals on the Libyan political landscape are the Islamic Martyrdom Movement and the Libyan Islamic Group. Both of these mysterious organizations seem to be focusing their recruiting efforts on poverty-stricken Libyan veterans of the Afghan conflict.[46]

During the past few years, anti-regime violence by Islamic extremists has reached new levels of intensity. Guerrilla forces have clashed with Libyan troops and are rumored to have attempted to assassinate Qaddafi.[47] Although the level of violence has not reached the same scale as it has in neighboring Algeria, the ability of the Islamic guerrillas to obtain advanced weapons and conduct raids against Qaddafi's security forces are reasons for the regime to worry.

Despite the recent surge of extremist violence, the army still holds the key to the future of the regime. Qaddafi's ill-fated adventures in Chad have caused considerable discontent among officers as has his attempts to reduce the power of the army by creating an alternative popular militia. Although the military has the power to challenge Qaddafi, it lacks a coherent ideology to legitimize its rule and attract support from other disaffected groups. This has led military challengers to seek an alliance with an opposition group that possesses legitimacy and ideological appeal—the Islamic extremists.[48]

The Primacy of Oil

Qaddafi has long known the political power of oil. His regime maintains a monopoly on the distribution of oil revenues, the country's primary source of income. He has used these revenues to bankroll spectacular, if wasteful, development. Billions of petrodollars have gone to finance the causes of liberation, terrorism, and Islam throughout the world and have paid for Libya's nuclear, chemical, and biological weapons programs. Qaddafi has distributed oil revenues in ways to influence tribal leaders and placate those who question his eccentric political concepts, foreign policy adventures, and lack of economic planning. But Libya is a slave to the price of oil. Depressed oil prices and a production complex hobbled from embargoes have put Qaddafi is a difficult position.[49]

Qaddafi is running out of money. The state runs almost all the economy and does so badly. Black marketeering and corruption are rampant. Huge sums are spent on eccentric schemes such as the construction of a $25 billion "Great Man-Made River Project" across the Sahara.[50] Qaddafi will find it difficult, if not impossible, to keep his support base content without the huge inflow of petrodollars to which he has been accustomed.

Weapons of Mass Destruction (WMD)

In spite of sanctions, embargoes, and a moribund economy, (not to mention the Non-Proliferation Treaty which Libya ratified in 1981), Qaddafi continues to pursue attainment of nuclear, biological, and chemical weapons. In his own words, the primary threat to Libya is "Israel's arsenal of nuclear weapons and missiles capable of hitting targets in Libya."[51] He evidently believes that these weapons can raise his international stature, deter U.S. and Israeli attack, intimidate his neighbors, and serve as cheaper alternatives to more expensive conventional forces. But even after 30 years of trying to develop a nuclear weapon, Libya's nuclear program remains in the embryonic stage. It has succeeded only in providing some training to a number of students and technicians and the establishment of a nuclear research center, which includes a small Soviet-supplied research reactor under International Atomic Energy Agency safeguards.[52] Progress has been hampered from mismanagement, lack of spare parts, and the reluctance of foreign suppliers to provide assistance.

Qaddafi does not appear to have abandoned his goal of acquiring nuclear weapons. There are reports that Libya tried to buy a nuclear bomb from China in 1970 and Russia in 1992.[53] Libya assisted Pakistan in its development of nuclear weaponry, through direct financial aid as well as by serving as an intermediary in the procurement of Niger-mined uranium. This was no doubt with the hope that Pakistan would one day provide Qaddafi with a nuclear weapon or at least the expertise for him to develop his own.[54] With the execution of Pakistani prime minister Ali Bhutto in 1979, Libya's hopes for an "Islamic Bomb" from Pakistan appear to have diminished.[55]

Although Libya is a signatory of the Biological Weapons Convention, it has pursued development of biological weapons for many years. Its program remains in the early research and development status though, primarily for want of an adequate scientific and technical base. The program suffers from the same difficulties as the nuclear program in acquiring needed foreign equipment and technical expertise.[56] This is scant reassurance, since biological weapons are a great deal easier to produce than nuclear weapons and can be done clandestinely with equipment otherwise used for commercial industry.

Available evidence suggests that only Libya's chemical warfare program has made any real progress. During the 1980s, it succeeded in producing up to 100 tons of blister and nerve agent at its Rabta facility, although many of the precursor chemicals were obtained from foreign sources.[57] The focus of intense media attention, Rabta was shut down in 1990—ostensibly because of a fire—only to be reopened in 1996. While Rabta was inoperative, Qaddafi's efforts shifted to the construction of a hardened, deeply buried facility at Tarhunah, southeast of Tripoli.[58] Over a hundred tons of mustard and nerve gases are believed to be stockpiled at Tarhunah. As if this were not enough, the facility is reported to be capable of producing up to 1,000 tons of mustard gas, 90 tons of sarin, and 1,300 tons of soman nerve agent per year.[59]

In addition to his quest for WMD agents, Qaddafi has been shopping for suitable delivery vehicles. Libya's only operational ballistic missile system is the Scud-B, acquired from the Soviet Union in the mid-1970s. These missiles are at the end of their service life and suffering from a host of maintenance problems. In January 2000, only a few days after Libya and Britain exchanged ambassadors for the first time in 15 years, Libya was caught trying to smuggle Scud components from China through London.[60] Efforts to procure the North Korean No Dong missile have been unsuccessful. U.N. sanctions have stymied Libya's efforts to develop the Al Fatah, a missile of its own design.[61]

WMD Strategies and Scenarios

Five WMD strategies have been identified that might be used by a state like Libya against the U.S. and its allies.[62] The first would be to fracture the allied coalition. Within the range of Libya's missiles and aircraft lie North Africa, southern Europe, Israel, and Turkey. By holding these nations at risk, Qaddafi could coerce them into refraining from joining any coalition against him. Without the participation of North African and Mediterranean members, a U.S.-led coalition against Libya would suffer from a perceived lack of legitimacy or even be labeled as U.S. aggression.

The second WMD strategy would be to defeat the U.S. at home. High U.S. and Allied casualties caused by WMD attack, or merely the fear of high casualties, could damage U.S. public support of the war effort. Qaddafi surely took note of the quick U.S. withdrawals from Lebanon in 1983 and Somalia in 1993 that were spurred by the deaths of U.S. servicemen.

The third strategy involves using WMD to shatter a U.S. expeditionary force. Qaddafi's armed forces are weak and would be no match for those of a U.S.-led force in a conventional engagement. A massive WMD attack against the invading army would go a long way toward leveling the playing field. Aimed at troop concentrations, either on the battlefield or at a point of debarkation, the WMD attack could inflict thousands of casualties and set the U.S. war effort back months (if it doesn't provoke nuclear retaliation). During the time it would take to rebuild the expeditionary force, U.S. public opinion might force a compromised peace to be negotiated.

Another strategy would be the use of WMD to secure the endgame. Qaddafi, when faced with an impending military defeat, could gain negotiating leverage by threatening to go down in a blaze of WMD glory. U.S. and Allied leaders, even though victorious on the battlefield, might be tempted to allow Qaddafi to remain in power rather than suffer additional casualties.

A final strategy for Qaddafi might be to use WMD to avenge the defeat of his regime. Samson-like, he could strike out against those nations he perceives as responsible for his overthrow. With nothing left for Qaddafi to lose there would be little that could be done to deter him.

When these strategies are applied to Libya's domestic and foreign affairs situation, three WMD scenarios become evident. The first involves Qaddafi employing WMD to defeat or repel an invading force or, as discussed above, to secure the endgame after his forces have been overrun. The only known instance of Libyan use of WMD occurred in 1987 during Libya's military operation in Chad. Chadian forces, with French and U.S. support, had turned the tide against their Libyan opponents and launched a surprise attack against a military base inside Libya. In response, Qaddafi ordered a chemical weapons attack—mustard gas delivered by a transport aircraft.[63] This suggests what the Libyan response would be against an attack by the U.S. or Egypt.

Warning signs preceding such a response are difficult to predict given the shroud of secrecy that cloaks the Qaddafi regime. Increased activity at the Tarhuna and Rabta facilities might be an indicator. So might be a protective withdrawal of his air force which, until his missile capability improves, is his most reliable chemical weapons delivery capability.

There have been unconfirmed reports that the Great Man-Made River Project, with its hundreds of miles of tunnels, is not merely an eccentric irrigation scheme but a method to store and transport WMD out of sight of Western intelligence sensors.[64] If this is the case, close attention must be paid to that system's nodes and service points.

The second WMD scenario involves a revenge attack against Western or Israeli targets. Following the 1986 U.S. air strikes, Libya launched two Scud missiles at the Italian island of Lampedusa.[65] Although both missiles fell short of their target (intentionally?), the attack demonstrated Qaddafi's willingness to lash out at third party populations in an attempt to fracture coalitions and shake public resolve. A twist to this scenario might have Qaddafi utilizing his terrorist connections to carry out the attack. This could even be ordered after his overthrow, either from a hiding place within Libya or while in exile abroad. An intelligence community observation:

> *Whereas Tripoli employs its own intelligence officers to eliminate opposition figures, it employs surrogates for its nastiest operations. Deviation from this norm, as in the Lockerbie bombing, has proved disastrous. Consequently, if Tripoli wishes to mimic the Tokyo underground gassing, it will turn to a third party like the Abu Nidal faction.*[66]

The third scenario has Qaddafi using WMD to eradicate opposition groups. According to dissident and diplomatic sources, armed opposition to the regime is growing. Libyan air force fighter-bombers and helicopter gunships have repeatedly struck suspected militant hideouts in the Green Mountain region.[67] It is difficult to determine how effective these operations have been but, given the weakness of the Libyan military and the growing threat from dissident groups—both tribal and religious, it is conceivable that Qaddafi might one day be forced to take a page from Saddam Hussein's playbook and employ chemical weapons against his own people.

Since no single opposition appears capable of ousting Qaddafi, a coalition of groups would have to be formed. A WMD attack against one group would likely discourage other dissident groups from joining the cause. Such an attack would probably be prompted by an opposition victory over regime forces and prefaced by an increase in Qaddafi's revolutionary rhetoric, both through speeches and the state-sponsored media. His favorite euphemism for enemies that he desires to kill is "Mad Dogs," a label he has applied to Islamic extremists. He is also prone to accuse his enemies—before he eliminates them—of collaborating with U.S. or Israeli intelligence. [68]

Is Qaddafi Deterrable?

Qaddafi has frequently been characterized by Western governments as being irrational or insane. His policies often seem senseless and counterproductive. His most brazen acts of terror—the Pan Am and UTA bombings—are nihilistic and self-destructive. He has used chemical weapons; he continuously defies international norms; he sponsors terrorist groups. For these reasons, he might be deterrable only to a degree.

A study of Qaddafi's personal history does not show a leader who is willing to go down in flames for his beliefs, but one who has repeatedly modified his ideology to safeguard his position as the Leader of the Revolution. His variable standing on Islam, is an example. When it was necessary to legitimize his ideology, he embraced Islam and was an enthusiastic proponent of strict Koranic law. But when the Muslim clerics criticized his Third Universal Theory, arguing that it was counter to

Islamic doctrine, Qaddafi jailed them and proclaimed that, with Islam, people could speak directly with Allah and therefore did not require clergymen as intermediaries.

Qaddafi, although complicated and difficult to read, seems to possess a degree of pragmatism. He will adjust the mix of his ideology—a little socialism one day, some Islam the next, a heavy dose of populism—to keep the revolution (i.e., his life and power) alive. He is not likely to do anything that will destroy all he has worked for. Hobbled by UN sanctions and his pariah status, he appears to have come around to the view that conciliatory diplomacy might be more effective in furthering Libya's influence than proclamations of support for terrorists and revolutionaries.

To deter Qaddafi, something of his that he holds dear must be held at risk. His military would make a poor target as it has become so weak and ineffectual that it is incapable of harming anyone except perhaps his own regime. Counterforce strategies against Libya's WMD facilities could be useful if the weapons were stored someplace more accessible than Tarhunah, the design of which is said to have been constructed from Soviet bomb shelter blueprints and therefore virtually impregnable to conventional air attack.[69] Pressure applied to Qaddafi's international support base would be effective if such a base existed. Qaddafi has been so ostracized by the leaders of the Arab world that they are unlikely to jeopardize their international standing to support him. Although Qaddafi claims that Libya is the gateway to Africa and that he is an African above all else, the affinity displayed toward him by African leaders exists only in proportion to how much financial aid Libya doles out. Qaddafi's domestic support base is provided chiefly by the three tribes from which his inner circle members hail. Tribal support depends a great deal on how well the tribes fare economically under the regime. They are not likely to cause trouble if their leaders and members are well cared for. All things considered, there appears only one prop holding up the Qaddafi regime—oil.

As we have seen with the U.N. sanctions and the decline in oil prices, when oil revenues dry up, so does the ability of the Qaddafi regime to provide financial benefits to its support base—tribal leaders, the urban poor, and politicized youth. Oil revenues finance his security police and military, placate potential opponents, and keep his friends happy. Oil is clearly Qaddafi's source of power and the key to deterring him.

Before we go any further, we must consider what a Libya without Qaddafi would look like and if such a situation would be more desirable than the one that exists now. Qaddafi has succeeded in disturbing the political environment in such a way as to prevent the emergence of a civilian opposition. The greatest threat to his regime is a coalition of Islamic extremist groups and the military. If and when these factions link up, Qaddafi's days are numbered. Given the regional destabilization threatened by Islamic extremism and the specter of religious fanatics in possession of Libya's chemical weapons stocks, it can be argued that the region would be worse off without Qaddafi than with him.

Military strikes against Libya's oil industry could target the pipelines, port facilities and the oil fields themselves. But with any military operation there exists the risk of WMD retaliation, either against the U.S. or its allies. And even if Qaddafi does not lash out with WMD, he can improve upon his pariah status by claiming that the U.S. is bullying him and, by destroying his oil industry, is responsible for the suffering of thousands of Libyans.

The method to deterring Qaddafi appears to be the judicious use of sanctions. Sanctions applied directly toward Libyan WMD production are difficult to enforce since many of the technologies involved have legitimate applications within civilian industry. This is especially true for chemical and biological weapons, less so for nuclear. The sanctions should take advantage of the Qaddafi regime's dependence upon petrodollars and specifically target Libya's oil production industry—production equipment, technical assistance, access to foreign markets, etc.

For these sanctions to be effective, they must be multilateral. This is evident by the relative ineffectiveness of the U.S. embargo against Libya, in effect since 1986. Even in the face of American pressure, there have always been nations—some of them U.S. allies—willing to trade with Libya. It was only with the U.N. sanctions, in effect from 1992 to 1999, that Qaddafi was squeezed into what resembled respectable behavior. For the first time, Libyans could not blame solely the U.S. and Israel for their problems but had to face the fact that they were international outcasts. In April 1999, the sanctions produced their desired effect with the turnover of the two Libyan suspects in the Pan Am bombing, and were suspended.

The key to preventing Qaddafi from misbehaving in the future is an efficient process of reinstating the sanctions. A healthy level of fear for the survival of his regime will keep Qaddafi on his best behavior.

Notes

1. Geoff Simons, *Libya--The Struggle for Survival* (New York: St. Martin's Press, 1996), 257.

2. Robert Waller, "Libyan Threat Perception," *Jane's Intelligence Review*, Vol. 7, No. 9 (September 1995), 408.

3. Dirk Vandewalle, *Libya Since Independence*, (Ithaca and London: Cornell University Press, 1998), 41-46.

4. David Blundy and Andrew Lycett, *Qaddafi and the Libyan Revolution*, (Boston: Little, Brown and Company, 1987), 61.

5. John K. Cooley, *Libyan Sandstorm*, (New York: Hold, Rinehard & Winston, 1982), 14.

6. Ibid.

7. Blundy and Lycett, *Qaddafi and the Libyan Revolution*, 44.

8. Ibid., 46-47.

9. Lisa Anderson, *The State and Social Transformation in Tunisia and Libya, 1830-1980*, (Princeton: Princeton University Press, 1986), 260-263.

10. Milton Viorst, "The Colonel in his Labyrinth," *Foreign Affairs*, Vol. 78, Issue 2, (Mar/Apr 99), 72-73.

11. George Joffé, "Qadhafi's Islam in Local Historic Perspective," *Qadhafi's Libya 1969-1994*, ed. Dirk Vandewalle, (New York: St. Martin's Press, 1995), 149-150.

12. Mansour O. El-Kikhia, *Libya's Qaddafi—the Politics of Contradiction*, (Gainesville: University Press of Florida, 1997), 45-55.

13. Viorst, "The Colonel in his Labyrinth," 71.

14. *1998 Human Rights Report-Libya Country Report*, U.S. Department of State, 1999, 1.

15. Waller, "Libyan Threat Perception," 408.

16. Thomas Omestad and Warren P. Strobel, "Here Come the Sons," *U.S. News & World Report*, Vol. 126, Issue 7 (22 February 1999), 41-43.

17. El-Kikhia, *Libya's Qaddafi—the Politics of Contradiction*, 89-92.

18. Ibid.

19. Ibid.

20. Ibid.

21. Viorst, "The Colonel in his Labyrinth," 71.

22. El-Kikhia, *Libya's Qaddafi*, 86-92.

23. Ibid., 170.

24. Viorst, "The Colonel in his Labyrinth," 65.

25. Ibid., 105.

26. Ibid., 105-106.

27. Ibid., 148.

28. Raymond Tanter, *Rogue Regimes*, (New York: St. Martin's Press, 1997), 132.

29. Ronald Bruce St John, *Qaddafi's World Design, Libyan Foreign Policy 1969-1987*, (London: Saqi Books, 1987), 60.

30. Vandewalle, *Libya Since Independence*, 145.

31. St John, *Qaddafi's World Design, 98-99*.

32. *Ibid,*. 149.

33. Simons, *Libya—The Struggle for Survival*, 14-17.

34. Scott Peterson, "Col. Qaddafi Seeks to Lead New Club—Africa," *Christian Science Monitor*, 9 September 1999.

35. Blundy and Lycett, *Qaddafi and the Libyan Revolution*, 150.

36. Robert Waller, "The Libyan Threat to the Mediterranean," *Jane's Intelligence Review*, (May 1996), 227.

37. Simons, *Libya: The Struggle for Survival*, 336.

38. Scott Peterson, "Trying to shed Pariah Status, Libya Warms to West," *Christian Science Monitor*, 13 September 1999.

39. Henry W. Prunckun, Jr. and Philip B. Mohr, "Military Deterrence of International Terrorism: An Evaluation of Operation El Dorado Canyon," *Studies in Conflict & Terrorism*, Vol. 20 (July-September 1997), 267-280.

40. Viorst, "The Colonel in his Labyrinth," 67-71.

41. Martin Sicker, *The Making of a Pariah State—the Adventurist Politics of Muammar Qaddafi*, (New York: Praeger, 1987), 33.

42. *1998 Human Rights Report-Libya Country Report*, U.S. Department of State, 1999, 1.

43. Alan George, Ghaddaffi: "Trouble in the Extended Family," *Jane's Intelligence Review*, vol.8, no.11 (November 1996), 525.

44. Ray Takeyh, "Qadhafi and the Challenge of Militant Islam," *Washington Quarterly*, vol.21, no.3 (Summer 1998), 162.

45. Ibid., 167.

46. Ibid., 167-168.

47. Viorst, "The Colonel in His Labyrinth," 62.

48. Ibid., 166.

49. "Muddling On," *Economist* Vol.352, No.8135, (4 September 1999), 47.

50. Viorst, "The Colonel in His Labyrinth," 62.

51. Waller, "Libyan Threat Perception," 408.

52. *Proliferation: Threat and Response*, U.S. Department of Defense, November 1997, 35.

53. Waller, "The Libyan threat to the Mediterranean," 228.

54. Simons, *Libya: Struggle for Survival*, 257. Also see Weissman and Krosney, *The Islamic Bomb*.

55. Steve Weissman and Herbert Krosney, *The Islamic Bomb*, (New York: Times Books, 1981), 211-213.

56. *Proliferation: Threat and Response*, 37.

57. Ibid., 35

58. Ibid.

59. Waller, "The Libyan Threat to the Mediterranean," 228.

60. T.R. Reid, "Britain Catches Libya Trying to Skirt Arms Ban," *Washington Post*, (10 January 2000).

61. *Proliferation: Threat and Response*, 37.

62. Barry R. Schneider, "Strategies for Coping with Enemy Weapons of Mass Destruction," *Airpower Journal*, (Special Edition 1996), 36-47.

63. Joshua Sinai, "Ghadaffi's Libya: the Patient Proliferator," *Jane's Intelligence Review*, Vol. 10, No. 12, (December 1998), 27.

64. Ibid.

65. Waller, "The Libyan threat to the Mediterranean," 228.

66. Ibid.

67. James Bruce, "Gaddafi tunnels into trouble both within and without," *Jane's Defence Weekly* (11 September 1996), 24.

68. Waller, "Libyan Threat Perception," 407.

69. Sinia, "Ghadaffi's Libya: the Patient Proliferator," 28.

CHAPTER 10

The Need for Influence Theory and Actor-Specific Behavioral Models of Adversaries*

Alexander L. George

This analysis begins with a discussion of problems of employing deterrence and coercive diplomacy in intra-state conflicts, drawing on those aspects of experience with these strategies during the Cold War relevant for dealing with intra-state conflicts, and adding some reflections on problems of employing these strategies in the post-Cold War environment.

The special characteristics of intra-state conflicts, identified in this analysis, call attention to the need for several types of indirect deterrence and coercive diplomacy. Emphasis is placed on including deterrence and coercive diplomacy within a broader influence framework that considers the utility and sometimes the necessity for coupling these strategies with positive initiatives.

Influence theory also requires that consideration be given to the role of reassurances to adversaries under several well-defined circumstances. An influence framework must also consider the possible utility of a strategy of conciliation (a term preferable to the discredited concept of appeasement). Similarly, the concept of influence theory also includes the strategy of conditional reciprocity, which limits risks of conciliatory efforts and which, also, can be employed in pursuing the ambitious long-range objective of re-socializing "rogue" leaders and "outlaw" states.

Attention is given in this analysis also to the problem of dealing with "spoilers" in intra-state conflicts, those who complicate or attempt to defeat efforts by mediators to end such struggles. The efforts of mediators will be facilitated if they distinguish between different types of spoilers

* Helpful comments on an earlier draft were provided by Barry Schneider and Brad Roberts.

and devise strategies appropriate for dealing with each type. This is followed with a discussion of a basic requirement for effective use of all the above strategies, namely the need to replace the simplistic assumption that adversaries are "rational, unitary" actors with more specific "actor-specific behavioral models" essential for understanding and attempting to influence different adversaries.

Deterrence and Coercive Diplomacy: Some Lessons of Experience

From an early stage in the Cold War it became evident that the theory and practice of deterrence and coercive diplomacy should be incorporated into a broader theory of influence.[1] Experience indicated that reliance on deterrence alone was not a substitute for a more rounded and well-conceptualized foreign policy towards adversary states. Deterrence was often a necessary part of foreign policy, but it was not a sufficient basis for dealing with many adversary states or for all situations with a particular adversary. Similarly, reliance exclusively on deterrence as the handmaiden of containment could not suffice. The originator of containment policy towards the Soviet Union, George Kennan, emphasized the need for utilizing positive measures as well as negative measures to reinforce containment.

Deterrence and coercive diplomacy are better conceived as parts of a broader influence theory, one that may often combine threats in some way with positive inducements and with other diplomatic efforts, to be discussed later in detail, to explore the possibility and feasibility of moving towards mutually acceptable ways of reducing the potential for conflict in relations with an adversary.

To do so, as will be indicated in our discussion of the need for "actor-specific" models, requires understanding the adversary's motives, needs, and goals. This is necessary not only to ascertain whether, how, and what kind of a deterrence, coercion, or accommodation may be possible, but also to assure that the effort to make use of positive incentives to influence the adversary will not degenerate into appeasement. (A discussion of appeasement, or "conciliation" as it might be better designated, will be addressed later.)

Viewed from this perspective, deterrence is often best viewed as a time-buying strategy, one that creates or awaits opportunities to explore

272

and possibly achieve at least a partial accommodation of interests and at least a substantial reduction of the danger of war.

Unfortunately, deterrence is not always easily achieved when conducting foreign policy even in situations in which it is most needed. There are several sobering examples of the failure of the United States to assert effective deterrence despite substantial warning that an attack might be in the works. Indeed, America's failure in 1950 to attempt to deter North Korea from attacking South Korea and its inability to mount a strong deterrent effort against Saddam Hussein before he attacked Kuwait in 1990 exemplify a disturbing paradox. The United States responded to these two aggressions with strong military action. However, what the U.S. was willing and able to do after the attacks, it was not able for various reasons to threaten to do beforehand.[2]

Timely reassessment of existing deterrence commitments or reconsidering the absence of such commitments, are necessary to take account of changes in the situation, in the adversary's intentions, and with regard to supplementing deterrence with other means of influencing the adversary. The assessment should consider emerging situations – as in U.S. policy in the months prior to the North Korean attack on South Korea – to ascertain whether a deterrence commitment, thus far lacking, should be made.

Experience with efforts to employ coercive diplomacy during the Cold War and thereafter also led to recognition that it, too, should be incorporated into a broad theory of influence. Comparative study of past efforts to employ coercive diplomacy indicates that it is risky to rely solely on threats of punishment for noncompliance with one's demands and that offering positive incentives as well may be of critical importance. Using a "carrot and stick" approach – as President Kennedy did in the Cuban Missile Crisis and as the United States did in developing the 1994 Agreed Framework with North Korea – may increase the possibility of a mutually acceptable, peaceful resolution of a war-threatening crisis.

Coercive diplomacy is best viewed as a flexible strategy in which what the stick cannot, or is not likely to achieve by itself, can possibly be obtained by adding an appropriate carrot.

In both deterrence and coercive diplomacy, the offer of conditional, positive inducements must, as with threats, be credible and sufficiently potent to influence the adversary.[3]

273

It must be emphasized that offering positive incentives to an adversary, as well as threats, is highly context dependent in both deterrence and coercive diplomacy. There can be no assurance that a combination of carrot and stick will be effective. The outcome depends on many characteristics of the two actors, the nature of the conflict between them, how well carrots and sticks are chosen and employed, and situational variables. For example, if important divisions exist in the leadership group of the adversary, a carrot and stick approach may encourage those leaders who favor some kind of settlement. When important domestic constituents of the leadership of the adversary state favor termination of the crisis, their views and actions may become more influential on decisions if their state is offered carrots as well as sticks.

Indirect Deterrence and Coercive Diplomacy

The conventional way of attempting to achieve successful deterrence or coercive diplomacy is to attempt to persuade leaders of an adversary state to desist or to comply with demands. This may be characterized as direct deterrence and coercive diplomacy. Most efforts to employ these strategies during the Cold War were direct efforts of this kind. Direct deterrence continues to have a role to play in post-Cold War crises as well.

However, intra-state conflicts have assumed greater prominence in the post-Cold War period. Direct deterrence is less likely to be effective in intra-state conflicts and against non-state actors. This is especially so, as we have learned, against terrorists and suicide bombers, especially those who regard conflict as a zero-sum conflict and who feel they have no other strategies available.

Against such non-state actors and participants in internal conflicts within a state, more attention needs to be given to the possibility of indirect modes of deterrence and coercive diplomacy.

In conventional deterrence and coercive diplomacy, the aim is to persuade the leaders of an adversary state that the costs and risks of a contemplated action or one already underway will outweigh its expected benefits. In contrast to direct deterrence and coercive diplomacy, three indirect forms of these strategies are available for attempting to influence the leaders of a weak state whose freedom of action and "rational" decision-making are limited. Namely:

1. An attempt may be made to influence the behavior of leaders in a weak state indirectly through a third party which has some influence with those leaders.

2. Indirect deterrence or coercive diplomacy may be exercised by attempting to strengthen the hand of moderates in a divided leadership in the target state.

3. Indirect deterrence or coercive diplomacy may be exercised by encouraging important constituents of the opposing regime to put pressure on their leaders.

Reassurance

It will be helpful at this point to consider whether an alternative strategy of influence, namely reassurance, can be helpful.[4] In judging whether resort to deterrence or coercive diplomacy is appropriate in a particular situation, consideration should be given to trying to reassure the adversary that one is not contemplating actions harmful to its interests.

What can one say on the basis of past experience as to when a strategy of reassurance is preferable to exerting deterrence or using coercive diplomacy? President Harry Truman placed misguided reliance on giving the Peoples Republic of China reassurances of historical U.S. friendship and non-hostile intentions in response to Chinese threats to intervene in the Korean War if U.S. forces went beyond the 38th parallel in pursuit of the retreating North Korean forces. Truman mistakenly relied on reassurances instead of using threats to attempt to deter Chinese entry into the war. Similarly, in 1990 when it appeared that Saddam Hussein might be getting ready to invade Kuwait, President Bush attempted to combine reassurance with deterrence. His administration was able to mount only a very weak deterrence effort, the efficacy of which was further diluted by the effort to assure Saddam Hussein of a United States desire to continue the policy of peaceful relations.

275

There is a need for more systematic analysis of the conditions and modalities for choosing between deterrence and reassurance, or combining them in an optimal manner. A hypothesis has been advanced that reassurance of some kind might be more appropriate than deterrence when the adversary's motivation for possibly taking a hostile action is defensive and stems from a sense of weakness, vulnerability, or mistaken concern that hostile actions are about to be directed towards it. An example of effective, appropriate reassurance is that given to the Chinese by the Kennedy administration when Chinese leaders mistakenly believed that the U.S. was preparing hostile action. Clarifying for a concerned opponent that one's actions are not preparation for hostile action has a rich history in international relations.

Conversely, another hypothesis holds that deterrence is more appropriate than reassurance when the adversary's motivation to undertake a hostile action is derived not from an undue, unwarranted preoccupation with threats directed towards it or a pervasive sense of vulnerability, but, rather, from a belief that an opportunity is available for gain or aggrandizement at acceptable cost and risk. A correct image of the opponent and good intelligence is needed to distinguish between the need for deterrence or for reassurance, and for sensitivity to the possibility that elements of both are appropriate in some situations.

Conciliation as a Strategy for Resolution or Avoidance of Conflict

Appeasement was a familiar strategy that was often employed in the era of classical diplomacy. It acquired a highly invidious connotation in the Western world as a result of Chamberlain's abortive effort to appease and re-socialize Hitler into becoming a responsible member of the European state system.

The classic definition of appeasement is a simple one. In the language of diplomacy employed in the European balance-of-power system, appeasement referred to a policy of attempting to reduce tension between two states by the methodical removal of the principal causes of conflict between them. In this sense, appeasement was regarded as a strategy for eliminating the potential for war in a conflict-ridden relationship between two states.[5]

In contemporary writings on conflict resolution, the terms *conciliation* and *accommodation* are often employed instead of *appeasement*. The latter term has acquired such a bad odor that specialists who write on these matters seem to gingerly steer clear of it.

It is important to recognize that there are a number of significantly different goals and strategies in which some form of conciliation can be employed. Thus, as Stephen Rock notes, conciliation can be (1) a short-term strategy aimed at crisis resolution; (2) a longer-term strategy aimed at crisis prevention; (3) a short-term effort to secure a limited political trade; and (4) a long-term strategy for a significant alteration of the status quo that may lead the two parties into a more peaceful relationship. Thus, different motivations and goals may lead a state to adopt some kind of conciliatory strategy and, indeed, such a policy may have both a minimum short-term goal as well as a longer-range one. Preserving a favorable balance of power was often a principal aim of opposing states employing conciliation earlier in history, but this is not the only goal that can be pursued.

Resort to conciliation does not exclude the possibility, or the desirability, of combining it with deterrent threats in a mixed influence strategy. Whatever the goal and variant of conciliation, it falls under the general umbrella of influence strategy. It should be recognized that when conciliation is part of a mixed influence strategy it can overlap with the strategy of "conditional reciprocity," to which we will turn shortly.

Actor-specific knowledge is of critical importance in determining whether conciliation of an adversary should be considered. In assessing its possible relevance, attention should be given to three factors: the adversary's motives and the extent of his desires; the nature of inducements, if any, that can be offered to opponents with different motives; and reasons other than inducements offered that may impel the target to accept or reject the offers. Taking account of these three factors will have important implications for whether and what kind of conciliation is offered.[6]

Policymakers may consider a strategy of conciliation when confronted by (1) a *revisionist* opponent who advances what it believes are legitimate claims for a change in a status quo situation, (2) an aggressive *expansionist* adversary, or (3) an opponent who is both revisionist and expansionist.

Policymakers must have a correct image of the opponent, his intentions, aspirations, and behavioral style to differentiate among these three situations, but ascertaining the true character of the opponent may be difficult. In addition to trying to determine whether the adversary is revisionist or expansionist or both, it is important to decide whether one is dealing with an outlaw state whose leaders essentially reject the norms and practices of the international system and are disposed to behave in ways that will undermine the order and stability of the system. Conciliation of such actors is neither desirable nor feasible, given their destructive orientation to the existing international system.[7]

On the other hand, when the adversary is not an outlaw but advances either revisionist or expansionist claims, the basic policy choices are conciliation, deterrence, or some combination of the two. Conciliation need not and often should not attempt to satisfy all of the revisionist or expansionist aims of the other party in a single grand settlement. It may be preferable and less risky to implement conciliation in a careful, incremental fashion. It can be incorporated into a strategy of incremental conditional reciprocity by means of which one secures at each stage compensating concessions or assurances of one kind or another from the adversary.

Until recently, systematic research on past efforts to employ conciliation has been lacking. A major comparative study is now available which compares cases of successful and ineffective efforts to conciliate opponents and provides useful guidelines.[8] This enables us to formulate a number of questions when deciding between conciliation and deterrence (or some combination of the two) in the face of demands for a change in the status quo.

1. Are the adversary's objectives revisionist or expansionist? If expansionist, are they perhaps legitimate and of a limited, acceptable character?

2. Will the adversary view concessions as evidence of goodwill, friendship, and recognition of the legitimacy of his revisionist claims, or as evidence of irresolution and weakness and therefore tempt him to seek greater gain?

3. Can the adversary be conciliated in such a way as to avoid giving the impression at home and abroad that one has yielded to blackmail? Will conciliating the adversary result in serious damage to one's reputation in the eyes of other states and encourage them to advance revisionist or expansionist demands of their own?

4. How can one limit or control the various risks of conciliating another state? By drawing a line as to the extent of concessions that will be made? By appeasing individual claims incrementally? By obtaining credible formal assurances from the adversary that his demands for changes in the status quo are limited? Can tests be devised to assess the scope of the adversary's intentions?

5. Is the expected benefit of conciliating the adversary limited to the short-term objective of avoiding a crisis or war? Or can short-term conciliation on a specific issue be built into a longer-range strategy of turning the entire conflictful relationship into a cooperative one?

6. Is reliance on deterrence instead of conciliation or coupling the two in a mixed strategy better for coping with the adversary's hopes for a change in the status quo? Will reliance solely on deterrence induce the adversary to give up hopes and efforts for changing the status quo in the future? Or will it only strengthen his motivation and lead him to prepare for challenging deterrence more effectively in the future? Beyond its possible psychological impact, will a change in the status quo in the adversary's favor that is being considered significantly alter the relative power balance?

Adopting one of Stephen Rock's suggestions, four possible situations and scenarios can be identified for analytical purposes, though it may be quite difficult for policymakers to judge which of these four possibilities correctly identifies the case at hand.

1. Either conciliation or deterrence can succeed in a given case, at least in the short run. A possible example is the Falkland Islands crisis, in which the British might have avoided the need to invade the islands and the ensuing war through either a more robust deterrence effort or timely conciliation.

2. Neither deterrence nor conciliation is likely to succeed when an adversary has hegemonic ambitions and is bent on employing military force. An example is Hitler's determination to go to war against Poland in the autumn of 1939.

3. Only deterrence can possibly succeed, because the adversary would respond to conciliation by generating new demands. A possible example is Chamberlain's appeasement of Hitler on the Sudetenland question, which did not prevent him from occupying the rest of Czechoslovakia later.

4. Only conciliation can succeed, either because the defender lacks capability or will or both to mount a robust deterrence effort or, if war breaks out, a willingness to pursue it effectively. A possible example is what Barbara Tuchman regards as England's "missed opportunity" to appease and thereby retain its American colonies.[9]

Comparative studies of successful and unsuccessful conciliation (such as the recent one by Stephen Rock) can help identify the conditions under which it may be a viable strategy, the risks of the strategy, and ways of coping with the risks.

In sum, although the critique of appeasement is deeply ingrained in the American consciousness, largely because of the experience of the 1930s, there is no reason to believe that concessions never work, that it is impossible to satisfy a dissatisfied state or leader. Certainly, however, careful thought needs to be given to the feasibility of conciliation of various states and non-state actors. As always, the risks of conciliation in any case must be carefully weighed and ways of safeguarding or limiting them are necessary. One way of controlling such risks is the strategy of "conditional reciprocity," to which we now turn.

Conditional Reciprocity[10]

The policy of conditional reciprocity for re-socializing outlaw states is not unfamiliar in diplomacy. An adaptation of it was employed for a less ambitious goal in the Agreed Framework of 1994 between the United States and North Korea.[11]

Great Powers have frequently been confronted by ambitious states that are not socialized into the norms of the international system and pose a threat to its orderly workings and stability. Addressing this problem at the outset of his book, *A World Restored*, Henry Kissinger held it to be of critical importance for the stability of the international system that all major states and their leaders hold a common concept of "legitimacy," which he defined as "international agreement about the nature of workable arrangements and about the permissible aims and method of foreign policy." Kissinger referred to states that rejected the norms and practices of the existing international system as "revolutionary" states.[12] "Revolutionary" or "outlaw" states differ from "revisionist" states, which seek merely to rectify the status quo and do not reject the norms and practices of the international system.

Rogue leaders and their outlaw states refuse to accept and abide by some of the most important norms and practices of the international system. Leaders of such states may seek to dominate and reshape the system to their own liking, and may aim at global or regional hegemony. Some resort to practices such as terrorism, taking as hostages citizens or official representatives of other states.

Great powers traditionally have accepted some responsibility for maintaining an orderly international system. Their incentive to find ways of coping with the threat to order by revolutionary powers, outlaw states, and rogue leaders is understandably accentuated when their own important national interests are threatened by the aims and behavior of such actors.

It should be noted, however, that there exists no clear and commonly accepted definition of an outlaw or rogue state. These concepts have no standing in international law, and the United Nations works imperfectly to single out such offenders and deal with them. In fact, members of the international community may disagree among themselves whether the behavior of a certain state justifies its being regarded as an outlaw and treated as a pariah. Even behavior that violates a particular norm may be condoned by some as an understandable way of pursuing legitimate grievances or ambitions.

Much of the task of recognizing and coping with outlaws, then, is undertaken by individual states, usually one or more of the Great Powers, which have a stake in preserving the system that they helped to create and that they subscribe to, as well as in protecting interests threatened or damaged by an outlaw. At the same time, it should be recognized that efforts by one or more states to cope with outlaws do not always win agreement and support from other states. Re-socialization of the rogue leader then becomes all the more difficult.

What strategies are available for dealing with revolutionary and outlaw states and their rogue leaders? Which strategies have been tried in the past and with what results? At present, there does not appear to be any systematic, comparative study of these questions that would provide today's policymakers with theory and empirical knowledge of this phenomenon.[13]

It is not difficult to make a list of possible strategies. Some of the possibilities are the following:

- Military action, coercive pressures, or covert action, or all three, to replace the outlaw regime with a more acceptable government or to eliminate its rogue leader.[14]

- Containment, which, if pursued effectively and long enough, might help to bring about, as it did in the case of the Soviet Union, changes in ideology and the internal composition of the regime that lead to moderation in its foreign policy orientation and behavior.

- A strategy of rewards and punishments designed to bring about fundamental changes in behavior and attitudes, a form of behavior modification via diplomacy. Such a behavior modification strategy probably must be accompanied by containment that prevents the outlaw state from achieving flagrantly expansionist aims.

It should be noted that conciliation is not listed as a strategy for dealing with outlaw states. When an outlaw state not only rejects important norms of the international system, but also seeks major changes in the status quo, conciliation of even its legitimate and seemingly reasonable demands is unlikely to contribute to re-socializing it into accepting the norms of the international system. In fact, such a strategy is much more likely to reinforce the rogue leader's ambitions and strengthen his predisposition to challenge the system.

This appeared to be the case, for example, of Saddam Hussein of Iraq, who saw concessions and conciliatory actions as signs of weakness or who, at least, had little hesitancy about attacking former allies when they did not suit his plans and ambitions.

Nevertheless, limited conciliation may have to be resorted to occasionally as a time-buying strategy for determining the true character of the adversary, strengthening one's capabilities, or generating domestic and international support for resisting the outlaw more effectively later.

In this connection, the strategy of *conditional reciprocity*, demanding some meaningful change in policy and behavior in return for each concession or benefit, is safer and likely to be more effective than pure conciliation in achieving re-socialization in the long run. In scholarly writings, conditional reciprocity is usually treated as a tactic to be employed in negotiating a particular issue or in encouraging changes in one or more of an adversary's policies.

Here, however, we point also to its strategic use as part of a long-range effort for bringing about fundamental change in the nature of the outlaw state and its leadership, that is, the gradual replacement of its antipathy to the norms and practices of the international system with attitudes and behavior more supportive of that system.

In other words, conditional reciprocity may be used as a lever for implementing a long-range strategy of behavior modification that has the objective of re-socializing the outlaw state and reforming its rogue leadership. At the same time, one should keep in mind that conditional reciprocity can also be used, as in developing the 1994 Agreed Framework with North Korea, for the lesser objective of inducing a change in the policies of another actor.

In any case, the strategy of re-socializing and the levers it employs must be conceptualized in a sophisticated way and carefully implemented. This is easier said than done, in part because we have as yet virtually no systematic analyses of past efforts of this kind.

GRIT: Graduated Reciprocation Tension-Reduction

Nonetheless, it is possible to differentiate the use of rewards and punishments in a strategy of re-socialization from the use of rewards and punishments in two other strategies: (1) GRIT, or graduated reciprocation in tension-reduction; and (2) "tit-for-tat," which have different and more limited aims than the re-socialization strategy.

GRIT is not a strategy for re-socialization and reforming outlaw states. Rather, it has the much more limited aim of removing distrust between states and thereby paving the way for a relaxation of tensions.[15] GRIT attempts to do so by taking a series of meaningful conciliatory actions, which may include concessions, carefully chosen to impress on the adversary that one genuinely desires to bring about an improvement in the relationship. These conciliatory actions are intended to encourage the adversary to replace his distrust with a more trusting, open attitude that will result in a relaxation of tensions, thereby creating an opportunity for dealing with some of the underlying disagreements that divide the two sides.

Unlike conditional reciprocity, GRIT initiates conciliatory actions without demanding that the adversary respond to the first conciliatory action with one of his own. And in contrast to the strategy of behavior modification, which rewards the subject only after he makes the desired change in behavior, GRIT offers its conciliatory actions beforehand, to induce a change in the adversary's perceptions and attitudes.

Given the striking differences between GRIT, conditional reciprocity, or behavior modification, policymakers have a clear choice between options that differ both in the objective sought and in the way in which they offer positive inducements for that purpose. The risks of GRIT, should it fail, are supposedly limited by choosing conciliatory actions that, though meaningful in the eyes of the adversary, do not give away anything of major importance. Further implementation of GRIT is abandoned if, after several conciliatory gestures, the adversary gives no sign of adopting a more trustful attitude and desiring to cooperate in a relaxation of tensions.[16]

In principle, therefore, GRIT is not to be confused with the practice of offering bribes to secure the more ambitious aim of a change in the adversary's policies and behavior. Neither is offering a reward in advance of a change in behavior (i.e., a bribe) consistent with the principle of behavior modification. Conditional reciprocity, on the other hand, can be more flexible than behavior modification: it can encompass initiating a positive action in order to elicit an appropriate reciprocating move from the adversary. But if the adversary does not reciprocate, it is highly questionable whether additional positive moves would be consistent with the strategy of conditional reciprocity.

This somewhat abstract conceptual discussion of several alternative strategies is useful only up to a point in policymaking. There are uncertainties in gauging whether the adversary is likely to be more receptive to one approach than to another or, indeed, to any of them. Policymakers may have to operate without reliable knowledge of the opponent's receptivity and likely response. And it may be difficult to correctly interpret the adversary's response. Intelligence sources and diplomatic communication may be helpful in reducing these uncertainties, but are not likely to eliminate them. As with other strategies discussed in this chapter, conditional reciprocity, too, requires good actor-specific behavior models of the adversary.

Thus, willingness to experiment and rely on trial and error may be necessary. However, the differences among the strategies should not be ignored or blurred in practice. For example, it is possible that at various times the Bush administration's policy of friendship toward Saddam Hussein prior to his attack against Kuwait blurred the important differences among GRIT, bribes, conditional reciprocity, and behavior modification. To the extent that blurring occurred, it further complicated the already difficult task of evaluating the efficacy of the policy of friendship and taking appropriate corrective measures.

Eye-for-an-Eye Strategies

As for the time-honored, if not always effective, practice of "tit-for-tat," it received fresh attention during the Cold War as a possible strategy for eliciting cooperative behavior between actors who recognize that their mutual interests call for cooperating to avoid the worst possible outcome for both, but who cannot easily do so because they are caught in a "prisoners' dilemma" (PD) situation. The relationship between a Great Power and the outlaw state it is attempting to reform, however, is not at all similar to the relationship between actors caught in a prisoners' dilemma. The PD game is built on the premise that in a given situation the two sides recognize their interest in cooperating to avoid the worst possible outcome of their interaction; the challenge of the game for them is to act toward each other in ways that secure the better outcome that both prefer. The results of a computer simulation devised by Robert Axelrod indicated that in repeated plays of the PD game, the tit-for-tat strategy performed best in achieving cooperation. This strategy bears a resemblance to some forms of conditional reciprocity in calling for each side to reward a conciliatory move by the other with a conciliatory move of its own and responding to a hostile move with a negative one of its own until the two sides eventually converge in trading only positive moves; hence, "cooperation" is established.[17]

285

Behavior Modification Strategy or Conditional Reciprocity

However, unlike tit-for-tat, which is a symmetrical game, re-socialization or an attempt to modify behavior is an asymmetrical game in which one actor attempts to bring about fundamental changes in the attitudes as well as the behavior of the other. The use of rewards and punishments after the adversary has taken some action, in re-socialization strategy, has to be much more refined and more finely calibrated than in tit-for-tat.

Efforts to use conditional reciprocity on behalf of the re-socialization objective are more likely to make headway when leaders of the "opposing" state have begun to question the results of their antipathy to certain norms and practices of the international system and, having become somewhat disenchanted with their earlier policies, are now willing to question the assumptions on which those policies were based.

Consideration needs to be given to building into the practice of conditional reciprocity "tests" designed to find out whether the leaders of the opposing state are genuinely moving toward abandoning earlier hostile attitudes and are ready to accept the norms and constraints of the international system. If they are not, the conclusion may be justified that the opposing leader cannot be re-socialized and that the only alternatives are containment or efforts to bring about their replacement by more tractable leaders.

In employing conditional reciprocity as a lever, what one "gives" the "outlaw" state and what one demands in return require sophisticated strategic planning. A series of incremental steps must be planned or improvised, as in the Agreed Framework between the United States and North Korea, yet the strategy must be implemented flexibly on the basis of monitoring and feedback. There must be awareness of the risks of the strategy and ways of minimizing and controlling those risks, and sensitivity to indications that the strategy is not working and needs prompt reassessment.[18]

What, then, are some of the risks of the strategy of conditional reciprocity and ways of minimizing them? It is not yet possible to derive firm answers to this question from studies of historical cases in which something like the strategy of conditional reciprocity was employed. In

286

the meanwhile, by drawing on general principles of behavior modification and learning theory, some hypotheses can be formulated as to the risks of the strategy and possible ways of minimizing or avoiding them.[19]

1. Concessions and benefits bestowed should not be linked merely with general injunctions to improve behavior; they should not be provided simply on the basis of the "outlaw's" vague assurances of better behavior. Rather, benefits offered but not yet given should be coupled with a demand (however, diplomatically conveyed) for quite specific changes in behavior that the outlaw state understands and agrees to. This approach is consistent with a cardinal principle of the psychological technique of behavior modification, which emphasizes that the therapist must identify for the subject the specific behavior that is to be extinguished and the more appropriate, acceptable behavior that should replace it. (Of course, it is possible that the "outlaw" state will refuse to accept the linkage of benefits to be received with some or all of the behavior changes demanded.)

2. Benefits should not be bestowed on an "outlaw" state in advance for reciprocity at some later date. Doing so violates another basic principle of behavior modification, which emphasizes positive reinforcement by means of a reward *after* the subject has performed required behavior and rejects the alternative practice of offering a bribe in advance to elicit the required behavior.[20]

3. The concessions and benefits bestowed on an "outlaw" state should be capable of being withdrawn or at least terminated if its leaders renege on their part of the reciprocal arrangement. If the concessions are not reversible, they should be in the nature of acceptable losses and the "outlaw" state should be punished in some other way for its delinquency.

4. Insofar as possible, concessions and benefits should give leaders of the "outlaw" state and its people a stake in continuing the process of conditional reciprocity and an awareness of the advantages of accepting and participating in the international system. (This is probably what Henry Kissinger had in mind

287

when, during the détente of the early 1970s, he spoke of weaving a "web of incentives" to encourage Soviet leaders to enter into playing a more "constructive" role in international affairs).

This analysis has provided a provisional sketch of conditional reciprocity, its general requirements, and some of its risks. It should be obvious that this strategy is not assured of success and that its chances of succeeding may depend on a slow, incremental, patient application of conditional reciprocity. In addition, we must recognize three complicating factors that may jeopardize efforts to pursue this strategy or a formal agreement such as the Agreed Framework with North Korea which lays out a sequence.

1. The Great Power may need the outlaw state's support to orchestrate an effective balance of power against an aggressive third party. A possible example of this is the Bush administration's reluctance to take a tougher policy towards Saddam Hussein prior to his invasion of Kuwait because it needed Iraq to balance Iran.

2. The Great Power may mistake tactically motivated good behavior by the outlaw state as evidence of a strategic change for the better in that state's orientation to the norms of the international system.

3. Even a coherent, well-conceptualized long-range policy for attempting to re-socialize the outlaw state may not be implemented consistently for various reasons. For example, the Great Power may be distracted by other foreign policy problems; obtaining and maintaining domestic and international understanding and support for the long range re-socialization policy may be difficult; bureaucratic officials may fail to implement policy fully or to correctly understand the policy laid down by top policymakers; and intra-administration disagreements on specific policies toward the outlaw state may undermine a more purposeful and consistent use of rewards and punishments. (These difficulties of implementation, of course, are not unique to the task of carrying out a policy of re-socialization; they are also encountered in the conduct of foreign policy more generally.)

I noted earlier the absence of any systematic scholarly study of past efforts to reform outlaw states and to draw their leaders into acceptance of the norms and practices of the international system. The several hypotheses provided in this chapter about the requirements and modalities of re-socialization need to be assessed through comparative studies of past efforts of this kind, some successful and others not. The absorption of Kemal Ataturk's Turkey into the international system is an example of successful integration of what was regarded initially, particularly by the British, as a possible outlaw state, or at least, as one situated outside the international community. In the contemporary era, efforts to deal with North Korea, Iran, Vietnam, and Cambodia will be worth studying from this standpoint.

The Nixon-Kissinger détente policy probably constitutes an example of a flawed version of the strategy of re-socialization insofar as its objectives included the long-range one of encouraging the Soviets to mend their ways and enter into a new "constructive relationship" with the United States. The development of a more constructive relationship between two superpowers was to serve as the foundation for a new international system, what Nixon vaguely referred to as "a stable structure of peace."

However, as many commentators noted, Nixon and Kissinger do not appear to have clearly conceptualized or elaborated what they had in mind in this respect. To be sure, the grand strategy for achieving this long-range objective combined rewarding the Soviets for good behavior with punishing them for unacceptable behavior. In other words, it was a carrot-and-stick strategy that attempted to employ, although imperfectly, behavior modification and conditional reciprocity.

The conciliatory component of the strategy offered the Soviet Union a number of benefits it prized: the possibility of greater trade and more access to western credits, grain, and technology; and the possibility of enhanced international status and recognition as a superpower equal to the United States; and the possibility of agreeing to the Soviet's long-standing desire for more formal recognition of the territorial changes in Eastern Europe and acceptance of the Soviet Union's dominant position in that area.

In return, Nixon and Kissinger hoped that once the Soviet Union acquired a strong stake in the détente process it would act with restraint in the Third World lest it jeopardize benefits it was receiving from the evolving relationship. In the meantime, when the Soviets misbehaved in the Third World, Nixon attempted to react sharply. In this context, U.S. leaders urged on the Soviets in general terms the necessity to adhere to a new set of norms and rules of conduct for restraining competition and avoiding conflict throughout the world. The underlying premise, presumably, was that if these efforts were effective, not only would such norms and rules evolve over time, but they would eventually be internalized by Soviet leaders and shape their behavior thereafter.

The strategy of re-socialization in this case was flawed both conceptually and in implementation. Aside from attempting to weave a web of incentives to induce restraint in Soviet foreign policy – or, as one commentator put it, to create a new type of Soviet self-containment – it was not clear what reshaping of the international system Nixon and Kissinger had in mind.

The détente policy foundered for other reasons as well. The two sides did not hold the same understanding of détente, and they held divergent expectations of its benefits. And the Nixon administration was not successful in achieving and maintaining domestic understanding and support for what it was trying to accomplish.[21]

The more recent substantial change in Soviet foreign policy and in its orientation to the international system associated with Gorbachev's "New Thinking" evolved more in line with George Kennan's 1947 "Mr. X" analysis, which held that effective containment supplemented with rewards and punishments for a period of years could eventually bring about internal changes in the ideology and domestic system of the Soviet Union that would result in a mellowing of its foreign policy.

As an example of a failed attempt to reform a rogue leader, one should look closely at Neville Chamberlain's policy toward Hitler. Sometimes forgotten or overlooked is the fact that Chamberlain did not aim only at appeasing Germany's legitimate claims, but also hoped to bring Germany as a responsible actor into a reconstituted European system. As already noted, the Bush administration's policy toward Saddam Hussein prior to his invasion of Kuwait reflects another unsuccessful, and in many respects, poorly conceived and implemented effort to re-socialize and reform him.

Other states and rulers that have been and still seem seriously at odds with the existing international system include the Iran of Ayatollah

Khomeini's successors, Khaddafi's Libya, Syria, and North Korea. It would be desirable to include in a comparative study an analysis of the policies the United States has employed to deal not only with the threats it perceives these states and their rulers pose for its own interests, but also with their challenge to the norms and practices of the international system.

More systematic knowledge regarding the uses, limitations, and risks of the strategy of attempting to reform an outlaw state is not merely of historical or theoretical interest. Rather, it has considerable relevance for contemporary U.S. foreign policy. For example, in early 1992 the administration formally reviewed U.S. policy toward Iran in order to consider adopting a strategy of constructive engagement that would entail lifting some economic sanctions. According to the *New York Times*, the policy review, completed in April, concluded that any gesture that "might be politically meaningful in Tehran – lifting the ban on oil sales to America, for example – would have been politically impossible at home.

On the other hand, a reward small enough to be painless in American political terms, such as lifting the ban on exports of carpets and pistachios, would have seemed too petty to Tehran." The policy review's conclusion that the time was not propitious for adopting a new policy is said to have been influenced by the earlier failure of constructive engagement toward Iraq.

According to the *New York Times*, "even those analysts who defend the use of incentives to moderate behavior are bewildered about how to treat Iran," recognizing that the Iranian government's moves to curb radical elements and to expand ties with the West may be only a tactical maneuver that could be reversed when Iran succeeded in reconstructing its economy.[22]

Dealing With "Spoilers" in Mediating Intra-State Conflicts

A problem often encountered by mediators in civil wars conflicts is that one or more of the contending local actors attempt to disrupt such efforts. A major source of risk encountered by mediators comes from "spoilers" – leaders and parties who believe that a peaceful resolution of the conflict threatens their power and interests. Such spoilers may resort to violence to undermine efforts to mediate the conflict. When spoilers succeed, as they did in Angola in 1992 and in Rwanda in 1994, the results are catastrophic. However, not all would-be spoilers succeed. In Mozambique, one of the local parties, the Mozambique National Resistance (RENAMO) delayed meeting its commitments, threatening to boycott elections and to resort once again to war. In the end, however, it accepted losing an election and disarmed. In Cambodia, peace efforts eventually overcame resistance from the Khmer Rouge.

An important difference between the success and failure of spoilers is how well international actors mediating such disputes play their role. A recent comparative study of such conflicts by Stephen Stedman emphasizes the importance of distinguishing different types of spoilers and identifying appropriate strategies for dealing with each type.[23]

Efforts to create peace in civil conflicts often creates spoilers because rarely in such conflicts do all internal leaders and parties see the terms of an emerging peace settlement as acceptable. Not every civil war easily finds a solution that satisfies the demands of all parties.

Stedman's analysis of a number of such conflicts identifies different types of spoilers. Successful management or mediation of spoiler problems is facilitated by recognition that they differ in their goals and in the level of commitment to achieving their goals. Three types of spoilers can be identified: "limited," "greedy," and "total." Limited spoilers have limited goals, for example, redress of a grievance, a share of power or a preference for how political differences will be allowed expression after the conflict is ended, and a concern for their basic security thereafter. However limited their goals, they may be non-negotiable to begin with and buttressed by a willingness to endure heavy sacrifice on their behalf.

The "greedy" spoiler tends to hold goals that are sensitive to cost and risk calculations; their goals may be limited but capable of expanding or restricting in the face of expected costs and risks.

At the extreme is the "total" spoiler who pursues extreme or total power, more or less exclusive recognition of his authority, and goals and preferences that are immutable. Total spoilers tend to see things in all-or-nothing terms and reject pragmatic compromise.

Spoiler types, therefore, present different problems for peacemaking. Limited spoilers may be included in a settlement if their limited demands can be accommodated. Greedy spoilers can also be accommodated if their limited goals are met and they are constrained from pushing for additional advantages. Total spoilers are difficult to satisfy by compromise arrangements; if they make what appears to be a concession or acceptance of a compromise, it is likely to be tactical in an effort to gain an opportunity later for total success.

This identification of types of demonstrates once again a central theme of this analysis, namely the importance of having reasonably valid "actor-specific" models of adversaries in order to enhance the possibility of coping with them. Different strategies must be adopted by would-be mediators for dealing with each type of spoiler.

As Stedman notes, custodians of peace processes in civil conflicts have pursued three different general strategies in efforts to manage spoilers. These strategies, varying from conciliation to coercion, were: (1) inducement, that is giving a spoiler what it wanted; (2) socialization, or attempting to change the behavior of the spoiler to make it more willing to adhere to a set of norms the mediator is attempting to establish; and (3) coercion, or punishing spoiler behavior and/or reducing its capacity to subvert the effort to establish peace.

Several different coercive strategies have been employed. Coercive diplomacy has not been used very often, an exception being NATO's air strikes against Bosnian Serbs in 1995. The use of force to defeat a spoiler has also been attempted infrequently, as for example when the U.N. tried to defeat the forces of Somali warlord Mohammed Farah Aidid in 1993.

Stedman identifies two more common varieties of coercion. A "departing-train" strategy, based on the finding that the spoiler's demands are unacceptable, conveys that the effort to establish peace will go irrevocably forward, leaving the spoiler behind if it forgoes joining. The "withdrawal" variant of coercion comes into play when the spoiler clearly wants an outside international presence involved in the peace process. "Withdrawal" works by threatening to punish such a spoiler by making credible threats to withdraw international support and outside peacekeepers.

Stedman holds that a correct diagnosis of spoiler type is critical for the choice of an appropriate strategy for dealing with it. The utility of these strategies, and problems that may be encountered in attempting to utilize them, are discussed and illustrated in five systematically compared case studies:

1. "Threatened Withdrawal" in Rwanda;

2. The "Departing Train" strategy in dealing with the Khmer Rouge in Cambodia;

3. The use of "inducement," later against the State of Cambodia;

4. The failure of "inducement" vis-à-vis UNITA in the Angolan Civil War;

5. Successful "inducement" vis-à-vis RENAMO in Mozambique.

In concluding, Stedman emphasizes that his study is a first step in developing a typological theory of spoiler management and makes a number of suggestions for additional work. To this, one might add that the analytical framework for such studies might be expanded to consider more explicitly the possible role of deterrent or threatened retaliatory threats in dealing with spoilers. Indeed, in Stedman's analysis, the line between coercion and deterrence occasionally appears to be blurred. What he does provide is a convincing demonstration of the importance of identifying different types of spoilers, the need for sound actor-specific knowledge of would-be spoilers, and the importance of matching strategies with spoiler types.

The Need for Actor-Specific Behavioral Models[24]

The abstract, general models of deterrence and coercive diplomacy rest on the assumption that the adversaries towards whom they are directed are *rational, unitary* actors. Such abstract models are not strategies in themselves, but merely the starting point for constructing specific, operational strategies that may be appropriate for dealing with specific adversaries in specific situations. Strategies of deterrence and coercive diplomacy are, therefore, highly "context-dependent." As used in social science research, this term indicates that the phenomenon of interest is affected by complex causation. That is, many variables and the interaction between them combine to explain or predict outcomes that result from efforts to employ deterrence and coercive diplomacy.

Abstract models based on the assumption that one is dealing with a rational unitary adversary identify only the general logic that must be induced into the adversary's calculations for the strategy to be successful.

For example, decision-makers at the top may not make their decisions only on the logic of a situation. They may share power and have to strike compromises that reflect the power arrangement that could skew the overall decisions made. Decision outcomes can be affected by logic, psychological dynamics, bureaucratic politics, or organizational procedures. Therefore, abstract decision models assuming rational unitary actors do not indicate what the policymakers on one side must do to induce that "logic" into the adversary's calculation of costs and risks. To achieve the desired result, policymakers have to convert the abstract notion of deterrence or coercive diplomacy into a specific strategy for inducing the adversary to believe that the costs and risks of pursuing a course of action outweigh the hoped for benefits.

The general logic of deterrence is that the adversary be persuaded that the costs and risks of an initiative he may be considering outweigh its expected benefits. The general logic of coercive diplomacy is that the adversary be persuaded that the costs and risks of continuing an initiative already undertaken outweigh its expected benefits.

As already noted, both of these two concepts assume that the adversary is a *rational, unitary* actor. However, both components of this assumption are likely to seriously oversimplify, thereby greatly complicate, the task of formulating and applying effective strategies of deterrence or coercive diplomacy.

Consider first the limitations of the assumption of a *rational* opponent. The adversary may, in fact be a small group of individuals who differ from one another in values, beliefs, perceptions, and judgment. To be sure, the calculus of deterrence rests upon the assumption of a rational opponent who can be deterred from a given course of action if made aware of the costs and risks of pursuing it clearly outweigh the benefits to be gained thereby. For the deterring power to act solely on the basis of such a general assumption may lead to grave error in designing and implementing a deterrence strategy. Not all actors in international politics calculate utility in making decisions in the same way. Differences in values, political culture, attitudes toward risk taking, and so on, may vary greatly. There is no substitute for specific knowledge of each adversary's mind-set and behavioral style, and this is often difficult to obtain or to apply correctly in assessing his intentions or predicting his responses.

The possibility of effective deterrence or coercive diplomacy, therefore, requires a more differentiated behavioral model of the opponent. The general notion of a rational opponent must be replaced by an "actor-specific" model of the opponent's way of calculating costs and risks and deciding what level of costs and risks are acceptable in striving for desired gains. This also requires policymakers to estimate the value an adversary places on obtaining those benefits which influence the level of costs and risks he is willing to accept. The greater the value the adversary attaches to an objective, the stronger his motivation to pursue it and, therefore, the stronger the credible threat must be to persuade him to desist.

Attributing "irrationality" to an opponent when he acts at odds with the coercer's expectation of rational behavior is a questionable way of filling the vacuum of knowledge about his approach to rational behavior. What is needed and often very difficult to develop is a more differentiated understanding of the opponent's values, ideology, culture, and mind-set. This is what is meant by an "actor-specific behavioral model of an opponent."

Policy specialists and academic scholars have no difficulty in agreeing on the need for a better understanding of the adversary's behavioral style. They both emphasize the necessity to try to see events *and, indeed, one's own behavior* from the perspective of the adversary. In a conflict situation, one's self-image often exercises a subtle influence in shaping one's foreign policy. Such a self-image, however, is seldom the same image of you perceived by the adversary that influences his perceptions, calculations, and behavior in ways that make conflict avoidance or crisis management more difficult. Only by being alert to these conflicting images of the self can one diagnose an emerging situation accurately and select appropriate ways of influencing an adversary. Faulty images of each other are a source of serious misperceptions and miscalculations that have often led to major errors in policy, avoidable catastrophes, and missed opportunities.[25]

Consider now the limitations of the assumption of a *"unitary"* actor. This assumes that the opponent is a single, homogenous actor, that there are no significant differences among the members of the ruling elite that influence and complicate the ruler's estimates, calculations, decision-making, and conflict behavior. The assumption of a unitary actor implies that the top leaders have effective control over all subordinate actors. This is a beguiling assumption to make since it dangerously simplifies efforts to use deterrence or coercive diplomacy.

When the assumption of a unitary actor is incorrect, it can contribute to faulty efforts to influence adversaries. Such an assumption can also contribute to the erroneous belief that the adversary operates with an uncomplicated approach to rationality.

Faulty assumptions that the adversary is a rational, unitary actor often occur in inter-state conflict situations. During the Cold War and since, when one has little information about an adversary's mind-set, it is common practice to attribute to rivals a sort of basic, simplified rationality, to see the rival leaders as a mirror image of one's own, decision-makers who ought to perceive the logic of a situation pretty much the same way as does the deterring side. If, in fact, the adversary regime's behavior turns out to be flagrantly at odds with one's expectations of a rational actor, one is tempted to regard the rival leadership as irrational as well as dangerous.

This is not to say that faulty assumptions about an opponent can be easily replaced by sophisticated actor-specific behavioral models. At the same time, however, one must forgo the temptation to regard efforts to develop better actor-specific models as unpromising, if not hopeless. At the very least, even imperfect actor-specific models can be useful, if only to make policymakers aware of relevant uncertainties as to the correct image of the opponent and the need for caution in efforts to employ deterrence and coercive diplomacy, or other strategies that have been discussed.

Simple assumptions that one is dealing with a rational opponent are particularly damaging when one is dealing with *non-state actors*, such as local warlords, terrorists, or rivals in intra-state conflicts and civil wars. Several characteristics of such non-state actors and their implications for counter-terrorist policy can be identified:[26]

1. Non-state actors may lack many identifiable or valuable assets that can be located and targeted in efforts to deter or coerce them;

2. Non-state actors' mind-sets, goals, motivations, and behavioral patterns may be especially difficult to ascertain. As a result, efforts to formulate coercive strategies directed towards them are likely to lack adequate understanding of how non-state actors make cost-benefit calculations. When reliable information

on terrorist motivations is lacking, the coercing power may develop simplified stereotypes of them that emphasize fanaticism and irrationality, particularly when their acts of terrorism are highly destructive.

3. Non-state actors generally lack well-developed decision-making structures, well-defined and reliable lines of authority, and command and control. In some cases, there may be competing power centers within the non-state apparatus. As a result, leaders of non-state actors may have imperfect control over operational units and, therefore, efforts to employ coercion against non-state leaders may not lead to desired changes in the behavior of their subordinates.

4. Coercive efforts against a multi-headed adversary, in which sub-actors have divergent interests, may have the unexpected result of strengthening the hand of the most radical elements. Coercive threats and actions against terrorists may lack credibility and efficacy insofar as some terrorists may not regard force as punishment, but believe it enhances their legitimacy and increases their support.

5. Non-state actors and terrorists often have stronger motivation than does the coercing state. Asymmetrical motivation may also favor some state supporters of terrorism, although such sponsors are locatable and may have other interests that limit such support, and make them more susceptible to pressure or inducements by the coercing power to terminate or significantly limit their support for terrorists. To be sure, non-state actors and terrorists may be largely autonomous and may have ambiguous or complicated relations with states that provide some support. This possibility can be taken into account in devising coercive strategies and offers of conditional inducements to state sponsors of terrorism. But it may be difficult to tailor such efforts to specific situations in which there is considerable uncertainty as to relations between sponsors and terrorists.

6. Efforts to coerce a non-state actor indirectly, by persuading states friendly to the non-state actor to exert pressure against it,

298

may work sometimes, but such efforts of indirect coercion are often difficult and may be counterproductive.

7. Non-state actors and terrorists are often adept in finding ways of exploiting constraints under which coercing states must labor. They can manipulate international opinion, exploit domestic constraints in coercing states, use "human shields" to deter actions against them, and counter efforts to coerce them by engaging in unpredictable or unconventional ways such as by detaining peacekeepers or humanitarian actors as hostages.

Implications for Policy

What are the general implications of the preceding analysis for U.S. foreign policy? In the first place, the distinction must be kept in mind between *concepts* of deterrence and coercive diplomacy and the various *strategies* each of these concepts can take. Concepts indicate only the general logic of deterrence and coercive diplomacy. Concepts do not tell us what must be done in various situations with regard to specific adversaries in order to achieve deterrence or successful coercive diplomacy. For this purpose, policymakers must convert the concept into a particular strategy considered to fit the adversary and the situation at hand.

Second, the effectiveness of deterrence and coercive diplomacy is highly *context dependent*. That is, outcomes of these strategies are influenced by many variables and the interaction between them. As a result, to choose a particular variant of the strategy and to tailor it to a specific situation and a particular adversary is laden with considerable uncertainty.

There is simply no single or simple set of "rules" for dealing with this problem. This lesson was clearly stated by former President George Bush in an address at West Point towards the end of his administration on January 5, 1993:

. . . when the stakes warrant, where and when force can be effective, where no other policies are likely to be effective, where its application can be limited in scope and time, and where the potential benefits justify the potential costs and sacrifice. There can be no single or simple set of fixed rules for using force . . . Each and every case is unique.

Similar conclusions have been drawn by other experienced policymakers and analysts as to whether any useful "decision rules" or specific guidelines can be formulated and agreed upon for dealing with the challenges and dilemmas of using force or threats of force in support of diplomacy. General Colin Powell, for example, also emphasized that there can be "no fixed set of rules" in answering this question.[27]

The question arises whether and how scholarly analysis of the problem of making effective use of deterrence, coercive diplomacy, and other strategies can be helpful to decision-makers. If every case is unique, as President Bush and others have emphasized, can useful lessons of a general kind be drawn from past experience and, if so, how can they be employed by policymakers in addressing new situations?

Scholars who address this task believe that useful lessons can be drawn from systematic study of each of the many generic problems repeatedly encountered in the conduct of foreign policy. This applies not only to generic problems such as deterrence and coercive diplomacy that are of particular interest here, but also to crisis management, war termination and, indeed, crisis avoidance, mediation, and cooperation. To the extent scholars are successful in doing so, their findings contribute to bridging the gap between theory (another word for "generic knowledge") and the practice of policymakers.

In past interviews with policy specialists this author quickly discovered that whenever the word *theory* was used, their eyes would quickly glaze. However, when the term "generic knowledge" was substituted for theory they nodded approvingly. Why? The answer, quite simply, is that policy specialists know that certain generic problems, such as deterrence and coercive diplomacy, repeatedly arise in the conduct of foreign policy. They thus are favorably disposed to efforts to develop generic knowledge of each of these tasks.

Of what value in policymaking is such generic knowledge? How ought it to be used in making decisions? Generic knowledge is most useful when it takes the form of conditional generalizations derived from analysis of past cases. Such generalizations identify the conditions under

300

which, for example, deterrence or coercive diplomacy is likely to be effective and when it is likely to fail.

Such conditional generalizations, it should be emphasized, are *not* prescriptions for action. Their relevance and value is, rather, that they can help policymakers *diagnose* new situations. The proper analogy here is the relationship of knowledge to practice in clinical medicine. In medicine, before powerful drugs were developed, a doctor attempted to diagnose the patient's problem before prescribing for it. Policymakers, like doctors, must diagnose a new situation as aptly as possible before deciding how to deal with it. Helpful in making such diagnoses is generic knowledge of deterrence and coercive diplomacy that identifies the conditions under which, judging from past experience, deterrence is likely to work or not work. Armed with such conditional generalizations, policy specialists are better able to judge whether such "favoring" conditions are present or can be created in the case at hand.

Generic or theoretical knowledge should therefore be useful to those intelligence and policy analysts within the government who are responsible for diagnosing emerging situations for the benefit of decision-makers. However, I would like to emphasize here, as in previous writings,[28] the fact that a gap exists between even the best generic knowledge (or theory) of deterrence and coercive diplomacy and practice and this gap cannot be eliminated, it can only be bridged.

One must have a realistic view of the limited, indirect, but still quite important, impact that generic knowledge about such strategies as deterrence and coercive diplomacy, or of activities such as crisis management or war termination can have on policymaking. Generic knowledge is best viewed as an input to policy analysis of specific situations within the government. Generic knowledge is an *aid* rather than a *substitute* for judgments that decision-makers must exercise when choosing a policy.

In other words, it is a mistake to view theory or generic knowledge as capable of providing policymakers with detailed, high-confidence prescriptions for action in each contingency that arises. Such policy-relevant knowledge does not exist and is not feasible. Rather, as noted above, we must think in terms of the analogy with traditional medical practice, which calls for a correct diagnosis of the problem before prescribing a treatment. In accord with this analogy, I have argued that the major function and use of theory and generic knowledge is to contribute to the diagnosis of specific problematic situations with which policymakers must deal, rather than to provide prescriptions or general "decision rules" for action. Like the medical doctor, the policymaker acts as a clinician who strives to make correct diagnosis of a certain problem before determining how best to deal with it.[29]

It is in this way that the unique nature of each situation, which President Bush emphasized in his West Point speech, can be diagnosed and better understood in order to decide whether and how force or threats of force may apply.

Thus far, I have called attention to two types of knowledge relevant for policy analysis of emergent situations in which consideration is given to employing deterrence, coercive diplomacy, or other strategies discussed in this chapter (reassurance, conciliation, conditional reciprocity). These are, first, the somewhat abstract conceptual models of the strategy and, second, generic knowledge of the strategy. To this, the third type of knowledge emphasized throughout the chapter is actor-specific behavioral knowledge of the adversary in question.[30]

What remains to be emphasized is that these three types of policy-relevant knowledge do not suffice. Policy analysts must also make use of specific information about the situation provided by intelligence and journalistic sources in order to diagnose the situation and prescribe appropriated options. The job of policy analysis is to provide an *analytic judgment* as to what is likely to be the best policy option and the uses and limitations of alternative options. The policymaker, however, has to exercise a broader *political judgment* as to what is most appropriate or more acceptable in the circumstances.

As Charles Hitch, who organized and led the Economics Department at the RAND Corporation repeatedly emphasized, even the results of the best systems analysis should be regarded as an *aid* to the preparation of policy decisions and not a *substitute* for the "judgment" of the decision-maker. One of the most important judgments a policymaker must make concerns the trade-off between the analytical quality of the policy to be chosen and the need to obtain sufficient support, domestic and often international, for the option finally chosen.

Another familiar trade-off problem arises from having to decide how much time and policymaking resources to allocate to an effort to select the best possible policy option.

A third trade-off problem arises from having to decide how much political capital and influence resources to expend in an effort to increase the level of support for an option finally chosen.[31]

The contributions of these three types of knowledge and specific intelligence to policy analysis and the role of the policymaker's judgment of trade-offs is depicted in Figure 1.

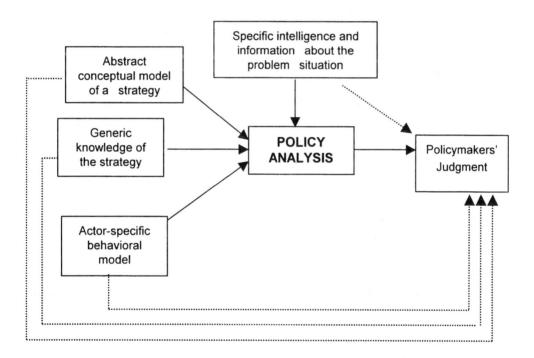

Figure 1: Ways in which the three types of knowledge together with specific information about the situation contribute to the policy analysis that precedes the various judgments policymakers must make.

Finally, I have emphasized in this chapter the need to place deterrence, coercive diplomacy, and the possible use of military force into a broader influence theory, one which encompasses the possible use of strategies of reassurance, conciliation, and conditional reciprocity. These strategies are alternatives that may recommend themselves in situations in which resort to deterrence, coercive diplomacy, or military force is laden with considerable uncertainty and risk.

At the same time, deterrence and coercive diplomacy, although often difficult to implement, remain helpful strategies in certain situations and against certain opponents. Despite their limitations, these strategies have a role to play, however restricted or complicated, in many post-Cold War contexts.

The policymaker needs both the velvet glove of diplomacy and the iron fist of armed forces, both carrots and sticks, to achieve state ends. In some cases, conciliatory means will suffice. In others, both positive and coercive incentives are necessary. In still others, only force or its threatened use can achieve the desired outcome.

The Bush administration's new emphasis on a declaratory policy that threatens preventive actions, involving either preventive war or preemption, considered for use against Saddam Hussein's Iraq, should be seen as an effort to reinforce deterrence and coercive diplomacy in some situations as well as to replace unqualified reliance on such policies.[32]

Notes

1. This point was emphasized in *Deterrence in American Foreign Policy*, published in 1974 by Alexander L. George and Richard Smoke. See Chapter 21, "From Deterrence to Influence in Theory and Practice." A major early contribution stressing the importance of inducement was David A. Baldwin, "The Power of Positive Sanctions," *World Politics* Vol. 24, No. 1 (1971), 19-38.

2. Other "lessons" of experience derived from efforts to employ deterrence are discussed in A. L. George, "The Role of Force in Diplomacy: A Continuing Dilemma for U.S. Foreign Policy," in H.W. Brands, ed., *The Use of Force After the Cold War* (College Station, TX: Texas A & M University Press, 2000), 59-92. Some recent books on deterrence which contain relevant material for this chapter include Keith B. Payne, *The Fallacies of Cold War Deterrence and a New Direction* (Lexington, Kentucky: University of Kentucky Press, 2001); Barry R. Schneider, *Future War and Counterproliferation* (Westport, Connecticut: Praeger, 1999), see Chapter 4, "Deterring Adversary Attacks"; Kenneth Watman and Dean Wilkening, *U.S. Regional Deterrence Strategies* (Santa Monica: RAND Corporation, 1995).

3. Additional discussion of the lessons of experience with coercive diplomacy are summarized in A.L. George, *op. cit.,* 80-85. An important new contribution which includes eight post Cold-War studies and policy recommendations is Robert J. Art and Patrick Cronin, eds., *The United States and Coercive Diplomacy After the Cold War* (tentative title) (Washington, D.C.: United States Institute of Peace Press, forthcoming). Other important recent works on coercive diplomacy and coercive strategies include Daniel L. Byman, Matthew C. Waxman, and Eric Larson, *Air Power as a Coercive Instrument* (Santa Monica: RAND Corporation, 1993); Lawrence Freedman, ed., *Strategic Coercion: Concepts and Cases* (Oxford, England: Oxford University Press, 1998); Peter Viggio Jakobsen, *Western Use of Coercive Diplomacy After the Cold War* (New York: St. Martin's Press, 1998); Donald C.F. Daniel and Bradd C. Hayes, *Coercive Inducement and the Containment of International Crises* (Washington, D.C.: U.S. Institute of Peace, 1999). The normative, political, and policy dilemmas associated with use of coercive diplomacy are incisively analyzed by Bruce W. Jentleson, *Coercive Prevention,* Peaceworks No. 35, (Washington, D.C.: United States Institute of Peace Press, October 2000). I do not discuss in the present chapter the important constraints on the ability of U.S. policymakers to employ deterrence and coercive diplomacy more effectively. There are occasions in which domestic and/or international constraints on the use of force made it advisable for U.S. leaders to begin with economic sanctions and/or coercive diplomacy even though they were not expected to be effective, but in order to move later, as in the war against Iraq in 1990, to the use of military force. Eric Larson provides an excellent discussion of the variety of domestic constraints on the use of coercive strategies by the United States and notes how these constraints can be exploited by adversaries in Chapter 4, in the book edited by Byman, Waxman, and Larson, noted above. See also the excellent contribution by Robert Art in Art and Cronin, eds., *op. cit.*

4. The best discussion of various reassurance strategies is Janice Gross Stein, "Deterrence and Reassurance," in Philip E. Fetlock, et. al., *Behavior, Society, and Nuclear War* (New York: Oxford University Press, 1991), 8-72.

5. For a detailed discussion of the role of appeasement in the classical era of European diplomacy, see Chapter 18, "Détente," in Gordon A. Craig and Alexander L. George, *Force and Statecraft: Diplomatic Problems of Our Time* (New York: Oxford University Press, Third Edition, 1995).

6. Rock discusses these considerations in some detail in *Appeasement in International Politics* (Lexington: University of Kentucky Press, 2000).

7. For a detailed analysis of the problems of dealing with so-called "rogue" states, see Robert S. Litwak, *Rogue States and U.S. Foreign Policy* (Woodrow Wilson Center Press, 2000); also Chapter 4, "Reforming Outlaw States and Rogue Leaders," A.L. George, *Bridging the Gap.*

8. Stephen R. Rock has provided the first analytical systematic study of historical experience with efforts at appeasement in a variety of contexts. He employs an incisive analytical framework for comparing cases of effective and unsuccessful efforts at appeasement. These cases are successful British appeasement of the United States, 1896-1903; unsuccessful British appeasement of Germany, 1936-1939; ineffective Anglo-American appeasement of the Soviet Union, 1941-1945; ineffective U.S. appeasement of Iraq, 1989-1990; possibly effective appeasement of North Korea, 1988-1994. *Appeasement in International Politics* (Lexington: University of Kentucky Press, 2000).

9. Barbara Tuchman, *The March of Folly* (New York: Knopf, 1984), Chapter 4. A related, fifth scenario is suggested by Stephen Stedman (in a personal communication): a situation in which appeasement might have succeeded at an early stage in the dispute but became more difficult because reliance on deterrence or force hardened the adversary's position.

10. This discussion of conditional reciprocity draws explicitly from that provided in Chapter 4, "Reforming Outlaw States and Rogue Leaders," in A.L. George, *Bridging the Gap: Theory and Practice in Foreign Policy* (Washington, D.C.: United States Institute of Peace Press, 1993).

11. For a discussion of the Agreed Framework, see Litwak, *op. cit.,* John Lewis Gaddis notes that George Kennan coupled the strategy of containment he recommended for dealing with the Soviet Union with a version of what might be called behavior modification. Gaddis notes in this connection that Kennan recommended that modifying Soviet behavior required both positive and negative reinforcement; it was important to reward the Kremlin for conciliatory gestures as it was to oppose aggressive moves. Gaddis, *Strategies of Containment* (New York: Oxford University Press, 1982), 71. Quoted in Robert S. Litwak, *op. cit.,* 10.

12. Henry Kissinger, *A World Restored: Europe After Napoleon* (Magnolia, MA: Peter Smith, 1973).

13. Yehezkel Dror's *Crazy States* (1971) provides suggestive observations but eschews empirical analysis of past experience. Charles Doran, *The Politics of Assimilation: Hegemony and its Aftermath* (Baltimore: Johns Hopkins Press, 1971), deals with the task of assimilating defeated hegemonic powers back into the international system and should be consulted for hypotheses in studies of the problem of re-socializing outlaw states.

14. A former official who was in the government in 1984-85 when the Reagan administration was attempting to coerce Khaddafi into stopping assistance to terrorists recalled in an interview that the administration sent naval forces into the Gulf of Sidra in a deliberate effort to provoke him; the administration hoped to shoot down his planes,

thereby humiliating and discrediting him so that he might be ousted. For a detailed account of the Bush administration's last minute effort before the cease-fire of February 28 to use two specially prepared deep penetration bombs to "get" Saddam in one of his hardened bunkers, see *U.S. News and World Report*, "Triumph Without Victory," 3-6. An incisive, balanced analysis of the option of assassinating rival leaders is provided by Stephen T. Hosner, *Operations Against Enemy Leaders* (Santa Monica: The RAND Corporation, 2001).

15. The distinguished psychologist, Charles Osgood, originated the strategy of GRIT many years ago in his *An Alternative to War and Surrender* (Urbana: University of Illinois Press, 1962).

16. For a fuller discussion of the nature of GRIT and tit-for-tat, see A.L. George, P.J. Farley, and A. Dallin, eds., *U.S.-Soviet Security Cooperation* (New York: Oxford University Press, 1988), 702-707.

17. Robert Axelrod, *Evolution of Cooperation* (New York: Basic Books, 1984).

18. Helpful for this purpose would be a list of explicit indicators that the adversary does not accept the norms of the international system and subscribes to and is preparing to achieve the goal of regional hegemony.

19. For a more general discussion, see Thomas W. Milburn and Daniel J. Christie, "Rewarding in International Politics," *Political Psychology* Vol. 10, No. 4 (December 1989), 625-645.

20. Precisely this objection was raised by members of the National Security Council (NSC) in April 1987 to proposals by Ross Perot that the Reagan administration make conciliatory actions toward North Vietnam to show "good faith," overcome its leaders' distrust of the United States, and thereby encourage Hanoi's cooperation in locating American POWS and MIAs. NSC officials objected on the grounds that such actions would be granting "concessions without performance." In an interview, one former NSC staff member added, "History has shown that concession prior to performance is death. They'll take and take. We've learned that over 25 years." Patrick E. Tyler, *New York Times* (July 5, 1992).

21. Many writers have analyzed the flaws in the conceptualization of the détente policy and the problems encountered in implementing it. For accounts focusing on aspects of the policy that resembled the reform and re-socialization strategies discussed in this chapter, see A.L. George, ed., *Managing the U.S.-Soviet Rivalry* (Boulder, CO: Westview Press, 1983), especially Chapters 1, 5, 6, and 13; also A.L. George, "Domestic Constraints on Regime Change in U.S. Foreign Policy: The Need for Policy Legitimacy," O.R. Holsti, R.M. Siverson, and A.L. George, eds., *Change in the International System* (Boulder, CO: Westview Press, 1980), 233-262.

22. Elaine Sciolino, *New York Times* (June 7, 1992).

23. Stephen John Stedman, "Spoiler Problems in Peace Processes," in Paul C. Stern and Daniel Druckman, eds., *International Conflict Resolution After the Cold War*, (Washington, D.C.: National Academy Press, 2000), Chapter 5.

24. I have emphasized the need for actor-specific behavioral models for many years. See, for example, A.L. George, D. Hall, and W.E. Simons, *The Limits of Coercive Diplomacy* (Boston: Little, Brown, and Company, 1971), xiv; A.L. George and R. Smoke, *Deterrence in American Foreign Policy* (New York: Columbia University Press, 1974); A.L. George, *Presidential Decisionmaking in American Foreign Policy* (Boulder, Colorado: Westview Press, 1980), 242; as well as A.L. George, *Bridging the Gap* (Washington, D.C.: U.S. Institute of Peace Press, 1993).

25. Examples of questionable or incorrect images of an opponent include Washington's image of Saddam Hussein and the role it played in several failed strategies and policies adopted towards him prior to his attack on Kuwait, Stalin's incorrect image of Hitler prior to his attack on the Soviet Union in 1941, Truman's incorrect image of China's threat to intervene in the Korean War in the fall of 1950, the different images of the Soviets held by top-level U.S. policymakers engaged in mid-1961 in efforts to assess Khrushchev's threat against Berlin. Contrast these and other cases with President's Kennedy's correct image of Khrushchev in the Cuban Missile Crisis. (For a more detailed discussion, see *Bridging the Gap*, 126-130.)

26. Examples and analysis of these characteristics of non-state actors and terrorists, and of the difficulties they create for deterrence and coercion against them are provided in a number of excellent studies. See particularly several studies by analysts of the RAND Corporation: Daniel L. Byman and Matthew C. Waxman, *The Dynamics of Coercion: American Foreign Policy and the Limits of Military Might* (Cambridge, U.K.: Cambridge University Press, 2002); Daniel L. Byman, Matthew C. Waxman, and Eric Larson, *Air Power As A Coercive Instrument* (Santa Monica, California: The RAND Corporation, 1999), see especially Chapter 6, "Coercing Nonstate Actors: A Challenge"; Ian O. Lesser, Bruce Hoffman, John Arquilla, David Ronfeldt, Michele Zanina, with a Foreword by Brian Michael Jenkins, *Countering the New Terrorism* (Santa Monica: The RAND Corporation, 1999).

An important contribution to this subject is Martha Crenshaw, "Coercive Diplomacy and the Response to Terrorism," in Art and Cronin, eds., *The United States and Coercive Diplomacy After the Cold War* (tentative title). See also additional items cited in Footnotes 2 and 3.

A detailed, well-informed, broad analysis of the entire set of problems involved in dealing with terrorism is provided by a former senior counter-terrorist official at the Central Intelligence Agency, Paul R. Pillar, *Terrorism and U.S. Foreign Policy* (Washington, D.C.: Brookings Institution, 2001). See also the comprehensive analysis by Jessica Stern, "Terrorist Activities and Unconventional Weapons," in Peter R. Lavoy, Scott D. Sagan, and James J. Wirtz, eds., *Planning the Unthinkable: How New Powers Will Use Nuclear, Biological, and Chemical Weapons* (Ithaca and London: Cornell University Press, 2000), Chapter 8.

See also the detailed analysis and proposals in Chapter 9, "Preventing Catastrophic Terrorism," in David A. Hamburg, *No More Killing Fields: Preventing Deadly Conflict* (Lanham, Maryland: Rowman & Littlefield, 2002). This book builds upon and significantly extends the work of the Carnegie Commission on Preventing Deadly Conflict, which Dr. Hamburg co-chaired with Cyrus Vance.

27. General Colin L. Powell, "U.S. Forces: Challenges Ahead," *Foreign Affairs* Vol. 71 (Winter 1992) 19-93, 32-36. For additional discussion, see A.L. George, "The Role of Force in Diplomacy: A Continuing Dilemma for U.S. Foreign Policy."

28. These ideas are developed in greater detail and illustrated in A.L. George's *Bridging the Gap: Theory and Practice in Foreign Policy* (Washington, D.C.: U.S. Institute of Peace, 1993).

29. The importance of the diagnostic use of theory and generic knowledge for policymaking has been emphasized in all my previous publications beginning with Alexander George's *Propaganda Analysis* (1959), *The Limits of Coercive Diplomacy* (1971). Richard K. Herrmann also emphasizes the diagnostic value of policy-relevant theory in "Policy-Relevant Theory and the Challenge of Diagnosis: The End of the Cold War," *Political Psychology* Vol. 15, No. 1 (March, 1994), 111-142.

30. Many writers have emphasized the imperatives of what is referred to here as "actor-specific behavioral models." Post-mortems conducted after a major intelligence failure usually give particular emphasis to the need for better "images" of adversaries in order to avoid "surprise." Recent efforts to develop novel approaches to this task include Richard K. Herrmann and Michael Fischerkeller, "Beyond the Enemy Images and Spiral Model: Cognitive-Strategic Research After the Cold War" *International Security* Vol. 49, No. 3 (Summer 1995), 15-450; and Caroline F. Ziemke, "Strategic Personality and the Effectiveness of Nuclear Deterrence: Deterring Iraq and Iran," IDA Paper P-3658 (September 2001) Alexandria, Virginia: Institute of Defense Analysis.

31. These and other trade-offs in high-level policymaking that complicate purely rational decision-making are discussed in Chapter 2 of A.L. George, *Bridging the Gap*.

32. Preventive war and preemption are general concepts that need clarification and operationalization. "Preventive war" involves a decision in peacetime to launch an attack, hopefully with the benefit of strategic or at least tactical surprise. In contrast, "preemption" can take several different forms: (1) an attack which is based in the belief that the opponent has already made a decision to initiate war, is making appropriate

preparations, but has not yet initiated the attack; (2) an attack based on the belief that an enemy attack is being launched and is in its early phase; (3) an attack based on the belief that an enemy attack is on the way and that its effectiveness can be diminished and/or that retaliation for it can be better assured by preemptive strike; (4) an attack based on the belief that an enemy attack is underway which may not have been authorized by top opponent leaders but is undertaken by subordinates - i.e., the possibility of "accidental war."

CHAPTER 11

Precise Assessments of Rivals
Vital in Asymmetric War Threat Environment

Jerrold M. Post and Barry R. Schneider

Rogue states and terrorist organizations, some armed with weapons of mass destruction or geared to acquire them, pose a new and alarming danger to the United States, its allies and vital interests. As the late U.S. Air Force General Robert Linhard once observed, we are now entering an era where small groups or even single individuals with WMD are now capable of inflicting the kind of damage and casualties that once could only have been inflicted by large and powerful states.

A new group of states and groups of concern, all with a common unpleasant mix of traits, now face the United States as adversaries. States like Iran, Iraq, North Korea, Libya, and Syria, and terror groups such as al Qaeda share a common lineage.

Each is a dictatorship or revolutionary group headed by a strong man who rules largely by fear and coercion. Each is a state sponsor of terrorism or is a terrorist group. Each is a self-professed extreme enemy of the United States. Each of the "states of concern" possess at least one form of weapon of mass destruction, and most pursue a mix of nuclear explosives, radiological weapons, biological arms, and chemical weapons for the future. There is also ample evidence of terrorist interest in acquiring mass casualty weapons.

Each of these rogue nations or terrorist organizations is prone to violent solutions to international problems and pose regional threats to their neighbors, some of which are U.S. allies such as the Republic of Korea, Israel, and the more moderate Arab states like Egypt, Jordan, and Saudi Arabia.

Avoiding A Holy War

Further, all but one of these adversary states or hostile groups are predominantly Muslim. None of the 25 Arab states in the world can be considered full fledged democracies that share a common political system with the United States. Only half of the 20 other Muslim, but non-Arab states are democracies. Much of the "Arab street" and remainder of the Muslim world is hostile to the United States. We are frequently viewed by them as from an alien culture, associated with their enemy, Israel, and partners with their former colonial masters in Europe. Further, the United States is rich where many of them are desperately poor, powerful where they are militarily weak, and are westernized infidels whose very presence is seen as an affront to their God and threat to their way of life.

One of the many challenges in confronting the Muslim rogue states and radical Islamists in terroristic groups is in finding a way of deterring, disarming, and defeating such adversaries. The problem is how to take them on without mobilizing the entire Muslim world against us.

It would be a costly mistake to make the contest one between the United States and Islam instead of differentiating among radical and moderate Muslim governments, nations, and groups.

The fight must be conducted against the radicals by separating and isolating them from the larger Muslim ranks. Every effort should be made to win or at least neutralize the majority of Muslims who remain moderate, peaceful, and who are either allies or who are willing to remain on the sidelines. Every effort must also be made to isolate the radical Islamists, clearly differentiate them from the moderates and neutral followers of Islam, and defeat and neutralize them.

The first step in that process is to more clearly understand their leaders, who they are, what they believe, the action program they have adopted, and their modus operandi.

Asymmetric Warfare Probable

All these adversaries, whether they be North Korea or Iraq or al Qaeda, when faced with the overwhelming military power of the United

312

States, are likely to adopt asymmetrical warfare strategies in an attempt to level the playing field in conflicts with the world's military superpower.

Therefore, they may adopt such means as terrorism, guerrilla warfare and other low intensity war strategies. In a regional war, such opponents might also attempt to reduce the U.S. advantage by attacking with nuclear, biological, and chemical weapons to offset superior U.S. conventional military power.

Some might attempt counter-space strikes to neutralize U.S. overhead reconnaissance and communications. Others may use information operations to disrupt the operations of U.S. forces and to concern U.S. citizens about their own safety. Asymmetric attacks may be aimed at vulnerable U.S. and allied critical infrastructure or key targets that, when struck, create panic and may influence the U.S. public to reconsider its support for U.S. international policies.

In such dangerous, challenging and interesting times, it is important to know who you are dealing with, how they think, and ways they act and fight. The United States Government leaders need to acquire a nuanced understanding of the leadership and strategic culture of such heavily armed U.S. adversaries. Indeed, the frequency of threats arising from relatively unknown and unfamiliar sources increases our need for a rapid and sophisticated profiling and modeling of a new group of unfamiliar foes.

The Rise Of Rogue Leaders And International Outlaws

The end of the Cold War has been destabilizing, producing not a "peace dividend" but an unpredictable international climate in which major political crises frequently have been precipitated by rogue leaders of outlaw nations. The relatively stable and predictable superpower rivalry has been replaced by a series of regional conflicts often precipitated by the actions of previously unknown or poorly understood leaders. There has been a proliferation of destructive power, with more destructive power in the hands of small, independent leadership with hostile agendas toward the United States. The most worrisome nations—Iran, Iraq, North Korea, Libya, and Syria—are ruled by unpredictable dictatorships. The headlines of the past few years have been dominated by such names as Saddam

313

Hussein, Kim Chong-il, Mohammad Farah Aideed, Radovan Karadzic, and Slobodan Milosevic.

Several of these leaders either already have or are actively seeking weapons of mass destruction. During the 1990-91 Gulf Crisis, a nuclear-armed Saddam Hussein would have entirely changed the dynamics of the conflict. Former Secretary of Defense Perry has referred to the "nightmare scenario" of a nuclear-armed North Korea. And just a few short years ago, an extremist nationalist contended for the presidency of Russia, a possibility at the time that was not entirely out of the question given Yeltsin's failing health and his tenuous hold on power. The prospect of a future Vladimir Zhirinovskiy-like figure with his finger on the nuclear button would be truly terrifying. The same could be said if leaders like Muammar Qaddafi of Libya or Ayotollah Khamenei of Iran were to acquire WMD capabilities mated with effective delivery means.

Avoiding Deadly Conflict

Earlier in this volume, in addressing the challenge of conducting effective coercive diplomacy, Dr. Alexander George stressed the importance of having clear models of the psychology of our adversaries. As with information campaigns, effective diplomacy in conflict situations cannot proceed effectively without clear and accurate understanding of leadership psychology.[1] International analysts have stressed the critical role of leadership, both in promoting deadly conflict and in avoiding it. In order to effectively counter leaders such as Saddam Hussein and Slobodan Milosevic as they promote deadly conflict, clear actor-specific models of their psychology and decision-making is an absolute requisite.

Precise adversary leader assessments are helpful, particularly when confronting unique rogue state and terrorist group leaders. To be effective against them, the U.S. should tailor a deterrence package that maximizes the influence it can wield against a particular leader and his group of associated sub-leaders.

Profiling – A Sound Investment

Assembling expert interdisciplinary teams that combine to give a clearer view of the personality and strategic views of rival political leaders is relatively inexpensive and can yield dividends far beyond the moderate cost of bringing a group of profilers together on common studies. Such multi-disciplinary intelligence groups, used properly and heeded, may well provide a "much greater bang for the proverbial buck" than adding an additional jet aircraft or other similar military force improvements. Such profiles can help U.S. decision-makers make more intelligent policy and strategic choices in times of crisis or war, helping them to anticipate and influence the behavior of adversaries. Such profiling helps U.S. Presidents to have a nuanced understanding of a rival leader like Saddam Hussein.

For example, a political and psychological analysis of Saddam's personality and operating methods described him as a rational calculator, a power maximizer who brooks absolutely no rivals and entertains very little contrary opinion. His profilers simultaneously describe him by a myriad of adjectives: calculating, Machiavellian, cunning, secretive and violent. He has been identified as highly suspicious, fearful of opposition, sadistic, and thuggish. He is seen as a survivor, vindictive, filled with murderous hate, guarded, and secretive, possessing a messiah complex, and totalitarian. He is understood to be extremely dangerous, lethal, callous, manipulative, and very egocentric. He was mistreated as a child, was poor and abused, and as a consequence, possesses a "wounded self" that protects itself by a search for even more acclaim and who eliminates all potential rivals whether they are forming against him or not at the time. He either kills, jails, tortures or exiles them. Having executed literally tens of thousands of his own countrymen, Saddam, of necessity, has become acutely aware of possible coups, assassins, and plots and uses extreme security measures, employing food tasters at all meals to avoid being poisoned. According to reports, he does not sleep in the same bed on consecutive nights, constantly moving around to present less of a target to his perceived enemies. He surrounds himself with bodyguards and doubles, and never advertises his schedule in advance.[2] He has created a terroristic police state and a cult of personality and his reward is to be

315

constantly having to protect his back against the families and friends of his legions of victims.

Saddam Hussein has spent his entire life pursuing and clinging onto political power. While capable of tactical retreats to preserve that power, he has never been faced with the choice of sure death or exile, but all his tendencies would likely incline him to fight to the last rather than surrender - a bunker mentality. Exile is probably not a psychologically viable option and any subordinate who might suggest that he give up power and flee is likely to meet an untimely end. Saddam has not been reluctant to use chemical weapons on the Kurds and Iranians and is thought likely to elect to use all remaining Iraqi mass casualty weapons to defend or avenge himself in a military end game. Compromise, surrender, or withdrawal from Iraq are not likely decisions by Saddam Hussein even if the opponent's vise is closing on him.

Profiles such as the one on Saddam Hussein help us understand who we are dealing with. They help get us inside the mind of a dictator.[3] They, at least, shed more light on answers to questions about whether or not he could be deterred from use of his weapons of mass destruction during a crisis or war. Profiling might help answer whether or not he could, in impending defeat, be persuaded to go quietly into the night if allowed to survive and go into exile or whether he would instead choose to go out in a blaze of biological and chemical attacks on his enemies as they closed in upon him.

Leadership profiling and the understanding of terrorist and rogue state strategic cultures also gives us insights that can help guide U.S. and allied PSYOPs or psychological operations.

The Requirement to Counter Low-Intensity Conflict

Psychological operations doctrine, developed and applied in conventional warfare, has an important role to play in countering terrorism, but its powerful techniques have not been adapted to the changing battlefield of low intensity conflict such as insurgencies and terrorism. In order to apply psychological operations effectively to terrorism, the attributes of the target must be specified, particularly the attributes of specific leaders and their pattern of decision-making. One

316

cannot effectively target and influence a group without a clear understanding of its leaders and decision structures, which vary widely from group to group.

Understanding the enemy commander and his supreme leader can provide decisive advantages to the United States if it allows us to anticipate and counter their decisions and tendencies. This should be part of the intelligence preparation of the battlefield or the counter-terrorism campaign.

This is an age of the information revolution and technological innovations have fueled a new revolution in military affairs (RMA).[4] In the U.S. military's <u>Joint Vision 2010</u> information superiority is the key enabler in allowing forces to achieve dominant maneuver, precision engagement, focused logistics, and full-spectrum protection.[5] However, perhaps the most important thing to understand is the mind of the enemy supreme leader. It is also useful to know how to use information to influence the perceptions and actions of others, including potential allies and adversaries.

Information is also a tool of psychological or information warfare. Until very recently, the battle for control of the information battlefield, vis-à-vis Iraq's non-compliance with U.N. Resolutions, was largely left uncontested as Saddam Hussein effectively re-framed the conflict for his radical Arab constituents and enhanced his reputation and leadership standing. Similarly, by his control of the information environment, for a time Slobodan Milosevic effectively countered the military superiority of the NATO air campaign to reframe the contest in such a manner as to increase his support and steel the will of the Serbian people. The ability of Saddam Hussein and Slobodan Milosevic to manipulate the information environment so adroitly and successfully caused serious problems for the United States and its allies.

Further, consider how rapidly the support of the American public changed concerning support for the intervention into Somalia. Initially, the televised spectacle of starving Somali children deeply touched the heart strings of the American public, which strongly supported the humanitarian intervention. But later, the sight of American soldiers' bodies being hauled behind the Somali warlord's jeeps rapidly led to pressure to withdraw to prevent further loss of American life. Whether purposeful or not, this assuredly was a highly effective psychological operation by the Somali warlord Mohammad Farah Aideed.

As major resources are being devoted to information warfare and psychological operations, it is crucial to incorporate state of the art techniques for specifying the behavioral attributes of the adversary's leadership. One cannot intelligently influence an adversary one does not understand. What deters one opponent may be an incitement for another. Actions must be taken and messages delivered that influence the perceptions, thoughts, and decisions of the adversary leadership. To achieve maximum results, such verbal and non-verbal communications must be based on a correct understanding of how they will influence the minds of the rival leaders. This requires the ability rapidly and accurately to model psychologically the adversary's leadership.

The Importance of Effective Methods for Profiling Political Leaders

Profiling techniques chart a pathway to this end. They have been used to assess the personalities of foreign political and military leaders to assist in summit meetings and other high-level negotiations, in crisis situations, and in estimative intelligence. These methods have been employed to evaluate the intentions of foreign political and military leaders, to evaluate the impact of foreign policy events on their psychological state and political attitudes, and to analyze changes in their threat potential.

The rapidity with which international conflicts can "go critical" and the catastrophic consequences of miscalculation make it imperative that accurate evaluations of rival leader psychology be developed swiftly and be monitored closely during crises. Encouraging progress is being made by some experts in this field in utilizing computer-assisted content analysis, so that the capacity to evaluate on-line key leader psychological states is considered attainable in the near future.

In a complex politico-military crisis, such as the crisis in the Gulf precipitated by Saddam Hussein's 1990 invasion of Kuwait, the capacity to closely monitor fluctuations in the leader's mental state can valuably inform crisis managers.

Similarly, in a terrorist hostage and barricade crisis, rapid changes in integrative cognitive complexity could signal a sharp increase in hazard to the hostages' lives, suggesting a shift from hostage negotiations to a SWAT team intervention. This and other measures could also be employed to identify crucial moments in international negotiations, predicting the negotiating adversary's readiness to compromise.

And, most importantly, the President and cabinet level officials, who see people as the essence of politics, are strongly interested in what makes their adversaries and allies tick. A better-informed leadership will better negotiate the treacherous shoals of national and international waters, and sound methods of evaluating the psychology of political leaders can assist in that important task.

This collection of studies has focused on the states of concern and terrorist groups that appear to offer the most immediate threat to the United States and its allies and vital interests. In late 2002, these appear to be the rivals in Iraq, Iran, North Korea, Libya, Syria, the parts of Pakistan not under central control, among radical terrorist groups like al Qaeda and inside organizations like the Muslim Brotherhood that breed such radicals who later join terrorist/revolutionary movements.

There is no claim here that we have exhausted the list of all the international rivals to the United States and its allies. There are others that bear close scrutiny including China, Cuba, Sudan, and dozens of terrorist organizations. Other new rivals will confront us that we are not expecting. Indeed, the unanticipated enemy has become the norm. Before the events, how many U.S. leaders or international affairs analysts predicted we would be at war with Slobodan Milosevic in Serbia, Mohammad Farah Aideed in Somalia, Osama bin Laden of al Qaeda, or Shoko Ashahara of the Aum Shinrikyo prior to their attacks on U.S. and allied targets? Who would have predicted a year before the 2001 attack on the World Trade Centers that the United States would prosecute a war in Afghanistan in 2002? Or that we would decisively win such a war in a few short months?

And who would have predicted how far the United States and Russia have come to being allies rather than adversaries in the decade following the demise of the former Soviet Union? Lord Palmerson once noted that states have no permanent allies, just permanent interests. Today's rival may become tomorrow's ally, and vice versa. However, given the enormous stakes involved in an era of weapons of mass destruction and international terrorist organizations capable of inflicting immense physical and economic harm, we are compelled to better understand our adversaries and their strategic cultures in order to anticipate them, deter the worst attacks, influence them, and if necessary, defeat them on the battlefields of the present and future.

Notes

1. This theme was carried forward in the work of the Carnegie Commission on Preventing Deadly Conflict, of which Alexander George was a member, 1994-1999 (Hamburg, Germany: George & Ballentine 1999).

2. See Ibrahim Al-Marashi, "Saddam's Security and Intelligence Network," CNS, Monterey Institute of International Studies, October 21, 2002. See on Internet: http://cns.miis.edu/research/iraq/iraqint.htm.

3. See Sonni Efron and Sebastian Rotella, "Inside the Mind of a Dictator," *London Times*, October 12, 2002. They conclude that Saddam Hussein "is ruthless but afraid, cunning but error prone. And he's eerily unpredictable."

4. For a comprehensive list of previous RMA's in military history see Andrew F. Krepinevich, "Cavalry to the Computer: The Pattern of Military Revolutions," *The National Interest*, Fall 1994, 30-42.

5. Joint Chiefs of Staff, <u>Joint Vision 2010</u>, (Washington, D.C.: Joint Staff, Pentagon, 2000), 19.

Contributors

Ms. Merrily Baird, from 1970 to 1997, was a specialist on Korea and Japan for the Central Intelligence Agency. During that period she held positions as Special Assistant to the Inspector General, Branch Chief and Senior Analyst for leadership analysis, North Korea, and specialized in foreign government management of nuclear weapons programs. Ms. Baird also served as Chief of the Japan-Korea Section at the Bureau of Intelligence and Research at the State Department, as a Proliferation Specialist at the National Intelligence Council, and has had a tour as attaché at the U.S. embassy in Tokyo. Ms. Baird is currently a lecturer on Japanese art, assistant curator of the Japanese print exhibit at Agnes Scott College, Atlanta, and consultant on Asian art to the American Museum of Papermaking, Atlanta. She is the author of books and articles on Japanese art. Ms. Baird is the recipient of the National Intelligence Medal of Achievement for work on North Korea and Counterproliferation.

Dr. Amatzia Baram is a professor of Middle Eastern History at the University of Haifa, Israel. He received his Ph.D. in Middle Eastern Studies from The Hebrew University of Jerusalem in 1986. He is the author of *Culture , History and Ideology in the Formation of Ba'thist Iraq: 1968-1989*, (London; Oxford; New York, 1991); *Building Toward Crisis: Saddam Husayn's Strategy for Survival* (Washington, DC, 1998), and joint editor of *Iraq's Road to War* (New York, London, 1993). He has also published numerous articles, monographs and chapters in academic magazines and volumes, as well as in encyclopedias. Recently, Dr. Baram also presented a position paper and provided testimony on Saddam Hussein and Weapons of Mass Destruction, to the U.S. House of Representatives Hearing on "Combating Terrorism: Preventing Nuclear Terrorism," Before the Subcommittee on National Security, Veterans Affairs and International Relations of the Committee on Government Reform, Washington DC, September 24, 2002.

Commander Craig Black is a U.S. Naval Aviator assigned to the Defense Intelligence Agency, undergoing attaché training. He graduated from the University of Missouri-Kansas City in 1982 with a Bachelor of Arts Degree in History. He received his commission as a Navy officer from Aviation Officers Candidate School in 1982, earning his pilot's wings in 1984. He is a 2000 graduate of the Air War College and the Armed Forces Staff College.

Dr. Stephen F. Burgess is Assistant Professor of International Security, Air War College, and an Associate of the USAF Counterproliferation Center (CPC). Previously, he was a faculty member at the University of Zambia, Vanderbilt University, and Hofstra University. Dr. Burgess completed his Ph.D. at Michigan State University, was a Fulbright-Hays fellow, and a Research Associate at the University of Zimbabwe. His two books are *Smallholders and Political Voice Zimbabwe*, University Press of America, 1997, and *The United Nations Under Boutros Boutros-Ghali, 1992-97*, Scarecrow Press, 2002. Dr. Burgess and Dr. Helen Purkitt collaborated on a monograph, *The Rollback of the South African Chemical and Biological Warfare Program* for the CPC and the Institute of National Security Studies (INSS), U.S. Air Force Academy. They are writing a book, *South Africa and Weapons of Mass Destruction*, which will be published by Indiana University Press in 2003. Recently, Dr. Burgess completed research on "India's Emerging Security Strategy and Defense Capabilities" for CPC and INSS.

Professor Alexander L. George is the Graham H. Stuart Professor Emeritus of International Relations at Stanford University. He did his undergraduate and graduate studies at the University of Chicago where he received a Ph.D. degree in Political Science. He has been with Stanford since 1968 where, in addition to courses on International relations, he taught seminars on decision-making, political leadership, and the presidency. His first book, *Woodrow Wilson and Colonel House*, written with his wife Juliette L. George, is widely regarded as a classic study on the role of personality in politics. His recently completed books include *Avoiding War; Problems of Crisis Management* (1991); *Forceful Persuasion: Coercive Diplomacy as an Alternative to War* (1992); and (with Juliette George) *Presidential Personality and Performance* (1999). Professor George was a member of the Carnegie Commission on Preventing Deadly Conflict, 1994-1999; Chair of the Committee on Conflict Resolution, National Academy of Sciences, 1995-1999.

Mr. Greg Giles is an Assistant Vice President of Science Applications International Corporation and Manager of its Weapons Proliferation

Analysis Division. His analytical work has focused on strategic personality and the military integration of weapons of mass destruction in the developing world. Mr. Giles recently authored "The Islamic Republic of Iran and Nuclear, Biological, and Chemical Weapons," in Planning the Unthinkable, Scott Sagan, Peter Lavoy, and James Wirtz, editors. Mr. Giles is a regular guest lecturer at the Defense Nuclear Weapons School and the USAF Counterproliferation Center.

Dr. Christopher Hemmer is an Assistant Professor in the Department of Strategy and International Security at the Air War College. Prior to that, he taught at Cornell University and Colgate University. He received his Ph.D. in 1998 from the Department of Government at Cornell University with a specialty in International Relations. He received his B.A. from the State University of New York at Albany, where he majored in political science and minored in psychology. His major teaching and research areas are political psychology, American foreign policy, and the Arab-Israeli Conflict. His publications include: "Historical Analogies and the Definition of Interests: The Iranian Hostage Crisis and Ronald Reagan's Policy Toward the Hostages in Lebanon," *Political Psychology* 20, 2 (June 1999): 267-298; *Which Lessons Matter? American Foreign Policy Decision Making in the Middle East, 1979-1987*, (State University of New York Press, 2000); and "Empire Without Tears: The Sequel?" *The Brown Journal of World Affairs* 7, 2 (Summer/Fall 2000): 163-171. His most recent article, co-written with Peter Katzenstein, entitled, "Why Is There No NATO in Asia? Collective Identity, Regionalism and the Origins of Multilateralism" will be forthcoming in *International Organization*.

Dr. Jerrold Post is Professor of Psychiatry, Political Psychology and International Affairs, and Director of the Political Psychology Program at the George Washington University. Dr. Post has devoted his entire career to the field of political psychology, coming to George Washington after a 21-year career with the U.S. government where he founded and directed the Center for the Analysis of Personality and Political Behavior. At George Washington, he co-founded and directs the George Washington University Institute for Crisis and Disaster Management. Dr. Post received his B.A. magna cum laude from Yale College. After receiving his M.D. from Yale, where he was elected to Alpha Omega Alpha, honor medical society, he received post-graduate training in psychiatry at Harvard Medical School and the National Institute of Mental Health, and in international studies from Johns Hopkins. A practicing psychiatrist, he is a Life Fellow of the American Psychiatric Association, a member of the American Academy of Psychiatry and the Law, and the American College of Psychiatrists. A leading expert on Saddam Hussein, Dr. Post has testified before the House Armed Services Committee and the House Foreign Affairs Committee on Saddam's personality and political behavior. He is a frequent commentator on national and international radio and television on world events, and he is the co-author of *When Illness Strikes the Leader: The Dilemma of the Captive King*, Yale, 1995, and *Political Paranoia: The Psychopolitics of Hatred*, Yale, 1997.

Lieutenant Colonel Gary Servold is a native of Lyons, CO. He was early commissioned as a Corps of Engineers Second Lieutenant in the U.S. Army Reserves in November 1979. In May 1981, he received a Regular Army Commission as a Second Lieutenant upon graduating as a Distinguished Military Graduate with a Bachelor of Science Degree in Civil Engineering from Colorado State University. He is a 2002 graduate of the Air War College and is currently a faculty member in the Department of Warfighting. Preceding his attendance at Air War College, he served as an aviation battalion task force commander for SFOR 8 in Bosnia where his unit supported the Multi-National Divisions and the Portuguese and Italian SFOR Operation Reserve. His awards include the Meritorious Service Medal (four awards), the Army Commendation Medal (three awards), the Army Achievement Medal, the Air Force Achievement Medal, Armed Forces Expeditionary Medal, Humanitarian Service Medal, the NATO Medal, and the AGOS Instructor on the Quarter. He is Airborne, AH-64 Apache, and UH-60 Blackhawk qualified.

Dr. Barry R. Schneider is the Director of the USAF Counterproliferation Center at Maxwell AFB, and is a Professor of International Relations at the Air War College. Dr. Schneider specializes in NBC counterproliferation and nonproliferation issues. He is the author of *Future War and Counterproliferation: U.S. Military Responses to NBC Proliferation Threats* (Praeger, 1999) and contributor to and co-editor of *Pulling back from the Nuclear Brink: Reducing and Countering Nuclear Threats* (Frank Cass Ltd., 1998), *Battlefield of the Future: 21st Century Warfare Issues* (Air University Press, 1998), *Missiles for the Nineties: ICBMs and Strategic Policy* (Westview, 1984), and *Current Issues in U.S. Defense Policy* (Praeger, 1976). He has served as a Foreign Affairs

Officer (GS-14) and Public Affairs Officer (GS-15) at the U.S. Arms Control and Disarmament Agency, as a Congressional staffer on arms control and defense issues, and was a Senior Defense Analyst at The Harris Group and the National Institute for Public Policy. He has taught at the Air War College since 1993. As a faculty member of the Department Warfighting (DFW), he teaches the DFW core course of instruction and elective courses such as International Flashpoints, Counterproliferation Issues, and CBW Issues for the USAF. He has taught at six other colleges and universities, and has a Ph.D. in International Relations from Columbia University.